KU-781-351

'This is absolutely the best exposition of CRM. I can't think of a better guide to increasing your performance and profits. This book belongs on the desk of every company that is serious about CRM. The wealth of information and insight is astounding.'

Professor Philip Kotler, S.C. Johnson & Son Distinguished Professor of International Marketing, Kellogg School of Management, Northwestern University, USA

'Francis Buttle and Stan Maklan's third edition of *Customer Relationship Management* is a comprehensive, soup-to-nuts compendium of information and guidance that ought to be a desk reference for every CRM professional in business today, whether you sell products or services, to consumers or businesses.'

Don Peppers, Founding Partner, Peppers & Rogers Group

'This lucid and content-packed book reads and informs like a charm. Francis Buttle and Stan Maklan's refreshing treatment of CRM as a core business strategy is destined to become a classic. Highly recommended.'

Fred Wiersema, Customer Strategist, Chair of the B2B Leadership Board, and top-selling author of The Discipline of Market Leaders

'This book is crisp, practical and stimulating. It combines Francis Buttle and Stan Maklan's considerable insights with practical examples and provides a step-by-step pragmatic approach to the application of CRM in business. Their coverage of CRM technology is an enhancing feature of the book. All senior management would benefit from reading it, particularly those who realize that profitable customers are their company's greatest asset and require foolproof guidance to retain them. Well-grounded academically, this book is equally beneficial for management students. Overall, it sets out a comprehensive reference/ guide to business success.'

Professor John A. Murphy, United Utilities Professor of Customer Management, Manchester Business School, UK

'A reference work to understand the ever-changing field of CRM. Especially demystifying what CRM is, what it is not, and offering a very comprehensive view on how to approach it and unlock its true value.'

Greg Lecointe, Director CX Applications Business Group, Oracle Corporation

'A great tour of the CRM landscape that covers the vastness between Operational and Strategic CRM while providing a robust overview of customer-related data and data mining. A definite reference for managers looking to take customer-centred strategies to the next level.'

Ian Di Tullio, Director Loyalty and Relationship Marketing Air Canada

CUSTOMER RELATIONSHIP MANAGEMENT

Customer Relationship Management: Concepts and Technologies, third edition, is a much-anticipated update of a bestselling textbook, including substantial revisions to bring its coverage up to date with the very latest in CRM practice. The book introduces the concept of CRM, explains its benefits, how and why it is used, the technologies that are deployed, and how to implement it, providing you with a guide to every aspect of CRM in your business or your studies.

Both theoretically sound and managerially relevant, the book draws on academic and independent research from a wide range of disciplines including information systems, marketing, human resources, project management, finance, strategy and more. Buttle and Maklan, clearly and without jargon, explain how CRM can be used throughout the customer lifecycle stages of customer acquisition, retention and development. The book is illustrated liberally with screenshots from CRM software applications and case illustrations of CRM in practice.

New to this edition:

* Updated instructor support materials online.
* Full colour interior.
* Brand new international case illustrations from many industry settings.
* Substantial revisions throughout, including new content on:
    - social media and social CRM
    - big data and unstructured data
    - recent advances in analytical CRM including next best action solutions
    - marketing, sales and service automation
    - customer self-service technologies
    - making the business case and realizing the benefits of investment in CRM.

Ideal as a core textbook for students on CRM or related courses such as relationship marketing, database marketing or key account management, the book is also essential to industry professionals, managers involved in CRM programmes and those pursuing professional qualifications or accreditation in marketing, sales or service management.

Francis Buttle, BSc, MA, PhD, is founder and principal consultant of Francis Buttle & Associates, and Honorary Adjunct Professor at Macquarie Graduate School of Management, Sydney, Australia.

Stan Maklan, BSc, MBA, PhD, is a Reader in Strategic Marketing, Cranfield School of Management, UK.

CUSTOMER RELATIONSHIP MANAGEMENT

Concepts and technologies

Third edition

**FRANCIS BUTTLE AND
STAN MAKLAN**

Routledge
Taylor & Francis Group

LONDON AND NEW YORK

First published 2003
by Butterworth-Heinemann, an imprint of Elsevier

Second edition 2009
Authored by Francis Buttle

Third edition published 2015
by Routledge
2 Park Square, Milton Park, Abingdon, Oxon OX14 4RN

and by Routledge
711 Third Avenue, New York, NY 10017

Routledge is an imprint of the Taylor & Francis Group, an informa business

© 2015 Francis Buttle and Stan Maklan

The right of Francis Buttle and Stan Maklan to be identified as author of
this work has been asserted by them in accordance with sections 77 and
78 of the Copyright, Designs and Patents Act 1988.

All rights reserved. No part of this book may be reprinted or reproduced
or utilized in any form or by any electronic, mechanical, or other means,
now known or hereafter invented, including photocopying and recording,
or in any information storage or retrieval system, without permission in
writing from the publishers.

Every effort has been made to contact copyright holders for their
permission to reprint material in this book. The publishers would be
grateful to hear from any copyright holder who is not here acknowledged
and will undertake to rectify any errors or omissions in future editions of
this book.

Trademark notice: Product or corporate names may be trademarks or
registered trademarks, and are used only for identification and
explanation without intent to infringe.

British Library Cataloguing in Publication Data
A catalogue record for this book is available from the British Library

Library of Congress Cataloging in Publication Data
Buttle, Francis.
    Customer relationship management: concepts and technologies/
    Francis Buttle and Stan Maklan. – Third edition.
        pages cm
    Includes bibliographical references and index.
    1. Customer relations – Management. I. Maklan, Stan. II. Title.
    HF5415.5.B875 2015
    658.8′12–dc23
    2014028109

ISBN: 978-1-138-78982-1 (hbk)
ISBN: 978-1-138-78983-8 (pbk)
ISBN: 978-1-315-76459-7 (ebk)

Typeset in Minion Pro and Futura Book
by Florence Production Ltd, Stoodleigh, Devon, UK
Printed in Great Britain by Ashford Colour Press Ltd, Gosport, Hampshire

Francis: *I dedicate this book to the memory of my brother Nick who died far too young from multiple myeloma, and to newborn Caitlin Rose who has an entire life ahead of her. One life ends and another begins.*

Stan: *I dedicate this book to my family and the support that they provide to enable such endeavours. My wife Anne's tireless support for which I need to say thank you more often and my daughter Alice whom I hope to inspire to achieve her goals, provide great motivation. I also dedicate this book to my mother, who passed away during the writing of this book, for all that she did for me and for what I have become.*

CONTENTS

List of figures		*xiv*
List of tables		*xvii*
About the authors		*xix*
Preface and acknowledgements		*xxi*

Part I UNDERSTANDING CUSTOMER RELATIONSHIPS | | **1**

1 Introduction to CRM | 3
Chapter objectives | 3
Introduction | 3
Strategic CRM | 5
Operational CRM | 7
Analytical CRM | 11
Where does social CRM fit? | 13
Misunderstandings about CRM | 13
Defining CRM | 15
CRM constituencies | 16
Commercial contexts of CRM | 18
The not-for-profit context – the 'third sector' | 18
Models of CRM | 20
Summary | 22
Notes and references | 23

2 Understanding relationships | 24
Chapter objectives | 24
What is a relationship? | 24
Relationship quality | 28
Why companies want relationships with customers | 28
Customer lifetime value | 32
When might companies not want relationships with customers? | 37
Why customers want relationships with suppliers | 39

	Customer satisfaction, loyalty and business performance	*41*
	Relationship management theories	*47*
	Summary	*52*
	Notes and references	*53*
3	**Managing the customer lifecycle – customer acquisition**	**58**
	Chapter objectives	*58*
	Introduction	*58*
	What is a new customer?	*60*
	Portfolio purchasing	*61*
	Prospecting	*63*
	Key performance indicators of customer acquisition programmes	*77*
	Making the right offer	*78*
	Operational CRM tools that help customer acquisition	*79*
	Summary	*82*
	Notes and references	*83*
4	**Managing the customer lifecycle – customer retention and development**	**84**
	Chapter objectives	*84*
	Introduction	*84*
	What is customer retention?	*85*
	Economics of customer retention	*88*
	Which customers to retain?	*89*
	Strategies for customer retention	*90*
	Positive customer retention strategies	*90*
	Context makes a difference	*106*
	Key performance indicators of customer retention programmes	*108*
	The role of research in reducing churn	*108*
	Strategies for customer development	*109*
	Strategies for terminating customer relationships	*111*
	Summary	*113*
	Notes and references	*114*
Part II	**STRATEGIC CRM**	**117**
5	**Customer portfolio management**	**119**
	Chapter objectives	*119*
	What is a portfolio?	*119*
	Who is the customer?	*121*
	Basic disciplines for CPM	*121*

CPM in the business-to-business context 141
Customer portfolio models 142
Additional customer portfolio management tools 146
Strategically significant customers 148
The seven core customer management strategies 150
Summary 151
Notes and references 151

6 How to deliver customer-experienced value 153
Chapter objectives 153
Introduction 153
Understanding value 154
When do customers experience value? 156
Modelling customer-perceived value 157
Sources of customer value 159
Customization 159
Value through the marketing mix 163
Summary 184
Notes and references 185

7 Managing customer experience 188
Chapter objectives 188
Introduction 188
What is customer experience? 189
Customer experience concepts 195
How to manage customer experience 197
What distinguishes customer experience management from customer
    relationship management? 200
How CRM software applications influence customer experience 202
Summary 205
Notes and references 206

Part III OPERATIONAL CRM 209

8 Sales force automation 211
Chapter objectives 211
Introduction 211
What is SFA? 212
The SFA eco-system 213
SFA software functionality 215
SFA adoption 226

How SFA changes sales performance 227
Summary 228
Notes and references 229

9 Marketing automation 231
Chapter objectives 231
Introduction 231
What is marketing automation? 231
Benefits of marketing automation 232
Software applications for marketing 234
Summary 260
Notes and references 260

10 Service automation 262
Chapter objectives 262
Introduction 262
What is customer service? 262
Modelling service quality 263
Customer Service Excellence certification 264
What is service automation? 266
Benefits from service automation 268
Software applications for service 270
Summary 285
Notes and references 285

Part IV ANALYTICAL CRM 287

11 Developing and managing customer-related databases 289
Chapter objectives 289
Introduction 289
Corporate customer-related data 290
Structured and unstructured data 290
Developing a customer-related database 292
Data integration 303
Data warehousing 305
Data marts 306
Knowledge management 307
Summary 308
Notes and references 308

12 Using customer-related data   310
    Chapter objectives   *310*
    Introduction   *310*
    Analytics for CRM strategy and tactics   *312*
    Analytics throughout the customer lifecycle   *313*
    Analytics for structured and unstructured data   *316*
    Big data analytics   *319*
    Analytics for structured data   *321*
    Three ways to generate analytical insight   *323*
    Privacy issues   *334*
    Summary   *336*
    Notes and references   *337*

Part V REALIZING THE BENEFITS OF CRM   **339**

13 Planning to succeed   341
    Chapter objectives   *341*
    The logic of the business case   *341*
    Organizing for benefits   *345*
    Network and virtual organizations   *349*
    Person-to-person contacts   *351*
    Key account management   *351*
    Summary   *356*
    Notes and references   *357*

14 Implementing CRM   359
    Chapter objectives   *359*
    Introduction   *359*
    Phase 1: Develop the CRM strategy   *361*
    Phase 2: Build CRM project foundations   *366*
    Phase 3: Needs specification and partner selection   *373*
    Phase 4: Project implementation   *380*
    Phase 5: Performance evaluation   *381*
    Summary   *382*
    Notes and references   *382*

Part VI LOOKING TO THE FUTURE   **385**

15 The future   387
    Notes and references   *389*

    Index   *391*

FIGURES

1.1	The CRM Value Chain	20
1.2	Payne's model of CRM	21
1.3	Gartner's CRM model	22
2.1	The satisfaction–profit chain	41
2.2	Two-dimensional model of customer loyalty	43
2.3	Market share versus share of customer	44
2.4	The American Customer Satisfaction Index (ACSI) model	45
2.5	Non-linear relationship between customer satisfaction and repeat purchase	47
2.6	The Six-Markets Model	51
3.1	The CEOExpress portal	65
3.2	Samsung merchandising	74
3.3	Customer acquisition email campaign	76
4.1	Using satisfaction and importance data to guide service improvement	92
4.2	Kano's model for creating customer delight	93
4.3	Nectar loyalty programme	95
4.4	Harley Owners Group	98
4.5	Cash-back sales promotion	99
4.6	Body Shop's core values	106
5.1	Bivariate segmentation of the chocolate market	126
5.2	McKinsey/GE customer portfolio matrix	130
5.3	Activity-based costing in a claims processing department	134
5.4	Decision tree output	140
5.5	The Pareto principle, or 80:20 rule	141
5.6	Customer profitability by sales volume quintile	142
5.7	Shapiro *et al.*'s customer portfolio matrix	143
5.8	Fiocca's CPM model: step 1	144
5.9	Fiocca's CPM model: step 2	145
5.10	Turnbull and Zolkiewski's three-dimensional customer classification matrix	146
5.11	Boston Consulting Group matrix	148
6.1	Different forms of mass customization	161
6.2	The marketing mix	163
6.3	Repositioning Lucozade as a sports drink	165
6.4	The SERVQUAL gaps model	169

6.5	Scandinavian Airline's understanding of customer expectations	170
6.6	Service level agreement scorecard	172
6.7	Information availability online at www.buzgate.org	179
6.8	Southwest Airline's blog	180
7.1	Evolution towards the experience economy	190
7.2	Layered model of customer experience	194
7.3	Experience map of a hotel guest	198
7.4	Typical CRM architecture, showing Web, back-office integration and mobile	204
8.1	Components of Oracle's SFA solution	213
8.2	Customer overview configured for iPad	214
8.3	Account management screenshot	216
8.4	Contact management screenshot	217
8.5	Lead management screenshot	220
8.6	Opportunity management report	221
8.7	Oracle pipeline overview screenshot	222
8.8	Sales management report	225
9.1	Closed-loop marketing	233
9.2	Oracle (Eloqua) multi-channel campaign management application	237
9.3	Email campaign management workflow	240
9.4	Marketing optimization: scenario testing	242
9.5	Technology Hype Cycle	247
9.6	Google Analytics dashboard report	251
9.7	Oracle's Loyalty Management software application	254
9.8	NetSuite partner management screenshot	255
9.9	Email campaign report	259
10.1	The International Customer Service Standard	265
10.2	Full visibility into customer service history (Oracle RightNow screenshot)	269
10.3	Trouble-ticket screenshot	273
10.4	Agent response to Twitter feed	274
10.5	Job management application	280
10.6	Customer service scripting screenshot	282
10.7	Oracle inbound telephony dashboard	283
10.8	Chat window (Oracle Smart technologies) screenshot	284
11.1	Relational database model	291
11.2	Steps in creating a relational database	292
11.3	SugarCRM screenshot	294
11.4	Email marketing application	295
11.5	Output from merge–purge operation	300
11.6	Single view of the customer	304
12.1	Basic data configuration for CRM analytics	311
12.2	Social media sentiment analytics	317
12.3	The 3Vs of big data	319
12.4	Standard report example	324
12.5	Example of a star schema: fact table and dimensions	325
12.6	Dendrogram output from hierarchical clustering routine	332

12.7	K-means clustering output	333
13.1	Benefit Dependency Network example	345
13.2	Category management at Kraft	348
13.3	Matrix organization structure	349
13.4	A model of KAM development	354
13.5	Bow-tie structure for early KAM	355
13.6	Virtual organization for synergistic KAM	355
14.1	The five-step implementation process	360
14.2	Customer strategy cube	361
14.3	Customer interaction map	363
14.4	Governance structure	367
14.5	The Competing Values model of organizational culture	369
14.6	The buy-in matrix	370
14.7	CRM project Gantt chart	371
14.8	Campaign management process for high interest saving account	375

TABLES

1.1	Definitions of CRM	4
1.2	Types of CRM	4
1.3	Operational CRM – some applications	7
2.1	The effect of customer retention on customer numbers	28
2.2	Retention rate and average customer tenure	30
2.3	The customer journey	31
2.4	Profit from customers over time	33
2.5	Impact of discount rate on CLV	35
2.6	Computing cohort value	37
3.1	Sources of B2B prospects	64
5.1	Intuitive and data-based segmentation processes	122
5.2	Criteria for segmenting consumer markets	124
5.3	ACORN geo-demographic household classification (UK)	125
5.4	How business markets are segmented	127
5.5	Examples of ISIC codes	127
5.6	Criteria for appraising segmentation opportunities	130
5.7	Sales forecasting using moving averages	132
5.8	Margin multiples	136
5.9	Credit risk training set	139
5.10	Cross-tabulation of dependent and independent variables	139
5.11	How costs vary between customers	143
5.12	Factors influencing the customer's attractiveness	145
6.1	How customers try to reduce perceived risk	156
6.2	Holbrook's typology of consumer value	158
6.3	Customization can be applied to any part of the offer	160
6.4	Grönroos model of service quality	168
6.5	SERVQUAL components	168
6.6	What customers want from service recovery	174
6.7	Xerox's 14 key business processes	175
6.8	How to improve complaints management processes	177
7.1	The 4Is of customer engagement	196
8.1	Classification of SFA vendors	213
8.2	Functionality offered by SFA software	215

8.3	Examples of reports available from SFA software	224
8.4	Motivations for implementing SFA	227
9.1	Functionality offered by MA software	234
10.1	Functionality offered by service automation software	271
11.1	Data transformation	306
12.1	CRM strategic goals and related tactics	312
12.2	Sample criteria used in prospect scoring	314
12.3	Selected techniques used by data miners	328
12.4	SERVQUAL's latent variables revealed by factor analysis	333
14.1	Strategic goals for CRM	364
14.2	Immediate and latent benefits from CRM	365
14.3	Critical success factors for successful CRM strategies	372
14.4	Evaluating processes	375
14.5	Comparing laptops and tablets	379

ABOUT THE AUTHORS

Francis Buttle, BSc, MA, PhD, is founder and principal consultant of Francis Buttle & Associates, a Sydney, Australia-based business that helps organizations become more skilled and successful at CRM, customer experience management, customer acquisition, retention and development (francisbuttle.com.au). Francis has spent most of the last 30 years in various academic roles around the world. He has been a Professor of Customer Relationship Management, Professor of Marketing, Professor of Relationship Marketing, and Professor of Management at a number of leading graduate schools of management, including Manchester Business School (UK), Cranfield School of Management (UK) and Macquarie Graduate School of Management (MGSM) (Australia). He was appointed as the world's first Professor of CRM in 1995, and remains an Honorary Adjunct Professor at MGSM.

Francis has authored, co-authored or edited 11 books, and over 125 peer-reviewed academic journal articles or conference papers. In addition, he is a frequent contributor to practitioner magazines, presenter at business conferences and blogger.

Francis has developed, run or contributed to many management development programmes, and has advised or provided consultancy to numerous for-profit and not-for-profit organizations in the UK, Australia, USA, Hong Kong, Singapore and New Zealand.

Although no longer a full-time academic, he still conducts and publishes customer-related research in partnership with mentees and associates in a number of universities. Francis lives on Sydney's Northern Beaches, is a qualified but reluctantly retired rugby union referee, enjoys cycling and kayaking, and rides a Suzuki.

Francis has degrees in management science, marketing and communication. His PhD was earned at the University of Massachusetts. He is an elected Fellow of the Chartered Institute of Marketing. He can be contacted at francis@francisbuttle.com.au or by mail at PO Box 243, Newport, NSW, 2106, Australia.

Stan Maklan, BSc, MBA, PhD, is Reader in Strategic Marketing, Cranfield School of Management, UK. Stan is an experienced academic, marketer and management consultant with senior, international line management experience in blue chip consumer and business marketing companies. Stan lectures on Cranfield's full-time MBA and MSc in Marketing programmes in addition to open and in-company executive courses.

Stan's research focuses on IT-led marketing change: what the marketing function must do to lead and ensure their organizations benefit from what is an ever-increasing role of technology in the practice of marketing. Much of this research centres on CRM, customer experience and developing new capabilities for marketing.

He is on the Editorial Advisory Board of the *International Journal of Market Research.* Stan has worked with leading telecommunications, computing, consumer products, defence, automotive, electricity, water and professional services companies.

Stan began his career with Unilever Canada. He subsequently moved with that firm to the UK and then Sweden, where he was Marketing Director of its Toiletries business. He then spent ten years as a management consultant with global leaders in information technology: Computer Sciences Corporation (CSC) and then Sapient. He established CSC UK's Customer Relationship Management practice and then moved to a role within its European Consulting and global management research units.

Stan completed a PhD that explores how firms change their marketing competencies when developing direct relationships with consumers online. He subsequently joined the faculty at Cranfield where he has authored numerous articles, conference papers and books.

Stan was awarded honours for academic excellence when he obtained a Master's of Business Administration from the University of Western Ontario – Ivey School of Management (Canada) and has a Bachelor of Science (Economics) from the Université de Montréal.

Learn more at www.stanmaklan.com or http://www.som.cranfield.ac.uk/som/p2323/People/Faculty/Academic-Faculty-Listing-A-Z/Last-Name-M/Stan-Maklan.

PREFACE AND ACKNOWLEDGEMENTS

Welcome to the third edition of *Customer Relationship Management: Concepts and technologies*. Welcome also to a new author team. Stan Maklan has joined Francis Buttle as co-author.

This book provides a comprehensive and balanced review of Customer Relationship Management. It explains what CRM is, the costs it creates and the benefits it delivers, the many varied contexts in which it is used, the technologies that are deployed, and how CRM can be implemented. It shows how CRM practices and technologies are used to enhance the achievement of marketing, sales, and service objectives throughout the customer lifecycle stages of customer acquisition, retention and development, whilst simultaneously supporting broader organizational goals.

The book has been written to meet the demand for an impartial, academically sound examination of CRM. It is a learning resource both for students of CRM and for managers wanting a better appreciation of the role that CRM can play in their own organizations.

CRM, and the business strategies it supports, have changed dramatically since the previous edition was published. No longer do businesses set the rules about how they will interact with customers through their control of communication channels and brand messaging. Customers now decide when and how they will interact with companies. Customers create and communicate their own messages that may be very different from the brand owner's and that appear on social media platforms like Facebook and Twitter.

CRM was made possible by advances in Information Technology, namely the ability to capture, store, interpret and distribute customer-related data cost-effectively so that organizations could enact their relationship management strategies. CRM practice has conventionally relied on its exploitation of structured data about customers, prospects and partners housed in company-owned databases. This is changing rapidly. Much of the data customers generate, for example on social media platforms, are unstructured and require complex new technologies if they are to be useful in executing relationship management strategies. Equally the sheer volume and variety of data that organizations can access is growing exponentially. This 'big data' phenomenon, the move from Web 1.0 to a Web 2.0 environment, is impacting the practice of relationship marketing and CRM more particularly. The third edition of this book aims to capture this disruptive change to relationship management practices, whilst accepting that the field is evolving very quickly.

Information is driving changes in customer relationship management practices. Information technology was first deployed by businesses to streamline administration with a strong focus on accounting, billing and financial reporting, resulting in IT heads reporting to the Chief Financial Officer (CFO) or Vice President of Finance. The next waves of IT deployment focused on personal productivity (desktop computing) and supply chain management (e.g. Enterprise Resource Planning – ERP). Next, IT was applied to customer relationship management, and most recently to customer experience management (CXM). As we explain in the book, CRM and CXM are two sides of the same coin. We feel confident that the next wave of technology-supported innovation in CRM will feature new business models founded on real-time, mobile data, particularly customer data. CRM, the most mature of the IT-enabled customer-facing management disciplines, has an enhanced role in such an environment and we believe remains the cornerstone for marketing, sales and customer service in the future.

In producing this third edition we knew we had to reflect this evolving landscape, and in true customer-oriented manner, we also surveyed readers and adopters of the previous edition. They told us what they wanted in this revision, and much of it was a reflection of Web 2.0's influence on CRM. We have added content on the following:

- How CRM practitioners in sales, marketing and service can understand and make use of social media platforms like Twitter and Facebook, and the customer-related data they offer.

- Big data. These are data that are typified by their volume, velocity and variety. The data that are held by social media platforms are only one type of big data.

- Social CRM. Technology firms are promoting new solutions that are collectively known as Social CRM solutions. We explore how Social CRM fits into the CRM landscape, and particularly whether it is a fundamental type of CRM, equivalent to strategic, operational and analytical CRM.

- How to analyze and make use of unstructured data such as transcripts of telephone calls, call centre agent notes and survey participants' responses to open-ended questionnaire items.

- Advances in CRM technologies, including customer self-service technologies. Although there are a number of chapters dedicated to CRM technologies, and technology matters are considered throughout the book, the book puts technology into a managerial context. This is not a book about technologies, but it is about how marketers, salespeople, service staff and their managers can use technologies to better understand and meet the requirements of customers, whilst also meeting organizational goals and objectives.

- More and updated case illustrations and screenshots from CRM software applications.

- How to prepare a business case for investment in CRM.

We have also refined the focus of the book. We have removed content that was not valued by readers and adopters, and streamlined what has been retained. This third edition continues to draw on academic and independent research to ensure that it is both theoretically sound and managerially relevant. Research from a wide range of academic disciplines contributes to the book. These include marketing, sales, customer service, human resources, technology management, strategy, change management, project management, leadership, operations, management accounting, finance, and organizational behaviour. Supplementing these academic credentials, the book also makes use of research conducted by independent analysts such as Gartner and Forrester, two organizations that conduct leading-edge, state-of-the-art research into CRM and related areas.

AUDIENCE FOR THE BOOK

This book has been written for a number of audiences, all of whom share an interest in improving their understanding of CRM.

- MBA and Master's students, and upper-level undergraduates studying CRM or related advanced courses such as relationship marketing, database marketing, customer management, customer portfolio management, customer experience management, sales management, key account management, strategic management, customer value management, and customer service management.
- Those pursuing professional qualifications or accreditation in marketing through international organizations such as the Chartered Institute of Marketing, the Digital Marketing Institute, and the Institute of Direct and Digital Marketing, or national bodies such as the Marketing Institute of Ireland or the Canadian Institute of Marketing.
- Senior and mid-level managers who are involved in CRM programmes and system implementations, whether in a marketing department, the sales force or the service centre.
- Students pursuing professional qualifications or accreditation in sales management or key account management through international organizations such as the Institute of Sales & Marketing Management, or corporate-based sales academies.
- CRM users who want a better understanding of this complex area. CRM tools are deployed across all customer-facing parts of organizations. Users include sales representatives and account managers, marketing managers, market analysts, campaign managers, market managers, customer relationship managers, and customer service managers. These users are exposed to just a fragment of the CRM universe. This book can put their role into broader context.

KEY FEATURES OF THE BOOK

- The book provides a helicopter view, an overview, of the domain of CRM. As an impartial review of the field, it is not tied to any particular perspective on CRM. Indeed, the book identifies a number of holistic models that provide different and competing overviews of CRM.
- Although CRM is in widespread use, there is still some misunderstanding about what CRM is. The book identifies three different types of CRM – strategic, operational and analytical. The book is structured so that the chapters on each of these types of CRM are clustered together. Several chapters are dedicated to each type of CRM.

- The book defines CRM as the core business strategy that integrates internal processes and functions, and external networks, to create and deliver value to targeted customers at a profit. It is grounded on high-quality customer-related data and enabled by information technology. This definition serves as a central point-of-reference throughout the book.

- We don't assume that customers value or want relationships with suppliers. If CRM is about developing and maintaining relationships with customers, it is important to have a clear understanding of what a relationship looks like, and how, if at all, it can be managed. We discuss what is meant by 'relationship' and question whether customers want relationships with suppliers and vice versa. We also identify attributes of successful relationships and review five different schools of thought that have influenced relationship management in a business context.

- The book emphasizes a managerial perspective on CRM. Although there is plenty of content on technology, it is not a book about technology, per se. The technology content of the book has been written so that readers who are unfamiliar with technology, or who are technophobes, can still understand what CRM technologies can deliver. Technology is secondary to management throughout the book. You don't need a degree in information systems to benefit from the book!

- The book has a strong academic foundation provided by research from a number of disciplines.

- The book contains many examples of CRM technologies and their application in marketing, selling or service functions. Screenshots are a feature of the book.

- Every chapter contains case illustrations. These are not problem-based cases, but examples of CRM in practice, so that readers can better appreciate how CRM is deployed.

- All chapters follow a common format: learning objectives, text, case illustrations, summary, notes and references.

ACKNOWLEDGEMENTS

We would like to acknowledge the contributions of many people to the production and publication of this book. We thank the editorial team at Taylor and Francis for their confidence in commissioning this third edition, their editorial diligence, and the detailed work of tracking down copyright owners and obtaining permission to use their materials. We thank the owners of all copyright materials for those permissions. We have made every effort to track down copyright owners, and to cite them correctly in notes or in the text. If we have failed to identify and cite any copyright material correctly, we apologise, and advise copyright owners to contact our publishers so corrections can be made in future editions. We thank associates around the world who have read drafts of chapters and made helpful suggestions. We thank the stars of the academic and business worlds who have graciously endorsed and lent their authority to our book. We thank our clients and students on whom many of our ideas have been stress tested. We thank our colleagues who have given moral and practical support to this writing venture. Finally, we thank our families who have put up with long periods of absence from family duty as we worked to keep to our publication deadline.

We hope you enjoy the book, and find it a satisfying read. Writing a book is a little like painting a picture, or tending a garden. You never reach a point where you can safely say that the job is finished. There is always more you can do. With that in mind, we invite you to write to us at francis@francisbuttle.com.au or stanmaklan@gmail.com or s.maklan @cranfield.ac.uk. We look forward to hearing from you.

Francis Buttle, Sydney
Stan Maklan, London

Part I

UNDERSTANDING CUSTOMER RELATIONSHIPS

This book is organized into six parts. Part I consists of four chapters that introduce you to the fundamentals of CRM. Chapter 1 explains what CRM is, picks out three different types of CRM, identifies CRM's main stakeholders and describes a number of different contexts in which CRM is used. Chapter 2 explores what we know about relationships and asks why companies and customers might want to develop relationships with each other, and why they sometimes do not. Chapters 3 and 4 investigate the three main stages of the customer lifecycle – customer acquisition, customer retention and customer development.

CHAPTER 1

INTRODUCTION TO CRM

CHAPTER OBJECTIVES

By the end of this chapter you will be aware of:

- Three major perspectives on CRM: strategic, operational and analytical.
- Where social CRM fits in the CRM landscape.
- Several common misunderstandings about CRM.
- A definition of CRM.
- The seven constituencies having an interest in CRM.
- How CRM contributes to performance in different industries.
- Four models of CRM.

INTRODUCTION

The expression, Customer Relationship Management (CRM), has been in use since the early 1990s. Since then, there have been many attempts to define the domain of CRM, a number of which appear in Table 1.1. As a discipline hotly contested by various information technology (IT) vendors, consultants and academics, a clear consensus has not yet emerged. Even the meaning of the three-letter acronym CRM is contested. For example, although most people would understand that CRM means Customer Relationship Management, others have used the acronym to mean Customer Relationship Marketing.[1]

Information technology companies have tended to use the term CRM to describe the software applications that are used to support the marketing, selling and service functions of businesses. This equates CRM with technology. Although the market for CRM software is now populated with many players, its commercialization was greatly boosted in 1993 when Tom Siebel founded Siebel Systems Inc. (now part of Oracle). Use of the term CRM can be traced back to that period. Gartner Inc., the information technology research and advisory firm, estimated that annual spending on CRM technology was $14 billion in 2013, and

Table 1.1 Definitions of CRM

- CRM is an information industry term for methodologies, software and usually Internet capabilities that help an enterprise manage customer relationships in an organized way.[2]

- CRM is the process of managing all aspects of interaction a company has with its customers, including prospecting, sales and service. CRM applications attempt to provide insight into and improve the company/customer relationship by combining all these views of customer interaction into one picture.[3]

- CRM is an integrated approach to identifying, acquiring and retaining customers. By enabling organizations to manage and coordinate customer interactions across multiple channels, departments, lines of business and geographies, CRM helps organizations maximize the value of every customer interaction and drive superior corporate performance.[4]

- CRM is an integrated information system that is used to plan, schedule and control the pre-sales and post-sales activities in an organization. CRM embraces all aspects of dealing with prospects and customers, including the call centre, sales force, marketing, technical support and field service. The primary goal of CRM is to improve long-term growth and profitability through a better understanding of customer behaviour. CRM aims to provide more effective feedback and improved integration to better gauge the return on investment (ROI) in these areas.[5]

- CRM is a business strategy that maximizes profitability, revenue and customer satisfaction by organizing around customer segments, fostering behaviour that satisfies customers, and implementing customer-centric processes.[6]

predicted that it would top $18.4 billion in 2016.[7] Others, with a managerial rather than technological emphasis, claim that CRM is a disciplined approach to developing and maintaining profitable customer relationships, and that technology may or may not have a role. That said, it is hard to conceive of a large organization dealing with millions of customers across multiple channels that can implement a customer strategy cost-effectively without the use of Information Systems technology and carefully designed business processes.

We can resolve the debate between managerial and technological schools by conceiving of CRM as taking three main forms: strategic, operational and analytical, as summarized in Table 1.2 and described below.

Table 1.2 Types of CRM

Type of CRM	Dominant characteristic
Strategic	Strategic CRM is a core customer-centric business strategy that aims at winning and keeping profitable customers.
Operational	Operational CRM focuses on the automation of customer-facing processes such as selling, marketing and customer service.
Analytical	Analytical CRM is the process through which organizations transform customer-related data into actionable insight for either strategic or tactical purposes.

STRATEGIC CRM

Strategic CRM is focused upon the development of a customer-centric business culture dedicated to winning and keeping customers by creating and delivering value better than competitors. The culture is reflected in leadership behaviours, the design of formal systems of the company, and the myths and stories that are created within the firm. In a customer-centric culture you would expect resources to be allocated where they would best enhance customer value, reward systems to promote employee behaviours that enhance customer satisfaction and retention, and customer information to be collected, shared and applied across the business. The heroes of customer-centric businesses deliver outstanding value or service to customers. Many businesses claim to be customer-centric, customer-led, customer-focused or customer-oriented but few are. Indeed there can be very few companies of any size that do not claim that they are on a mission to satisfy customer requirements profitably. Customer-centricity competes with other business logics. Kotler identifies three other major business orientations: product, production and selling.[8]

- *Product-oriented* businesses believe that customers choose products with the best quality, performance, design or features. These are often highly innovative and entrepreneurial firms. Many new business start-ups are product-oriented. In these firms it is common for the customer's voice to be missing when important marketing, selling or service decisions are made. Little or no customer research is conducted. Management makes assumptions about what customers want and/or provides visionary leadership for the market. Perhaps the most iconic example of product-orientation is Apple. Apple has created huge demand for products that customers did not know they needed, for example the iPad. Leading fashion houses tend to be product-oriented and try to establish new fashion trends rather than respond to consumer research about what should be next year's look. However, these are exceptional. Product-oriented companies often over-specify or over-engineer for the requirements of the market, and therefore are too costly for many customers. The subset of relatively price-insensitive customers marketers dub 'innovators', who are likely to respond positively to company claims about product excellence, is a relatively small segment, perhaps 2.5 per cent of the potential market.[9]

- *Production-oriented* businesses focus on operational excellence.[10] They seek to offer the customers the best value for money, time and/or effort. Consequently, they strive to keep operating costs low, and develop standardized offers and routes to market. Complexity, customization and innovation are very costly and unappealing to production-oriented businesses. Production-oriented firms rarely are first to market with the best new offer. They focus their innovation on supply chain optimization and simplification. They tend to serve customers who want 'good-enough', low-priced products and services. Production-oriented businesses choose not to believe that customers have unique needs or wants. It is possible to be highly profitable by being the lowest cost business player, for example Wal-Mart. There is a price and convenience segment in most markets but the majority of customers have other requirements. Moreover, an excessive focus on operational efficiency might make you blind to disruptive changes just over the horizon; making cheap products that no one wants to buy is not a sustainable strategy.

- *Sales-oriented* businesses make the assumption that if they invest enough in advertising, selling, public relations (PR) and sales promotion, customers will be persuaded to buy. Very often, a sales orientation follows a production orientation. The company produces low-cost products and then has to promote them heavily to shift inventory – a 'make and sell' approach. The deal-maker and persuader is king in such firms. In markets that are growing rapidly, such an approach can promote strong market share growth and attendant economies of scale. Many large technology firms have promoted an emphasis on selling. The risks of this orientation are twofold: (1) winning large contracts is not the same thing as making money from them and (2) focus on the immediate sale rarely allows enough slack resources to experiment and innovate to serve emerging needs and wants not yet articulated by customers.

- A *customer or market-oriented* company shares a set of beliefs about putting the customer first. It collects, disseminates and uses customer and competitive information to develop better-value propositions for customers. A customer-centric firm is a learning firm that constantly adapts to customer requirements and competitive conditions. There is evidence that customer-centricity correlates strongly to business performance.[11]

CASE STUDY 1.1

STRATEGIC CRM AT HONDA AUSTRALIA[12]

Honda manufactures and markets a successful range of motorcycle, power equipment and marine products. The Honda brand has a reputation for quality, technology and performance. Honda Australia recognized that while it was diligently nurturing individual relationships with partners, dealers and customers, each was closed off from the others. Inevitably, this meant valuable customer data being trapped in pockets within the organization and not available to potential users.

Honda realized that consolidating and freeing up the flow of data could have a huge positive impact on the effectiveness and efficiency of the business. Honda developed a strategy themed *Customers For Life*, based on data integration and a whole-of-customer view. Honda found customer-related data in numerous spreadsheets and databases across the business. These were integrated into a single CRM platform, supplied by salesforce.com, and hosted in the cloud. This was enriched with customer information from Honda Australia Rider Training (HART), Automobile Association memberships and several other sources to create a single comprehensive data source and reporting system. Honda then removed responsibility for managing customer relationships from individual departments, and moved it to the CRM unit.

An integrated view of the customer has allowed Honda to stop different operating units from bombarding customers with multiple communications. Instead, Honda now consolidates outbound customer contact into meaningful and relevant communications, and accurately measures communications effectiveness. Honda has built workflows into customer touchpoints, for example customer satisfaction surveys, guaranteeing follow-up of any negative comments. The immediate effect was a reduction in complaint resolution time from months to minutes. Honda has shifted closer to becoming a unified brand that really knows and understands its customers.

Many managers would argue that customer-centricity must be right for all companies. However, at different stages of market or economic development, other orientations may have stronger appeal.

OPERATIONAL CRM

Operational CRM automates customer-facing business processes. CRM software applications enable the marketing, selling and service functions to be automated and integrated. Some of the major applications within operational CRM appear in Table 1.3.

Table 1.3 Operational CRM – some applications

Marketing automation

- Campaign management
- Event-based (trigger) marketing
- Marketing optimization

Sales force automation

- Account management
- Lead management
- Opportunity management
- Pipeline management
- Contact management
- Quotation and proposal generation
- Product configuration

Service automation

- Case (incident or issue) management
- Customer communications management
- Queuing and routing
- Service level management

Although we cover the technological aspects of operational CRM in Part III, it is worth making a few observations at this point.

Marketing automation

Marketing automation (MA) applies technology to marketing processes.

Campaign management modules allow marketers to use customer-related data in order to develop, execute and evaluate targeted communications and offers. Customer segmentation for campaigning purposes is, in some cases, possible at the level of the individual customer, enabling unique communications to be designed.

In multi-channel environments, campaign management is particularly challenging. Some fashion retailers, for example, have multiple transactional channels including free-standing stores, department store concessions, e-tail websites, home shopping catalogues, catalogue stores and perhaps even a television shopping channel. Some customers may be unique to a single channel, but most will be multi-channel prospects, if not already customers of several channels. Integration of communication and offer strategies, and evaluation of performance, requires a substantial amount of technology-aided coordination across these channels.

Event-based, or trigger, marketing is the term used to describe messaging and offer development to customers at particular points in time. An event triggers the communication and offer. Event-based campaigns can be initiated by customer behaviours, or contextual conditions. A call to a contact centre is an example of a customer-initiated event. When a credit-card customer calls a contact centre to enquire about the current rate of interest, this can be taken as indication that the customer is comparing alternatives, and may switch to a different provider. This event may trigger an offer designed to retain the customer. Examples of contextual events are the birth of a child or a public holiday. Both of these indicate potential changes in buyer behaviour, initiating a marketing response. Event-based marketing also occurs in the business-to-business context. The event may be a change of personnel on the customer-side, the approaching expiry of a contract or a request for information (RFI).

Real-time marketing (automation), combining predictive modelling and work-flow automation, enables companies to make relevant offers to customers as they interact with company technologies at different touchpoints such as website and retail outlet. As consumers share more data with companies, and as the company's ability to analyze those data improves, online marketing increasingly occurs in real time. The choices the customer makes as she navigates through the Web, the enquiries she makes and her profile enable firms to predict which products and services will be most appealing to her: the so-called Next Best Offer or NBO. This offer can be refreshed in real time as a result of customer behaviour online. E-retailers such as Amazon continually refresh their recommendations as a result of customer searches, and Google changes the advertising it pushes to you as a function of your location and search behaviours.

More information about marketing automation appears in Chapter 9.

Sales force automation

Sales force automation (SFA) was the original form of operational CRM. SFA systems are now widely adopted in business-to-business environments and are seen as 'a competitive imperative'[13] that offers 'competitive parity'.[14]

SFA applies technology to the management of a company's selling activities. The selling process can be decomposed into a number of stages such as lead generation, lead qualification, lead nurturing, needs identification, development of specifications, proposal generation, proposal presentation, handling objections and closing the sale. SFA software can be configured so that it is modelled on the selling process of any industry or organization.

Automation of selling activities is often linked to efforts to improve and standardize the selling process. This involves the implementation of a sales methodology. Sales methodologies allow sales team members and management to adopt a standardized view of the sales cycle, and a common language for discussion of sales issues.

SFA software enables companies to assign leads automatically and track opportunities as they progress through the sales pipeline towards closure. Opportunity management lets users identify and progress opportunities-to-sell from lead status through to closure and beyond, into after-sales support. Opportunity management software usually contains lead management and sales forecasting applications. Lead management applications enable users to qualify leads and assign them to the appropriate salesperson. Sales forecasting applications generally use transactional histories and salesperson estimates to produce estimates of future sales.

Contact management lets users manage their communications programme with customers. Digital customer records contain customer contact histories. Contact management applications often have features such as automated customer dialling, the salesperson's personal calendar and email functionality.

Quotation and proposal generation allow the salesperson to automate the production of prices and proposals for customers. The salesperson enters details such as product codes, volumes, customer name and delivery requirements, and the software automatically generates a priced quotation.

Product configuration applications enable salespeople, or customers themselves, automatically to design and price customized products, services or solutions. Configurators are useful when the product is particularly complex, such as IT solutions. Configurators are typically based on an 'if . . . then' rules structure. The general case of this rule is 'If X is chosen, then Y is required or prohibited or legitimated or unaffected'. For example, if the customer chooses a particular feature (say, a particular hard drive for a computer), then this rules out

CASE STUDY 1.2

SALES FORCE AUTOMATION AT ROCHE

Roche is one of the world's leading research-based healthcare organizations, active in the discovery, development and manufacture of pharmaceuticals and diagnostic systems. The organization has traditionally been product-centric and quite poor in the area of customer management. Roche's customers are medical practitioners prescribing products to patients. Customer information was previously collected through several mutually exclusive sources, ranging from personal visits to handwritten correspondence, and not integrated into a database, giving incomplete views of the customer.

Roche identified the need to adopt a more customer-centric approach to better understand their customers, improve services offered to them and to increase sales effectiveness. Roche implemented a sales force automation system where all data and interactions with customers are stored in a central database which can be accessed throughout the organization. This has resulted in Roche being able to create customer profiles, segment customers and communicate with existing and potential customers. Since implementation Roche has been more successful in identifying, winning and retaining customers.

certain other choices or related features that are technologically incompatible or too costly or complex to manufacture.

More information about sales force automation appears in Chapter 8.

Service automation

Service automation involves the application of technology to customer service operations. Service automation helps companies to manage their service operations, whether delivered through a call centre, contact centre, field service, the Web or face-to-face, with high levels of efficiency, reliability and effectiveness.[15] Service automation software enables companies to handle inbound and outbound communications across all channels. Software vendors claim that this enables users to become more efficient and effective, by reducing service costs, improving service quality, lifting productivity, enhancing customer experience and lifting customer satisfaction.

Service automation differs significantly depending upon the product being serviced. The first point of contact for service of consumer products is usually the retail outlet, or a call centre. People working at these touchpoints often use online diagnostic tools that help identify and resolve the problem. A number of technologies are common in service automation. Call routing software can be used to direct inbound calls to the most appropriate handler. Technologies such as Interactive Voice Response (IVR) enable customers to interact with company computers. Customers can input to an IVR system after listening to menu instructions either by telephone keypad (key 1 for option A, key 2 for option B), or by voice. If first contact problem resolution is not possible, the service process may then involve authorizing a return of goods, or a repair cycle involving a third-party service provider.

Companies are beginning to learn to respond to customer complaints in social media such as Facebook and Twitter in close to real time. Social media have greatly increased the risks of consumer complaints remaining unanswered. Real-time engagement in the social conversation enables companies to intervene immediately and resolve an issue before a social media storm erupts. A case can be made that companies consider employing people and/or

CASE STUDY 1.3

CUSTOMER SERVICE AT JETBLUE

JetBlue is a successful US low-cost carrier known not only for its prices, but for friendly and helpful customer service, winning multiple JD Power customer service awards. It created its first Twitter account in 2007.[16] Initially, like so many new technology users, the company felt that Twitter would be a sales promotion channel. Indeed, JetBlue has been imaginative in building its following and promoting ticket sales over the new channel. As its competence grew, JetBlue was able to use Twitter for real-time customer service. An anecdote is that a customer tweeted that he had left sunglasses at one of the stages before boarding and head office team monitoring the Twitter-feed was able to arrange for them to be found and returned to the passenger prior to boarding the aircraft. Customer frustrations, experiences and pleasant surprises are easier to capture at the moment they are experienced, and JetBlue's active engagement with customers over Twitter improves its ability to feel the experience as a customer does and make necessary improvements quickly.

technologies to monitor and respond to tweets and other social media content. However, other participants in the conversation, for example other users of Twitter, might also be able to contribute to the resolution of a consumer's problem, through what is known as crowd-sourced customer service.

Service automation for large capital equipment is quite different. This normally involves diagnostic and corrective action taken in the field, at the location of the equipment. Examples of this type of service include industrial air conditioning and refrigeration. In these cases, service automation may involve providing the service technician with diagnostics, repair manuals, inventory management and job information on a laptop or mobile device. This information is then synchronized at regular intervals to update the central CRM system. An alternative strategy for providing service for capital equipment is for diagnostics to be built into the equipment, and back-to-base issue reporting to be automated. Rolls-Royce aero-engines, for example, are offered with a service contract that involves Rolls-Royce engineers monitoring engines in flight to help airlines maximize efficiencies, reduce service cost and, most importantly, reduce downtime of the airplane through preventive service interventions. Rolls-Royce calls this 'Power-by-Hour'. GE, its chief competitor in aircraft engines, offers a similar service. Turning products into services, or developing combined 'product-service systems',[17] is known as 'servitization'. This is not a new strategy; indeed, IBM famously made a transition from selling computers to providing solutions and systems. In all such cases, the nature of the customer relationship changes. Modern operational CRM systems permit the delivery of such solutions in a cost-effective manner.

Many companies use a combination of direct and indirect channels especially for sales and service functions. When indirect channels are employed, operational CRM supports this function through partner relationship management (PRM). This technology allows partners to communicate with the supplier through a portal, to manage leads, sales orders, product information and incentives.

More information about service automation appears in Chapter 10.

ANALYTICAL (OR ANALYTIC) CRM

Analytical CRM, also called analytic CRM, is concerned with capturing, storing, extracting, integrating, processing, interpreting, distributing, using and reporting customer-related data to enhance both customer and company value.

Analytical CRM builds on the foundation of customer-related information. Customer-related data may be found in enterprise-wide repositories: sales data (purchase history), financial data (payment history, credit score), marketing data (campaign response, loyalty scheme data) and service data. To these internal data can be added data from external sources: geo-demographic and lifestyle data from business intelligence organizations, for example. These are typically structured datasets held in relational databases. A relational database is like an Excel spreadsheet where all the data in any row is about a particular customer, and the columns report a particular variable such as name, postcode and so on. See Chapter 11 for more detail. With the application of data mining tools, a company can then interrogate these data. Intelligent interrogation provides answers to questions such as: Who are our most valuable customers? Which customers have the highest propensity to switch to competitors? Which customers would be most likely to respond to a particular offer?

In recent years, we have seen the emergence of 'big data'. Although the expression 'big data' has been around since 2000, it is only since 2010 that businesses have become seriously interested in these huge datasets. According to IBM, Big data comes from everywhere: from sensors used to gather climate information, posts to social media sites, digital pictures and videos posted online, transaction records of online purchases, and from cell phone GPS signals to name a few'.[18] Big data extends beyond structured data, including unstructured data of all varieties: text, audio, video, click streams, log files and more. The tools for searching, making sense of, and acting on unstructured data differ from those available for data-mining structured datasets.

CASE STUDY 1.4

ANALYTICAL CRM AT AXA SEGUROS E INVERSIONES (AXA)[19]

Spanish insurer AXA Seguros e Inversiones (AXA) has revenues of over €1.8 billion (US$2.3 billion), two million customers and is a member of global giant The AXA Group.

AXA runs marketing campaigns in Spain for its many products and services. The company wanted a better understanding of its customers, in order to be able to make more personalized offers and implement customer loyalty campaigns.

AXA used CRM vendor SAS's data mining solution to build a predictive policy cancellation model. The solution creates profiles and predictive models from customer data that enable more finely targeted campaign management, call centre management, sales force automation and other activities involved in customer relationship management.

The model was applied to current and cancelled policies in various offices, so as to validate it before deploying it across Spain. Moreover, the model was used to create two control groups (subdivided into high and low probability) that were not targeted in any way, while other groups, similarly divided into high and low probability, were targeted by various marketing actions. The outcome was that the auto insurance policy cancellation rate was cut by up to nine percentage points in specific targeted segments.

With the customer insight obtained from the model, AXA is now able to design and execute personalized actions and customer loyalty campaigns tailored to the needs and expectations of high-value customers.

Analytical CRM has become an essential part of many CRM implementations. Operational CRM struggles to reach full effectiveness without analytical information about customers. For example, an understanding of customer value or propensities to buy underpins many operational CRM decisions, such as:

- Which customers shall we target with this offer?
- What is the relative priority of customers waiting on the line, and what level of service should be offered?
- Where should I focus my sales effort?

Analytical CRM can lead companies to decide that selling approaches should differ between customer groups. Higher potential value customers may be offered face-to-face selling; lower value customers may experience telesales.

From the customer's point of view, analytical CRM can deliver timely, customized solutions to the customer's problems, thereby enhancing customer satisfaction. From the company's point of view, analytical CRM offers the prospect of more powerful cross-selling and up-selling programmes, and more effective customer retention and customer acquisition programmes.

WHERE DOES SOCIAL CRM FIT?

We have identified three different types of CRM – strategic, operational and analytical. Another expression that has recently found widespread traction is 'social CRM'. This expression is widely used by technology firms with solutions to sell, but we do not regard it as a fundamental type of CRM, equivalent to strategic, operational and analytical. We suspect that this term will in time be subordinated by a larger discussion of big data which we cover in this book. Social CRM technologies, which we discuss in more detail in Chapter 9, essentially enable users to exploit social network data for customer management purposes. Interactions between individuals within social networks have produced a colossal amount of data, often unstructured, which some businesses are now trying to collect, interpret and use to create and maintain long-term beneficial relationships with their customers. CRM as a management practice was popularized by the advances in database technology that allowed a single view of the customer for most firms and the analytical tools and operational systems (e.g. call centres) that enabled firms to exploit those data. The data that fuelled CRM were largely generated and held within organizations' operational systems: sales, call centres, service requests, etc. Now, data about customers are as likely to be found in their Facebook or Twitter activities and user-generated content posted to YouTube. There is, therefore, a desire to integrate organization 'owned' data with that generated socially to create a more comprehensive view of the customer.

When social media generate customer-related data that are used by companies to manage customer relationships, social media support and enhance analytical CRM. Where consumers use social media (e.g. Facebook) to make purchases, social media become part of operational CRM. Social media also feature heavily in crowd-sourced customer service. At a strategic level, we believe that only a limited number of firms are currently poised to replace an overall relationship strategy with one purely activated through social media, but interesting new business models will develop undoubtedly.

MISUNDERSTANDINGS ABOUT CRM

As with all major management initiatives, there are a number of common misunderstandings about the nature of CRM. Sometimes, to scope a phenomenon, it is useful to say what it is not. These misunderstandings are described below.

Misunderstanding 1: CRM is merely database marketing

Database marketing is concerned with building and exploiting high-quality customer data-bases for marketing purposes. Companies collect data from a number of sources. These data are verified, cleaned, integrated and stored on computers, often in data warehouses or data-marts. They are then used for marketing purposes such as market segmentation, targeting, offer development and customer communication.

Whereas most large and medium-sized companies do indeed build and exploit customer databases, CRM is much wider in scope than database marketing. A lot of what we have described above as analytical CRM has the appearance of database marketing. However, database marketing is less evident in strategic and operational CRM.

Misunderstanding 2: CRM is a marketing process

CRM software applications are used for many marketing activities: market segmentation, customer acquisition, customer retention and customer development (cross-selling and up-selling), for example. However, operational CRM extends into selling and service functions.

The deployment of CRM software to support a company's mission to become more customer-centric often means that customer-related data are shared more widely throughout the enterprise than the marketing function alone. Operations management can use customer-related data to produce customized products and services. People management (HR) can use customer preference data to help recruit and train staff for the front-line jobs that interface with customers. Research and development management can use customer-related data to focus new product development.

Customer data can not only be used to integrate various internal departments but can also be shared across the extended enterprise with outside suppliers and partners.

Misunderstanding 3: CRM is an IT issue

In the authors' experience, this is the most serious of the misunderstandings. There is no doubt that IT is a necessary enabler of CRM in most organizations, given the need to store, analyze and distribute huge amounts of data quickly throughout the organization and its business partners. CRM technology keeps advancing and can be costly (see discussion above on social CRM). It is therefore too easy for senior management to look to the IT function for CRM leadership. Too many CRM implementations are framed at the outset as IT initiatives, rather than broader strategic initiatives.

CRM technology provides tools that can be used to generate better value for customers and company alike. However, two other important parts of most CRM projects are people and process. People develop and implement the processes that are enabled by the IT. IT cannot compensate for bad processes and inept people. Successful CRM implementations involve people designing and implementing processes that deliver customer and company value. Often, these processes are IT-enabled. IT is therefore a part of most CRM strategies.

That said, not all CRM initiatives involve IT investments. An overarching goal of many CRM projects is the development of relationships with, and retention of, highly valued customers. This may involve behavioural changes in store employees, education of call centre staff, and a focus on empathy and reliability from salespeople. IT may play no role at all.

Misunderstanding 4: CRM is about loyalty schemes

Loyalty schemes are commonplace in many industries: car hire, airlines, food retail and hotels, for example. Customers accumulate credits, such as air miles, from purchases. These are then redeemed at some future point. Most loyalty schemes require new members to complete an application form when they join the programme. This demographic information is typically used together with purchasing data to help companies become more effective at customer communication and offer development. Whereas some CRM implementations are linked to loyalty schemes, not all are.

Loyalty schemes may play two roles in CRM implementations. First, they generate data that can be used to guide customer acquisition, retention and development. Second, loyalty schemes may serve as an exit barrier. Customers who have accumulated credits in a scheme may be reluctant to exit the relationship. The credits accumulated reflect the value of the investment that the customer has made in the scheme, and therefore in the relationship.

Misunderstanding 5: CRM can be implemented by any company

Strategic CRM can, indeed, be implemented in any company. Every organization can be driven by a desire to be more customer-centric. Chief executives can establish a vision, mission and set of values that bring the customer into the heart of the business. CRM technology may play a role in that transformation. Some companies are certainly more successful than others. The banking industry has implemented CRM very widely, yet there are significant differences between the customer satisfaction ratings and customer retention rates of different banks.

Any company can also try to implement operational CRM. Any company with a sales force can automate its selling, lead management and contact management processes. The same is true for marketing and service processes. CRM technology can be used to support marketing campaigns, service requests and complaints management.

Analytical CRM is a different matter, being based on customer-related data. At the very least, data are needed to identify which customers are likely to generate most value in the future, and to identify within the customer base the segments or customers that have different requirements. Only then can different offers be communicated to each customer group to optimize company and customer value over the long term. If these data are missing then analytical CRM cannot be implemented.

DEFINING CRM

Against this background of three types of CRM, and the misunderstandings about CRM, it is no easy matter to settle on a single definition of CRM. However, we can identify a number of core CRM attributes, and integrate them into a definition that underpins the rest of this book.

> **CRM is the core business strategy that integrates internal processes and functions, and external networks, to create and deliver value to targeted customers at a profit. It is grounded on high-quality customer-related data and enabled by information technology.**

CRM is a 'core business strategy' that aims to 'create and deliver value to targeted customers at a profit'. This clearly denotes that CRM is not just about IT. CRM 'integrates internal process and functions'. That is, it allows departments within businesses to dissolve the silo walls that separate them. Access to 'customer-related data' allows selling, marketing and service functions to be aware of each other's interactions with customers. Furthermore, back office functions such as operations and finance can learn from and contribute customer-related data. Customer-related data allow suppliers and members of their 'external network', for example distributors, value-added resellers and agents, to align their efforts with those of the focal company. Underpinning this core business strategy in the majority of cases is IT – software applications and hardware.

Historically, most companies were located close to the markets they served, and knew their customers intimately. Very often there would be face-to-face, even day-to-day, interaction with customers, through which knowledge of customer requirements and preferences grew. However, as companies have grown larger, they have become more remote from the customers they serve. The remoteness is not only geographic; it may be cultural also. Even some of the most widely admired American companies have not always understood the markets they served. Disney's development of a theme park near to the French capital, Paris, was not an initial success because they failed to deliver to the value expectations of European customers. For example, Disney failed to offer visitors alcohol on-site. Europeans, however, are accustomed to enjoying a glass or two of wine with their food.

Geographic and cultural remoteness, together with business owner and management separation from customer contact, means that many companies, even small companies, do not have the intuitive knowledge and understanding of their customers so often found in micro-businesses such as neighbourhood stores and hairdressing salons. This has given rise to demand for better customer-related data, a cornerstone of effective CRM.

In summary, we take the view that CRM is a technology-enabled approach to management of the customer interface. Most CRM initiatives expect to have impact on the costs-to-serve and revenues streams from customers. The use of technology also changes the customer's experience of transacting and communicating with a supplier. For that reason, the customer's perspective on CRM is an important consideration in this book. CRM influences customer experience, and that is of fundamental strategic significance.

CRM CONSTITUENCIES

There are several important constituencies having an interest in CRM:

1   *Companies* implementing CRM. Many companies have implemented CRM. Early adopters were larger companies in financial services, telecommunications and

manufacturing in the USA and Europe. Medium-sized businesses are following. There is still potential for the CRM message to reach smaller companies, other worldwide markets, not-for-profits and new business start-ups.

2   *Customers and partners* of those companies. The customers and partners of companies that implement CRM are a particularly important constituency. Because CRM influences customer experience, it can impact on customer satisfaction ratings, and influence loyalty to the supplier.

3   *Vendors of CRM systems*. Vendors of CRM include Oracle, IBM, SAP and SAS. There has been considerable consolidation of the CRM vendor marketplace in recent years. PeopleSoft and Siebel, two of the pioneering CRM vendors, are now integrated into Oracle. IBM has been integrating analytic solution providers as it builds a more comprehensive analytical CRM capability. Vendors sell licences to companies, and install CRM software on the customer's servers. The client's people are trained to use the software.

4   *CRM cloud solutions providers*. Companies implementing CRM can also choose to access CRM functionality on a subscription basis through hosted CRM vendors such as salesforce.com, RightNow (part of Oracle), Microsoft Dynamics and NetSuite. Clients upload their customer data to the host's servers and interact with the data using their web browsers. These service providers deliver and manage applications and other services from remote sites to multiple users via the Internet. These companies are also known as Software as a Service (SaaS) firms or Application Service Providers (ASPs). Clients access CRM functionality in much the same way as they would use eBay or Amazon.

5   *Social media players*. Facebook, Twitter and some other platforms are building enormous communities that generate valuable data about people's preferences, activities, friends and wants. We predict a major battle between the major social media players and companies with large numbers of customers for the analysis and use of that data.

6   *Vendors of CRM hardware and infrastructure*. Hardware and infrastructure vendors provide the technological foundations for CRM implementations. They supply technologies such as servers, computers, hand-held and mobile devices, call centre hardware and telephony systems.

7   *Management consultants*. Consultancies offer clients a diverse range of CRM-related capabilities such as strategy, business, application and technical consulting. Consultants can help companies implementing CRM in several ways: systems integration, choosing between different vendors, developing implementation plans and project management as the implementation is rolled out. Most CRM implementations are composed of a large number of smaller projects, for example: systems integration, data quality improvement, market segmentation, process engineering and culture change. The major consultancies such as Accenture, McKinsey, Bearing Point, Braxton Group and CGEY all offer CRM consultancy. Smaller companies sometimes offer specialized expertise. Peppers and Rogers provide strategy consulting. Dunnhumby is known for its expertise in data mining for segmentation purposes.

COMMERCIAL CONTEXTS OF CRM

CRM is practised in a wide variety of commercial contexts, which present a range of different customer relationship management problems. We'll consider four contexts: banks, automobile manufacturers, technology solution vendors and consumer goods manufacturers.

- *Banks* deal with a large number of individual retail customers. They want CRM for its analytical capability to help them manage customer defection (churn) rates and to enhance cross-sell performance. Data mining techniques can be used to identify which customers are likely to defect, what can be done to win them back, which customers are hot prospects for cross-sell offers and how best to communicate those offers. Banks want to win a greater share of customer spend (share-of-wallet) on financial services. In terms of operational CRM, many banks have been transferring service into contact centres and online in an effort to reduce costs, in the face of considerable resistance from some customer segments.

- *Auto manufacturers* sell through distributor/dealer networks. They have little contact with the end-user owner or driver. They use CRM for its ability to help them develop better and more profitable relationships with their distribution networks. Being physically disconnected from drivers, they have built websites that enable them to interact with these end-users. This has improved their knowledge of customer requirements. Ultimately, they hope CRM will enable them to win a greater share of end-user spend across the car purchase, maintenance and replacement cycle.

- *Technology solution vendors* manufacture or assemble complex bundles of hardware, software and implementation that are generally sold by partner organizations. For example, small innovative software developers have traditionally partnered with companies such as IBM to obtain distribution and sales. Other companies have copied Michael Dell's direct-to-customer (DTC) channel strategy for personal computers. CRM helps these DTC companies to collect customer information, segment their customer base, automate their sales processes with product configurator software and deliver their customer service online.

- *Consumer goods manufacturers* deal with the retail trade. They use CRM to help them develop profitable relationships with retailers. CRM helps them understand costs-to-serve and customer profitability. Key account management practices are applied to strategically significant customers. IT-enabled purchasing processes deliver higher levels of accuracy in stock replenishment. Manufacturers can run CRM-enabled marketing campaigns that are highly cost-effective.

THE NOT-FOR-PROFIT CONTEXT – THE 'THIRD SECTOR'

Most of this chapter has been concerned with CRM in the for-profit context. However, CRM is also found in the not-for-profit context. The 'third sector', the not-for-profit community (charity, non-government organization (NGO), education and government), is very active in implementing CRM. Universities wish to maintain relationships with alumni, charities campaign to raise income and government increasingly is interested in changing citizens' behaviour gently, through 'nudges' (behavioural economics). It is sometimes difficult to translate concepts developed for commercial, profit-centric organizations to the third sector. Fundamental to CRM is the customer selection and targeting process: there are some customers for whom we do more, and some customers for whom we do less. Governments interact with citizens, not customers. Governments typically provide more services to the most vulnerable citizens; in terms of profit maximization, these are 'unprofitable' customers, but government does not exist to maximize profit – we consent to be governed for our mutual benefit. This includes helping those in most need. Operational CRM solutions are often used to improve government service delivery. The UK's annual licensing of private road vehicles is online, and charities segment donors by regularity and size of gift, trying to manage small givers up a donation value tree to major bequests.

CASE STUDY 1.5

THE UK DRIVER AND VEHICLE LICENSING AGENCY

The UK's Driver and Vehicle Licensing Agency (DVLA) organizes the annual taxation of road vehicles through the issuance of a 'tax disc' that private car owners must display in their windscreen so that authorities know a vehicle is licensed. Owners must prove that they are insured and that their vehicle is roadworthy; the latter is achieved by passing a test at an authorized service point that issues roadworthiness certificates. The process for most Britons used to consist of waiting for hard-copy papers to be mailed from the DVLA as the tax disc reached its expiry, paying for a certificate of insurance, getting a roadworthiness certificate. The bundle of papers would then be taken to a Post Office, where other forms would be completed, evidence presented and payment made. A call centre in Wales managed a large volume of calls to support car owners as they engaged this process. The DVLA re-engineered the process such that roadworthiness certificates were stored online and insurers allowed the DVLA access to sufficient data so that it could verify the insurance on each vehicle. Today, the about-to-lapse notification comes to the car owner, who can go online and enter the reference number from the notification; computer systems verify that the vehicle is insured and roadworthy, the owner is asked to pay online and the tax disc comes via the post in a few days. For the government, compliance is improved and costs reduced. For car owners, time, effort and errors are taken out of the process. Such self-service online is an example of operational CRM (Citizen Relationship Management, rather than Customer Relationship Management) systems improving outcomes for both parties in a not-for-profit context.

MODELS OF CRM

A number of comprehensive CRM models have been developed. We introduce four of them here.

The IDIC model

The IDIC model was developed by Don Peppers and Martha Rogers, of the Peppers & Rogers Group, and has featured in a number of their books.[20] The IDIC model suggests that companies should take four actions in order to build closer one-to-one relationships with customers:

- *Identify* who your customers are and build a deep understanding of them.
- *Differentiate* your customers to identify which customers have most value now and which offer most for the future.
- *Interact* with customers to ensure that you understand customer expectations and their relationships with other suppliers or brands.
- *Customize* the offer and communications to ensure that the expectations of customers are met.

The CRM Value Chain

Francis Buttle's model, shown in Figure 1.1, consists of five primary stages and four supporting conditions leading towards the end goal of enhanced customer profitability.[21] The primary stages of customer portfolio analysis, customer intimacy, network development, value proposition development and managing the customer lifecycle are sequenced to ensure that a company, with the support of its network of suppliers, partners and employees, creates and

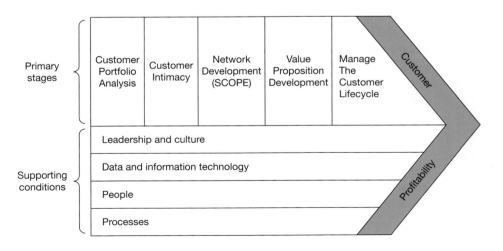

Figure 1.1 The CRM Value Chain

delivers value propositions that acquire and retain profitable customers. The supporting conditions of leadership and culture, data and IT, people and processes enable the CRM strategy to function effectively and efficiently.

Payne and Frow's 5-process model

Adrian Payne and Pennie Frow developed the 5-process model of CRM.[22] This model (Figure 1.2) clearly identifies five core processes in CRM: the strategy development process, the value creation process, the multi-channel integration process, the performance assessment process and the information management process. The first two represent strategic CRM; the multi-channel integration process represents operational CRM; the information management process is analytical CRM.

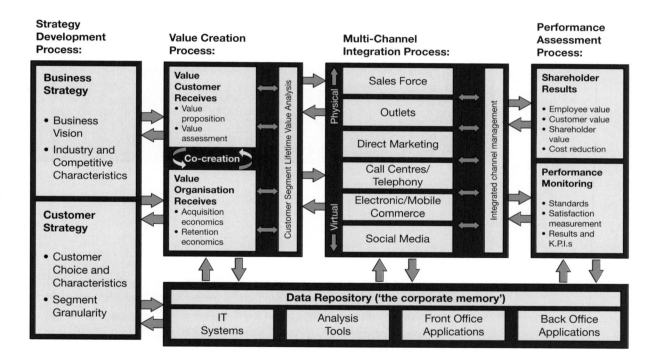

Figure 1.2 Payne's model of CRM

The Gartner competency model

The final comprehensive CRM model comes from Gartner Inc. Gartner Inc. is a leading IT research and advisory company that employs some 1,450 research analysts and consultants in 85 countries, and has a significant place in CRM research. Figure 1.3 presents Gartner's CRM competency model.

The model suggests that companies need competencies in eight areas for CRM to be successful. These include building a CRM vision, developing CRM strategies, designing valued customer experiences, intra- and extra-organizational collaboration, managing customer lifecycle processes, information management, technology implementation and developing measures indicative of CRM success or failure.

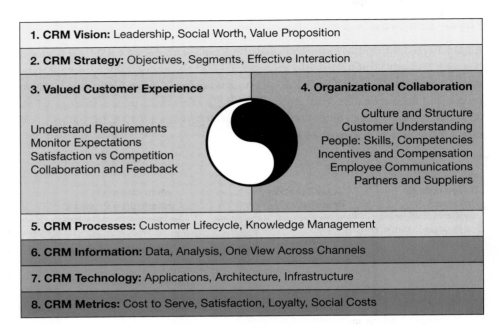

1. CRM Vision: Leadership, Social Worth, Value Proposition

2. CRM Strategy: Objectives, Segments, Effective Interaction

3. Valued Customer Experience

Understand Requirements
Monitor Expectations
Satisfaction vs Competition
Collaboration and Feedback

4. Organizational Collaboration

Culture and Structure
Customer Understanding
People: Skills, Competencies
Incentives and Compensation
Employee Communications
Partners and Suppliers

5. CRM Processes: Customer Lifecycle, Knowledge Management

6. CRM Information: Data, Analysis, One View Across Channels

7. CRM Technology: Applications, Architecture, Infrastructure

8. CRM Metrics: Cost to Serve, Satisfaction, Loyalty, Social Costs

Figure 1.3 Gartner's CRM model

SUMMARY

In this chapter you have learned that the expression CRM has a variety of meanings. Three major types of CRM have been identified: strategic, operational and analytical. There are many misunderstandings about CRM. For example, some people wrongly equate CRM with loyalty programmes, whereas others think of CRM as an IT issue. Although CRM is generally thought of as a business practice it is also applied in the not-for-profit context. A number of different constituencies have an interest in CRM, including CRM consultancies, CRM software vendors, CRM cloud solutions providers, CRM hardware and infrastructure vendors, companies that are implementing CRM and their customers.

We have produced a definition that underpins the rest of this book. We define CRM as the core business strategy that integrates internal processes and functions, and external networks, to create and deliver value to targeted customers at a profit. It is grounded on high-quality customer-related data and enabled by information technology.

Finally we have introduced a few models of CRM that try to scope the field.

NOTES AND REFERENCES

1   Gamble, P., Stone, M. and Woodcock, N. (1999). *Customer relationship marketing: up close and personal.* London: Kogan Page; Jain, S.C. (2005). CRM shifts the paradigm. *Journal of Strategic Marketing*, 13 (December), 275–91; Evans, M., O'Malley, L. and Patterson, M. (2004). *Exploring direct and customer relationship marketing.* London: Thomson.

2   http://whatis.techtarget.com/definition/0,289893,sid9_gci213567,00.html (Accessed 29 November 2005).

3   http://onlinebusiness.about.com/cs/marketing/g/CRM.htm (Accessed 29 November 2005).

4   http://www.siebel.com/what-is-crm/software-solutions.shtm (Accessed 29 November 2005).

5   http://computing-dictionary.thefreedictionary.com/CRM (Accessed 29 November 2005).

6   http://www.destinationcrm.com/articles/default.asp?ArticleID=5460 (Accessed 29 November 2005). This definition is attributed to Gartner Inc. (www.gartner.com).

7   Gartner Inc. (2012). Reported in: www.crmsearch.com/crm-market.php (Accessed 24 January 2014).

8   Kotler, P. (2000). *Marketing management: the millennium edition.* Englewood Cliffs, NJ: Prentice-Hall International.

9   Rogers, E.M. (1962). *Diffusion of innovations.* New York: Free Press.

10 Treacy, M. and Wiersema, F. (1995). *The discipline of market leaders.* London: Harper-Collins.

11 Deshpandé, R. (1999). *Developing a market orientation.* London: Sage.

12 http://www.salesforce.com/au/customers/stories/honda-australia.jsp (Accessed 21 February 2014).

13 Morgan, A. and Inks, S.A. (2001). Technology and the sales force. *Industrial Marketing Management*, 30(5), 463–72.

14 Engle, R.L. and Barnes, M.L. (2000). Sales force automation usage, effectiveness, and cost-benefit in Germany, England and the United States. *Journal of Business and Industrial Marketing*, 15(4), 216–42.

15 Contact centres differ from call centres in that they handle not only phone calls, but communications in other media such as mail, fax, email and Short Message Service (SMS).

16 Amplifying perceptions: how JetBlue uses Twitter to drive engagement and satisfaction. Case Clearing House: M-336 (2010), Stanford Graduate School of Business.

17 Baines, T.S., Lightfoot, H.W., Evans, S., Neely, A., Greenough, R., Peppard, J., *et al.* (2007). State-of-the-art in product-service systems. *Proceedings of the Institution of Mechanical Engineers – Part B – Engineering Manufacture (Professional Engineering Publishing)*, 221(10), 1543–52.

18 http://www-01.ibm.com/software/au/data/bigdata/ (Accessed 24 January 2014).

19 http://www.sas.com/success/axaseguros.html (Accessed 20 January 2007).

20 Peppers, D. and Rogers, M. (1996). *The 1-to-1 future: building business relationships one customer at a time.* London: Piatkus; Peppers, D. and Rogers, M. (1998). *Enterprise 1-to-1.* London: Piatkus; Peppers, D. and Rogers, M. (1999). *The 1-to-1 fieldbook.* London: Piatkus; Peppers, D. and Rogers, M. (2000). *The 1-to-1 manager.* London: Piatkus; Peppers, D. and Rogers, M. (2001). *One-to-one B2B: CRM strategies for the real economy.* London: Piatkus; Peppers, D. and Rogers, M. (2004). *Managing customer relationships: a strategic framework.* Hoboken, NJ: John Wiley; Peppers, D. and Rogers, M. (2005). *Return on customer: creating maximum value from your scarcest resource.* New York: Doubleday.

21 Buttle, F. (2004). *Customer relationship management: concepts and tools.* Oxford: Elsevier Butterworth-Heinemann.

22 Payne, A. and Frow, P. (2013). Strategic customer management: integrating CRM and relationship marketing. Cambridge: Cambridge University Press, p. 211. See also Payne, A. (2005). *Handbook of CRM: achieving excellence through customer management.* Oxford: Elsevier Butterworth-Heinemann; Payne, A. and Frow, P. (2005). A strategic framework for customer relationship management. *Journal of Marketing*, 69 (October), 167–76.

CHAPTER 2

UNDERSTANDING RELATIONSHIPS

CHAPTER OBJECTIVES

By the end of this chapter you will understand:

- How to recognize a relationship.
- Attributes of successful relationships.
- The importance of trust and commitment within a relationship.
- Why companies and customers are sometimes motivated to establish and maintain relationships with each other, and sometimes not.
- The meaning and importance of customer lifetime value.
- The five different schools of thought that contribute to our understanding of relationships and relationship management.

WHAT IS A RELATIONSHIP?

The 'R' of CRM stands for 'relationship'. But what do we really mean by the expression 'relationship'? Certainly, most of us would understand what it means to be in a personal relationship, but what is a relationship between a customer and supplier?

At the very least a relationship involves interaction over time. If there is only a one-off transaction, like buying a vacuum cleaner from a specialist outlet, most of us wouldn't call this a relationship. Thinking in terms of a dyadic relationship, that is a relationship between two parties, if we take this interaction over time as a critical feature, we can define the term 'relationship' as follows:

A relationship is composed of a series of interactive episodes between dyadic parties over time.

Let's be clear about what is meant by 'interactive episode'. Episodes are time bound (they have a beginning and an end) and are identifiable; you can put names to the episodes. Within a sales representative–customer relationship it is often possible to identify a number of discrete episodes, such as making a purchase, enquiring about a product, making a sales call, negotiating terms, dealing with a complaint, resolving an invoicing dispute and playing a round of golf. For consumers taking on a mobile phone contract there is the enquiry-to-purchase episode, the on-boarding (getting connected), billing and other customer service episodes – mostly over the phone.

Each episode in turn is composed of a series of interactions. Interaction consists of action, and response to that action. Within each episode, each participant will act towards, and interact with, the other. The content of each episode is a range of communicative behaviours including speech, deeds (actions) and body language.

Some authorities think that it is insufficient, even naive, to define a relationship as interaction over time. Jim Barnes, for example, suggests that there needs to be some emotional content to the interaction.[1] This implies some type of affective connection, attachment or bond.

Similarly, a relationship has been said to exist only when the parties move from a state of independence to dependence or interdependence.[2] When a customer buys an occasional latte from a coffee shop, this is a transaction, not a relationship. If the customer returns repeatedly because she likes the store's atmosphere, the way the coffee is prepared or has taken a shine to the barista, this looks more like a relationship. And whilst in this instance there is dependence (of customer on coffee shop), there is no interdependence.

This suggests the parties may have very different ideas about whether they are in a relationship. For example, in a professional procurement context for a multinational organization, corporate buying staff may think they are being tough and transactional. Their suppliers may feel that they have built a relationship. Woodburn and McDonald have explored the potential mismatching of buyer and seller preferences for their relationship.[3] They identify five hierarchical levels of relationship: exploratory, basic, cooperative, interdependent and integrated. Suppliers and buyers each have their own preference of the level they wish to achieve. Ideally they match, but often they don't. The zone of delusion is when a supplier is investing in building a higher-level partnership with the customer, whilst the buyer is merely interested in the basic transaction. Conversely, the zone of frustration is where the buyer would like to partner but the supplier is focused only on the next transaction.[4]

Of course, modern business relationships are typically more complex than simple dyads. In a business-to-business (B2B) relationship, there may be many interpersonal relationships formed between people on both sides. The CEOs may be talking about building a formalized partnership; the customer's engineers may be talking with the supplier's product management about product quality; the customer's product users may be talking to the supplier's customer service team about product training, and so on. Sometimes, when purchasing large complex business solutions a customer will build relationships with companies in the supplier's own supply chain, so as to ensure that the right levels of product functionality, quality and innovation are built into future offerings. And to make it even more complex, one can imagine many customers dealing with many suppliers in a collaborative network of relationships. However, we will begin by focusing upon the single dyad: a customer and a supplier.

Change within relationships

Relationships change over time. Parties become closer or more distant; interactions become more or less frequent. Because they evolve, they can vary considerably, both in the number and variety of episodes, and the interactions that take place within those episodes. Dwyer has identified five general phases through which customer–supplier relationships can evolve.[5]

1   Awareness.

2   Exploration.

3   Expansion.

4   Commitment.

5   Dissolution.

Awareness is when each party comes to the attention of the other as a possible exchange partner. Exploration is the period of investigation and testing during which the parties explore each other's capabilities and performance. Some trial purchasing takes place. If the trial is unsuccessful the relationship can be terminated with few costs. This exploration phase is thought to comprise five sub-processes: attraction; communication and bargaining; development and exercise of power; development of norms; and the development of expectations. Expansion is the phase in which there is increasing interdependence. More transactions take place and trust begins to develop. The commitment phase is characterized by increased adaptation on both sides and mutually understood roles and goals. Automated purchasing processes are a sure sign of commitment.

Not all relationships will reach the commitment phase. Many are terminated before that stage. There may be a breach of trust that forces a partner to reconsider the relationship. Relationship termination can be bilateral or unilateral. Bilateral termination is when both parties agree to end the relationship. They will probably want to retrieve whatever assets they invested in the relationship. Unilateral termination is when one of the parties ends the relationship. Customers exit relationships for many reasons, such as repeated service failures or changed product requirements. Suppliers may choose to exit relationships because of the relationship's failure to contribute to sales volume or profit goals. One option to resolve this problem and continue the relationship may be to reduce the supplier's cost-to-serve the customer.

This discussion of relationship development highlights two attributes of highly developed relationships: trust and commitment. These have been the subjects of a considerable amount of research.[6]

Trust

Trust is focused. That is, although there may be a generalized sense of confidence and security, these feelings are directed. One party may trust the other party's:

- *Benevolence*. A belief that one party acts in the interests of the other.
- *Honesty*. A belief that the other party's word is reliable or credible.

- *Competence*. A belief that the other party has the necessary expertise to perform as required.

The development of trust is an investment in relationship-building which has a long-term payoff. Trust emerges as parties share experiences, and interpret and assess each other's motives. As they learn more about each other, risk and doubt are reduced. For these reasons, trust has been described as the glue that holds a relationship together across time and different episodes.[7]

When mutual trust exists between partners, both are motivated to make investments in the relationship. These investments, which serve as exit barriers, may be either tangible (e.g. property) or intangible (e.g. knowledge). Such investments may or may not be retrievable when the relationship dissolves.

If trust is absent, conflict and uncertainty rise, whilst cooperation falls. Lack of trust clearly provides a shaky foundation for a successful customer–supplier relationship.

Commitment

Commitment is an essential ingredient for successful, long-term relationships. Morgan and Hunt define relationship commitment as follows:

> **Commitment is shown by 'an exchange partner believing that an ongoing relationship with another is so important as to warrant maximum effort to maintain it; that is, the committed party believes the relationship is worth working on to ensure that it endures indefinitely'.[8]**

Commitment arises from trust, shared values and the belief that partners will be difficult to replace. Commitment motivates partners to cooperate in order to preserve relationship investments. Commitment means partners forgo short-term alternatives in favour of more stable, long-term benefits associated with current partners. Where customers have choice, they make commitments only to trustworthy partners, because commitment entails vulnerability, leaving them open to opportunism. For example, a corporate customer that commits future purchasing of raw materials to a particular supplier may experience the downside of opportunistic behaviour if that supplier raises prices.

Evidence of commitment is found in the investments that one party makes in the other. One party makes investments in the promising relationship and if the other responds, the relationship evolves and the partners become increasingly committed to doing business with each other. Investments can include time, money and the sidelining of current or alternative relationships. A partner's commitment to a relationship is directly represented in the size of the investment in the relationship, since these represent termination costs. Highly committed relationships have very high termination costs since some of these relationship investments may be irretrievable, for example, investments in capital equipment made for a joint venture. In addition there may be significant costs incurred in switching to an alternative supplier, such as search costs, learning costs and psychic (stress, worry) costs.

RELATIONSHIP QUALITY

This discussion of trust and commitment suggests that some relationships can be thought to be of better quality than others. Research into relationship quality generally cites trust and commitment as core attributes of a high-quality relationship.[9] However, a number of other attributes have also been identified, including relationship satisfaction, mutual goals and cooperative norms.

Relationship satisfaction is not the same as commitment. Commitment to a supplier comes as investments are made in the relationship, and investments are only made if the committed party is satisfied with their transactional history. In other words, investments are made in relationships that are satisfactory.[10] Mutual goals are present when the parties share objectives that can only be achieved through joint action and relationship continuity. Cooperative norms are seen when relational parties work together constructively and interdependently to resolve problems.

Given that CRM implementations are often designed to build closer, more value-laden relationships with customers, it makes sense for managers to be aware of variance in the quality of the relationships they have with customers.

WHY COMPANIES WANT RELATIONSHIPS WITH CUSTOMERS

The fundamental reason that companies want to build relationships with customers is economic. Companies generate better results when they manage their customer base in order to identify, acquire, satisfy and retain profitable customers. These are key objectives of many CRM strategies.

Improving customer retention rates has the effect of increasing the size of the customer base. Table 2.1 compares two companies. Company A has a churn rate (customer defection rate) of 5 per cent per annum; company B's churn rate is 10 per cent. Put another way, their respective customer retention rates are 95 per cent and 90 per cent. Starting from the same position and acquiring an identical number of new customers each year, company A's customer base is 19 per cent larger than company B's after four years: 1,268 customers compared to 1,066 customers.

Table 2.1 The effect of customer retention on customer numbers

Year	Company A (5% churn)			Company B (10% churn)		
	Existing customers	New customers	Total customer base	Existing customers	New customers	Total customer base
1	1,000	100	1,100	1,000	100	1,100
2	1,045	100	1,145	990	100	1,090
3	1,088	100	1,188	981	100	1,081
4	1,129	100	1,229	973	100	1,073
5	1,168	100	1,268	966	100	1,066

Churn rates vary considerably. Energy utilities supplying electricity and gas typically have enjoyed very low churn levels because of their monopoly positions. However, industry deregulation changed that. In the UK about 25 per cent of utility customers changed suppliers within two years of industry deregulation. The industry had been expecting 5–10 per cent churn, and were surprised at the actual levels. Most switchers were looking for better prices and to achieve a dual-fuel (gas and electricity) discount.

There is little merit in growing the customer base aimlessly. The goal must be to retain existing customers, and recruit new customers, who have future profit potential, or are important for other strategic purposes.[11] Not all customers are of equal importance. Some customers may not be worth recruiting or retaining at all, for example those who have a high cost-to-serve, are debtors, late payers or promiscuous in the sense that they switch frequently between suppliers.

Other things being equal, a larger customer base does deliver better business performance. Similarly, as customer retention rates rise (or churn rates fall), so does the average tenure of a customer, as shown in Table 2.2. Tenure is the term used to describe the length of time a customer remains a customer. The impacts of small improvements in customer retention are hugely magnified at the higher levels of retention. For example, improving the customer retention rate from 75 per cent to 80 per cent grows average customer tenure from ten years to 12.5 years. Managing tenure by reducing defection rates can be critical. For example, it can take 13 years for utility customers to break even by recovering the costs of their initial recruitment.

CUSTOMER CHURN AT EIRCOM[12]

CASE STUDY 2.1

Eircom is one of Ireland's biggest telecommunications service providers with over two million fixed-line and mobile customers, just under 5,000 employees and an annual turnover of around €1.5 billion. Eircom has 20 per cent share of the country's mobile market, and 40 per cent of the broadband market. Ireland's economic recession following the 2008 financial crisis led to increasing competition between mobile network operators and higher levels of customer churn as customers sought better value.

Eircom routinely collects structured data on important issues for customers, such as dropped calls, and customer satisfaction with service interactions, such as customer on-boarding onto the network. The company's customer satisfaction instrument allows customers to explain in free-text boxes why they have assigned a particular satisfaction score. Eircom has a team of analysts working with data mining tools that allow them to explore both structured and unstructured data. Text analytics help eircom to understand customer sentiment at different points along their journey, as reported in the free-text boxes.

Eircom uses automated churn prediction modelling to enable a quick response when a customer's patterns of behaviour indicate a high probability of churn. Eircom has also improved in-store processes and staff training. The analytics team discovered that customer experience during the on-boarding process had a significant effect on the likelihood of churn. As a result, eircom introduced a new in-store process to enhance the on-boarding experience, based on improving the import of contacts from an old phone to a new one.

Table 2.2 Retention rate and average customer tenure

Customer retention rate (%)	Average customer tenure (years)
50	2
67	3
75	4
80	5
90	10
92	12.5
95	20
96	25
97	33.3
98	50
99	100

Managing customer retention and tenure intelligently generates two key benefits for companies – reduced marketing costs, and better customer insight.

Reduced marketing costs

Improving customer retention reduces a company's marketing costs. Fewer dollars need to be spent replacing churned customers.[13] For example, it has been estimated that it costs an advertising agency at least 20 times as much to recruit a new client than to retain an existing client. Major agencies can spend up to $4 million on research, strategic analysis and creative work in pitching for one major international client, with up to four creative teams working on different executions. An agency might incur these costs several times over as it pitches to several prospective clients to replace a lost client.[14] In addition to reducing the costs of customer acquisition, costs-to-serve existing customers also tend to fall over time. Ultimately, as in some business-to-business markets, the relationship may become fully automated. Some supply-chain relationships, for example, employ electronic data interchange (EDI). EDI is the computer-to-computer exchange of business documents in a standard electronic format – such as ANSI, EDIFACT, TRADACOMS and XML – between business partners. EDI fully automates the ordering, inventory and invoicing processes. EDI is a relationship investment that acts as an exit barrier.

Better customer insight

As customer tenure lengthens, suppliers are able to develop a better understanding of customer requirements and expectations. Customers also come to understand what a supplier can do for them. Consequently, suppliers are better placed to identify and satisfy customer requirements profitably, selling more product and service to the retained customer.

Over time, as relationships deepen, trust and commitment between the parties is likely to grow. Under these circumstances, revenue and profit streams from customers become more secure. One study, for example, shows that the average online clothing customer spends 67 per cent more, and grocery customers spend 23 per cent more, in months 31–36 of a relationship than in months 0–6.[15] McKinsey has found that retained customers are significantly less likely to shop around for a new auto insurance policy than newly recruited customers. Retention is improved if car insurance is bundled with another insurance product.[16]

In sum, both the cost and revenue sides of the profit equation are impacted by customer retention.

Some companies employ a model that has been variously known as a value ladder[17] or value staircase[18] to help them understand where customers are positioned in terms of their tenure with the company. Customers typically buy from a portfolio of more-or-less equivalent offers or suppliers. For example, large and medium-sized businesses often do business with more than one bank, and consumers may select a soft drink from a small portfolio of branded carbonated beverages. When customers climb the ladder, their value to your company grows. Your share of their portfolio expands. Put another way, your share of customer spending, or customer wallet, grows. In Table 2.1 we present a seven-stage customer journey from suspect status to advocate status.

As in the Dwyer model cited earlier, not every customer progresses uniformly along the path from 'never-a-customer' to 'always-a-customer'. Some may have a long maturity phase (i.e. loyal customer) and others will have a shorter life, perhaps never shifting from first-time customer to repeat customer; others might never convert from prospect to first-timer. CRM software allows companies to trace where customers are on this pathway and to allocate resources intelligently to advance suitable customers along the value trajectory.

Costs and revenues vary from stage to stage of the journey. In the early stages, a company may invest significant sums in converting a prospect into a first-time customer. The investment in initiating a relationship may not be recovered for some time. For example, Reichheld and Sasser have shown that it takes a credit card company approaching two years

Table 2.3 The customer journey

Suspect	Does the potential customer fit your target market profile?
Prospect	The customer fits the target market profile and is being approached for the first time.
First-time customer	The customer makes a first purchase.
Repeat customer	The customer makes additional purchases. Your offer plays a minor role in the customer's portfolio.
Majority customer	The customer selects your company as supplier of choice. You occupy a significant place in the customer's portfolio.
Loyal customer	The customer is resistant to switching suppliers, and has a strong positive attitude to your company or offer.
Advocate	The customer generates additional referral dollars through positive word-of-mouth.

to recover the costs of customer acquisition.[19] Another study shows that the average online clothing customer takes four purchases (12 months) to recover the costs of their acquisition, whereas online grocery customers take 18 months to break even.[20]

CUSTOMER LIFETIME VALUE

This leads to the core CRM idea that a customer should not be viewed as a set of independent transactions but as a lifetime income stream. In the auto industry, for instance, it has been estimated that a General Motors retail customer is worth $276,000 over a lifetime of purchasing cars (11 or more vehicles), parts and service. Fleet operators are worth considerably more.[21] When a GM customer switches to Ford the revenue streams from that customer may be lost for ever. This makes customer retention a strategically important goal for GM. Customer lifetime value (CLV) is even more important if you consider that a small number of customers may account for a high proportion of the entire value generated by all customers. Tukel found that the top 28 per cent of customers generate 80 per cent of the total value of all customers.[22]

CASE STUDY 2.2

CUSTOMER LIFETIME VALUE IN THE BANKING INDUSTRY[23]

One in five banking executives does not measure CLV. Couple this with the 22 per cent who do not measure portfolio or share-of-wallet, and it is easy to see why cross-selling is such a challenge for financial service providers. Unless a banker knows which of a customer's financial needs are being met, it is exceedingly difficult to suggest additional services. A robust business intelligence system can provide a financial services firm with a 360-degree view of the customer. Transactions can be consolidated with demographic and psychographic data, revenue and profit measures, as well as historical customer service incidents and queries. With this total picture, the provider can see the customer from multiple perspectives and craft programmes that will satisfy a broad range of client requirements. Part of this multifaceted view of the customer is the ability to aggregate multiple customers into a household perspective. The benefits of this consolidated view are clear and strong. Multiple financial service needs can be seen *in toto*, investment opportunities can be tied to life events for cohabiting family members and marketing costs can be driven down by providing a single, comprehensive marketing message.

Customer lifetime value is a measure of a customer's profit-generation for a company. CLV can be defined as follows:

Customer lifetime value is the present-day value of all net margins earned from a relationship with a customer, customer segment or cohort.

CLV can be estimated at the level of the individual customer, customer segment or cohort. A cohort of customers is a group that has some characteristic or set of characteristics in common. These might be customers recruited in a single year, or recruited through a single campaign or channel. This type of cohort analysis is useful, for example, to find out whether certain channels are more effective or more efficient at recruiting high value customers. A European motoring organization knows that it costs an average of $105 to recruit a new member. However, recruitment costs vary across channels. The organization's member-get-member (MGM) referral scheme costs $66, the organization's direct response TV campaign costs $300, and door-drops cost $210 per newly acquired member. The MGM scheme is most cost-effective at customer acquisition, but if these customers churn at a high rate and cost significantly more to serve, they may turn out to be less valuable than customers generated at higher initial cost. In fact, customers acquired through the MGM referral scheme remain members longer, buy more and also generate word-of-mouth referrals.

To compute CLV, all historic net margins are compounded up to today's value and all future net margins are discounted back to today's value. Estimates of CLV potential look to the future only, and ignore the past.

The focus on free cash flow rather than gross margins is because a customer that appears to be valuable on the basis of the gross margins generated can become less profitable once cost-to-serve the customer is taken into account. Companies that do not have the processes in place to allocate costs (e.g. ABC – Activity Based Costing) to customers cannot use free cash. They must work either with gross margin or sales revenue data.

For most companies, an important strategic objective is to identify and attract those customers or segments that have the highest CLV potential. They are unconcerned with the past. What matters is the future.

Research by Reichheld and Sasser indicates why it is important to look forward to compute CLV.[24] Their data suggest that profit margins tend to accelerate over time, as shown in Table 2.4. This has four causes.

Table 2.4 Profit from customers over time

	Profit (loss) per customer over time ($)					
	Year					
Service	0	1	2	3	4	5
Credit card	(51)	30	42	44	49	55
Industrial laundry		144	166	192	222	256
Industrial distribution		45	99	121	144	168
Auto servicing		25	35	70	88	88

1   *Revenues grow* over time, as customers buy more. In the credit card example in Table 2.4, users tend to grow their balances over time as they become more relaxed about using their card for an increasing range of purchases. Also, a satisfied customer may look to buy additional categories of product from a preferred supplier. An insurance company that has a loyal car insurance customer is likely to experience some success cross-selling other personal lines, for example home, property and travel insurance.

2   *Cost-to-serve is lower* for existing customers, because both supplier and customer understand the other. For example, customers do not make demands on the company that it cannot satisfy. Similarly companies do not communicate offers that have little or no value to customers.

3   *Higher prices may be paid* by existing customers. This is partly because they are not offered the discounts that are often promised to new customers, and partly because they are less sensitive to price offers from other potential suppliers because they are satisfied with their experience.

4   *Value-generating referrals* are made by satisfied customers. Every customer not only has their own CLV, but also, potentially, a Customer Referral Value or CRV. That is, satisfied customers can generate additional value for their supplier by giving positive word-of-mouth to their friends and associates. Word-of-mouth can be powerfully persuasive when it is regarded as independent and unpaid.

Computing CLV

The computation of CLV potential is very straightforward in principle, but can be complicated in practice. Several pieces of information are needed. For an existing customer, you need to know:

1   What is the probability that the customer will buy products and services from the company in the future, period-by-period?

2   What will be the gross margins on those purchases period-by-period?

3   What will be the cost of serving the customer, period-by-period?

For new customers an additional piece of information is needed:

4   What is the cost of acquiring the customer?

Finally, to bring future margins back to today's value, another question needs to be answered for both existing and new customers:

5   What discount rate should be applied to future net margins?

Some commentators suggest that CLV estimates should not be based on future purchasing only, but on word-of-mouth (WOM) influence too. The logic is that a satisfied and retained customer not only buys but also influences others to buy. Lee and colleagues show that incorporation of WOM effects increased customer value significantly.[25] Not all customers have the same Customer Referral Value. Kumar and his co-authors found that the customers with the highest CRV at a telecommunications company were not the customers with the highest personal CLV, but those in the mid-levels of CLV. For example, customers in the top decile with an average CLV of $1,933 generated an additional $40 of value through referrals, whilst customers in the 5th decile, having a CLV of $313, generated $1,020 of referral value for their telecommunications.[26] As more and more customers interact with each other over social media, the impact of WOM is likely to grow substantially.

Table 2.5 demonstrates the impact that discount rate has on customer value. Without discounting future profits, the customer appears to have a CLV of $235. However, once a 15 per cent discount rate is applied, the customer's CLV in today's dollar is only $127.43. A common practice is to use the weighted average cost of capital (WACC) as the discount factor. WACC takes into account the costs of the two sources of capital – debt and equity. Each usually has a different cost, and therefore the average cost of capital for a business will reflect the degree to which the business is funded by the two sources. Equally, an argument can be made for differentiating discount rates by the inherent risk of the customer segment targeted. Customers in segments that have inherently high churn might attract a greater discount rate to reflect their higher risk. Whilst we are not aware of many firms practising such fine-tuning in their CLV calculations overtly, credit-scoring processes used by credit card companies and banks essentially provide a similar assessment of individual risk.

Table 2.5 Impact of discount rate on CLV

1.	Undiscounted profit earned over 5 years		2.	Discounted profit earned over 5 years (15% discount rate)	
		$			$
Year	0	−50	Year	0	−50
	1	+30		1	$+30 \div 1.15 = 26.09$
	2	+40		2	$+40 \div 1.15^2 = 30.25$
	3	+55		3	$+55 \div 1.15^3 = 36.16$
	4	+72		4	$+72 \div 1.15^4 = 41.17$
	5	+88		5	$+88 \div 1.15^5 = 43.76$
Totals		$235			$127.43

The net present value of 5 years' profit earned from this customer is $127.43

Computation of a meaningful CLV estimate requires companies to be able to forecast customer buying behaviour, product and service costs and prices, the costs of capital (for determining the discount rate) and the costs of acquiring and retaining customers. This is very demanding, especially at the level of the individual customer, but is a challenge that analytical CRM implementations often take on.

A number of companies have developed models that produce approximate CLV estimates. US Bancorp, for example, calculates a customer profitability metric called Customer Relationship Value (CRV) in which they use historical product ownership to generate 'propensity to buy' indices. Overhead costs are not factored in to the computation. Within their customer base, they have been able to identify four CRV segments, each having different value, cost, attrition and risk profiles:

- top tier, 11 per cent of customers
- threshold, next 22 per cent

- fence sitters, next 39 per cent
- value destroyers, bottom 28 per cent.

Each of these segments is treated to different value propositions and customer management programmes: product offers, lending decisions, fee waivers, channel options and retention efforts. North Carolina's Centura Bank has two million customers. The top customers receive special attention from service staff and senior management, including an annual call from the CEO.

For situations where the cost of generating accurate CLV data is thought not to be prohibitive, Berger and Nasr have developed a number of mathematical models that can be used in CLV estimation.[27]

CASE STUDY 2.3

HIGH LIFETIME VALUE CUSTOMERS AT BARCLAYS BANK

Barclays is a UK-based bank with global operations. As part of the bank's CRM strategy, it undertook an analysis of its customer portfolio to identify which retail segments were most strategically significant. The analysis found that customers within the 25–35-year age group, who were professionally employed and who had a mortgage and or credit card product, were most strategically significant. These were the bank's most profitable customers.

The bank also found that this segment represented the highest potential customer lifetime value for the bank, 12 per cent greater than any other segment. CLV is derived from the bank's estimates of future income from fees, interest and other charges over their lifetime as a customer.

Table 2.6 shows how to compute CLV for a cohort of customers. In year 0, the company spent $10 million in marketing campaigns to generate new customers. The result was 100,000 new customers added to the customer base at an acquisition cost of $100 per customer.

In year 1 the company lost 40 per cent of these new customers, but the remaining 60 per cent each generated $50 contribution to profit. If this is discounted at 15 per cent, each retained customer's profit contribution is $43.48. In year 2, the retention rate rises from 60 per cent to 70 per cent, and each of the remaining customers contributes $70 ($52.93 at discounted rate) to profit. You can see from the right-hand column in Table 2.6 that it takes nearly five years to recover the costs of acquiring this cohort. The data demonstrate a couple of well-established phenomena. First, profit per customer rises over time – for reasons set out earlier in this chapter. Second, customer retention rate rises over time.

It is feasible to use data such as these to manage a business for improved profitability. Several strategies are available:

1   Improve customer retention rate in the early years of the relationship. This will produce a larger number of customers to generate higher profits in the later years.

Table 2.6 Computing cohort value

Year	Profit per customer ($)	Net present value at 15% discount ($)	Customer retention rate (%)	No. of customers	Total annual profit ($)
1	50	43.48	60	60,000	2,608,800
2	70	52.93	70	42,000	2,223,062
3	100	65.75	75	31,500	2,071,125
4	140	80.00	80	25,200	2,016,000
5	190	94.53	85	21,420	2,024,776
6	250	108.23	90	19,278	2,086,034
7	320	120.30	92	17,736	2,133,654
8	400	130.72	94	16,672	2,179,346
9	450	127.84	95	15,838	2,024,744
10	500	123.15	96	15,204	1,872,372

2   Increase the profit earned per customer by:

a   reducing cost-to-serve;

b   cross-selling or up-selling additional products and services.

3   Become better at customer acquisition by:

a   using more cost-effective recruitment channels;

b   better qualification of prospects. Customers who defect early on perhaps should have not been recruited in the first place;

c   careful nurturing of prospects with high CLV potential;

d   recruiting new customers matched to the profiles of current customers having a high CLV.

You should not leave this discussion of CLV by believing that if you improve customer retention, business performance will automatically lift. It depends entirely upon which customers are retained and how you manage those relationships. We have more to say about customer retention in Chapter 4.

WHEN MIGHT COMPANIES NOT WANT RELATIONSHIPS WITH CUSTOMERS?

Despite the financial benefits that can accrue from a relationship, companies sometimes resist entering into relationships with customers. We look at both business-to-business (B2B) and business-to-consumer (B2C) contexts. In the business-to-business context there are a number of reasons for this resistance.

- *Loss of control.* A mature customer–supplier relationship involves give and take on both sides of the dyad. In bilateral relationships, suppliers may have to give up unilateral control over their own business's resources. For example, a supplier of engineering services might not want to provide free pre-sales consultancy for a new project with an established client because of the high costs involved. However, the customer might have clear expectations of the activities that should be performed and the resources deployed by the supplier.

- *Exit costs.* Not all relationships survive. It is not necessarily easy or cost-effective to exit a relationship. Sometimes, investments that are made in a relationship are not returned when a relationship breaks down, for example, investments in Electronic Data Interchange (EDI). Relationship investments vary from the insignificant (e.g. co-branding of promotional literature) to highly significant (e.g. setting up a new production line to service a particular customer's requirements). A company might justifiably be concerned about the security of a relationship-based investment in new manufacturing operations.

- *Resource commitment.* Relationships require the commitment of resources such as people, time and money. Companies have to decide whether it is better to allocate resources to customer management or some other area of the business such as operations or research and development. Once resources are committed, they can become sunk costs. Sunk costs are unrecoverable past expenditures. These would not normally be taken into account when deciding whether to continue in a relationship, because they cannot be recovered whether the relationship endures or not. However, it is a common instinct to consider them.

- *Opportunity costs.* If resources are committed to one customer, they cannot be allocated to another. Relationships imply high opportunity costs. If you commit resources to customer A, you may have to give up the possibility of a relationship with customer B, even if that does seem to be a better proposition. An engineering consultancy that commits consultants to pre-sales activities with a current client might incur the opportunity cost of losing more lucrative work in business opportunities from other prospective clients.

When businesses interact with consumers (the B2C market) they have many opportunities to collect customer-related data that are useful for CRM purposes. Transaction data, warranty data and loyalty programme data are examples of the types of data that many B2C companies routinely collect. The majority of consumer marketers would like to establish closer, even one-to-one, relationships with their customers, but customer focus is not the only strategy available to consumer goods and services companies. Some adopt a product leadership strategy and focus on innovating and bringing to market leading-edge products. Apple, whilst providing a uniformly high level of customer service and experience, does not mine its customer database to generate differential treatments for individual customers aligned to their needs, wants and preferences. Other companies opt for an operational excellence strategy and seek to reduce costs through outstanding operational expertise, rather than investing in customer relationships. Low-cost airlines, for example, rarely manage individual relationships actively; they compete on cost rather than on excellence at relationship management. Many of the 'fun fashion' retailers do not invest in loyalty programmes but focus on design and supply chain for competitive advantage.

WHY CUSTOMERS WANT RELATIONSHIPS WITH SUPPLIERS

We now reverse the question and examine why customers may want to build relationships with suppliers. First, we look at the business-to-business context. A relationship with a supplier can reduce the customer's sense of perceived risk. Perceived risk takes many forms – performance, physical, financial, social and psychological risk. High levels of perceived risk are uncomfortable for many customers. A relationship can reduce or eliminate perceived risk. Here are a number of circumstances when perceived risk may be high and a relationship desirable:

- *Product complexity*. If the product or its applications are particularly complex, for example networking infrastructure, a relationship can reduce performance risk – the risk that the technology will not work as desired or expected.
- *Product strategic significance*. If the product is strategically important or mission-critical, for example supply of essential raw materials for a continuous process manufacturer, performance risk may be high.
- *Service requirements*. If there are downstream service requirements, for example for machine tools, a relationship can ensure that the tools will remain serviced and functional.
- *Purchase cost*. If a purchase is particularly costly, for example purchases of large pieces of capital equipment such as earth-moving equipment, financial risk is high.
- *Reciprocity*. A financial audit practice may want a close relationship with a management consultancy, so that each party benefits from referrals by the other.

In the business-to-consumer context, relationships with suppliers are likely to be valued by customers if the relationship delivers customer benefits over and above those directly derived from acquiring, consuming or using the product or service. Risk may play a role here, too. For example, an automobile owner may develop a relationship with a service station to reduce the perceived performance, financial and physical risk attached to having a car serviced. The relationship provides the assurance that the job has been skilfully performed and that the car is safe to drive. There are other motives behind consumers' desires to build relationships with suppliers, too:

- *Recognition*. Customers may feel more valued when recognized and addressed by name, for example at a retail bank branch, or as a frequent flyer.
- *Personalization*. Relationships mean that suppliers have enough customer insight to customize products or services. For example, over time, a hairdresser may come to understand a customer's particular preferences or expectations.
- *Power*. Relationships with suppliers can be empowering. For example, some of the usual power asymmetry in relationships between banks and their customers may be reversed when customers feel that they have personal relationships with particular bank officers or branches.

- *Status*. Customers may feel that their status is enhanced by a relationship with a supplier, such as an elite health club or platinum credit card company.

- *Affiliation*. People's social needs can be met through commercially based, or non-commercially based, relationships. Many people are customers (members) of professional or community associations, for example.

Customer segments can vary in their desire to have relationships with suppliers. In the banking industry, for example, large corporations have their own treasury departments and often get little value from a bank relationship; small private account holders have no need for the additional services that a relationship provides; small and medium-sized business and high net worth individuals may have most to gain from a closer relationship.

A number of B2C organizations deliver incremental benefits by building closer relationships with their customers. The Harley Owners Group (HOG) offers a raft of benefits to Harley Davidson owners including club outings and preferential insurance rates. Nestlé's mother and baby club offers advice and information to new mothers.

When might customers NOT want relationships with suppliers?

Whilst companies generally want long-term relationships with customers for the economic reasons already described, it is far less clear that customers universally want relationships with their suppliers. B2B customers cite a number of concerns.[28]

- *Fear of dependency*. This is driven by a number of worries. Customers are concerned that the supplier might act opportunistically, once they are in a preferred position, perhaps introducing price rises. They also fear the reduction in their flexibility to choose alternative suppliers. There may also be concerns over a loss of personal authority and control.

- *Lack of perceived value in the relationship*. Customers may not believe that they will enjoy substantial savings in transaction costs, or that the relationship will help them create a superior competitive position, generate additional revenue or that there will be any social benefits. In other words, there is no perceived value above and beyond that obtained from the product or service.

- *Lack of confidence in the supplier*. Customers may choose not to enter a relationship because they feel the potential partner is unreliable, too small, has a poor reputation or is insufficiently innovative.

- *Customer lacks relational orientation*. Not all company cultures are equally inclined towards relationship-building. Some are much more transactional. For example, some retailers make it a policy to buy a high proportion of their merchandise on special. This preference for transactional rather than relational business operations will be reflected in the company's buying processes, and employee reward systems.

- *Rapid technological changes*. In an industry with rapidly changing technology, commitment to one supplier might mean that the customer misses out on new developments available through other suppliers.

In the B2C context, consumers buy hundreds of different convenience, shopping and speciality products and services. Whereas consumers might want a relationship with their financial service adviser or their physician, they can often find no good reason for developing closer relationships with the manufacturer of their household detergent, snack foods or toothpaste. However, for consumer products and services that are personally important, customers can become more involved and become more emotionally engaged.

CUSTOMER SATISFACTION, LOYALTY AND BUSINESS PERFORMANCE

An important rationale for CRM is that it improves business performance by enhancing customer satisfaction and driving up customer loyalty, as shown in Figure 2.1. There is a compelling logic to the model, which has been dubbed the 'satisfaction–profit chain'.[29] Satisfaction increases because customer insight allows companies to understand their customers better, and create improved customer value propositions and better customer experiences. As customer satisfaction rises, so does customer intention to repurchase.[30] This in turn influences actual purchasing behaviour that has an impact on business performance.

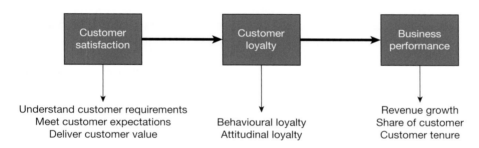

Figure 2.1 The satisfaction–profit chain

We will examine the variables and linkages between them. First we will define the major variables: customer satisfaction, customer loyalty and business performance.

Customer satisfaction

Customer satisfaction has been the subject of considerable research, and has been defined and measured in many ways.[31] We define customer satisfaction as follows:

Customer satisfaction is the customer's fulfilment response to a customer experience, or some part thereof.

Customer satisfaction is a pleasurable fulfilment response. Dissatisfaction is an unpleasurable fulfilment response. The 'experience, or some part of it' component of the definition suggests that the satisfaction evaluation can be directed at any or all elements of the customer's experience. This can include product, service, process and any other components of the customer experience.

The most common way of operationalizing satisfaction is to compare the customer's perception of an experience, or some part of it, with their expectations. This is known as the expectations–disconfirmation model of customer satisfaction. This model suggests that if customers believe their expectations have been met, they are satisfied. If their expectations are underperformed, this is negative disconfirmation, and they will be dissatisfied. Positive disconfirmation occurs when perception exceeds expectation. The customer might be pleasantly surprised or even delighted. This model assumes that customers have expectations, and that they are able to judge performance. The expectations–disconfirmation model adopts a cognitive perspective on customer satisfaction. A customer satisfaction paradox has been identified by expectations–disconfirmation researchers. At times customers' expectations are met but the customer is still not satisfied. This happens when the customer's expectations are low. 'I expected the plane to be late. It was. I'm unhappy!'

Many companies research customer requirements and expectations to find out what is important for customers, and then measure customers' perceptions of their performance compared to the performance of competitors.

The expectations–disconfirmation model is not without its detractors despite its widespread use. Some experts do not accept that customers make satisfaction judgements by comparing each experience to prior expectations; rather, they form judgements over multiple episodes and across numerous channels – in other words, satisfaction judgements are associated with overall customer experience.[32] Satisfaction, from this perspective, is an overall assessment or attitude rather than a gap.[33]

Equally, customer satisfaction judgements may have a strong emotional or affective content that is not picked up when the expectations–disconfirmation approach is used. Customers may simply like or not like their experience, and may be unable or unwilling to articulate why in terms of having specific expectations being met or not. Some researchers suggest that emotion and cognition interact, and that the interaction effects on customer satisfaction are both complex[34] and dynamic; that is, they change over time.[35] Affect has a strong influence on satisfaction in the early stages of judgement formation but its role declines as the customer has further experiences.[36] Hence, we should be cautious about viewing customer satisfaction as a simple episodic assessment of performance versus expectations.

Customer loyalty

Customer loyalty has also been the subject of considerable research. There are two major approaches to defining and measuring loyalty, one based on behaviour, the other on attitude.

Behavioural loyalty is measured by reference to customer purchasing behaviour. Loyalty is expressed in continued patronage and buying. There are two behavioural aspects to loyalty. First, is the customer still active? Second, have we maintained our share of customer spending? In portfolio purchasing environments, where customers buy products and services from a number of more-or-less equal suppliers, the share of customer spending question is more important.

Many direct marketing companies use RFM measures of behavioural loyalty. The most loyal are those who have high scores on the three behavioural variables: Recency of purchases (R), Frequency of purchases (F) and Monetary value of purchases (M). The variables are generally measured as follows:

R = Time elapsed since last purchase

F = Number of purchases in a given time period

M = Monetary value of purchases in a given time period

Attitudinal loyalty is measured by reference to components of attitude such as beliefs, feelings and purchasing intention. Those customers who have a stronger preference for, involvement in or commitment to a supplier are the more loyal in attitudinal terms.

These perspectives on loyalty have been combined by Dick and Basu, as shown in Figure 2.2.[37] These authors identify four forms of loyalty according to relative attitudinal strength and repeat purchase behaviour. 'Loyals' are those who have high levels of repeat buying and a strong relative attitude. 'Spurious loyals' have high levels of repeat purchase but weak relative attitude. Their repeat purchasing can be explained by inertia, high switching costs or indifference. 'Latent loyalty' exists when a strong relative attitude is not accompanied by repeat buying. This might be evidence of weakness in the company's distribution strategy, the product or service not being available when and where customers want.

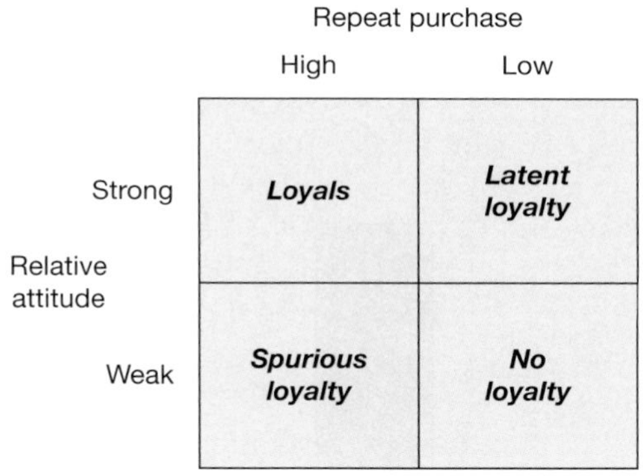

Figure 2.2 Two-dimensional model of customer loyalty

From a practical point-of-view, the behavioural definition of loyalty is attractive because sales and profits derive from actions not attitudes. However, taking the trouble to understand the causes of weak or negative attitudes in customers can help companies identify barriers to purchase. It is equally true that knowledge of strong or positive attitudes can help companies understand the causes of competitor-resistant commitment. However, it is not clear from the Dick and Basu model whether attitude precedes behaviour or behaviour precedes attitude. Researchers generally accept that causation is circular rather unidirectional. In other words, attitudes influence behaviour, and behaviour influences attitude.

Business performance

Business performance can be measured in many ways. The recent trend has been away from simple short-term financial measures such as quarterly profit or earnings per share. Leading companies have moved towards a more rounded set of performance indicators, such as represented by the triple bottom line[38] and balanced scorecard.[39]

The balanced scorecard employs four sets of linked key performance indicators (KPI): financial, customer, process, and learning and growth. The implied connection between these indicators is that people (learning and growth) do things (process) for customers (customer) that have effects on business performance (financial).

Customer-related KPIs that can be used to evaluate business performance following the adoption of CRM include: customer satisfaction levels, customer retention rates, customer acquisition costs, number of new customers acquired, average customer tenure, customer loyalty (behavioural or attitudinal), sales per customer, revenue growth, market share and share of customer spending (wallet).

The balanced scorecard is highly adaptable to CRM contexts. Companies need to ask the following questions: What customer outcomes drive our financial performance? What process outcomes drive our customer performance? What learning and growth outcomes drive our process performance? The satisfaction–profit chain suggests that the customer outcomes of satisfaction and loyalty are important drivers of business performance.

Share of customer spend (share-of-wallet or SOW) is a popular measure of CRM performance. If your company makes a strategic CRM decision to serve a particular market or customer segment, it will be keen to measure and grow its share of the chosen customers' spending. As indicated in Figure 2.3, share of customer spend focuses on winning a greater share of targeted customers' or segments' spending, rather than market share.

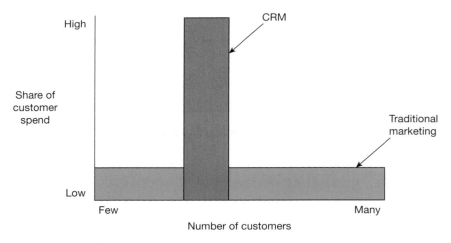

Figure 2.3 Market share versus share of customer

Researching the satisfaction–profit chain

We will now look at some of the research into the links between customer satisfaction, loyalty and business performance. Analysis has been done on international data, national data, industry data, corporate data and individual customer data.

The American Customer Satisfaction Index (ACSI) was established in 1994. It has tracked the relationships between customer satisfaction and a number of antecedents and consequences, including customer loyalty as measured by customers' probability of buying at different price points. The ACSI model appears in Figure 2.4. Data are collected in telephone interviews with approximately 250 current customers of the larger companies in a number of industries.[40] Results from the multi-industry study show that there is a strong correlation between customer satisfaction scores and corporate earnings in the next quarter. According to the ACSI organization, 'the reason is that a satisfied customer is more profitable than a dissatisfied one. If satisfaction declines, customers become more reluctant to buy unless prices are cut. If satisfaction improves the opposite is true.'[41] An independent study, using data from the ACSI, has also found that customer satisfaction had a considerable effect on business performance, although there was variation across sectors.[42]

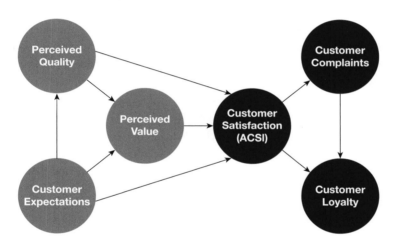

Figure 2.4 The American Customer Satisfaction Index (ACSI) model

The ACSI model underpins customer satisfaction research in Brazil, Colombia, Korea, Mexico, Portugal, Singapore, Turkey and the UK.

At the national level, customer data from the Swedish Customer Satisfaction Barometer (SCSB) have been correlated with corporate profit performance since 1989. A lagged relationship has been identified, indicating that current customer satisfaction levels impact on tomorrow's profit performance.[43] The SCSB database correlates customer-based measures with traditional financial measures of business performance, such as productivity and return on investment (ROI).

A number of studies in different industries and companies – telecommunications, banking, airline and automobile distribution – support the relationship between customer satisfaction, loyalty and business performance.

- *Telecommunications*. One study of the telecoms industry found that a 10 per cent lift in a customer satisfaction index predicted a 2 per cent increase in customer retention (a behavioural measure of loyalty) and a 3 per cent increase in revenues. The researchers concluded that customer satisfaction was a lead indicator of customer retention, revenue and revenue growth.[44]

- *Banking*. Another study found that customer satisfaction in retail banking correlated highly with branch profitability. Highly satisfied customers had balances 20 per cent higher than satisfied customers, and as satisfaction levels went up over time so did account balances. The reverse was also true: as satisfaction levels fell, so did account balances.[45]

- *Airlines*. A study in the airline industry examined the link between customer dissatisfaction, operating income, operating revenue and operating expense. The study identified the drivers of dissatisfaction as high load factors (i.e. seat occupancy), mishandled baggage and poor punctuality. The study concluded that as dissatisfaction rose, operating revenue (an indicator of customer behaviour) and operating profit both fell, and operating expense rose.[46]

- *Car distribution*. A study of Volvo car owners examined the links between customer satisfaction with the car purchase experience, workshop service and the vehicle itself, and dealer business performance. The results indicated that a one scale-point increase in overall customer satisfaction was associated with a 4 per cent increase in dealer profitability at next car purchase.[47]

- *Multi-industry*. Using 400 sets of matched corporate-level data obtained from two databases – the ACSI (see above, which provided customer satisfaction scores) and Standard and Poor's Compustat (which provided business profitability data) – Yeung and colleagues found a linear relationship between customer satisfaction scores and business profitability. They rise and fall together in the same time period.[48] Another study demonstrates that customer satisfaction improves cash flow and reduces its variability. Lower variability of cash flow is associated with lower risk. These two effects – improved cash flow and reduced risk – combine to enhance shareholder value.[49]

Research into the satisfaction–profit chain has also been performed at the level of the individual customer. Using data collected from both customers and exporters in the Norwegian fishing industry, Helgesen finds support for both steps in the satisfaction–profit chain.[50] Satisfaction is positively associated with behavioural loyalty, which in turn is positively associated with customer profitability. However, he notes that 'the satisfaction level has to pass a certain threshold if it is to have any influence on customer loyalty', and that as satisfaction increases it has a diminishing effect on loyalty. The same effects are observed in the relationship between loyalty and customer profitability.

According to one review, there is 'growing evidence that the links in the satisfaction–profit chain are solid'.[51] However, the relationships can be both asymmetrical and non-linear. The asymmetric nature of the relationships is found by comparing the impact of an increase in one variable with an equivalent decrease. For example, a one scale-point shift up in customer satisfaction (say from 3 to 4 on a five-point scale) may not have a comparable impact on customer retention rates as a one scale-point downward shift (say from 3 to 2 on the same five-point scale). Second, links can be non-linear. Non-linearity is sometimes reflected in diminishing returns, other times in increasing returns. For example, increasing returns may be observed in repeat purchase levels as customers progress up the customer satisfaction scale, as shown in Figure 2.5. Diminishing returns may set in if customer expectations are already largely met. Investments in increasing customer satisfaction at already high levels of performance do not have the same impact as investments at lower levels of performance.

Figure 2.5 Non-linear relationship between customer satisfaction and repeat purchase

RELATIONSHIP MANAGEMENT THEORIES

There are five main schools of thought that offer different perspectives on relationships between customers and suppliers. Although some schools are quite similar, they generally describe relationships in different terms and have different implications for relationship management. The major schools of thought are the Industrial Marketing and Purchasing (IMP) school, the Nordic school, the Anglo-Australian school, the North American school and the Asian (*guanxi*) school. Each is briefly reviewed in the following sections. Concepts and themes from these schools have been incorporated into the preceding discussion.

The Industrial Marketing and Purchasing school

The Industrial Marketing and Purchasing (IMP) school has a dedicated focus on B2B relationships. The IMP school first emerged in the late 1970s when a number of European researchers began investigating B2B relationships with the simple goal of describing them accurately. Some of the major contributors to the IMP school are Malcolm Cunningham, David Ford, Lars-Erik Gadde, Håkan Håkansson, Ivan Snehota, Peter Naudé and Peter Turnbull.[52]

The IMP school argues that B2B transactions occur within the context of broader, long-term relationships, which are, in turn, situated within a broader network of relationships. Any single B2B relationship between supplier and customer is composed of activity links, actor bonds and resource ties. IMP researchers were among the first to challenge the view that transaction costs determined which supplier would be chosen by a customer. IMP researchers identified the importance of the impact of relationship history on supplier selection.

The characteristics of B2B relationships, from an IMP perspective, are as follows:

- Buyers and sellers are both active participants in transactions, pursuing solutions to their own problems rather than simply reacting to the other party's influence.

- Relationships between buyers and sellers are frequently long term, are close in nature and involve a complex pattern of interaction between and within each company.

- Buyer–seller links often become institutionalized into a set of roles that each party expects the other to perform, and expectations that adaptations will be made on an ongoing basis.

- Interactions occur within the context of the relationship's history and the broader set of relationships each firm has with other firms – the firm's network of relationships.

- Firms choose which firms they interact with and how. The relationships that firms participate in can be many and diverse, carried out for different purposes, with different partners and have different levels of importance. These relationships are conducted within a context of a much broader network of relationships.

- Relationships are composed of actor bonds, activity links and resources ties, as now described.

Actor bonds are defined as follows:

Actor bonds are interpersonal contacts between actors in partner firms that result in trust, commitment and adaptation between actors.[53]

Actor bonds are a product of interpersonal communication and the subsequent development of trust. Adaptation of relationships over time is heavily influenced by social bonding.

Activity links can be defined as follows:

Activity links are the commercial, technical, financial, administrative and other connections that are formed between companies in interaction.

Activities might centre on buying and selling, technical cooperation or inter-firm projects of many kinds. Activities such as inter-partner knowledge exchange, the creation of inter-partner IT systems, the creation of integrated manufacturing systems such as Just-In-Time (JIT) and Efficient Consumer Response (ECR), the development of jointly implemented total quality management (TQM) processes, are investments that demonstrate commitment.

IMP researchers have focused on two major streams of activity-related research: the structure and cost-effectiveness of activity links, and the behavioural characteristics that enable relationships to survive. The reduction of transaction costs is an important consideration when customers form links with suppliers. Dyer argues that search costs, contracting costs, monitoring costs and enforcement costs (the four major types of transaction cost) can all be reduced through closer B2B relationships.[54]

Resources are defined as follows:

Resources are the human, financial, legal, physical, managerial, intellectual and other strengths or weaknesses of an organization.[55]

Resource ties are formed when these resources are deployed in the performance of the activities that link supplier and customer. Resources that are deployed in one B2B relationship may strengthen and deepen that relationship. However, there may be an opportunity cost. Once resources (for example, people or money) are committed to one relationship they might not be available to another relationship.

The Nordic school

The Nordic school emphasizes the role of service in supplier–customer relationships. The main proponents of the Nordic school are Christian Grönroos and Evert Gummesson.[56]

The Nordic school emerged from research into services marketing that began in the late 1970s particularly in Scandinavia. The key idea advocated by the Nordic school is that service is a significant component of transactions between suppliers and their customers. Their work became influential in the development of the field of relationship marketing, which presents a challenge to the transactional view of marketing that has been dominant for so long. The Nordic school's approach has application in both B2B and B2C environments.

Grönroos has defined relationship marketing as follows:

Relationship marketing is the process of identifying and establishing, maintaining, enhancing, and, when necessary, terminating relationships with customers and other stakeholders, at a profit, so that the objectives of all parties involved are met, where this is done by a mutual giving and fulfilment of promises.[57]

Gummesson goes further, redefining marketing as follows:

Marketing can be defined as 'interactions, relationships, and networks'.[58]

The Nordic school identifies three major characteristics of commercial relationships – interaction, dialogue and value – known collectively as the 'Triplet of Relationship Marketing',[59] and described further below.

- *Interaction*. Like the IMP school, the Nordic school suggests that inter-firm exchanges occur in a broader context of ongoing interactions. This is a significant departure from traditional notions of marketing where inter-firm exchanges are conceptualized as discrete, unrelated events, almost as if there is no history. From the Nordic school's perspective, interactions are service-dominant. As customers and suppliers interact, each performs services for the other. Customers supply information; suppliers supply solutions.

- *Dialogue.* Suppliers and customers are in dialogue with each other. Indeed, communication between partners is essential to the functioning of the relationship. Traditional marketing thinking has imagined communication to be one-way, from company to customer, but the Nordic school emphasizes the fact that communication is bilateral.

- *Value.* The concepts of 'value', 'value creation' and 'value creation systems' have become more important to managers over the past 20 years. The Nordic school stresses the mutual nature of value. To generate value from customers, companies need to generate customer-perceived value; that is, create and deliver something that is perceived to be of value to customers. Value creation therefore requires contributions from both buyer and seller. From the Nordic school's perspective, service performance is a key contributor to customer-perceived value.

The Nordic school is closely aligned with Service-Dominant Logic (SDL). SDL's main proponents are Robert Lusch and Stephen Vargo. SDL claims that all firms are service firms, even manufacturing firms. We can all appreciate that a patient visiting a doctor receives a service – medical advice. How can this also be true of manufacturing? SDL argues that although a manufacturer may build printers, the manufacturer is providing a service to users when they use the printer to convert images on a computer screen into text on a page. The printer has no value until it is used. SDL takes a relational view of customer value. Neo-classical economists generally suggest that value is created (or at least measured) at the point of exchange; this is known as value-in-exchange. SDL, however, proposes that value is created when customers use the goods or services; this is known as value-in-use. It is customers who co-create value when they use or interact with products or services; firms do not create value in their factories and ship it to market. This conceptualization of value is inherently grounded in productive supplier–customer relationships wherein the supplier (and its supply chain) helps the customer to extract this value-in-use by marketing goods and services that help the customer experience more and better value than the goods and services of competitors.[60] The worldview of SDL involves reframing goods as services; they are merely the vessels through which service is delivered to customers, the embodiment of the know-how of the firm's network of relationships (supply chain) in a format amenable to exchange. In such a worldview, every firm competes as part of a network, against other value networks, and relationships become critical.

The Anglo-Australian school

The Anglo-Australian school takes the view that companies not only form relationships with customers, but also with a wide range of other stakeholders including employees, shareholders, suppliers, buyers and governments. The main proponents of this school are Martin Christopher, Adrian Payne, Helen Peck and David Ballantyne.[61]

Stakeholder relationships vary in intensity, according to the level of relationship investment, commitment and longevity. Unlike the IMP school that takes a descriptive approach, the Anglo-Australian school takes a more prescriptive approach. Its work sets out to help managers improve relationships with stakeholder groups.

The major conceptual contribution of this school is their Six-Markets Model that has been revised several times (see Figure 2.6). The model suggests that firms must satisfy six major stakeholder 'markets': internal markets (employees), supplier/alliance markets (including major suppliers, joint venture partners and the like), recruitment markets (labour markets), referral markets (word-of-mouth advocates and cross-referral networks), influence markets (these include governments, regulators, shareholders and the business press) and customer markets (both intermediaries and end-users).

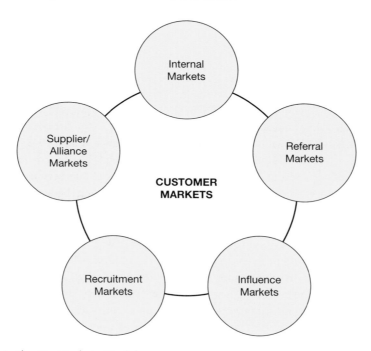

Figure 2.6 The Six-Markets Model

The school's researchers have focused on a number of topics: customer retention, customer loyalty, customer satisfaction, customer relationship economics and value creation. One of their major findings is that customer satisfaction and customer retention are drivers of shareholder value.[62]

The North American school

The North American school receives less emphasis as a separate school of relationship management than other schools. Significant contributors to this school are Jeffery Dyer, Sandy Jap, Shelby Hunt, Robert Dwyer, Jan Heide, Robert Morgan and Jagdish Sheth. A major theme flowing through this school's work is the connection between successful inter-firm relationships and excellent business performance. The school acknowledges that relationships reduce transaction costs,[63] and that trust and commitment are two very important attributes of successful relationships. Indeed, one of the more important theoretical contributions to come from the North American school is Morgan and Hunt's 'Commitment–Trust Theory of Relationship Marketing'. This was the first time that trust was explicitly linked to commitment in the context of customer–supplier relationships. According to the theory, trust is underpinned by shared values, communication, non-opportunistic behaviour, low functional conflict and cooperation. Commitment, on the other hand, is associated not only with high relationship termination costs, but also with high relationship benefits.[64]

The North American school tends to view relationships as tools that a well-run company can manipulate for competitive advantage. They also focus on dyadic relationships rather than networks, most commonly buyer–supplier dyads or strategic alliance/joint venture partnerships.

The Asian (*guanxi*) school

Guanxi (pronounced Gwan-She) is, essentially, a philosophy for conducting business and other interpersonal relationships in the Chinese, and broader Asian, context. Therefore, its effects have a significant impact on how Asian societies and economies work.

Guanxi has been known to Western business people since at least 1978. This was the time when the Chinese market began to open up to the West.[65] The foundations of *guanxi* are Buddhist and Confucian teachings regarding the conduct of interpersonal interactions. *Guanxi* refers to the informal social bonds and reciprocal obligations between various actors that result from some common social context, for example families, friendships and clan memberships. These are special types of relationship that impose reciprocal obligations to obtain resources through a continual cooperation and exchange of favours.[66]

Guanxi has become a necessary aspect of Chinese and, indeed, Asian business due to the lack of codified, enforceable contracts such as those found in Western markets. *Guanxi* determines who can conduct business with whom and under what circumstances. Business is conducted within networks, and rules based on status are invoked. Network members can only extend invitations to others to become part of their network if the invitee is a peer or a subordinate.

SUMMARY

In this chapter you have learned that there are differing beliefs about what counts as a relationship. Although interactions over time are an essential feature of relationships, some believe that a relationship needs to have some emotional content. Although the character of a relationship can change over time, successful relationships are based on a foundation of trust and commitment. The primary motivation for companies trying to develop long-term relationships with customers is the profit motive. There is strong evidence that long-term relationships with customers yield commercial benefits as companies strive to enhance customer lifetime value. The satisfaction–profit chain suggests that customers who are satisfied are more likely to become loyal, and high levels of customer loyalty are associated with excellent business performance. However, companies are advised to focus their customer acquisition and retention efforts on those who have profit-potential or are otherwise strategically significant. Although companies generally want to develop long-term relationships with customers, there are good reasons why customers don't always share the same enthusiasm. Finally, the chapter closes with a discussion of several schools of management or marketing theory that shed light on customer relationship management. These are the IMP, Nordic, Anglo-Australian, North American and Asian (*guanxi*) schools of thought.

NOTES AND REFERENCES

1   Barnes, J.G. (2000). *Secrets of customer relationship management.* New York: McGraw Hill.

2   Heath, R.L and Bryant, J. (2000). *Human communication theory and research: concepts, contexts and challenges.* Mahwah, NJ: Lawrence Erlbaum.

3   Woodburn, D. and McDonald, M. (2011). *Key account management: the definitive guide,* 3rd edn. Chichester: Wiley.

4   Professor Lynette Ryals uses the terms zone of delusion and frustration.

5   Dwyer, F.R., Schurr, P.H. and Oh, S. (1987). Developing buyer–seller relationships. *Journal of Marketing,* 51, 11–27.

6   See, for example, Morgan, R.M. and Hunt, S.D. (1994). The commitment–trust theory of relationship marketing. *Journal of Marketing,* 58(3), 20–38; Rousseau, D.M., Sitkin, S.B., Burt, R.S. and Camerer, C. (1998). Not so different after all: a cross-discipline view of trust. *Academy of Management Review,* 23(3), 393–404; Selnes, F. (1998). Antecedents of trust and satisfaction in buyer–seller relationships. *European Journal of Marketing,* 32(3/4), 305–22; Shepherd, B.B. and Sherman, D.M. (1998). The grammars of trust: a model and general implications. *Academy of Management Review,* 23(3), 422–37; de Ruyter, K., Moorman, L. and Lemmink, J. (2001). Antecedents of commitment and trust in customer–supplier relationships in high technology markets. *Industrial Marketing Management,* 30(3), 271–86; Walter, A. and Ritter, T. (2003). The influence of adaptations, trust, and commitment on value-creating functions of customer relationships. *Journal of Business & Industrial Marketing,* 18(4/5), 353–65; Gounans, S.P. (2005). Trust and commitment influences on customer retention: insights from business-to-business services. *Journal of Business Research,* 58(2), 126–40; Fullerton, G. (2011). Creating advocates: the roles of satisfaction, trust and commitment. *Journal of Retailing & Consumer Services,* 18(1), 92–100.

7   Singh, J. and Sirdeshmukh, D. (2000). Agency and trust mechanisms in consumer satisfaction and loyalty judgements. *Journal of Marketing Science,* 28(1), 255–71.

8   Morgan, R.M. and Hunt, S.D. (1994). The commitment–trust theory of relationship marketing. *Journal of Marketing,* 58(3), 20–38.

9   Buttle, F. and Biggemann, S. (2003). Modelling business-to-business relationship quality. Macquarie Graduate School of Management Working Paper #2003–3; Athanasopoulou, P. (2009). Relationship quality: a critical literature review and research agenda. *European Journal of Marketing,* 43(5/6), 583–610; Marquardt, A. (2013). Relationship quality as a resource to build industrial brand equity when products are uncertain and future-based. *Industrial Marketing Management,* 42, 1386–97.

10 Wilson, D.T. and Mummalaneni, V. (1986). Bonding and commitment in supplier relationships: a preliminary conceptualization. *Industrial Marketing and Purchasing*, 1(3), 44–58.

11 The idea of strategic significance is discussed in Chapter 5.

12 http://www-01.ibm.com/software/success/cssdb.nsf/CS/STRD-994E8F?OpenDocument&Site= default&cty=en_us (Accessed 29 January 2014).

13 Reichheld, F.F. and Detrick, C. (2003). Loyalty: a prescription for cutting costs. *Marketing Management*, September/October, 2425.

14 Ang, L. and Buttle, F.A. (2002). ROI on CRM: a customer journey approach. *Proceedings of the Inaugural Asia–Pacific IMP conference*, Bali, December.

15 Bain & Co/Mainline (1999). Customer spending on-line. Boston, MA: Bain & Co.

16 McKinsey and Co. (2012). Winning share and customer loyalty in auto insurance: insights from McKinsey's 2012 auto insurance customer insights research. www.mckinsey.com (Accessed 27 December 2012).

17 Christopher, M., Payne, A. and Ballantyne, D. (1991). *Relationship marketing*. Oxford: Butterworth-Heinemann.

18 Gordon, I. (1998). *Relationship marketing*. Ontario: John Wiley.

19 Reichheld, F. and Sasser, Jr., W.E. (1990). Zero defections: quality comes to services. *Harvard Business Review*, September/October, 105–11.

20 Bain & Co/Mainline (1999). Customer spending on-line. Bain & Co.

21 Ferron, J. (2000). The customer-centric organization in the automobile industry – focus for the 21st century. In S. Brown (ed.) *Customer relationship management: a strategic imperative in the world of e-business*. Toronto: John Wiley, pp. 189–211.

22 Tukel, O.A. and Dixit, A. (2013). Application of customer lifetime value model in make-to-order manufacturing. *Journal of Business & Industrial Marketing*, 28(6), 468–74.

23 IBM (2000) Business intelligence in the financial services industry: the case for differentiation. http://sysdoc.doors.ch/IBM/fss_business_intelligence_2.pdf (Accessed 20 January 2008).

24 Reichheld, F. and Sasser, Jr., W.E. (1990). Zero defections: quality comes to the services. *Harvard Business Review*, September/October, 105–11; see also Reichheld, F.F., Markey, R.G. and Hopton, C. (2000). The loyalty effect: the relationship between loyalty and profits. *European Business Journal*, 12(3), 134–9.

25 Lee, J., Lee J. and Fieck, L. (2006) Incorporating word of mouth effects in estimating lifetime value. *Journal of Database Marketing and Customer Strategy Management*, 14(1), 29–39.

26 Kumar, V., Petersen, J.A. and Leone, R.P (2007). How valuable is word-of-mouth? *Harvard Business Review*, October, 1–8.

27 Berger, P.D. and Nasr, N.I. (1998). Customer lifetime value: marketing models and applications. *Journal of Interactive Marketing*, 12(1), 17–30.

28 Biong, H., Wathne, K. and Parvatiyar, A. (1997). Why do some companies not want to engage in partnering relationships? In H.-G. Gemünden, T. Ritter and A. Walter (eds). *Relationships and networks in international markets*. Oxford: Pergamon, pp. 91–108.

29 Anderson, E.W. and Mittal, V. (2000). Strengthening the satisfaction–profit chain. *Journal of Service Research*, 3(2), 107–20.

30 Anderson, E.W. (1994). Cross-category variation in customer satisfaction and retention. *Marketing Letters,* 5 (Winter), 19–30.

31 Oliver, R.L. (1997). *Satisfaction: a behavioural perspective on the consumer*. Singapore: McGraw Hill International.

32 See two articles in support of this. Lemke, F., Clark, M. and Wilson, H. (2011). Customer experience quality: an exploration in business and consumer contexts using repertory grid technique. *Journal of the Academy of Marketing Science*, 39(6), 846–69. Klaus, P. and Maklan, S. (2012). EXQ: a multi-item scale for assessing service experience. *Journal of Service Management*, 23(1), 5–33.

33 Cronin, Jr., J. and Taylor, S. (1992). Measuring service quality: a reexamination and extension. *Journal of Marketing*, 56(3), 55–68.

34 White, C. (2010). The impact of emotions on service quality, satisfaction and positive word-of-mouth intentions over time. *Journal of Marketing Management*, 26(5–6), 381–94.

35 Homburg, C., Koschate, N. and Hoyer, W.D. (2006). The role of cognition and affect in the formation of customer satisfaction: a dynamic perspective. *Journal of Marketing*, 70(3), 21–31.

36 See Homburg *et al.* above.

37 Dick, A.S. and Basu, K. (1994). Customer loyalty: towards an integrated framework. *Journal of the Academy of Marketing Science*, 22(2), 99–113.

38 Savitz, A.W. and Weber, K. (2006). *The triple bottom line: how today's best run companies are achieving economic, social and environmental success*. San Francisco, CA: Jossey-Bass.

39 Kaplan, R.S. and Norton, D.P. (1996). *The balanced scorecard*. Boston, MA: Harvard Business School Press.

40 Fornell, C., Johnson, M.D., Anderson, E.W., Jaesung C. and Bryant, B.E. (1996). The American Customer Satisfaction Index: nature, purpose, and findings. *Journal of Marketing*, 60(4), 7–18.

41 http://www.theacsi.org/predictive_capabilities.htm (Accessed 30 November 2005).

42 Yeung, M.C.H. and Ennew, C.T. (2001). Measuring the impact of customer satisfaction on profitability: a sectoral analysis. *Journal of Targeting, Measurement and Analysis for Marketing*, 19(2), 106–16.

43 Anderson, E.W., Fornell, C. and Lehman, D.R. (1994). Customer satisfaction, market share and profitability: findings from Sweden. *Journal of Marketing*, July, 53–66.

44 Ittner, C.D. and Larcker, D.F. (1998). Are non-financial indicators of financial performance an analysis of customer satisfaction? *Journal of Accounting Research*, 36 (supplement), 1–46.

45 Carr, N.G. (1999). The economics of customer satisfaction. *Harvard Business Review*, 77(2), 15–18.

46 Behn, B.K. and Riley, R.A. (1999). Using non-financial information to predict financial performance: the case of the US airline industry. *Journal of Accounting, Auditing and Finance*, 14(1), 29–56.

47 Gustaffson, A. and Johnson, M.D. (2002). Measuring and managing the satisfaction–loyalty–performance links at Volvo. *Journal of Targeting, Measurement and Analysis for Marketing*, 10(3), 249–58.

48 Yeung, M.C.H., Ging, L.C. and Ennew, C. (2002). Customer satisfaction and profitability: a reappraisal of the relationship. *Journal of Targeting, Measurement and Analysis for Marketing*, 11(1), 24–33.

49 Gruca, T. and Rego, L. (2005). Customer satisfaction, cash flow and shareholder value. *Journal of Marketing*, 69(3), 115–30. Similar findings are reported in Aksoy, L. *et al.* (2008). The long-term stock market valuation of customer satisfaction. *Journal of Marketing*, 72(4), 105–22. There are inevitably dissenters: Jacobson, R. and Mizik, N. (2009). The financial markets and customer satisfaction: reexamining possible financial market mispricing of customer satisfaction. *Marketing Science*, 28(5), 810–19.

50 Helgesen, O. (2006). Are loyal customers profitable? Customer satisfaction, customer (action) loyalty and customer profitability at the individual level. *Journal of Marketing Management*, 22, 245–66.

51 Anderson, E.W. and Mittal, V. (2000). Strengthening the satisfaction–profit chain. *Journal of Service Research*, 3(2), 107–20.

52 The IMP group has its own dedicated website (www.impgroup.org), annual conference and is a prolific publisher of books and papers, a number of which follow. Cunningham, M. (1980). International marketing and purchasing: features of a European research project. *European Journal of Marketing*, 14(5–6), 5–21; Ford, D., Gadde, L.-E., Håkansson, H. and Snehota, I. (2003). *Managing business relationships*, 2nd edn. Chichester: John Wiley; Ford, D. and McDowell, R.

(1999). Managing business relationships by analyzing the effects and value of different actions. *Industrial Marketing Management*, 28, 429–42; Ford, D. and Redwood, M. (2004). Making sense of network dynamics through network pictures: a longitudinal case study. *Industrial Marketing Management*, 34(7), 648–57; Gadde, L.E., Huemer, L. and Håkansson, H. (2003). Strategizing in industrial networks. *Industrial Marketing Management*, 32, 357–64; Håkansson, H. and Ford, D. (2002). How should companies interact in business networks? *Journal of Business Research*, 55, 133–9; Håkansson, H. and Snehota, I. (1995). *Developing relationships in business networks*. London: Routledge; Håkansson, H.E. (1982). *International marketing and purchasing of industrial goods: an interaction approach*. Chichester: John Wiley; Turnbull, P.W. and Cunningham, M. (1980). *International marketing and purchasing: a survey among marketing and purchasing executives in five European countries*. London: Macmillan; Zolkiewski, J. and Turnbull, P. (2002). Do relationship portfolios and networks provide the key to successful relationship management? *Journal of Business and Industrial Marketing*, 17(7), 575–97.

53 Håkansson, H. and Snehota, I. (1995). *Developing relationships in business networks*. London: Routledge.

54 Dyer, J.H. (1997). Effective inter-firm collaboration: how firms minimize transaction costs and maximize transaction value. *Strategic Management Journal*, 18(7), 535–56; Dyer, J.H. and Chu, W. (2003). The role of trustworthiness in reducing transaction costs and improving performance: empirical evidence from the United States, Japan and Korea. *Organisation Science*, 14(1), 57–68.

55 Definition based on Barney, J.B. (1991). Firm resources and sustained competitive advantage. *Journal of Management*, 17(1), 99–120; and Wernerfelt, B. (1984). A resource-based view of the firm. *Strategic Management Journal*, 5(2), 171–80.

56 Christian Grönroos and Evert Gummesson are prolific authors. Amongst their works are the following. Grönroos, C. (1996). Relationship marketing logic. *Asia–Australia Marketing Journal*, 4(1), 7–18; Grönroos, C. (1997). Value-driven relational marketing: from products to resources and competencies. *Journal of Marketing Management*, 13, 407–20. Grönroos, C. (2000a). Creating a relationship dialogue: communication, interaction and value. *The Marketing Review*, 1, 5–14; Grönroos, C. (2000b). Relationship marketing: the Nordic School perspective. In J.N. Sheth and A. Parvatiyar (eds). *Handbook of relationship marketing*. London: Sage, pp. 95–120; Grönroos, C. (2004). The relationship marketing process: communication, interaction, dialogue, value. *Journal of Business and Industrial Marketing*, 19(2), 99–113; Gummesson, E. (1990). *The part-time marketer*. Karlstad, Sweden: Center for Service Research; Gummesson, E. (1987). The new marketing: developing long-term interactive relationships. *Long Range Planning*, 20(4), 10–20; Gummesson, E. (1994). Making relationship marketing operational. *International Journal of Service Industry Management*, 5(5), 5–20; Gummesson, E. (1996). Relationship marketing and imaginary organisations: a synthesis. *European Journal of Marketing*, 30, 31–44; Gummesson, E. (1997a). In search of marketing equilibrium: relationship marketing versus hypercompetition. *Journal of Marketing Management*, 13, 421–30; Gummesson, E. (1997b). Relationship marketing as a paradigm shift: some conclusions from the 30R approach. *Management Decision*, 35(4), 267–72; Gummesson, E. (1997c). Relationship marketing: the emperor's new clothes or a paradigm shift? *Marketing and Research Today*, 25(1), 53–61; Gummesson, E. (2002). Relationship marketing and a new economy: it's time for de-programming. *Journal of Services Marketing*, 16(7), 585–9.

57 Grönroos, C. (1997). Value-driven relational marketing: from products to resources and competencies. *Journal of Marketing Management*, 13, 407–20.

58 Gummesson, E. (1997). Relationship marketing as a paradigm shift: some conclusions from the 30R approach. *Management Decision*, 35(4), 267–72.

59 Grönroos, C. (2000). Creating a relationship dialogue: communication, interaction and value. *The Marketing Review*, 1, 5–14.

60 The definitive article that launched this perspective is Vargo, S. and Lusch, R. (2004). Evolving to a new dominant logic for marketing. *Journal of Marketing*, 68(1), 1–17. See also the range of resources about SDL at: http://www.sdlogic.net/.

61   Christopher, M., Payne, A. and Ballantyne, D. (1991). *Relationship marketing: bringing quality, customer service and marketing together*. Oxford: Butterworth-Heineman; Payne, A. (2000). Relationship marketing: the UK perspective. In J.N. Sheth and A. Parvatiyar (eds). *Handbook of relationship marketing*. London: Sage, pp. 39–67; Peck, H., Payne, A., Christopher, M. and Clark, M. (1999). *Relationship marketing: strategy and implementation*. Oxford: Butterworth-Heinemann.

62   Payne, A. and Frow, P. (2005). A strategic framework for customer relationship management. *Journal of Marketing*, 69, 167–76; Payne, A. and Holt, S. (2001). Diagnosing customer value: integrating the value process and relationship marketing. *British Journal of Management*, 12(2), 159–82.

63   Heide, J.B. (1994). Inter-organisational governance in marketing channels. *Journal of Marketing*, 58(1), 71–86; Heide, J.B. and John, G. (1990). Alliances in industrial purchasing: the determinants of joint action in buyer–supplier relationships. *Journal of Marketing Research*, 27(1), 24–36.

64   Morgan, R.M. and Hunt, S.D. (1994). The commitment–trust theory of relationship marketing. *Journal of Marketing*, 58(3), 20–39; Gao, T., Joseph S.M. and Bird, M.M. (2005). Reducing buyer decision-making uncertainty in organizational purchasing: can supplier trust, commitment, and dependence help? *Journal of Business Research*, 58(4), 397–406.

65   Ambler, T. (1995). Reflections in China: re-orienting images of marketing. *Marketing Management*, 4(1), 23–30.

66   Davies, H.A., Leung, T.K.P., Luk, S.T.K. and Wong, Y.H. (1995). The benefits of guanxi: an exploration of the value of relationships in developing the Chinese market. *Industrial Marketing Management*, 24, 207–14.

CHAPTER 3

MANAGING THE CUSTOMER LIFECYCLE

Customer acquisition

CHAPTER OBJECTIVES

By the end of this chapter you will understand:

- The meaning of the terms 'customer lifecycle' and 'new customer'.
- The strategies that can be used to recruit new customers.
- How companies can decide which potential customers to target.
- Sources of prospects in both business-to-business and consumer markets.
- How to communicate with potential customers.
- What offers can be made to attract new customers.
- Key performance indicators for customer acquisition strategies.
- The operational CRM applications that support customer acquisition.

INTRODUCTION

In the last chapter we explained why companies generally want to build long-term relationships with customers. In this and the following chapter you will be introduced to the idea of the customer lifecycle, and its management. The customer lifecycle is a representation of the stages that customers go through in their relationship with a company, as seen from the company's perspective. The core stages in the customer lifecycle are customer acquisition, customer retention and customer development. Companies develop strategies and processes for moving customers through these three stages, often but not always with the help of CRM technologies. These strategies and processes determine how companies identify and acquire new customers, grow their value to the business and retain them for the long term. We examine customer retention and development processes in the next chapter.

The focus of this chapter is customer acquisition, the first stage of the customer lifecycle. New customers have to be acquired to build companies. Even in well-managed companies there can be a significant level of customer attrition. These lost customers need to be replaced. We look at several important matters for CRM practitioners: which potential new customers to target, how to approach them and what to offer them.

The first task in managing the customer lifecycle is to acquire customers. In the context of CRM, one should acquire customers that have a strong likelihood of being profitable over time. Customer acquisition is always the most important goal during new product launches and with new business start-ups. For small businesses with ambitions to grow, customer acquisition is often as important as customer retention. A one-customer company, such as BICC (now part of Balfour Beatty plc) that supplied copper cable to a single customer, British Telecom (BT), could double its customer base by acquiring one more customer. On the other hand, the loss of that single customer could spell the end of the company. With such high stakes, all too often companies feel compelled to acquire as many new customers as possible only to find out that they face problems of retention, service demands that they cannot manage and low margins. Acquiring profitable customers, as measured by customer lifetime value (CLV), should be the goal of CRM strategy.

Even with careful targeted and well-developed and implemented customer retention plans, customers still need replacing. In a B2C context, customers may shift out of a targeted demographic as they age and progress through the family lifecycle; their personal circumstances may change and they no longer need and find value in your product; they may even die. In a B2B context, you may lose corporate customers due to merger and acquisition by another company with alternative supplier preferences; they may have stopped producing the goods and services for which your company provided input; they may have ceased trading. Customers lost to these uncontrollable causes indicate that customer acquisition will always be needed to replace natural attrition.

A number of important questions have to be answered when a company puts together a customer acquisition plan. These questions concern targets, channels and offers as below:

1   Which prospects (potential new customers) will be targeted?

2   How will these prospects be approached?

3   What offer will be made?

These issues need to be carefully considered and programmed into a properly resourced customer acquisition plan. Many marketing plans do not distinguish between customer acquisition and customer retention. Few consider lifetime value as a useful guide to customer acquisition, and often customer acquisition and retention are managed in different parts of the business, which runs the risk of recruiting customers who have little chance of becoming profitable. Acquisition should be guided by the same CLV considerations that underpin retention strategies.

WHAT IS A NEW CUSTOMER?

A customer can be new in one of two senses:

1   New to the product category.
2   New to the company.

New-to-category

New-to-category customers are customers who have either identified a new need or have found a new category of solution for an existing need. Consider the B2C context. When a couple have their first child, they have a completely new set of needs connected to the growth and nurturing of their child. This includes baby clothes, food, toys, for example. As the child grows, the parents are faced with additional new-to-category decisions, such as pre-school and elementary education. Sometimes, customers also become new-to-category because they find a new category to replace an existing solution. Cell phones have now largely replaced card- or cash-operated pay phones in many countries. Environmentally friendlier detergents and diapers are growing their share of market, as customers switch from current solutions.

Sometimes, customers beat marketers to the punch, by adopting established products for new uses. Marketers then catch on and begin to promote that use. Arm and Hammer baking soda was used by customers to deodorize fridges and trash cans, and as a mild abrasive for whitening teeth. The manufacturer, Church and Dwight, responded to this revelation and began promoting a variety of different applications. It is now an ingredient in toothpaste. Their website (www.armhammer.com) provides visitors with about 100 other tips for baking soda applications including cleaning, deodorizing, personal care and baking. The website encourages visitors to write in describing novel applications for the product. Auto manufacturers noticed that many utility vehicles were not being bought by tradesmen but as fun vehicles for weekend use. They began promoting this use whilst at the same time trying to innovate in product design to meet the requirements of that market segment. The result has been the emergence of a completely new market segment – the market for Sports Utility Vehicles (SUVs).

The same distinction between new needs and new solutions also exists in the B2B marketplace. A customer can be new-to-category if they begin an activity that requires resources that are new to the business. For example, when McDonald's entered the coffee shop market, they needed to develop a new set of supplier relationships. New-to-category customers may also be customers who find a new solution for an existing problem. For example, some clothing manufacturers now use computer-operated sewing machines to perform tasks that were previously performed by skilled labour and manual sewing machines.

New-to-company

The second category of new customers is customers who are new to the company. New-to-company customers are won from competitors. They might switch to your company because they feel you offer a better solution or because they value variety. Generally, new-to-company customers are the only option for growing customer numbers in mature markets where there are very few new-to-category customers. In developed economies, new players in grocery retail can only succeed by winning customers from established operators. They would not expect to convert those customers completely but to win a share of their spending by offering better customer-perceived value in one or more of important categories. Once the customer is in-store, the retailer will use merchandising techniques such as point-of-sale signs and displays to increase spending.

New-to-category customers are sometimes expensive to recruit; sometimes they are not. For example, when children leave home for university, banks compete vigorously for their patronage. They advertise heavily in media used by students, communicate direct-to-student, offer free gifts and low- or zero-cost banking for the duration of the studentship. On the other hand, supermarket retailers incur no direct costs in attracting these same students to their local stores.

New-to-company customers can be very expensive to acquire, particularly if they are strongly committed to their current supplier. Commitment is reflected in a strong positive attitude to, or high levels of investment in, the current supplier. These both represent high switching costs. A powerful commitment to a current supplier can be difficult, and often is too expensive, to break, as described in Chapter 2. High potential value customers are not always the most attractive prospects because of this commitment and investment. A lower value customer with a weaker commitment to the current supplier may be a better prospect.

PORTFOLIO PURCHASING

New customers can be difficult to identify in markets where customers exhibit portfolio purchasing behaviours. Customers buy on a portfolio basis when they buy from a choice set of several more or less equivalent alternatives. A customer who has not bought from one of the portfolio suppliers for a matter of months or even years, may still regard the unchosen supplier as part of the portfolio. The supplier, on the other hand, may have a business rule that says: 'If a customer has not bought for three months, mail out a special offer'. In the UK, many grocery customers shop at both Tesco and Sainsbury's, two of the major supermarket chains. These retailers do not simply compete to acquire and retain customers. Instead they compete for a larger share of the customer's spending; that is, to grow share-of-wallet (SOW).

Strategic switching

Companies may encounter evidence of strategic switching by customers. These are customers who shift their allegiances from one supplier to another in pursuit of a better deal. Banks know that their promotional pricing stimulates hot money. This is money that is moved from account to account across the banking industry in search of a better rate of interest. Sometimes the money may only be in an account overnight.

MCI, the telecoms company, discovered that about 70 per cent of customers newly acquired from competitors stayed for four months or less. These customers had been acquired when MCI mailed a cheque valued at $25, $75 or more to competitors' customers.

When the cheque was banked, this automatically triggered the transfer of service to MCI. A few months later these customers again switched suppliers when another deal was offered and the cheque was already cashed. MCI fixed the problem by adjusting the promotion. Instead of mailing an immediately cashable cheque, its promotion was relaunched as a 'staged rebate' promotion. The accounts of new customers who stayed for 3, 9 and 13 months were credited with sums equivalent to the cheque value that would previously have been sent.[1]

Sometimes, you can think of a customer that has been regained a second or further time as a new customer. For example, if the new parents mentioned previously were to have a second child after four years, they would most likely have been removed from the mother-and-baby databases. A new record would have to be created. The customer would need to be targeted afresh. In portfolio markets, a customer who has not purchased in Quarter 1 may be treated as a new customer for promotional purposes in Quarter 2, as the company attempts to reactivate the customer.

The Conversion Model®

Jan Hofmeyr has developed The Conversion Model®. This contains a battery of questions designed to assess whether a customer is likely to switch. His basic premise is that customers who are not committed are more likely to be available to switch to another provider. Commitment, in turn, is a function of satisfaction with the brand or offer, the attractiveness of alternatives and involvement in the brand or offer. Involvement is low if the product or its usage context is relatively unimportant to customers. The Conversion Model® allows customers to be segmented into four subsets according to their level of commitment: entrenched, average, shallow, convertible. There are two clusters of committed customers and two of uncommitted customers, as follows:

Committed customers:

- *Entrenched* customers are unlikely to switch in the foreseeable future.
- *Average* customers are unlikely to change in the short term but may switch in the medium term.

Uncommitted customers:

- *Shallow* customers have a lower commitment than average, and some of them are already considering alternatives.
- *Convertible* customers are most likely to defect.

Hofmeyr suggests that companies can measure customer commitment by asking just four questions:

1   How happy are you with < whatever it is > ?

2   Is this relationship something that you care about?

3   Is there any other < whatever it is > that appeals to you?

4   If so, how different is the one < whatever > from the other?

Non-customers are also segmented according to commitment scores into four availability subsets: available, ambivalent, weakly unavailable and strongly unavailable. There are two clusters that are open and two that are unavailable, as follows:

Open non-customers:

- *Available* non-customers prefer the alternative to their current offer though they have not yet switched, and are ready to switch.

- *Ambivalent* non-customers are as attracted to the alternative as they are to their current brand.

Unavailable non-customers:

- *Weakly unavailable* non-customers prefer their current brands.

- *Strongly unavailable* non-customers have a strong preference for their current brands.

Hofmeyr claims that these profiles can be used to guide both acquisition and retention strategies.[2] He suggests that where the number of open non-customers is greater than the number of uncommitted customers, companies should focus strongly on customer acquisition.

Companies need to nurture their relationships with committed customers, reassuring them that their decision is wise, and finding ways to enrich and enhance their customer experience. The strategy for uncommitted customers is to investigate why there is a low level of commitment and address the causes. Maybe it is a low-involvement category, or maybe customers are dissatisfied with their experience. Whether companies should appeal to open non-customers depends upon the value they can generate. Finally there are many potential reasons why some market segments are composed of unavailable non-customers. They may have tried your offer, and didn't find it satisfying; they may be committed to their current brand or supplier; they may be aware of your offer but find it unappealing; or, they may simply be unaware of your offer. You might be able to fix this last problem with advertising or other forms of customer communication, shifting these non-customers from the unavailable cluster to the open cluster. Customer experience research might reveal what customers do not like about your offer or doing business with you, and give you some clues about how to make their experience more satisfying.

A core principle of CRM is that customer-related data are used to target acquisition efforts accurately. By contrast, poorly targeted acquisition efforts waste marketing budget and may alienate more prospects than they gain through irrelevant and untimely messaging. We now turn to the practice of new customer prospecting.

PROSPECTING

Prospecting is, of course, a mining term. In that context it means searching an area thought likely to yield a valuable mineral deposit. In CRM, it means searching for opportunities that might generate additional value for the company.

Prospecting is an outcome of the market segmentation and targeting process. Market segmentation divides a heterogeneous market into homogenous subsets, even down to the level of the unique customer. Targeting is the process of choosing which market segments, clusters or individuals to approach with an offer. We explain the market segmentation and targeting processes in more detail in Chapter 5.

We will now look at prospecting from the business-to-business perspective.

Business-to-business prospecting

In the B2B environment, it is very often the task of marketers to generate leads, and for the salesperson to follow up allocated leads. Leads are individuals or companies that might be worth approaching. The lead then needs to be qualified so that sales and other resources are used wisely to nurture a relationship with higher value prospects.

Once leads are qualified, companies need to decide the best channels for initiating contact. A distinction can be made between *direct-to-customer* (DTC) channels such as salespeople, direct mail, email and telemarketing, and channels that are *indirect*, either because they use partners or other intermediaries or because they use bought time and space in media. The improved quality of databases has meant that direct channels allow access to specific named leads in target businesses.

Sources of business-to-business leads

Leads come from a variety of sources. In a B2B context this includes the sources identified in Table 3.1. Many companies turn to satisfied customers for *personal referrals*. Customer satisfaction scores enable companies to identify which current customers to approach for referrals. They may be prepared to write an email of introduction, provide a testimonial or receive a call to verify the credentials of a salesperson.

We discuss four main *online sources* of leads: search engines, company websites, portals and social media.

Table 3.1 Sources of B2B prospects

- Personal referrals from satisfied customers
- Online sources
  — Search engines
  — Company websites
  — Portals
  — Social media
- Networking
- Promotional activities
  — Attendee and delegate lists from exhibitions, seminars, workshops, tradeshows, conferences, events
  — Advertising response enquiries
  — Publicity
  — Email campaigning
- Lists and directories
- Canvassing
- Telemarketing

- *Search engines* provide an indexed guide to websites. Users searching for information type keywords into the search engine's web form. The engine then reports and lists the number of hits; that is, web pages that are associated with the keyed word or words. Users can then click on a hyperlink to take them to the relevant pages. To ensure that your site is hit when a prospect is searching for a supplier, your website needs to be registered with appropriate search engines or optimized for those search engines (for more information see Search Engine Optimization (SEO) in Chapter 9). Major search engines are Google, Yahoo and Bing (Microsoft).

- *Company websites* can be fruitful sources of new customers. The Internet enables prospective customers to search globally for products and suppliers.

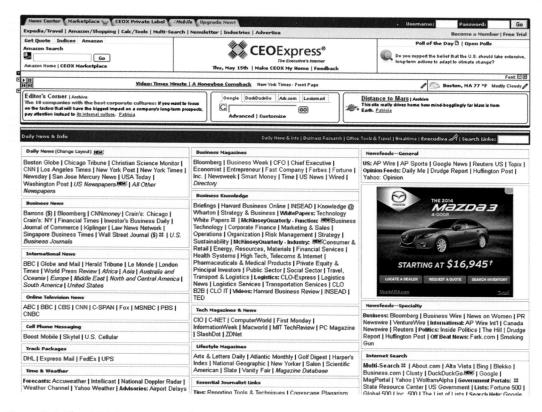

Figure 3.1 The CEOExpress portal[3]

- *Portals* are websites that act as gateways to the rest of the Internet. Portals tend to be focused on particular industries or user groups and offer facilities such as search engines, directories, customizable home pages and email. For example, the portal www.CEO Express.com provides a wealth of information and access to other sites that may be of use to busy chief executives (see Figure 3.1).

- An increasing number of suppliers in the B2B marketplace are developing a presence in *social media* such as Facebook and LinkedIn. For example, salesforce.com has a Facebook page that in part aims to appeal to potential customers.

When prospective customers reach an online destination they want to find engaging content that is relevant to their reasons for conducting the search. Content can include blogs, white papers, videos, presentations, podcasts, reports, case studies, testimonials, competitions and games, tools and surveys. Interactivity can help build engagement. To help qualify a lead, companies may want visitors to register prior to their accessing content. Registration effectively provides companies with permission to follow up and qualify the lead.

Networking can be defined as follows:

Networking is the process of establishing and maintaining business-related personal relationships.

A network might include members of a business association, chamber of commerce, friends from university or professional colleagues in other companies. In some countries it is essential to build and maintain personal networks. Much professional networking is now done online in social media such as LinkedIn. In China, for example, the practice of *guanxi*, covered in Chapter 2, means that it is well nigh impossible to do business without some personal connections already in place.

Referral networks are common in professional services. Accountants, banks, lawyers, auditors, tax consultants, estate agents will join together in a cross-referral network in which they undertake to refer clients to other members of the network.

Promotional activities can also generate useful leads. *Exhibitions, seminars, workshops, trade shows and conferences* can be productive sources. Companies that pay to participate in these events may either be able to obtain privileged access to delegate and attendee lists, or to generate lists of their own such as a record of visitors to their own stand at a trade show.

B2B marketers generally do little *advertising*, though this can generate leads. B2B advertising is generally placed in highly targeted specialist media such as trade magazines.

An important activity for some B2B companies is *publicity*. Publicity is an outcome of public relations (PR) activity. Publicity can be defined as follows:

Publicity is the generation of free editorial content relevant to a company's interests.

Successful PR can generate publicity for your product or company in appropriate media. This coverage, unlike advertising, is unpaid. Though unpaid, publicity does create costs. Someone has to be paid to write the story and submit it to the media. Many magazines, trade papers and online communities are run on a shoestring. They employ very few staff and rely heavily on stories submitted by companies and their PR staff to generate editorial matter. Editors are always looking for newsworthy items such as stories about product innovation, original customer applications or human interest stories about inventors and entrepreneurs. Editorial staff generally will edit copy to eliminate deceptive or brazen claims.

A growing number of B2B companies use *email* for new customer acquisition. Email offers several clear advantages. A very large proportion of business decision makers have email, although this does vary by country and industry. It is very cheap, costing just about the same to send one thousand emails as it does to send one single email. It is quick and simple for recipients to respond. Content can be personalized. Production values can be matched to audience preferences: you can use richly graphical or simple textual content. It is an asynchronous prospecting tool. In other words, it is not tied to a particular time frame, like a sales call. Email messages sit in mailboxes until they are read or deleted. It is a very flexible tool that can be linked to telesales follow-up, 'call-me' buttons or click-throughs.

When email is permission-based, response rates can be extraordinarily high.[4] On the other hand, there is growing resistance to spam email. Emails are spammed when they are sent to large numbers of recipients who have not been properly screened. What is spam to one recipient may be valuable information to another. An important ingredient in email marketing is a process by which prospects are encouraged or incentivized to provide email addresses for future contact. We have more to say about email marketing in Chapter 9.

Lists of prospects can be developed from many sources such as telephone *directories*, business lists, chamber of commerce memberships, professional and trade association memberships, website registrations and magazine circulation data. Lists can also be bought ready-made from list compilers and brokers. Lists of prospects, organized by their Standard Industrial Classification code, are widely used (see Chapter 5 for more detail). Some lists are of poor quality: out of date, containing duplications, omissions and other errors. High-quality lists with full contact details, including phone numbers and email addresses, tend to be more expensive. Lists can support direct marketing efforts by phone, mail, email or face-to-face.

Canvassing involves making unsolicited calls, sometimes known as cold calls. This can be a very wasteful use of an expensive asset – the salesperson. Some companies have banned their salespeople from cold-calling. Others outsource this activity to third parties. Some hotel chains, for example, use hospitality students to conduct a sales blitz that is essentially a telephone-based cold-calling campaign.

Telemarketing is widely used as a more cost-effective way of prospecting than use of a salesperson. Telemarketing, sometimes called telesales, is a systematic approach to prospecting using the telephone and, sometimes, other electronic media such as email or web chat. Telemarketing is usually done by staff in company-owned customer contact centres, or outsourced. Outbound telemarketers make outgoing calls to identify and qualify leads. Inbound telemarketers receive calls from prospective customers. In addition to prospecting, telemarketing can be used for other customer management purposes – cross-selling, handling complaints and winning back at-risk or churned customers, for example. We examine telemarketing in greater detail in Chapter 9.

Business-to-consumer lead generation

In B2C contexts, the distribution of customer acquisition effort is different. More emphasis is put on advertising, sales promotion, buzz or word-of-mouth, social media and merchandising. However, all of the techniques you have just read about are also used, but generally in a different way. We will turn to them later. First, we will look at advertising.

Advertising

Advertising is used as a prime method for generating new customers in B2C environments. Advertising can be defined as follows:

Advertising is the creation and delivery of messages to targeted audiences through the purchase of time or space in media owned by others.

Advertising can be successful at achieving two different classes of communication objective: cognitive and affective. Cognition is concerned with what audiences know; affect is concerned with what they feel. Advertising alone is often insufficient to generate behavioural outcomes such as trial purchasing. It can, however, predispose audiences to make an intention-to-buy based on what they learned about and felt towards the advertised product.

Cognitive advertising objectives include: raising awareness, developing understanding and generating knowledge. New customers generally need to be made aware of the product and to understand what benefits it can deliver prior to purchase. Affective advertising objectives include developing a liking for the product, and generating preference.

In high involvement purchasing contexts, where products or their usage context are personally significant and relevant to the consumer, prospects will normally progress through a learn–feel–do process when making their first purchase. In other words, before they buy, they acquire information that helps them learn about and compare alternatives, thus reducing perceived risk. They then develop a preference for, and intention-to-buy, a particular offer. Customers are essentially conducting a complex problem-solving process. Advertising is one of the sources they can use in the learn–feel part of that process. It is, however, not the only source of information, nor is it necessarily the most powerful.

High involvement advertising can employ long copy because prospects use advertising to learn about alternatives. Comparison advertising and copy featuring endorsements by opinion formers may be influential. Media that help prospects to acquire and process information are those that have a long dwell-time such as magazines and newspapers.

Advertising can also evoke powerful emotional responses in audiences. The type of response that advertisers seek in prospects is 'I like the look of that. I really must try it.' This is an affective response linked to a buying intention. Ads for fashion items, jewellery and vacation destinations often aim for an emotional response. TV ads evoke emotions by their clever mix of voice, music, images and sound effects. Advertisers can pre-test different executions to ensure that the right sort of emotional response is evoked.

In low involvement contexts, where the product category or its usage context is relatively unimportant, prospects are very unlikely to go through a complex and demanding learn–feel–do process. Rather, there will be little or no pre-purchase comparison of alternatives. The prospect is much more likely to simply become aware of the product and buy it. There may not even be post-purchase evaluation of the experience except in the most elementary of forms. Evaluation may only take place if the product fails to deliver the benefits expected. The purchase model is therefore learn–do. The role of advertising for low involvement products is to build and maintain brand awareness and recognition. Copy needs to be kept short – prospects won't read long advertising copy. Recognition can be achieved with the use of simple visual cues. Repetition of the ad in low involvement media such as TV and radio will be needed to build awareness and recognition.

Advertisers are concerned with two major issues as they attempt to generate new customers: message and media issues. Which messages will generate most new customers, and which media are most cost-effective at customer acquisition?

Message

Although precise measurement has not been conducted, it has been suggested that heavy media users are exposed to over one thousand ads per week.[5] Yet, how many can the person recall? In an increasingly communicated world, it is a first requirement that an advertisement must stand out from the background clutter and claim the audience's attention. Advertisers call this 'cut-through'. Without it, no cognitive, affective or behavioural outcomes can be achieved. An ad that stands out is one that differs from the many ads and other stimuli that compete for the prospect's attention. 'Standing out' is a matter both of message creativity and execution, and media selection. What stands out? Here are some examples: black and white ads in colour magazines, ads that feature movement in largely static media, image-based ads in text-dominated media, loud ads in quiet media, ads that leave you wondering 'what was that all about?' and ads that challenge your comprehension and emotions.

Message execution is an important issue in gaining an audience's attention. Messages can be executed in many different ways. Execution describes the way in which a basic copy strategy is delivered. Basic copy strategy is the core message or theme of the campaign. Execution styles can be classified in a number of ways: rational or emotional, factual or fanciful, funny or serious. Individual forms of execution include slice-of-life (product being used in a recognizable context), aspirational (associates the product with a desirable outcome or lifestyle), testimonial (the product is endorsed by an opinion-influencer) and comparative (the ad compares one or more alternatives with the advertised product).

Advertisements often close with a 'call to action', such as a suggestion that the audience clip a coupon, call a number or register online. These actions generate useful sources of prospects that can then be followed up.

Pre-testing messages on a sample of potential new customers is a way to improve the chances of an ad achieving its objectives. Among the criteria you can assess are the following:

- *Recall*. How much of the ad can the sample recall?
- *Comprehension*. Does the sample understand the ad?
- *Credibility*. Is the message believable?
- *Feelings evoked*. How does the sample feel about the ad?
- *Intention-to-buy*. How likely is it that the sample will buy?

If you buy space or time in media that have local or regional editions, you can conduct post-tests to assess the effectiveness of different executions in achieving the desired outcomes.

Creativity in message execution makes an important contribution to the visibility of an ad.

Media

Media selection for new customer acquisition is sometimes quite straightforward. For example, there are print media such as *What Digital Camera* (also online at: www.whatdigitalcamera.com) that are targeted specifically at new-to-category prospects for high involvement products. An uninvolved prospect will only learn passively about your product because there is no active search for and processing of information. Consequently, for low involvement prospects, frequency is a more important media consideration than reach. These are defined as follows:

Reach is the total number of a targeted audience that is exposed at least once to a particular ad or campaign.

Frequency is the average number of times that a targeted audience member is exposed to an ad or campaign.

The total number of exposures is therefore computed by multiplying reach by frequency. If your ad reaches two million people an average of four times, the total number of impressions or exposures is eight million. For high involvement products lower levels of frequency are generally sufficient. Advertising agencies should be able to offer advice on how many exposures (frequency) it takes to evoke a particular response in an audience member,[6] and what media are most appropriate.

You can compute various media efficiency statistics to help you get better value for money from your customer acquisition budget. These include response rates and conversion rates.

- *Response rates* provide a first-level indicator of ad effectiveness. Examples include the number of coupons clipped and returned, click-throughs from email campaigns or calls requesting information (RFI) made to a contact centre.

- *Conversion rates* offer a second-level indicator of ad effectiveness. Examples include sales made as a percentage of coupons returned, number of purchases made following click-through or proposals submitted as a percentage of RFIs.

Critics of the use of advertising for customer acquisition claim that ads are ineffective at customer acquisition. They argue that ads work on current and past customers and therefore impact more on retention.[7] Others point to the ineffectiveness of advertising at influencing sales at all. Len Lodish, for example, concluded that 'there is no simple correspondence between increased TV advertising weight and increased sales'.[8] In one study he found that the sales of only 49 per cent of advertised products responded positively to increases in advertising weight.[9]

Another media consideration is the timing of the ad exposure. Some electronic media allow messaging to be delivered at the time the customer is searching for a supplier or product. Relevant Google ads appear to the right of the screen when a user has entered a search term. Ads can be delivered to mobile phones based on the phone's location, as identified by the phone's global positioning system (GPS) data.

Sales promotion

Sales promotion can be defined as follows:

Sales promotion is any behaviour-triggering temporary incentive aimed at prospects, customers, channel partners or salespeople.

Although sales promotions can be directed at existing customers, salespeople and channel members, our concern here is only with sales promotions aimed at prospects. As the definition makes clear, sales promotions offer a temporary and immediate inducement to buy a product. They are not part of the normal value proposition. There are many forms of consumer sales promotion, including the following examples:

- *Sampling* is the provision of a free sample of the product. This can be delivered in a number of ways: mailed or dropped door-to-door, bound or packed with a related item, or delivered in response to a customer request. Sampling is expensive not only because of distribution costs but because it may be necessary to set up a special production run with unique promotional packaging. However, sampling is highly effective at generating trial, especially if the sample is accompanied with a voucher offering a discount off the first regular purchase. Sampling has been used for coffee, breakfast cereal and moisturizer products. It has also been used in the online context. Charles Schwab, the execution-only broker, offered free online share trading to new customers. It signed up 8,500 new customers; over 6,000 remained active clients once the three-month trial period ended.

- *Free trial.* Some companies offer products to customers on an approval basis. If they like the product they keep it and pay. Auto dealers offer test drives to prospective purchasers. One bedding retailer offers beds on a free trial basis to customers. They deliver the bed to the customer's home and let them try it for a month. If they don't like it the company collects the bed.

- *Discounts* or money-off deals are temporary price reductions. This reduces perceived risk and improves value for a first-time purchaser. Discounts can be promoted on-pack, at point-of-sale or in the media.

- *Coupons.* These act like money. They are redeemable on purchase, generally at the point-of-sale. Coupons may be available in print media, on-shelf at the point-of-sale, on the till receipt at checkout, online or delivered to a cell phone. Mobile coupons can be either pushed to the consumer's cell phone through SMS or Multi-Media Messaging (MMS), based on user demographics, purchase history or location, or consumers can request a coupon. Mobile apps such as Cellfire and Yowza give consumers access to mobile coupons from many retailers.

- *Rebates or cash-back.* In consumer goods markets, these are often offered on-pack and require collection of proofs of purchase. Their use has extended into automobile and mortgage markets. Take out a loan to buy a car, and get $500 in cash back from the dealer.

- *Bonus packs.* A bonus pack is a promotion in which the customer gets more volume at an unchanged price. A customer might get 2.5 litres of juice for the price of a 2-litre pack.

- *Banded packs.* A banded pack promotion offers two, or rarely three, products banded together at a bundled price. A customer might be offered a banded pack of shaving gel and after-shave balm.

- *Free premiums.* A free premium is a gift to the customer. The gift may be offered at the point-of-purchase, in packaging, or require the customer to mail, email, text or phone in a request.

- *Cross-promotions.* These occur when two or more non-competing brands create a mutual promotion. A proof-of-purchase from a theatre entitles the patron to a 25 per cent discount on a restaurant meal, and vice versa.

- *Lotteries.* A lottery is a game of chance, not involving skill. Consumers are invited to purchase the product and be entered into a draw for a prize. Prizes are highly variable. They range from low value items such as shopping vouchers to high value prizes such as personal makeovers, exotic vacations and even fully furnished houses.

- *Competitions.* Unlike a lottery, a competition requires skill or knowledge. The prizes are varied, as in the case of lotteries.

- *Buzz or word-of-mouth.* A growing number of companies are trying to attract new customers through word-of-mouth (WOM) influence, also known as buzz. Word-of-mouth can be defined as follows:

Word-of-mouth is interpersonal communication about a product or organization in which the receiver assumes the communicator to be independent of commercial influence.

WOM has been shown to influence receivers' knowledge, emotions, intentions and behaviours, and because of its apparent separation from commercial influence is regarded as independent and trustworthy.[10] Brands such as Body Shop, Amazon.com, YouTube.com and Krispy Kreme owe much of their success to WOM. Marketers can promote WOM by identifying and sponsoring opinion formers such as radio show hosts or bloggers. Giving people something to talk about is a high priority for buzz marketers – this includes ads, slogans and product innovations that are high in conversational value and capture people's attention and interest. An example is Budweiser's use of 'Whassup?' in its TV commercials – the expression caught on in everyday communication.

A number of agencies, such as Buzzador, Soup and Fizz now offer WOM marketing services. Typically, they maintain a panel of members who agree to sample new products, share them with friends and talk about them. Brand owners contract these agencies to kick-start word-of-mouth. Sometimes, brand owners take a simple multiplicative approach to computing the effects of a WOM Marketing (WOMM) campaign. They assume that if 200 campaign participants each tell 15 people and each of those tells a further 5 people, then the campaign has reached 15,000 people. However, there is evidence that transitivity of social ties constrains campaign reach. The more ties there are between members of a social network, the more transitive it is. Groeger and Buttle found that 21 per cent of all WOMM campaign-related conversations were multiple exposures – i.e. the conversation was with someone who had already been told about the campaign.[11]

Social media

Although we discussed social media in our earlier coverage of B2B prospecting, it is in the B2C context that social media are more widely used. Social media are Internet-based applications that allow the creation and exchange of user-generated content. There are a host of social media platforms aimed at individual consumers – Facebook, Twitter, flickr, YouTube and Tumblr, to name a few.

Companies can develop a page or create a channel that prospective customers can visit. Engaging, interactive content may motivate visitors to spend time on the page, eventually leading to trial purchase. Some companies offer valuable downloads to visitors – apps, offers or vouchers for example. Companies can also use social media as an advertising medium. Facebook ads, for example, can be targeted by location, age, gender and interest. Technology, in the form of social CRM applications, can be used to search social media for references to competitors' brands, and then join the conversation. Established customers may become fans and benefit from receiving up-to-date news feeds about the company and its products, passing on their enthusiasm in 'likes' and 'shares' to friends in their social network, thereby generating new customers for the brand.

It is sometimes suggested that encouraging key influencers in social media to promote a brand message into their social networks can be extremely powerful. The thinking is that you identify and build relationships with a small number of influential people who have a following of hundreds of thousands who in turn influence millions. This would be a highly concentrated social media based campaign and highly cost-effective. Whilst intuitively appealing, few firms have the data and capabilities required to map complex social networks to identify the key individuals and then track the subsequent cascading of influence. A Marketing Science Institute (MSI) report suggests that rather than targeting key influencers in social media, identifying a company's revenue leaders, its most profitable customers, can produce a similar effect.[12] The MSI report finds that people with similar characteristics tend to form close friendships (a phenomenon known as homophily) and hence a customer whose needs and wants are satisfied by your offer will tend to associate with others whose needs and wants could be satisfied by your offer.

innocent drinks is a London-based fruit juice and smoothie brand. innocent decided not to be on every social media platform, but to select the right platforms for its consumer demographic and then to build a strong interactive community, which through likes and shares would spread word-of-mouth about the brand, encouraging friends to try innocent. innocent's social media platforms include Facebook, Twitter, YouTube, Flickr, Instagram and Pinterest. The brand's Facebook page has over 400,000 likes. Innocent gives 10 per cent of its profits to charity, including the innocent foundation that supports sustainable agriculture projects, and emergency relief.

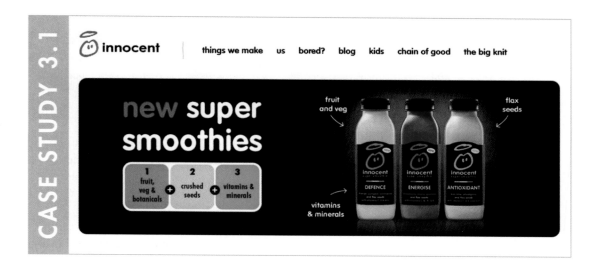

Merchandising

Merchandising can be defined as follows:

Merchandising is any behaviour-triggering stimulus or pattern of stimuli other than personal selling that takes place at retail or other points-of-sale.

Merchandising is designed to influence behaviour in store or at other points-of-sale such as restaurants, banks or gas stations. Merchandisers have available a large number of techniques. These include retail floor plans, shelf-space positioning, special displays, window displays and point-of-sale print. Some forms of merchandising are particularly useful for generating new customers, for example money-off signs, 'as used by' and 'as advertised' signs. Related item displays place two or more related items together, for example toppings next to icecream or dressings next to salads. Sales of one category assist sales of the other. Eye-level positions on shelves are generally more productive than 'reach' or 'stoop' positions. If merchandisers can position new products in these preferred positions sales will be positively influenced.

A study by Deloitte's has found that a growing percentage of shoppers use their smart phones in store, particularly for research, product reviews and price comparisons of big-ticket items.[13] This means that relevant in-store messaging and offers can be communicated to shoppers by SMS or MMS as they are in the process of making a buying decision.

Figure 3.2 Samsung merchandising
Photograph by Oonagh Reidy.

Other tools for B2C customer acquisition

As mentioned earlier in the section on B2B customer acquisition, B2C companies can also use referral schemes, promotions such as consumer exhibitions, publicity, telemarketing, email and canvassing to generate new customers.

Some companies believe that delighted or even completely satisfied customers will naturally speak well of the company. Eismann, the German frozen food manufacturer, estimates that 30 per cent of its new customers are recruited by *referrals* from satisfied customers.[14] Despite high levels of naturally occurring referral, companies may still choose to develop a Customer Referral Scheme (CRS). CRSs are also known as Member-Get-Member (MGM) and Recommend-A-Friend (RAF) schemes. These work by inviting

CASE STUDY 3.2

TRACKING REFERRALS USING GOOGLE ANALYTICS

Referral traffic is Google's method of reporting visits that came to a website from sources outside of Google itself, often when someone clicks on a hyperlink for example in an email or blog to go to a new page on a different website. Analytics tracks the click as a referral visit to the second site. The originating site is called a 'referrer' because it refers traffic from one place to the next. Referral traffic is one of three statistics tracked by Google Analytics. The others are Search traffic – visits from a search engine – and Direct traffic to a domain.

To understand where traffic comes from, website owners log onto their Google Analytics account. A graph displays traffic for a one-month period. Below it, a table displays the names of domains referring traffic to the site, as well as statistics on what visitors do on the site.

existing customers to recommend a friend and rewarding the recommender with a gift. It is important to choose the right customer and the right time to invite a referral. Broadly, schemes are more effective when targeted at a relevant section of the customer base, for example customers who are satisfied or customers who have just experienced excellent service. For example, companies offering roadside assistance to stranded motorists will ask for a referral when the vehicle is repaired and the customer's anxiety levels reduced.[15]

Lexus, the automobile manufacturer, invites up to 300 potential buyers to stylish *events* such as dinner-and-theatre shows or dinner-and-concert performances. The Lexus vehicles are on display. Also invited are current Lexus owners who sit among the prospects and talk to them. Lexus knows from customer satisfaction surveys which customers to invite. It is a very soft sell. Current owners receive no direct reward for participation other than the opportunity to enjoy the event itself.

Fashion retailers will organize fashion *shows* for current customers who are invited to bring along a friend who might be interested. Party plans have been popular for many years. Distributors of products such as 'Tupperware' and Anne Summers sex aids organize parties in their own homes. They invite friends and neighbours along. Refreshments are offered and products are exhibited and demonstrated.

Free *publicity* such as that obtained by Richard Branson, founder of the Virgin Group of companies, enables many companies to spend less than major competitors on advertising. Branson excels at gaining publicity. When Virgin cola was launched in the USA, he hired a tank to roll into Times Square and take a 'shot' at Coca-Cola's illuminated advertising sign. All the TV networks were invited to film the stunt, as were representatives of the press. A huge amount of free publicity was achieved as the brand sought to build its customer base.

Telemarketing and *cold canvassing* to people's homes is a contentious issue. Many customers feel that these methods are too intrusive, and in some countries privacy regulations prevent companies from engaging in these practices. For example, in Australia, people can register their landline and mobile telephone numbers on a 'Do Not Call' register. In some other countries, regulation is less restrictive, and some industries, for example telecoms and utilities, still use both telemarketing and door-to-door canvassing for lead generation. Outbound telemarketing can then be used for lead qualification. Selling door-to-door to well-targeted prospects is a different matter. Fuller Brushes, Avon Cosmetics, Collier's Encyclopedias and Prudential Insurance have a long tradition of door-to-door selling.

SMS messaging can also be used for customer acquisition. Because it is text and not voice, it does not have to be 'answered' in the traditional sense. SMS has been used very successfully for local bar and club promotions, amongst Generation Y consumers. As the medium is so immediate, offers can be switched on at the last minute for highly perishable cinema and retail offers. As mobile devices become more popular, so will the distribution of messaging in text and video formats, which will be increasingly targeted to the prospects' known profiles.

Email is also useful for B2C customer acquisition programmes. Over 95 per cent of people having Internet access at home use it for email, often on a daily basis.[16] In the UK, organizations such as Dell Computers, Barclays Bank, Comic Relief and Epson Printers have used email to acquire new customers. The same benefits and reservations outlined in the earlier discussion of email also apply in the B2C context.

Figure 3.3 Customer acquisition email campaign[17]

Recent innovations in new customer acquisition tactics are *product placement* and *product integration*. Product placement involves arranging for products to be shown on display or in use in TV, movies, videogames and web-cast productions. There is no explicit promotion of the product. It is simply seen in the production. Actors may use the product or it may be used as a background prop. There are three different compensation models for product placement. First, a company can pay for placement. Second, the product is donated in exchange for its appearance in the production – a form of barter. Third, the product is donated to the production company to strengthen the storyline or build character but is returned afterwards. A particular form of placement is product integration. This occurs where a product is integral to the storyline. Companies can pay considerable sums for their products to appear in movies. It is estimated that the product placement market was growing at a compound rate of over 16 per cent per annum to be worth over US$8.25 billion in 2012, and expected to rise substantially to 2016.[18] Over half of product placements are food and beverage, health and beauty, and household brands.[19]

Pitchers or pitchmen approach prospective customers and ask them to buy a product. Pitching is a well-known practice in street trading, but has now been extended into other forms of retail. For example, pitchers will approach dancers in a club and ask them if they have tried a new drink, then suggest that they buy some. Pitchers generally are expected to act as if they are unpaid advocates, therefore simulating genuine word-of-mouth.

KEY PERFORMANCE INDICATORS OF CUSTOMER ACQUISITION PROGRAMMES

CRM practitioners are concerned with the following three key performance indicators (KPIs) for customer acquisition activities:

1   How many customers are acquired?
2   What is the cost per acquired customer?
3   What is the value of the acquired customer over the longer term?

The ideal result would be a low-cost programme that generates lots of highly valuable customers.

Some customer acquisition programmes may require major capital investment, as well as marketing expense. A supermarket operator may build new stores to increase geographic coverage. A financial services institution may invest in IT infrastructure for a new online channel. A manufacturer of automotive parts may build a new factory close to prospective customers.

Customer referral schemes are very cost-effective methods for acquiring customers. They cost little to operate but they also generate few new customers. However, the customers generated by these schemes tend to be more loyal (less likely to churn) and higher spenders. Advertising can generate a lot of enquiries, but these may be very poor-quality prospects, with low conversion rates into first-time customers, and, ultimately, low customer value. This is particularly true if the advertising is poorly targeted. Customers won by a sales promotion may be deal-prone. In other words, they are not acquired for the long term, but switch whenever there is a better opportunity.

Companies can compare the relative costs of customer acquisition per channel before deciding how to spend their acquisition budget. For example, a motoring membership organization knows that its member-get-member scheme has a direct cost per new customer of £22 compared to £100 for Direct Response TV and £70 for door drops. The average is £35. A telecoms company reports that it costs £52 to win a new customer through its recommend-a-friend programme, compared to an average of £100 and an advertising-generated cost of £200.[20] The costs of acquiring new customers online are variable over time and across categories. Amazon.com claimed it was costing them $29 to acquire each new customer;[21] credit card operators thought it cost $50 to $75, and mortgage customers cost $100 to $250 to acquire.[22]

Companies have a choice of acquiring new customers through relatively costly but fast-acting marketing investments or through slower but low- or zero-cost WOM processes. Julian Villanueva and colleagues have researched the effects of marketing-induced versus word-of-mouth customer acquisition on firm performance. Using data from an Internet firm that provided free Web hosting to registered users during a 70-week-long observation period, they found that customers acquired through WOM were themselves productive at generating new customers through their own WOM. They also generated more word-of-mouth activity than those acquired by marketing-induced channels. Each customer acquired through marketing is expected to bring around 1.59 new customers throughout his or her lifetime, while a customer acquired through WOM is expected to bring 3.23 customers (including self).[23]

Costs of customer acquisition are one-off costs that are not encountered again at any stage in a customer's tenure. The costs might include prospecting costs, advertising costs, commissions to salespeople, collateral materials, sales promotion costs, credit referencing, supplying tangibles (e.g. credit cards) and database costs. Many sales managers incentivize their salespeople to find new customers. These incentives, whether cash or merchandise or some other reward, are a cost of acquisition.

MAKING THE RIGHT OFFER

In addition to carefully targeting new customers for acquisition, companies need to consider what offer they will make to the target. Some industries are consistent in their use of entry-level products for customer acquisition.

Insurance companies use automobile insurance to acquire new customers. Developed countries require drivers to be insured at least at third-party level. Since insurance expires annually, it offers the prospect of repeat purchase. Generally auto premiums are highly discounted and offer little or no margin to the insurer. However, auto insurance does give the company at least one year in which to cross-sell additional insurance products – home and contents insurance, travel insurance, health insurance, mortgage protection insurance and so on. Churn rates on auto insurance can be as high as 50 per cent, giving average customer tenure of only two years. This is the period that insurers have to make the cross-sales.

Banks will often use relatively high interest rates on deposit accounts or relatively low charges on credit cards to attract new customers. Supermarkets price high demand, frequently purchased items such as bread as loss leaders in order to build store traffic.

The 'right offer' might be influenced by the geographic location of the consumer. Mobile phones provide data on the geographic location of the phone. Location-relevant offers can be directed to the user, for example, special offers at a local supermarket.

OPERATIONAL CRM TOOLS THAT HELP CUSTOMER ACQUISITION

CRM software provides a number of operational tools that help in the customer acquisition process, including lead management, campaign management and event-based marketing. We cover these in more detail in chapters 8 and 9, but introduce them here.

Lead management

CRM software helps B2B companies to manage the selling process. An important part of that process is lead management. There are hundreds of different lead management software vendors. Many of these enable the recommended lead management practices of published sales methodologies to be implemented, amongst them the CustomerCentric Selling, Miller Heiman and Solution Selling methodologies.

The lead management process includes a number of sub-processes, including lead generation, lead qualification, lead allocation, lead nurturing and lead tracking.

Lead qualification processes prioritize leads so that a company can invest its selling and marketing resources where they generate the best returns. High value leads are those that will produce high margins, buy in quantity, have a higher likelihood for repeat sales, generate high levels of positive word-of-mouth due to customer satisfaction and are relatively easy to close because they are not committed to current suppliers. Other important questions for lead qualification are: Does our product or service solve a customer problem? What is the time frame for the prospect's purchase decision? Does the prospect have authority to buy? Authority to buy may be invested in a named individual, a decision-making unit composed of a group of employees, a group composed of internal employees and external adviser(s) or, in some rare cases, an external individual or group. Can the prospect pay? Ability to pay covers both cash and credit. The ability to pay of prospective customers can be assessed by subscribing to credit rating services such as Dun & Bradstreet, and Standard & Poor's. Being a well-known name is no guarantee that a prospect is credit-worthy, as suppliers to Lehman Brothers, the global financial services firm, found out when the company declared bankruptcy in 2008, precipitating a global financial crisis.

CRM software applications allow prospects to be scored against these and other relevant criteria. Higher ranked prospects are then allocated to salespeople. *Lead allocation* processes ensure that leads are routed to the right salesperson. *Lead nurturing* processes ensure that leads receive levels of service and support that help build trust and confidence prior to becoming buyers. *Lead tracking* processes trace the conversion of prospects into customers. Lead management software generally allows salespeople to customize their interactions by applying selling workflow rules that vary according to prospect attributes such as company size and level of qualification. Sales reps may want to reject leads, further qualify them, redefine them as opportunities or take other actions as required.

Successful lead management programmes are supported by analytics. Sales managers want to know which lead generation programmes generate high conversion rates and/or high revenues, which leads are costly to convert, and which territories and account teams have the greatest success at lead generation and conversion.

Campaign management

Campaign management software is widely deployed in B2C environments and increasingly in B2B environments for new customer acquisition. Campaign managers design, execute and measure marketing campaigns with the support of CRM technologies. Sometimes these are multimedia campaigns across direct mail, email, social media, outbound telephony and SMS platforms. The technology assists in selecting and grouping potential campaign targets, communicating the offer, measuring campaign results and learning from the results how to produce more effective and efficient campaigns in the future.

Campaign management software not only enables companies to manage and execute automated and personalized campaigns, generating leads for sales follow-up, but also to generate and manage contact lists, whilst simultaneously complying with anti-spam legislation.

Experimentation is a common feature of campaign management. Experiments can be performed on subsets of the customer database. For example, different cells of the recency–frequency–monetary value (RFM) matrix can be treated to different offers in order to develop an understanding of the propensities-to-buy of different customer groups. If the results were to show that women aged 15–25 were particularly responsive to a health-and-beauty bundled offer, you could search for prospects matching that profile, or buy additional lists to target.

Event-based marketing

Event-based marketing (EBM) is also used to generate new customers. EBM provides companies with opportunities to approach prospects at times that have a higher probability of leading to a sale.

In retail banking, an event such as a large deposit into a savings account might trigger an approach from the bank's investment division. A name-change might trigger an approach from a financial planner. A call from a customer enquiring about rates of interest on a credit card might trigger a call from a customer retention specialist.

Many B2C companies can link purchasing to life-stage events. For example, finance companies target mortgages at newlyweds and empty nesters whose children have left home. Clothing retailers target different offerings at customers as they age: branded fashion clothing at single employed females, baby clothes for new mothers and so on. If you can associate purchasing with particular life-stage events you will be well placed to target your customer acquisition efforts.

Public events such as interest rate falls or hikes, tax law changes and weather events or competitive events, such as new product launches, might signal an EBM opportunity. For example, an insurance company might launch a health insurance campaign following announcements in the press of an upcoming influenza epidemic.

Support from CRM analytics

Clearly, these operational CRM tools have to be supported by sound analytics to ensure that the right offer is made to the right prospect through the right channel at the right time.

It is often possible to query current customer-related databases for clues to guide customer acquisition. Supermarket operators can mine transactional data to provide insight into the baskets of goods that customers buy. If you were to find that 60 per cent of customers buying frozen apple pies also bought premixed custard, you might think it worthwhile targeting the other 40 per cent with an offer. A bank wanting to generate new customers for its savings account can develop a model predicting propensity to buy based upon current product ownership. In the B2B environment, salespeople may have entered data about

---

CASE STUDY 3.3

BONOBOS USES PREDICTIVE ANALYTICS TO OPTIMIZE CUSTOMER ACQUISITION STRATEGY[24]

Bonobos is a US men's apparel brand launched in 2007. Bonobos has become the largest apparel brand ever built on the Web in the USA. Bonobos is a data-driven, customer-focused retailer that has always recognized the importance of making business decisions around customer lifetime value (CLV). Initially the marketing team had used Excel to compute CLV metrics but, as the company experienced rapid growth and its customer base grew substantially, this became prohibitively time-consuming and tedious and the analysis was not completed as frequently as the team would have liked.

Not having access to real-time CLV insights made it difficult for Bonobos to make agile decisions about customer acquisition. Bonobos then began to use analytics to compute the lifetime value of customers acquired through every marketing channel. This allows Bonobos to understand which acquisition channels are bringing in the most valuable customers, and optimize their acquisition strategy accordingly.

For example, Bonobos discovered that its Guideshops, service-oriented e-commerce stores that enable men to try on Bonobos clothing in person before ordering online, were bringing in customers with the highest CLV across all of its marketing channels. This insight encouraged Bonobos to expand its marketing efforts to support the Guideshops.

Bonobos also uses predictive analytics to identify their highest CLV customers as early as their first purchase. Bonobos then uses this information to ensure these highly valued customers get the attention they deserve. 'Top customers' receive additional services, such as handwritten thank-you notes from the Bonobos customer service team. Bonobos measured the impact of these notes on incremental revenue and repeat purchase rate, and saw a positive lift. Top customers also receive perks such as exclusive event invites and early access to new merchandise.

prospects' satisfaction with competitors' offerings into their sales call records. Those who are less satisfied will likely show a higher propensity to switch, and may be worth targeting with an offer.

Affiliation data can also be used to guide customer acquisition. Customers may be members or otherwise associated with a number of organizations: a university, a sports club or a charity. Affinity marketers recognize membership as an opportunity. Banks like MBNA have led the way in affinity marketing of credit cards. MBNA, the organization and the member all benefit from the arrangement. MBNA offers a credit card to members of the organization. The organization receives a fee for allowing the bank access to its membership data. Members enjoy a specially branded card and excellent customer experience from the bank. Affinity groups include members of the World Wildlife Fund, fans of Manchester United and congregations of the Uniting Church.

SUMMARY

Customer acquisition is the first issue that managers face as they attempt to build a profitable customer base. There are three major decisions to be made: which prospects to target; how to communicate with them; and what offer to communicate to them. New customers are of two kinds. They are either new to the product category, or new to the company. In principle the best prospects are those that have potential to become strategically significant customers, but any customer that generates value over and above their acquisition cost is a net contributor. You will certainly want to recruit new customers that generate more profit than they consume in acquisition and retention costs.

Business-to-business prospects are generated in a number of ways, including referrals, interpersonal networks, online including social media, promotional activities such as exhibitions, trade shows and conferences, advertising, publicity and public relations, canvassing, telemarketing and email.

New customers for consumer companies can be generated from much the same sources as B2B prospects, but much greater effort is put into advertising, social media, sales promotion, buzz or word-of-mouth marketing and merchandising.

Operational CRM applications such as lead management, campaign management and event-based marketing are useful tools for customer acquisition. CRM analytics underpin the success of these applications. The transactional histories of current customers can be analyzed and the cost-effectiveness of different customer acquisition strategies can be computed. By analyzing customer data, companies are better informed about which prospects are most promising, and the offers to make. Predictive modelling can determine relationship-starter products, such as automotive insurance that is used to acquire customers in the personal insurance market. When sales have been made and the customer's permission to use their information has been obtained, other products can be cross-sold, turning acquisition into repeat purchase and subsequently into customer retention.

NOTES AND REFERENCES

1 Peppers, D. and Rogers, M. (1997). *Enterprise one-to-one*. London: Piatkus.

2 Hofmeyr, J. and Rice, B. (2000). *Commitment-led marketing: the key to brand profits is in the customer's mind*. Chichester: John Wiley.

3 CEOExpress.com (Accessed 7 February 2014).

4 Godin, S. (1999). *Permission marketing: turning strangers into friends and friends into customers*. New York: Simon and Schuster.

5 See discussion at: http://www.frankwbaker.com/adsinaday.htm.

6 Herbert Krugman claimed that three exposures was enough. See Krugman, H.E. (1975). What makes advertising effective? *Harvard Business Review*, March–April, p. 98.

7 Ehrenberg, A.S.C. (1974). Repetitive advertising and the consumer. *Journal of Advertising Research*, 14, 25–34; Barnard, N. and Ehrenberg, A.S.C. (1997). Advertising: strongly persuasive or just nudging? *Journal of Advertising Research*, 37(1), 21–31.

8 Lodish, L., Abraham, M., Kalmenson, S., Livelsberger, J., Lubetkin, B., Richardson, B. and Stevens, M.E. (1995). How TV advertising works: a meta-analysis of 389 real-world split cable TV advertising experiments. *Journal of Marketing Research*, 32 (May), 125–39.

9 Abraham, M.M. and Lodish, L. (1990). Getting the most out of advertising and promotion. *Harvard Business Review*, 68(3), 50–6.

10 Buttle, F. (1998). Word-of-mouth: understanding and managing referral marketing. *Journal of Strategic Marketing*, 6, 241–54.

11 Groeger, L. and Buttle, F. (2013). Word-of-mouth marketing influence on offline and online communications: evidence from case study research, *Journal of Marketing Communications*, 20(1–2), 21–41.

12 Haenlein, M. and Libai, B. (2013). *Targeting revenue leaders for a new product*. Report no. 13–101. Cambridge, MA: Marketing Science Institute.

13 Deloitte Digital (2013). Mobile Influence 2013: the growing influence of mobile in store. http://www2.deloitte.com/content/dam/Deloitte/ie/Documents/ConsumerBusiness/2013_mobile_influence_deloitte_ireland.pdf (Accessed 10 February 2014).

14 Naumann, E. (1995). *Creating customer value: the path to sustainable competitive advantage*. Cincinnati, OH: International Thomson Press.

15 Buttle, F. and Kay, S. (2000) RAFs, MGMs and CRSs: is £10 enough? *Proceedings of the Academy of Marketing Annual Conference*.

16 LBM Internet, UK. Personal communication.

17 http://www.sglc.com/images/sia_sample-email.gif (Accessed 22 January 2008).

18 http://www.pqmedia.com/globalproductplacementforecast-2012.html (Accessed 12 February 2014).

19 http://www.pqmedia.com/ppsm2005-es.pdf (Accessed 20 October 2007).

20 Buttle, F. and Kay, S. (2000) RAFs, MGMs and CRSs: is £10 enough? *Proceedings of the Academy of Marketing Annual Conference*.

21 Lee, J. (1999). Net stock frenzy. *Fortune*, 39(2), 148–51.

22 Gurley, J.W. (1998). The soaring cost of e-commerce. *Fortune*, 138(2), 226–8.

23 Villanueva, J., Yoo, S. and Hanssens, D.M. (2006). The impact of marketing-induced versus word-of-mouth customer acquisition on customer equity. Working paper 06–119. Cambridge, MA: Marketing Science Institute.

24 https://www.custora.com/customer_results/bonobos_predictive_customer_lifetime_value (Accessed 12 February 2014).

CHAPTER 4

MANAGING THE CUSTOMER LIFECYCLE

Customer retention and development

CHAPTER OBJECTIVES

By the end of this chapter you will understand:

- What is meant by the terms 'customer retention' and 'customer development'.
- The economics of customer retention.
- How to select which customers to target for retention.
- The distinction between positive and negative customer retention strategies.
- Several strategies for improving customer retention performance.
- Several strategies for growing customer value.
- CRM technologies that facilitate growth in customer value.
- Why and how customers are 'sacked'.

INTRODUCTION

In the last chapter we explained that the customer lifecycle is a representation of the stages that customers go through in their relationship with a company, as seen from the company's perspective. The core stages in the customer lifecycle are customer acquisition, customer retention and customer development. In the last chapter we explored customer acquisition. In this chapter, we turn to customer retention and development.

The major strategic purpose of CRM is to manage a company's relationships with customers profitably through three stages of the customer lifecycle: customer acquisition, customer retention and customer development.

A customer retention strategy aims to keep a high proportion of valuable customers by reducing customer defections (churn), and a customer development strategy aims to increase the value of those retained customers to the company. Just as customer acquisition is focused on particular prospects, retention and development also focus on particular customers. Focus is necessary because not all customers are worth retaining and not all customers have potential for development. We will deal with the issue of retention first, before turning to development.

A number of important questions have to be answered when a company builds its customer retention strategy. Which customers will be targeted for retention? What customer retention strategies will be used? How will the customer retention performance be measured?

We believe that these issues need to be considered carefully and programmed into a properly resourced customer retention plan. Many companies, perhaps as many as six out of ten, have no explicit customer retention plan in place.[1] Most companies spend a majority of their time, energy and resources chasing new business, with 75 per cent or more of marketing budgets being earmarked for new customer acquisition.[2]

WHAT IS CUSTOMER RETENTION?

Customer retention is the maintenance of continuous trading relationships with customers over the long term. Customer retention is the mirror image of customer defection or churn. High retention is equivalent to low defection.[3]

Conventionally, customer retention is defined as follows:[4]

Customer retention is the number of customers doing business with a firm at the end of a financial year expressed as percentage of those who were active customers at the beginning of the year.

However, the appropriate interval over which retention rate should be measured is not always one year. Rather, it depends on the customer repurchase cycle. Car insurance and magazine subscriptions are bought on an annual basis. Carpet tiles and hi-fis are not. If the normal hi-fi replacement cycle is four years, then retention rate is more meaningful if it is measured over four years instead of 12 months. An additional complexity is added when companies sell a range of products and services each with different repurchase cycles. Automobile dealers might sell cars, parts, fuel and service to a single customer. These products have different repurchase cycles that make it very difficult for the dealer to have a whole-of-customer perspective on retention.

Sometimes companies are not clear about whether an individual customer has defected. This is because of the location of customer-related data, which might be retained in product silos, channel silos or functional silos.

- *Product silos.* Consider personal insurance. Insurance companies often have product-based information systems. Effectively, they regard an insurance policy as a customer. If the policy is renewed, the customer is regarded as retained. However, take a customer who shops around for a better price and, after the policy has expired, returns to the original insurer. The insurer may take the new policy to mean a new customer has been gained, and an old customer has churned. They would be wrong.

- *Channel silos.* In the B2B context, independent office equipment dealers have formed into cooperative buying groups to purchase at lower prices and experience other economies of scale in marketing. When a dealer stops buying direct from Brother Electronics, and joins a buying group, Brother's customer data may report a defection, but all that has happened is that the dealer has begun to buy through a different channel.[5] Telecoms companies acquire customers through many channels. Consider a customer who buys a 12-month mobile telecoms contract from a Vodafone-owned retail outlet. Part-way through the year Vodafone launches a new pay-as-you-go product with no contractual obligation. The customer allows her current contract to expire, then buys the new pay-as-you-go product not from a Vodafone outlet but from a supermarket. Vodafone regards her as a lost customer because the contract was not renewed. They would be wrong.

- *Functional silos.* Customer-related data are often kept in functional silos that are not integrated to provide a whole-of-customer perspective. A customer might not have made a product purchase for several years, and is therefore regarded as a churned customer on the sales database. However, the same customer might have several open queries or issues on the customer service database, and is therefore regarded as still active.

The use of aggregates and averages in calculating customer retention rates can mask a true understanding of retention and defection. This is because customers differ in their sales, costs-to-serve and buying behaviours. It is not unusual for a small number of customers to account for a large proportion of company revenue. If you have 100 customers and lose 10 in the course of a year, your raw defection rate is 10 per cent. But what if these customers account for 25 per cent of your company's sales? Is the true defection rate 25 per cent? Consideration of profit makes the computation even more complex. If the 10 per cent of customers that defected produce 50 per cent of your company's profits, is the true defection rate 50 per cent?

What happens if the 10 per cent of customers lost are at the other end of the sales-and-profit spectrum? In other words, what if they buy very little and/or have a high cost-to-serve? It could be that the 10 per cent contributes less than 5 per cent of sales and actually generates a negative profit; that is, they cost more to serve than they generate in margin. The loss of some customers might enhance the company's profit performance. It is not inconceivable that a company could retain 90 per cent of its customers, 95 per cent of its sales and 105 per cent of its profit!

A solution to this problem is to consider three measures of customer retention:

1 *Raw customer retention rate.* This is the number of customers doing business with a firm at the end of a trading period expressed as a percentage of those who were active customers at the beginning of the period.

2 *Sales-adjusted retention rate.* This is the value of sales achieved from the retained customers expressed as a percentage of the sales achieved from all customers who were active at the beginning of the period.

3   *Profit-adjusted retention rate.* This is the profit earned from the retained customers expressed as a percentage of the profit earned from all customers who were active at the beginning of the period.

A high raw customer retention rate does not always signal excellent customer retention performance. This is because customer defection rates vary across cohorts of customers. Defection rates tend to be much higher for newer customers than longer tenure customers. Over time, as seller and buyer demonstrate commitment, trust grows and it becomes progressively more difficult to break the relationship.[6] Successful customer acquisition programmes could produce the effect of a high customer defection rate, simply because newly acquired customers are more likely to defect.

A high sales-adjusted customer retention rate might also need some qualification. Consider a corporate customer purchasing office equipment. The customer's business is expanding fast. It bought 30 computers last year, 20 of which were sourced from Apex Office Supplies. This year it bought 50 computers of which 30 were from Apex. From Apex's point of view it has grown customer value by 50 per cent (from 20 to 30 machines), which it might regard as an excellent achievement. However, in a relative sense, Apex's share of customer has fallen from 67 per cent (20/30) to 60 per cent (30/50). How should Apex regard this customer? The customer is clearly a retained customer in a 'raw' sense, has grown in absolute value, but fallen in relative value. Consider also a retail bank customer who maintains a savings account, but during the course of a year transfers all but a few dollars of her savings to a different institution in pursuit of a better interest rate. This customer is technically still active, but significantly less valuable to the bank.

Managing customer retention or value retention?

The discussion above indicates that companies should focus on retaining customers that contribute value. Sometimes this will mean that the focus is not on retention of customers, per se, but on retention of share-of-wallet. In the banking industry, for example, it may be more important for companies to focus on managing the overall downward migration of customer spending than customer retention. Many customers simply change their buying behaviour rather than defect. Changes in buying behaviour may be responsible for greater changes in customer value than defection. One bank, for example, lost 3 per cent of its total balances when 5 per cent of checking (or current) account customers defected in a year, but lost 24 per cent of its total balances when 35 per cent of customers reduced the amounts deposited in their checking accounts. The need to manage migration rather than defection is particularly true when customers engage in portfolio purchasing by transacting with more than one supplier.[7]

Improving customer retention is an important objective for many CRM strategies. Its definition and measurement need to be sensitive to the sales, profitability and value issues mentioned above. It is important to remember that the fundamental purpose of focusing CRM efforts on customer retention is to ensure that the company maintains relationships with value-creating customers. It may not be beneficial to maintain relationships with all customers. Some may be too costly to serve. Others may be strategic switchers constantly in search of a better deal. These can be value-destroyers, not value-creators.

ECONOMICS OF CUSTOMER RETENTION

There is a strong economic argument in favour of customer retention, which was first introduced in Chapter 2. The argument goes as follows:[8]

1 *Increasing purchases as tenure grows*. Over time customers come to know their suppliers. Providing the relationship is satisfactory, trust grows whilst risk and uncertainty are reduced. Therefore, customers commit more of their spending to those suppliers with which they have a proven and satisfactory relationship. Also, because suppliers develop deeper customer intimacy over time, they can enjoy better yields from their cross-selling efforts.

2 *Lower customer management costs over time*. The relationship start-up costs that are incurred when a customer is acquired can be quite high. It may take several years for enough profit to be earned from the relationship to recover those acquisition costs. For example, it can take six years to recover the costs of winning a new retail bank customer.[9] In the B2B context, in particular, ongoing relationship maintenance costs such as selling and service costs can be low relative to the costs of winning the account. Therefore, there is high probability that the account will become more profitable on a period-by-period basis as tenure lengthens. These relationship maintenance costs may eventually be significantly reduced or even eliminated as the parties become closer over time. In the B2B context, once automated processes are in place, transaction costs are effectively eliminated, and portals largely transfer account service costs to the customer. In the B2C context, especially in retailing, the assertion that acquisition costs generally exceed retention costs is hard to prove. This is in part because it is very difficult to isolate and measure customer acquisition costs.[10]

3 *Customer referrals*. Customers who willingly commit more of their purchases to a preferred supplier are generally more satisfied than customers who do not. They are therefore more likely to utter positive word-of-mouth (WOM) and influence the beliefs, feelings and behaviours of others. Research shows that customers who are frequent buyers are heavier referrers. For example, online clothing customers who have bought once refer three other people; after ten purchases they will have referred seven. In consumer electronics, the one-time customer refers four; the ten times customer refers 13. These referred customers spend about 50–75 per cent of the referrer's spending over the first three years of their relationship.[11] However, it is also likely that newly acquired customers, freshly enthused by their experience, would be powerful WOM advocates, perhaps more than longer-term customers who are more habituated.[12]

4 *Premium prices*. Customers who are satisfied in their relationship may reward their suppliers by paying higher prices. This is because they get their sense of value from more than price alone. Customers in an established relationship are also likely to be less responsive to price appeals offered by competitors. There is strong empirical evidence linking customer satisfaction to willingness-to-pay.[13]

These conditions mean that retained customers are generally more profitable than newly acquired customers. Drawing from their consulting experience, Dawkins and Reichheld report that a 5 per cent increase in customer retention rate leads to an increase in the net present value of customers by between 25 per cent and 95 per cent across a wide range of industries including credit cards, insurance brokerage, auto services and office building management.[14] In short, customer retention drives up customer lifetime value (CLV).

WHICH CUSTOMERS TO RETAIN?

Simply, the customers who have greatest strategic value to your company are prime candidates for your retention efforts. These are the customers who have high CLV, or are otherwise strategically significant as high volume customers, benchmarks, inspirations or door openers, as described in more detail at the end of Chapter 5.

You need to bear in mind that there may be a considerable cost of customer retention. Your most valued customers are also likely to be very attractive to your competitors. If the costs of retaining customers become too great then they might lose their status as strategically significant.

The level of commitment between your customer and you will figure in the decision about which customers to retain. If the customer is highly committed, they will be impervious to the appeals of competitors, and you will not need to invest so much in their retention. On the other hand, if you have highly significant customers who are not committed, you may want to invest considerable sums in their retention.

Some companies prefer to focus their retention efforts on their recently acquired customers. They often have greater future lifetime value potential than longer tenure customers. There is some evidence that retention rates rise over time, so if defections can be prevented in the early stages of a relationship, there will be a pay-off in future revenue streams and profitability.[15] Another justification for focusing on recently acquired customers comes from research into service failures. When customers experience service failure, they may be more forgiving if they have a history of good service with the service provider. In other words, customers who have been recently acquired and let down are more likely to defect or reduce their spending than customers who have a satisfactory history with the supplier.[16]

There is also some evidence that the most valuable customers change over time. The UK retail organization, John Lewis Partnership, for example, has found that 50 per cent of profits are produced by 5 per cent of their customers, but that the composition of the 5 per cent changes year on year. The company uses data from its loyalty programme and credit card to identify the 5 per cent, and directs its retention efforts accordingly.[17] John Lewis's 'Never Knowingly Undersold' market positioning is about 'a relationship with a customer over a lifetime, making a trade-off between making slightly more money on the sale of the fork versus the lifetime value that comes from the trust you can engender by making sure that the fork is sold at a price which is no greater than it could be, if bought anywhere else'.

Retention efforts where there is portfolio purchasing can be very difficult. Should effort be directed at retaining the high-share customer with whom you have a profitable relationship, the medium-share customer from whom you might lose additional share to competitors or the low-share customer from whom there is considerable CLV potential? The answer will depend on the current value of the customer, the potential for growing that value and the cost of maintaining and developing the relationship.

STRATEGIES FOR CUSTOMER RETENTION

Positive and negative retention strategies

An important distinction can be made between strategies that lock the customer in by penalizing their exit from a relationship, and strategies that reward a customer for remaining in a relationship. The former are generally considered negative, and the latter positive customer retention strategies.

Negative customer retention strategies impose high switching costs on customers, discouraging their defection. In a B2C context, mortgage companies have commonly recruited new customers with attractive discounted interest rates. When the honeymoon period is over, these customers may want to switch to another provider, only to discover that they will be hit with early redemption and exit penalties. Customers wishing to switch retail banks find that it is less simple than anticipated: direct debits and standing orders have to be reorganized. In a B2B context, a customer may have agreed to purchase a given volume of raw material at a quoted price. Some way through the contract a lower cost supplier makes a better offer. The customer wants to switch but finds that there are penalty clauses in the contract. The new supplier is unwilling to buy the customer out of the contract by paying the penalties.

Some customers find these switching costs are so high that they remain customers, though unwillingly. The danger for CRM practitioners is that negative customer retention strategies produce customers who feel trapped. They are likely to agitate to be freed from their obligations, taking up much management time. Also, they are likely to utter negative word-of-mouth; in today's social media environment it is easier than ever and highly effective. They are unlikely to do further business with that supplier. Companies that pursue these strategies argue that customers need to be aware of what they are buying and the contracts they sign. They argue that the total cost of ownership (TCO) of a mortgage should and does include early redemption costs.

When presented with dissatisfied customers complaining about high relationship exit (switching) costs, companies have a choice. They can either enforce the terms and conditions, or not. The latter path is more attractive when the customer is strategically significant, particularly if the company can make an offer that matches that of the prospective new supplier.

POSITIVE CUSTOMER RETENTION STRATEGIES

In the following sections we look at a number of positive customer retention strategies, including creating customer delight, adding customer-perceived value, creating social and structural bonds, and building customer engagement.

Customer delight

It is very difficult to build long-term relationships with customers if their needs and expectations are not understood and well met. It is a fundamental principle of modern customer management that companies should understand customers, and then ensure their satisfaction and retention. This is why CRM is grounded on detailed customer-related knowledge. Customers that a company cannot serve well may be better served by competitors.

Delighting customers, or exceeding customer expectations, means going beyond what would normally satisfy the customer. This does not necessarily mean being world class or best in class. It does mean being aware of what it usually takes to satisfy the customer and what it might take to delight or pleasantly surprise the customer. You cannot consciously delight the customer if you do not understand the customer's expectations. You may stumble onto attributes of your performance that do delight the customer but you cannot consistently expect to do so unless you have deep customer insight. Consistent efforts to delight customers show your commitment to the relationship. Commitment builds trust. Trust leads to relationship longevity.

Customer delight occurs when the customer's perception of their experience of doing business with you exceeds their expectation. In formulaic terms:

$$CD = P > E$$

where CD = Customer Delight, P = Perception of performance, and E = Expectation

This formula implies that customer delight can be influenced in two ways: by managing expectations or by managing performance. In most commercial contexts customer expectations exceed customer perceptions of performance. In other words, customers generally can find cause for dissatisfaction. You might think that this would encourage companies to attempt to manage customer expectations down to levels that can be delivered. However, competitors may well be improving their performance in an attempt to meet customer expectations. If your strategy is to manage expectations down, you may well lose customers to the better performing company. This is particularly likely if you fail to meet customer expectations on important attributes.

Customers have expectations of many attributes, for example product quality, service responsiveness, price stability, and the physical appearance of your people and vehicles. These are unlikely to be equally important. It is critical to meet customer expectations on attributes that are important to the customer. Online customers, for example, look for rapid and accurate order fulfilment, good price, high levels of customer service and website functionality. Online retailers must meet these basic requirements.

Dell Computers believes that customer retention is the outcome of their performance against three variables that are critical for customers: order fulfilment (on-time, in full, no error – OTIFNE), product performance (frequency of problems encountered by customers) and after-sales service (per cent of problems fixed first time by technicians). The comments in parentheses are the metrics that Dell uses.

Figure 4.1 identifies a number of priorities for improvement (PFIs) for a restaurant company. The PFIs are the attributes where customer satisfaction scores are low, but the attributes are important to customers. In the example, the PFIs are food quality and toilet cleanliness. There would be no advantage in investing in speedier service or more helpful staff.

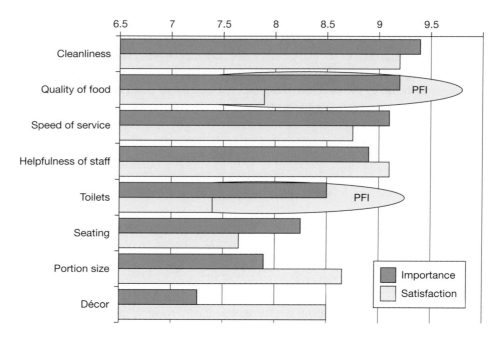

Figure 4.1 Using satisfaction and importance data to guide service improvement

Kano's customer delight model

Noriaki Kano has developed a product quality model that distinguishes between three forms of quality. *Basic qualities* are those that the customer routinely expects in the product. These expectations are often unexpressed until the product fails. For example, a car's engine should start first time every time, and the sunroof should not leak. The second form is *linear quality*. These are attributes of which the customer wants more or less. For example, more comfort, better fuel economy and reduced noise levels. Marketing research can usually identify these requirements. Better performance on these attributes generates better customer satisfaction. The third form is *attractive quality*. These are attributes that surprise, delight and excite customers. They are answers to latent, unarticulated needs and are often difficult to identify in marketing research. As shown in Figure 4.2, Kano's analysis suggests that customers can be delighted in two ways: by enhancing linear qualities beyond expectations and by creating innovative attractive qualities.[18]

Exceeding expectations need not be costly. For example, a sales representative could do a number of simple things for a customer, such as:

- Volunteer to collect and replace a faulty product rather than issuing a credit note and waiting for the normal call cycle to schedule a call on the customer.

- Offer better, lower cost solutions, even though that might reduce profit margin.

- Provide information about the customer's served market. A packaging company, for example, might alert a fast-moving consumer goods manufacturer customer to competitive initiatives in their served markets.

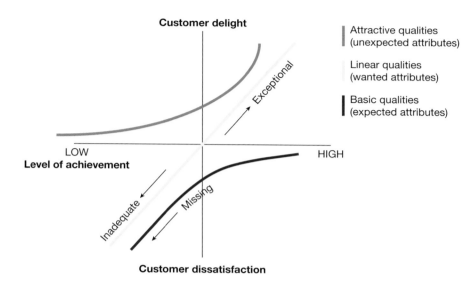

Figure 4.2 Kano's model for creating customer delight

Some efforts to delight customers can go wrong. For example, sooner is not necessarily better. For example, if a retail store customer has requested delivery between 1 p.m. and 3 p.m., and the driver arrives an hour early, the truck may clog up goods inwards and interfere with a carefully scheduled unload plan. Many contact centres play music while callers are waiting online. This is to divert the caller's attention, and create the illusion of faster passage of time. However, the cycle time of the selected music must not be too fast, otherwise callers will be exposed to the same songs repeatedly. Also, the music needs to be appropriate to the context. Customers may not appreciate 'I Can't Get No Satisfaction' by the Rolling Stones if they are waiting online to complain.

A number of companies have explicitly adopted 'Customer Delight' as their mission, including Audi Group, IHS (www.ihs.com) and, until recently, American Express and Kwik Fit, the auto service chain. Others pay homage to the goal but do not organize to achieve it. In the service industries, customer delight requires front-line employees to be trained, empowered and rewarded for doing what it takes to delight customers. It is in the interaction with customers that contact employees have the opportunity to understand and exceed their expectations. The service quality attributes of empathy and responsiveness are on show when employees successfully delight customers.

Companies sometimes complain that investing in customer delight is unproductive. As noted earlier, expectations generally increase as competitors strive to offer better value to customers. Over time, as customers experience delight, their expectations change. What was exceptional becomes the norm. In Kano's terms, what used to be an attractive attribute becomes a linear or basic attribute. It no longer delights. Delight decays into normal expectation, and companies have to look for new ways to pleasantly surprise customers. In a competitive environment, it makes little sense to resist the quest for customer delight if competitors will simply drive up expectations anyway.

Add customer-perceived value

Companies can explore ways for customers to experience additional value as they buy and use products and services. The ideal is to enable additional value to be experienced by customers without creating additional costs for the supplier. If costs are incurred then customers may be expected to contribute towards cost recovery. For example, an online customer community may be expected to generate a revenue stream from its membership.

There are three common forms of value-adding programmes: loyalty schemes, customer communities and sales promotions.

Loyalty schemes

Loyalty schemes reward customers for their patronage. A loyalty scheme or programme can be defined as follows:

A loyalty scheme is a customer management programme that offers delayed or immediate incremental rewards to customers for their cumulative patronage.

The more a customer spends, the higher the reward. Loyalty schemes have a long history. In 1844, the UK's Rochdale Pioneers developed a cooperative retailing operation that distributed surpluses back to members in the form of a dividend. The surpluses were proportionate to customer spend. S&H Pink stamps and Green Shield stamps were collected in the 1950s and 1960s, and redeemed for gifts selected from catalogues. In the 1970s, Southwest Airlines ran a 'Sweetheart Stamps' programme that enabled travellers to collect proofs of purchase and surrender them for a free flight for their partner.[19]

Today's CRM-enabled loyalty schemes owe their structure to the frequent flier programmes (FFP) that started with American Airlines' AAdvantage programme in 1981. The airline made a strategic decision to use its spare capacity as a resource to generate customer loyalty. Airlines are high fixed cost businesses. Costs do not change much, regardless of whether the load factor is 25 per cent or 95 per cent. American Airlines knew that filling empty seats would have little impact on costs, but could impact significantly on future demand. The airline searched its reservation system, SABRE, for details of frequent fliers in order to offer them the reward of free flights.

This basic model has migrated from airlines into many other B2C sectors – hotels, restaurants, retail, car hire, gas stations and bookstores, for example. It has also transferred into B2B contexts with many suppliers offering loyalty rewards to long-term customers.

The mechanics of these schemes have changed over time. Initially, stamps were collected. The first card-based schemes were anonymous; that is, they carried no personal data, not even the name of the participant. Then magnetic stripe cards were introduced, followed by chip-embedded cards that carried a lot of personal and transactional data. Innovators developed their own individual schemes. Eventually, these transformed into linked schemes, in which, for example, it was possible to collect air miles from various participating companies such as gas stations, credit cards and food retailers. Current schemes are massively different from the early programmes. For example, Nectar is a consortium loyalty scheme operating in the UK, with 19 million cards in circulation. It is managed not by the participants, but by an independent third party. Its core retail participants are all numbers one or two in their

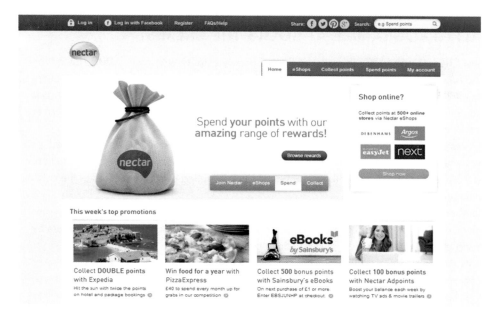

Figure 4.3 Nectar loyalty programme

respective markets, such as Sainsbury's, Homebase and BP. Points can also be earned from over 500 online retailers. Shoppers register in the scheme, then use their loyalty card to collect points that are redeemable in a wide range of retailers including supermarkets, liquor stores, catalogue retailers, restaurants, hotels, cinemas, travel outlets and tourist attractions. They can even be donated to charities.

Loyalty programmes provide added value to consumers at two points: during credit acquisition and at redemption. Although the credits have no material value until they are redeemed, they may deliver some pre-redemption psychological benefits to customers, such as a sense of belonging and of being valued, and an enjoyable anticipation of desirable future events. At the redemption stage, customers receive both psychological and material benefits. The reward acts to positively reinforce purchase behaviour. It also demonstrates that the company appreciates its customers. This sense of being recognized as valued and important can enhance customers' overall sense of well-being and emotional attachment to the firm. However, customers can become loyal to the scheme rather than to the company or brand behind the scheme.[20]

Loyalty schemes are not without critics. Critics question their cost and effectiveness. Certainly, they can be very expensive to establish and manage. In respect of operating costs, retail schemes typically reward customers with a cash rebate or vouchers equivalent to 1 per cent of purchases. This comes straight out of the bottom line, so a retailer that is making 5 per cent margin loses one-fifth or 20 per cent of its profit to fund the scheme. There may also be a significant investment in CRM technology to support the scheme, and marketing to launch and sustain the scheme. Supermarket operator Safeway dropped its UK loyalty programme that had been costing about £30 million annually. Shell is reported to have spent up to £40 million to develop its smart card scheme.[21] Unredeemed credits

LOYALTY PROGRAMME AT BOOTS THE CHEMIST

Boots the Chemist is the UK's largest health and beauty retailer with over 3,000 stores. The Boots Advantage Card loyalty scheme, launched in 1997, at an initial cost of £30 million, is a key element of the Boots customer offer, enabling customers to earn points on purchases for redemption at a later date. It provides Boots with valuable customer insight to further enhance its customer offer.

By March 2013, the number of active Boots Advantage Card members, defined as members who have used their card at least once in the last 12 months, reached 17.9 million. Around 90 per cent of active members are women, representing nearly two-thirds of the adult female population in the UK.

Members collect four points for every £1 spent in store or online. Boots periodically runs promotions offering additional points. Advantage Card members receive additional offers by mail or via email, including special promotions and invitations.

Boots Advantage Card members aged over 60 can also join the 'More treats for over 60s' scheme, which enables them to collect 10 points per £1 on Boots branded products, plus other benefits. The Boots Parenting Club, which at March 2013 had almost one million active members, is designed to support parents from the early stages of pregnancy to their baby's second birthday, and provides further opportunities to earn points.

Over 60 per cent of Boots retail sales are to Boots Advantage Card members. On average they spend over 60 per cent more per transaction than non-members. Boots's technology allows it to personalize customer offers, including till-generated promotional coupons.

represent liabilities for scheme operators. For example, it has been suggested that if all the unused air miles were redeemed on the same day it would take 600,000 Boeing 747s to meet the demand.[22]

Schemes are also criticized for their effectiveness.[23] Critics claim that schemes have become less distinctive and value-adding as many competitors now operate me-too programmes. Indeed, it is very hard to find any hotel chain that does not have a loyalty programme. Customers now expect to accumulate credits as part of the standard hotel value proposition. Many supermarket shoppers carry loyalty cards from more than one supermarket.[24] The customer's choice set when grocery shopping might include all suppliers with which they have a card-based relationship.

One major concern is that loyalty schemes may not be creating loyalty at all. As explained in Chapter 2, loyalty takes two forms – attitudinal and behavioural. Attitudinal loyalty is reflected in positive affect towards the brand or supplier. Behavioural loyalty is reflected in purchasing behaviour.[25] There is some longitudinal evidence about shifts in customer behaviour after they join a loyalty scheme. One study found that retail shoppers who were heavy buyers when they joined a loyalty programme did not change their patronage behaviour after joining. However, shoppers whose initial patronage levels were low or moderate gradually became more behaviourally loyal to the firm, spending more of their shopping dollar at the franchise. For light buyers, the loyalty programme encouraged shoppers to buy from additional categories, thus deepening their relationship with the franchise.[26]

Meyer-Waarden studied the effects of three loyalty programmes on retail customer behaviour over three years. He found that programme members had significantly higher purchase intensities in terms of total and average shopping baskets, share of category purchases, purchase frequencies and inter-purchase times than non-members.[27]

Whether or not they develop customer loyalty, these schemes certainly reward buying behaviour. Accumulated credits represent investments that the customer has made in the scheme or the brands behind the scheme. When customers get no return from this investment, they can be deeply distressed. Members of at least five airlines – Braniff, Midway, MGM Grand, Legend and Ansett – lost their air miles when their airlines folded. Members of Pan Am's FFP were fortunate to have their credits transferred into Delta Airlines when Pan Am stopped flying. Frequent fliers of Ansett forfeited their miles after the airline stopped flying in 2001. Passengers organized themselves into a group to lobby, ultimately unsuccessfully, for their loyalty to be recognized and rewarded by the company administrators, or prospective purchasers of the airline.

Additionally, loyalty schemes are successful enablers of customer insight. Personalized cards are obtained only after registering personal data. Then it becomes possible to monitor transactional behaviour. Chip-embedded smart cards carry the information on the card itself. A huge amount of data is generated that can be warehoused and subjected to data mining for insights into purchasing behaviour. These insights can be used to guide marketing campaigns and offer development. Boots, for example, ran a series of controlled experiments mailing health and beauty offers to select groups of carefully profiled customers. It achieved 40 per cent response rates in comparison to 5 per cent from the control group.[28]

Customer clubs

Customer clubs have been established by many organizations. A customer club can be defined as follows:

A customer club is a company-run membership organization that offers a range of value-adding benefits exclusively to members.

The initial costs of establishing a club can be quite high but thereafter most clubs are expected to cover their operating expenses and, preferably, return a profit. Research suggests that customer clubs are successful at promoting customer retention.[29]

To become a member and obtain benefits, clubs require customers to register. With these personal details, the company is able to begin interaction with customers, learn more about them, and develop customized offers and services for them. Customer clubs only succeed if members experience benefits they value. Club managers can assemble and offer a range of value-adding services and products that, given the availability of customer data, can be personalized to segment or individual level. Among the more common benefits of club membership are access to member-only products and services, alerts about upcoming new and improved products, discounts, magazines and special offers. For example, IKEA FAMILY, the home furnishing retailer's club, offers members discounts on selected IKEA products, restaurant and service offers, a free home furnishing magazine quarterly, free product insurance and news updates via email.

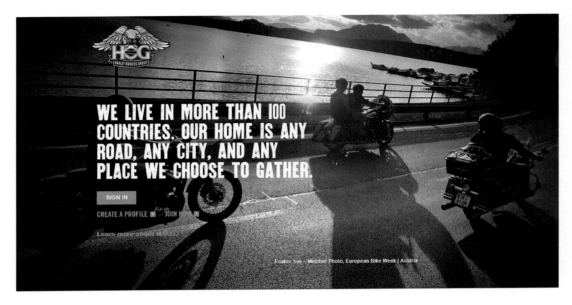

Figure 4.4 Harley Owners Group

There are a huge number of customer clubs. One report estimates that there are 'several hundreds' in Germany alone.[30] B2C clubs include:

- Swatch the Club (www.swatch.com)
- Harley Owners Group (HOG) (www.hog.com)
- Subaru Owners Club (www.subaruownersclub.com)
- Nestlé's mother and baby club (www.nestlebaby.com).

There are over a million paid-up members of the Harley Owners Group that was established in 1983. They choose from four types of membership, and a variable membership length from one year to lifetime. Among the many benefits are roadside assistance, a membership manual, a touring handbook, a dedicated website, magazines, a mileage recognition programme, a theft reward programme, a selection of pins and patches, membership in over 1,400 chapters, invitations to events and rallies, and a lot more.

Sales promotions

Whereas loyalty schemes and clubs are relatively durable, sales promotions offer only temporary enhancements to customer-experienced value. Sales promotions, as we saw in the last chapter, can be used for customer acquisition too. Retention-oriented sales promotions encourage the customer to repeat purchase, so the form they take is different. Here are some examples.

- *In pack or on-pack voucher.* Customers buy the product and receive a voucher entitling them to a discount off one or more additional purchases.

- *Rebate or cash-back.* Rebates are refunds that the customer receives after purchase. The value of the rebate can be adjusted in line with the quantity purchased, in order to reward customers who meet high volume targets.

- *Patronage awards.* Customers collect proofs of purchase, such as store receipts or bar codes from packaging, that are surrendered for cash or gifts. The greater the volume purchased, the bigger the award.

- *Free premium for continuous purchase.* The customer collects several proofs of purchase and mails them in or surrenders them at points of sale to obtain a free gift. Sometimes the gift might be part of a collectible series. For example, a manufacturer of preserves and jams developed a range of collectible enamel badges. Customers collected proofs of purchase and mailed them in to receive a badge. There were 20 different badges in the series. So popular was this promotion that a secondary market was established so that collectors could trade and swap badges to obtain the full set.

Figure 4.5
Cash-back sales promotion[31]

- *Collection schemes.* These are long-running schemes in which the customer collects items with every purchase. Kellogg's ran a promotion in which they inserted picture cards of carefully chosen sports stars into packets of cereals. Customers didn't know what card they had until they bought and opened the pack. These became collectible items.

- *Self-liquidating premium.* A self-liquidating promotion is one that recovers its own direct costs. Typically, consumers are invited to collect proofs of purchase and surrender them together with a sum of money. This entitles the customer to buy a discounted premium such as a camera or gardening equipment. The promoter will have reached a deal with the suppliers of the premiums to buy in bulk at a highly discounted rate, perhaps on a sale-or-return basis. Margins earned from the sale of product plus the money paid by the consumer cover the costs of running the promotion that, as a consequence, becomes self-liquidating.

Bonding

The next positive customer retention strategy is customer bonding. B2B researchers have identified many different forms of bond between customers and suppliers. These include interpersonal bonds, technology bonds (as in electronic data interchange – EDI), legal bonds and process bonds. These different forms can be split into two major categories: social and structural.[32]

Social bonds

Social bonds are found in *positive interpersonal relationships* between people. Positive interpersonal relationships are characterized by high levels of trust and commitment. Successful interpersonal relationships may take time to evolve as uncertainty and distance are reduced. As the number of episodes linking customer and supplier grows, there is greater opportunity for social bonds to develop. Suppliers should understand that if they act opportunistically or fail to align themselves to customer preferences, trust and confidence will be eroded.

Strong social bonds can emerge between employees in companies having similar sizes, cultures and locations. For example, small and medium-sized businesses generally prefer to do business with similar-sized companies, and Japanese companies prefer to do business with other Japanese companies. Geographic bonds emerge when companies in a trading area cooperate to support each other.

Social relationships between buyer and seller can be single-level or multi-level. A single-level relationship might exist between the supplier's account manager and the customer's procurement officer. The more layers there are between the dyad, the more resistant the relationship is to breakdown. For example, technical, quality and operations people talk to their equivalents on the other side.

Social bonds characterized by trust generally precede the development of structural bonds. Mutual investments in business relationships serve as structural bonds. These structural bonds can be formally recognized in an alliance or joint venture having legal status. Companies are unlikely to commit resources if there is a low level of trust in the partner's integrity and competence.

Structural bonds

Structural bonds are established when companies and customers commit resources to a relationship. Generally, these resources yield mutual benefits for the participants. For example, a joint customer–supplier quality team can work on improving quality compliance, benefiting both companies. Resources committed to a relationship may or may not be recoverable if the relationship breaks down. For example, investments made in training a customer's operatives are non-returnable. On the other hand, a chilled-products manufacturer that has installed refrigerated space at a distributor's warehouse may be able to dismantle and retrieve it when the relationship breaks down.

A key feature of structural bonding is investment in adaptations to suit the other party. Suppliers can adapt any element of the offer – product, process, price and inventory levels, for example – to suit the customer. Customers on the other hand also make adaptations. For example, they can adapt their manufacturing processes to accommodate a supplier's product or technology.

Power imbalances in relationships can produce asymmetric adaptations. A major multi-outlet retailer might force adaptations from small suppliers while making no concessions itself. For example, it could insist on a reduction in product costs, or co-branding of point-of-sale material, or even attempt to coerce the supplier not to supply competitors.

Different types of structural bond can be identified. All are characterized by an investment of one or both parties in the other:

- *Financial* bonds: where the seller offers a financial inducement to retain the customer. Insurance companies form financial bonds with customers by offering no-claims discounts, tenure related discounts and multi-policy discounts.

- *Legal* bonds: when there is a contract or common ownership linking the relational partners.

- *Equity* bonds: where both parties invest in order to develop an offer for customers, e.g. the owners of airports invest in the shells of the duty-free retail outlets; the retailer invests in the internal fixtures and fittings.

- *Knowledge-based* bonds: when each party grows to know and understand the other's processes and structures, strengths and weaknesses.

- *Technological* bonds: when the technologies of the relational partners are aligned, e.g. with EDI, Just-in-Time logistics and manufacturing.

- *Process* bonds: when processes of the two organizations are aligned, e.g. the quality assurance programme on the supplier side and the quality inspection programme on the customer side. Some suppliers manage inventory levels for their customers, ensuring inventory levels are optimized. This is known as Vendor Managed Inventory (VMI). The chemicals company, Solvay Interox, uses telemetry systems to perform VMI for its customers.

- *Values-based bonds*. Some companies are renowned for their strong values, e.g. the Body Shop is opposed to testing cosmetics on animals, and it will not source products from suppliers who do so.

- *Geographic* bonds: when companies in a trading area – street, city region or country – create a buyer–seller referral network that supports all members of their group. In the UK, retailers in the town of Royal Leamington Spa have combated out-of-town developments by creating a loyalty programme, known as Spa'kle, in which customers can collect and redeem loyalty credits at any member store.

- *Project* bonds: when the partners are engaged in some special activity outside of their normal commercial arrangements, e.g. a new product development project. There may be an exchange of resources to enable the desired outcome to be achieved, e.g. an exchange of engineers and technologists between the companies.

- *Multi-product* bonds: when a customer buys several products from a supplier, the bond is more difficult to break. There are economies for customers when they deal with fewer suppliers. When a relationship with a supplier of several products is dissolved, the customer may incur significant money, transaction and psychic costs in identifying one or more replacements. Further, the level of perceived risk attached to a new relationship may become uncomfortable.

Social bonds are generally easier to break than structural bonds. Structural bonds link organizations. Social bonds link people. If the account manager and procurement officer do not grow to trust each other, they may fall out, but this is unlikely to bring down a joint venture.

CUSTOMER RETENTION AT KOREA TELECOM

Korea Telecom places a high level of importance upon creating valuable relationships with customers, both business and consumer, in the telecommunications markets of South Korea and South East Asia.

The organization places significant emphasis on maintaining high retention rates in markets that are becoming increasingly competitive. To this end Korea Telecom estimates that it costs around US$185 to gain a consumer for a broadband Internet service. However, for an average customer it takes almost two years for the organization to break even with such a service. Consequently the organization undertakes a number of activities as part of its CRM strategy to retain customers including the bundling of a number of services such as Internet, mobile and home phone at a discount to customers who enter into service contracts for at least two years.

Build customer engagement

The final positive strategy for improving customer retention is to build customer engagement. Various studies have indicated that customer satisfaction is not enough to ensure customer longevity. For example, Reichheld reports that 65 per cent to 85 per cent of recently churned customers claimed to be satisfied with their previous suppliers.[33] Another study reports that one in ten customers who said they were completely satisfied, scoring 10 out of 10 on a customer satisfaction scale, defected to a rival brand the following year.[34] Having satisfied customers is increasingly no more than a basic requirement of being in the game. Today, many commentators are stressing the need for companies to lift levels of customer engagement instead of just focusing on customer satisfaction.

This concept of engagement has migrated into customer relationship management from psychology and organizational behaviour, where it was first explored in the context of the workplace–employee engagement. Although there is still is no clear consensus on a definition of *customer* engagement,[35] engaged consumers are generally thought to have a higher intensity of participation in and connection to a brand or organization.[36] They feel a strong sense of connection to the organization or brand based on their experiences of the firm's offerings, activities and reputation.

Customer engagement can be thought of as a multidimensional construct composed of four elements: cognitive engagement, affective engagement, behavioural engagement and social engagement. The cognitive and affective elements reflect the experiences and feelings of customers, and the behavioural and social elements capture brand or organizational participation by consumers, beyond merely buying the firms' offerings. Consumers who are engaged do more than just buy. They may perform acts of 'corporate citizenship', such as being an unpaid advocate by uttering positive word-of-mouth, providing frequent feedback on their experiences, participating in company research, contributing to a new product or service development, being more forgiving if the company makes a mistake or service fails, and participating in online communities and user groups.

CUSTOMER ENGAGEMENT AT JETBLUE[37]

JetBlue is a USA-based airline founded by David Neeleman in 1999. The company employs 17 individuals in its social media department, has a Twitter feed with 1.8 million followers and a Facebook page with more than 880,000 'likes'. Moreover, they have 200,000 potential passengers signed up for their cheap deals feed. JetBlue uses these mechanisms to communicate with and respond to customer issues more than to advertise. For example, in 2010, a disgruntled flight attendant exited a parked JetBlue flight via the emergency slide causing a public relations issue for the company. To relieve the situation, the company made light of the episode in a blog. The first customer comment on the blog read, 'I love you JetBlue.' That customer is engaged. When snowstorms led to flight cancellations in 2014 JetBlue announced in its blog 'Blue Tales' that 'We will reach out to customers directly via provided contact information to assist in re-accommodating them on . . . new flights. We've also established a compensation plan to address the inconveniences our customers faced. The plan addresses those customers who experienced multiple cancellations, and offers TrueBlue points, credit toward a future JetBlue flight, and/or monetary reimbursement based on the level of impact.' Passengers posted comments to the blog, and JetBlue responded individually to each comment whether the comments were favourable or unfavourable.

Preliminary research indicates that engaged consumers can exhibit greater loyalty to brands than unengaged consumers,[38] and may develop such a close affinity to the brand that they become highly resistant to competitive influence. One report, for example, indicates that the rate of account closure at a bank was 37 per cent lower for emotionally engaged customers than for rationally satisfied customers.[39]

Managers often try to build engagement by creating interactive relationships with consumers that get them more involved with and connected to their brand, as illustrated in Case study 4.3. Much of the interactivity is delivered through social media including blogs, Facebook pages and YouTube channels. A recent development that lifts interactivity is gamification of brands.

Gamification

Gamification can be defined as follows:

Gamification is the use of game-like mechanics in non-game contexts.

At its heart is the idea that competition and play will build consumer engagement with the brand. The more engaged the gamer, the more likely she is to remain active as consumer.

Customers may also feel a strong sense of connection to a brand or organization when they build close relationships with the firm's employees or when their personal values align with those of the firm.

CASE STUDY 4.4

EARN YOUR WINGS – GAMIFICATION AT AIR CANADA[40]

In 2013, Air Canada breathed new life into the hackneyed world of collecting points redeemable for flights or other goods and services (hotels, care hire). All but the discount airlines offer some version of 'loyalty' programmes, albeit the value of which has been questioned by academics.[41] Indeed so prevalent is the currency that the major airlines have grouped into three consortia that recognize each other's collected miles: Star Alliance, One World and SkyTeam. This makes it easy to question the branded benefits of an individual scheme: does it really generate loyalty or is it merely a price discount that has become universal?

Air Canada's game (run solely in Canada) offered ten million air miles split amongst the players who collected badges for destinations achieved (on Air Canada flights of course). A leaderboard was created and almost 7,000 loyalty cardholders participated. Leaderboards added a competitive and social aspect to traditional loyalty schemes and badges a more immediate sense of gratification and progress than quarterly statements and achievement of higher status levels; all of which are considered valuable elements of games. Air Canada estimates its ROI on this activity to be in excess of 500 per cent, recognizing a significant increase in the number of routes flown by participants. It plans to continue gamification with its cardholders to create a more engaging and branded loyalty scheme.

Source: Trademark used under license from Air Canada.

Relational attachment

Customers can become highly attached to a company's people. An emotional tie may be formed with an individual person, a work group or the generalized company as a whole. Customers who talk about 'my banker' or 'my mechanic' or 'my builder' are expressing this attachment. They feel a sense of personal identification with that individual. Often, these are employees who 'break the rules' or 'go the extra mile'. They are reliable, competent, empathic and responsive. When these employees recover an at-risk customer, they create a friend.

Customer-focused organizations make heroes out of these individuals. They are fêted and celebrated. For example, American Express tells the story of a customer service agent (CSA) who responded to a call from a customer who had been robbed, by arranging to have replacement travellers cheques delivered personally to the customer. The CSA also confirmed the customer's hotel reservation, arranged for a car to collect the customer from the phone booth and notified the police. All of this was above and beyond the CSA's call of duty. Customers can also become attached to a work group. In banking, for example, some customers are highly committed to a specific branch and prefer not to transact elsewhere. Finally, customers can become attached to an organization as a whole, believing its people to be better than competitors on dimensions that are important to the customer. They may provide 'the best service' or be 'the friendliest people'.

Values-based attachment

Customers may develop a strong sense of emotional attachment when their personal values are aligned with those of the company. Values can be defined as follows:

Values are core beliefs that transcend context and serve to organize and direct attitudes and behaviours.

Customers have many and varied core beliefs such as sustainability, honesty, child protection, independence, family-centredness and so on. Many of these values reflect cultural norms. Where these values coincide with those of an organization, the customer may develop a strong sense of emotional attachment to the organization.

Companies that are accused of using child labour, damaging the environment or otherwise acting unethically place themselves at risk. Nestlé had been accused of marketing infant formula in African countries where the infrastructure made its use dangerous. Many babies died as mothers used unclean water and unsterilized equipment. This is estimated to have cost the company $40 million.[42] When BP's Deepwater Horizon oilrig exploded, claiming 11 lives and releasing 4.9 million barrels of crude oil into the Gulf of Mexico, consumers responded by boycotting BP's products. This resulted in a 52 per cent fall in BP's share price in the 50 days following the catastrophe.[43] Just as customers can take action against companies that they feel are in breach of their values, so can they commit to companies that mirror their values. Research supports the claim that there is a hierarchical relationship from values to attitudes to purchase intention and ultimately to purchase.[44]

A number of companies benefit from values-based commitment, for example, Body Shop, Harley-Davidson and Virgin.

• *Body Shop International* is a health and beauty retailer that adheres to five core values in its operations. As shown in Figure 4.6, it is against animal testing, it supports community fair trade, it activates self-esteem, it defends human rights and it protects the planet. Body Shop's core customers align themselves with these values and feel a strong sense of brand affinity. Body Shop has influenced other retailers to become more sensitive to these issues.

• *Harley-Davidson*, the US motorcycle manufacturer, has a phenomenally committed customer base. When Harley riders replace their bikes, 95 per cent buy another Harley. The bike is a central part of a lifestyle that is grounded on fraternity, independence and rebellion. Image is critical to the Harley rider. In the USA, the average age of a Harley rider is 47 (up from 38 in the late 1980s), and a big challenge for Harley is to develop value propositions that appeal to a younger customer.[45]

Figure 4.6 Body Shop's core values

The *Virgin Group* is a family of over 200 privately owned strategic business units ranging across airlines, rail, cosmetics, telecoms, wines and financial services. In the year 2012 Virgin operated in 50 countries, employed 50,000 people and had group sales of £15 billion. The values of the Virgin brand are integrity, value for money, quality and fun. Virgin Group is chaired by its founder, the renegade but highly visible Sir Richard Branson. Customers are attracted to the brand because of its reputation for fairness, simplicity and transparency. Customers trust the brand and rely on it in markets that are new to them. For example, Virgin was a late mover into the UK's indexed-linked mutual fund marketplace. It still managed to become market leader in 12 months despite having no history as a financial institution.

CONTEXT MAKES A DIFFERENCE

Context makes a difference to customer retention in two ways. First, there are some circumstances when customer acquisition makes more, indeed the only, sense as a strategic goal. Second, customer retention strategies will vary according to the environment in which the company competes.

When launching a new product or opening up a new market a company's focus has to be on customer acquisition. In contexts where there are one-off purchases such as funerals, or infrequent purchases such as heart surgery, customer retention is subordinate to acquisition.

The impact of contextual conditions on the choice and timing of customer retention practices has not been thoroughly researched. However, we can see that a number of contextual considerations impact on customer retention practices:

- *Number of competitors.* In some industries, there is a notable lack of competitors, meaning that companies do not suffer badly from customer churn. This typically applies in state-provided services such as education and utilities such as gas, electricity, rail and telecoms, whether deregulated or not. When customers are dissatisfied they have few or no competitors to turn to. Customers may also believe that the competitors in the market are not truly differentiated by their service standards. In other words, each supplier is as bad as the others. The result is inertia; customers do not churn.

- *Corporate culture.* In corporate banking, the short-term profit requirement of both management and shareholders has resulted in a lack of genuine commitment to relationship banking. Banks have been very opportunistic in their preference for transactional credit-based relationships with customers.[46]

- *Channel configuration.* Sellers may not have the opportunity to maintain direct relationships with the final buyers and users of their products. Instead, they may rely on their intermediaries. Caterpillar, for example, does not have a relationship with the contractors that use its equipment. Instead, it works in partnership with over 1,500 independent dealers around the world to provide customer service, training, field support and inventories of spare parts.

- *Purchasing practices.* The purchasing procedures adopted by buyers can also make the practice of customer retention futile. Customers do not always want relationships with their suppliers, as explained in Chapter 2.

- *Ownership expectations.* The demands of business owners can subordinate customer retention to other goals. For example, Korean office-equipment manufacturers are very focused on sales volumes. They require their wholly owned overseas distributors to buy quotas of product from Korea, and sell them in the served market regardless of whether or not the products are well matched to local market conditions and customer requirements. The distributors are put in a position of having to create demand against competitors that do a better job of understanding and meeting customer requirements.[47]

- *Ethical concerns.* Public sector medical service providers cannot simply focus on their most profitable (or lowest cost-to-serve) customers. This would result in the neglect of some patients and a failure to address other areas of disease management. Private sector providers do not necessarily face this problem. The Shouldice Hospital in Ontario specializes in hernia repairs. Their website (www.shouldice.com) reports that they repair 7,000 hernias a year, with a 99.5 per cent success rate. They even organize annual reunions attended by 1,000 satisfied patients.

KEY PERFORMANCE INDICATORS OF CUSTOMER RETENTION PROGRAMMES

CRM practitioners may focus on a number of key performance indicators (KPIs) as they measure the impact of their customer retention strategies and tactics, among them the following:

1   Raw customer retention rate.

2   Raw customer retention rate in each customer segment.

3   Sales-adjusted retention rate.

4   Sales-adjusted retention rate in each customer segment.

5   Profit-adjusted retention rate.

6   Profit-adjusted retention rate in each customer segment.

7   Cost of customer retention.

8   Share-of-wallet of the retained customers.

9   Customer churn rate per product category, sales region or channel.

10   Cost-effectiveness of customer retention tactics.

The choice of KPI will vary according to context. Some companies do not have enough data to compute raw retention rate per segment. Others may not know their share-of-wallet (share of customer spending on the category).

THE ROLE OF RESEARCH IN REDUCING CHURN

Companies can reduce levels of customer churn by researching a number of questions:

1   Why are customers churning?

2   Are there any lead indicators of impending defection?

3   What can be done to address the root causes?

The first question can be answered by contacting and investigating a sample of former customers to find out why they took their business elsewhere.

Customers defect for all sort of reasons, not all of which can be foreseen, prevented or managed by a company. For example, Susan Keaveney identified eight causes of switching behaviours in the service industries: price, inconvenience, core service failures, failed employee responses to service failure, ethical problems, involuntary factors, competitive issues and service encounter failures.[48] Another industry-specific study found that between 20 per cent and 25 per cent of supermarket shoppers changed their primary store in a 12-month period. Twenty-four percent of switchers changed allegiance because a new competitive store had opened, 14 per cent because they had moved house, 11 per cent for better quality and 10 per cent for better choice.[49]

The second question attempts to find out if customers give any early warning signals of impending defection. If these were identified the company could take pre-emptive action. Signals might include the following:

- reduced RFM scores (Recency–Frequency–Monetary value)
- non-response to a carefully targeted offer
- reduced levels of customer satisfaction
- dissatisfaction with complaint handling
- reduced share of customer wallet (e.g. customer switches mobile phone service to another provider, but keeps fixed line service with your firm)
- inbound calls for technical or product-related information
- late payment of an invoice
- querying an invoice
- customer touchpoints are changed, e.g. store closes, change of website address
- customer change of address.

Customer researchers are advised to analyze the reasons for customer defection, and to identify the root causes.[50] Sometimes management can fix the problems causing churn. For example, if you lose customers because of the time taken to deal with a complaint, management can audit and overhaul the complaints management process. This might involve identifying the channels and touchpoints through which complaints enter the business, introducing complaints-management software to ensure issues are resolved to the customer's satisfaction, or training and empowering front-line staff. Root causes can be analyzed by customer segment, channel and product. The 80:20 rule may be applicable. In other words, it may be possible to eliminate 80 per cent of the causes of customer defections with relative ease.

STRATEGIES FOR CUSTOMER DEVELOPMENT

Customer development is the process of growing the value of retained customers. Companies generally attempt to cross-sell and up-sell products into the customer base whilst still having regard for the satisfaction of the customer. Cross-selling, which aims to grow share-of-wallet, can be defined as follows:

Cross-selling is selling additional products and services to an existing customer.

Up-selling can be defined as follows:

Up-selling is selling higher priced or higher margin products and services to an existing customer.

Customers generally do not respond positively to persistent and repeated efforts to sell additional products and services that are not related to their requirements. Indeed, there is an argument that companies should down-sell where appropriate. This means identifying and providing lower cost solutions to the customers' problems, even if it means making a smaller margin. Customers may regard up-selling as opportunistic and exploitative, thereby reducing the level of trust they have in the supplier, and putting the relationship at risk. However, multi-product ownership creates a structural bond that decreases the risk of relationship dissolution.

There are a number of CRM technologies that are useful for customer development purposes.

- *Campaign management* software is used to create up-sell and cross-sell customer development campaigns in single or multiple communication channels and track their effectiveness, particularly in terms of sales and incremental margin.

- *Event-based marketing.* Up-selling and cross-selling campaigns are often associated with events. For example, a bank will cross-sell an investment product to an existing customer if deposits in a savings account reach a trigger point.

- *Data mining.* Cross-sell and up-sell campaigns are often based on intelligent data mining. Transactional histories record what customers have already bought. Data mining can tell you the probability of a customer buying any other products (propensity-to-buy), based on their transactional history or profile. First Direct, an online and telephone bank, uses propensity to buy scores to run targeted, event-driven cross-sell campaigns through direct mail and call centres. They achieve high conversion rates by making follow-up out-bound telephone calls.

- *Customization.* Cross-sell and up-sell offers can be customized at segment or unique customer level, based upon the transactional history and profile of the target. Also personalized is the communication to the customer and the channel of communication – email, surface mail, social media, SMS or phone call, for example.

- *Channel integration.* Customer development activities can be integrated across channels. When different channels make different offers to the same customer at the same time, this creates bad customer experience. In retail, channel integration is observed when channels such as stores, Web and direct-to-consumer channels act in an integrated, customer-centric manner. For this to happen, customer information and customer development plans need to be shared across channels.

- *Integrated customer communications.* CRM practitioners generally prefer that the messages communicated to customers are consistent across all channels.

- *Marketing optimization.* Optimization software is available from CRM analytics organizations such as SAS. Optimization enables marketers to enjoy optimal returns from up-sell and cross-sell campaigns across multiple channels and customer segments, taking account of issues such as budget constraints, communication costs, contact policies (e.g. no more than two offers to be communicated to any customer in any quarter), and customers' transactional histories and propensities-to-buy.

In professional services, the client audit is often the foundation for cross-selling and up-selling of clients. In B2B environments, sales reps need to be alert to opportunities for cross- and up-selling. This means understanding customers' operations, and knowing their product/service innovation plans.

In mature markets, where customer acquisition is difficult or expensive, the development of retained customers is an important source of additional revenues. For example, in the mature mobile telecoms market, the penetration of handsets is at a very high level. Winning new-to-market customers is regarded as too difficult, since these are the laggards, and expensive to convert. Mobile telecommunication service providers tend to focus on selling additional data services to their existing customers, diversifying beyond voice services.

STRATEGIES FOR TERMINATING CUSTOMER RELATIONSHIPS

Companies rarely hesitate to terminate employee positions that serve no useful purpose. In a similar vein, a review of customer value might identify customers that are candidates for dismissal, including customers who will never be profitable or who serve no other useful strategic purpose. More specifically, these include fraudsters, persistent late payers, serial complainants, those who are capricious and change their minds with cost consequences for the supplier, and switchers who are in constant search for a better deal. This certainly happens in reverse; customers sack suppliers when they switch vendors.

Relationships dissolve when one partner no longer views the relationship as worth continuing investment. In a B2B context, activity links, resource ties and actor bonds would be severed. However, even if there is no strategic value in a customer, dissolution of the relationship is not always an attractive option because of contractual obligations, expectations of mutuality, word-of-mouth risks and network relationships.

McKinsey reports that between 30 per cent and 40 per cent of the typical company's revenues are generated by customers who would be unprofitable if their true cost-to-serve were applied.[51] It is therefore important to conduct regular reviews of the customer base to identify potential candidates for dismissal. If this is not done, sales, marketing and service resources will continue to be suboptimally deployed. Nypro, a plastic injection moulder, had 800 customers and sales of $50 million when it decided to move out of low value-added manufacturing. Many of these customers served no useful strategic purpose. Ten years later the company had only 65 customers, all of whom were large, and required value-added solutions rather than cheap moulded products. However, sales revenue had reached $450 million.

Sacking customers, sometimes called 'demarketing', needs to be conducted with sensitivity. Customers may be well connected and spread negative word-of-mouth about their treatment. UK banks began a programme of branch closures in geographic areas that were unprofitable. Effectively they were shedding low value customers in working-class and rural areas. There was considerable bad publicity, government intervened and the closure strategy was reviewed.

CUSTOMERS SACKED BY CBA

The Commonwealth Bank of Australia (CBA), like many other banks, has been criticized in the media for adopting a strategy of sacking unprofitable customers.

In recent years the bank has closed branches in many areas that were considered unprofitable, particularly in less populated areas of rural and regional Australia. For bank accounts that are believed to be unprofitable the bank introduced higher bank fees where the balance is less than $500. The bank charges transaction fees when customers withdraw their money over the counter in a branch.

The media have widely speculated that actions such as these by many banks will continue to occur as banks and other financial institutions attempt to shift customers to electronic banking channels where the cost to the bank of performing a simple deposit or withdrawal transaction can be just a few cents as opposed to a few dollars for similar over-the-counter service in a branch.

There are a number of strategies for shedding unprofitable customers:

- *Make them profitable by raising prices or cutting the cost-to-serve.* A company can simply increase prices to increase margin; customers who pay the higher price become profitable. If most customers are retained at the higher price, it suggests you were not charging enough in the first place! Customers unwilling to pay the higher price, find insufficient value in your product given the higher price, effectively remove themselves from the customer base when they stop transacting. Where price is customized this is a feasible option. When banks introduced transaction fees for unprofitable customers many left in search of a better deal. Similarly, you can reduce service costs, forcing customers to use lower cost channels, such as self-service online.

- *Un-bundle the offer.* You could take a bundled value proposition, un-bundle it, reprice the components and reoffer it to the customer. This makes transparent the value in the offer, and enables customers to make informed choices about whether they want to pay the un-bundled price.

- *Respecify the product.* This involves redesigning the product so that it no longer appeals to the customer(s) you want to sack. For example, the airline BA made a strategic decision to target frequent-flying business travellers they regarded as high value. They redesigned the cabins in their fleet, reducing the number of seats allocated to economy travellers.

- *Reorganize* sales, marketing and service departments so that they no longer focus on segments or customers you no longer wish to retain. You would stop running marketing campaigns targeted at these customers, prevent salespeople calling on them and discontinue servicing their queries.

- *Introduce ABC class service.* A business-to-business company could migrate customers down the service ladder from high-quality face-to-face service from account teams, to sales representatives, or even further to contact centre or web-based self-service.

This eliminates cost from the relationship and may convert an unprofitable customer into profit. In a B2C context, this equates to shifting customers from a high cost service channel into a low cost service channel. Frontier Bank, for example, introduced a no-frills telephone account for business customers who needed no cash processing facilities. A minimum balance was needed for the bank to cover its operating costs. Customers who did not maintain the targeted credit balance in their account were invited to switch to other products in other channels. If they refused the bank asked them to close their account.[52]

Empirical evidence on how companies terminate customer relationships is sparse. However, one study of German engineering companies reports that very few firms have a systematic approach to managing unprofitable customers. Most respondents confirm that unprofitable relationships are commonplace; indeed, a fifth of firms have a customer base more than half of which is not, or not yet, profitable. Companies fall into three clusters in respect of the customer-sacking behaviours:[53]

1   *Hardliners* take an active and rigorous stance in terminating unprofitable relationships, including the regular evaluation of their customer portfolio. Qualitative implications, such as a potential loss of trust in relationships with other customers or negative word-of-mouth do not seem to hinder their willingness to sack unprofitable customers.

2   *Appeasers* take a more cautious approach concerning the termination of unprofitable relationships, due to strategic considerations such as not playing customers into competitors' hands.

3   *The undecided* are reluctant to terminate unprofitable relationships, mainly because they fear the costs of attracting new customers.

SUMMARY

In this chapter we have looked at the important issues of how companies can retain, develop and, if necessary, sack customers. The economic argument for focusing on customer retention is based on four claims about what happens as customer tenure lengthens: the volume and value of purchasing increases, customer management costs fall, referrals increase and customers become less price sensitive. Measures of customer retention vary across industry because of the length of the customer repurchase cycle. There are three possible measures of customer retention. Raw customer retention is the number of customers doing business with a firm at the end of a trading period expressed as a percentage of those who were active customers at the beginning of the same period. This raw figure can be adjusted for sales and profit. Customer retention efforts are generally directed at customers who are strategically valuable. These same customers may be very attractive to competitors and may be costly to retain.

A number of alternative strategies can be used to retain customers. A distinction can be made between positive and negative retention strategies. Negative retention strategies impose switching costs on customers if they defect. Positive retention strategies reward customers for staying. There are four main forms of positive retention strategy. These are meeting and exceeding customer expectations, finding ways to add value, creating social and structural bonds, and building customer engagement. Companies have a number of methods for adding value including loyalty schemes, customer clubs and sales promotions. What is an appropriate customer retention strategy will be contextually defined. Not all strategies work in all circumstances. In addition to customer retention two other customer management activities were discussed in this chapter. These are developing and sacking customers. Customer development aims to increase the value of the customer by cross-selling or up-selling products and services to retained customers. The termination of customer relationships aims to improve the profitability of the customer base by divesting customers who show no signs of ever becoming profitable or strategically significant.

NOTES AND REFERENCES

1   Research conducted in Australia indicates that less than 40 per cent of companies had a customer retention plan in place. See Ang, L. and Buttle, F. (2006). Customer retention management processes: a quantitative study. *European Journal of Marketing*, 40(1/2), 83–99.

2   Weinstein, A. (2002). Customer retention: a usage segmentation and customer value approach. *Journal of Targeting, Measurement and Analysis for Marketing*, 10(3), 259–68; Payne, A.F.T. and Frow, P. (1999). Developing a segmented service strategy: improving measurement in relationship marketing, *Journal of Marketing Management*, 15(8), 797–818.

3   This section is based on Ahmad, R. and Buttle, F. (2001). Customer retention: a potentially potent marketing management strategy. *Journal of Strategic Marketing*, 9, 29–45.

4   Dawkins, P.M. and Reichheld, F.F. (1990). Customer retention as a competitive weapon. *Directors & Board*, Summer, 42–7.

5   Ahmad, R. and Buttle, F. (2002). Customer retention management: a reflection on theory and practice. *Marketing Intelligence and Planning*, 20(3), 149–61.

6   Reichheld, F.F. (1996). *The loyalty effect: the hidden force behind growth, profits, and lasting value.* Boston, MA: Harvard Business School Press.

7   Coyles, S. and Gorkey, T.C. (2002). Customer retention is not enough. *McKinsey Quarterly*, No. 2, 80–9.

8   Based on Reichheld, F.F. and Sasser, Jr, W.E. (1990). Zero defections: quality comes to services. *Harvard Business Review*, September–October, 105–11; Reichheld, F.F. (1996). *The loyalty effect.* Boston, MA: Harvard Business School Press.

9   Murphy, J.A. (1996). Retail banking. In F. Buttle (ed.) *Relationship marketing: theory and practice.* London: Paul Chapman, pp. 74–90.

10 East, R. and Hammond, K. (2000). Fact and fallacy in retention marketing. Working paper, Kingston Business School, UK.

11 Bain & Co./Mainline (1999). Consumer spending online. Boston, MA: Bain & Co.

12 East, R. and Hammond, K. (2000). Fact and fallacy in retention marketing. Working paper, Kingston Business School, UK. Reichheld (1996, *The loyalty effect: the hidden force behind growth,*

profits, and lasting value. Boston, MA: Harvard Business School Press) shows profit from customer referrals grows as tenure lengthens.

13   Homburg, C., Koschate, N. and Hoyer, W. (2005). Do satisfied customers really pay more? A study of the relationship between customer satisfaction and willingness to pay. *Journal of Marketing*, 69(2), 84–95.

14   Dawkins, P.M. and Reichheld, F.F. (1990) Customer retention as a competitive weapon. *Directors & Board*, Summer, 42–7.

15   Reichheld, F.F. (1996). *The loyalty effect: the hidden force behind growth, profits, and lasting value.* Boston, MA: Harvard Business School Press.

16   Bolton, R.N. (1998). A dynamic model of the duration of the customer's relationship with a continuous service provider: the role of satisfaction. *Marketing Science*, 17(1), 45–65.

17   Chahal, M. (2014). Profile: Sir Charles Mayfield. *Marketing Week*, 9 April.

18   Kano, N. (1995). Upsizing the organization by attractive quality creation. In G.H. Kanji (ed.). *Total Quality Management: proceedings of the First World Congress.* London: Chapman Hall.

19   Gilbert, D. (1996). Airlines. In F. Buttle (ed.) *Relationship marketing: theory and practice.* London: Paul Chapman, pp. 31–144.

20   Dowling, G. and Uncles, M. (1997). Do customer loyalty programs really work? *Sloan Management Review*, 38(4), 71–82.

21   Dignam, C. (1996). Being smart is not the only redeeming feature. *Marketing Direct*, September, 51–6.

22   Quoted in Gilbert, D. (1996). Airlines. In F. Buttle (ed.). *Relationship marketing: theory and practice.* London: Paul Chapman, pp. 31–144.

23   Shugan, S.M. (2005). Brand loyalty programs: are they shams? *Marketing Science*, 24(2), 185–93.

24   Reed, D. (1995). Many happy returns. *Marketing Week*, 17 November, 7–11.

25   Dick, A.S. and Basu, K. (1994). Customer loyalty: towards an integrated framework. *Journal of the Academy of Marketing Science*, 22(2), 99–113.

26   Liu, Y. (2007). The long-term impact of loyalty programs on consumer purchase behaviour and loyalty. *Journal of Marketing*, 71 (October), 19–35.

27   Meyer-Waarden, L. (2008). The influence of loyalty programme membership on customer purchase behaviour. *European Journal of Marketing*, 42(1/2), 87–114.

28   For more information on the history and development of these schemes see Worthington, S. (2000). A classic example of a misnomer: the loyalty card. *Journal of Targeting, Measurement and Analysis for Marketing*, 8(3), 222–34.

29   Stauss, B., Chojnacki, K., Decker, A. and Hoffmann, F. (2001). Retention effects of a customer club. *International Journal of Service Industry Management*, 12(1), 7–19.

30   Stauss, B., Chojnacki, K., Decker, A. and Hoffmann, F. (2001). Retention effects of a customer club. *International Journal of Service Industry Management*, 12(1), 7–19.

31   http://www.warcom.com.au/blog/printers/brother-cash-back-offer-on-printers-and-ink/ (Accessed 27 May 2014).

32   Buttle, F., Ahmad, R. and Aldlaigan, A. (2002) The theory and practice of customer bonding. *Journal of Business-to-Business Marketing*, 9(2), 3–27.

33   Reichheld, F.F. (1993). Loyalty-based management. *Harvard Business Review*, March–April, 63–73.

34   Mitchell, A. (1998). Loyal yes, staying no. *Management Today*, May, 104–5.

35   Hollebeek, Linda (2011). Demystifying customer brand engagement: exploring the loyalty nexus. *Journal of Marketing Management*, 27(7–8), 785–807.

36   Vivek, S.D., Beatty, S.E. and Morgan, R.M. (2012), Customer engagement: exploring customer relationships beyond purchase. *Journal of Marketing Theory and Practice,* 20(2), 127–45.

37   Vivek, S.D., Beatty, S.E. and Morgan, R.M. (2012). Customer engagement: exploring customer relationships beyond purchase. *Journal of Marketing Theory and Practice,* 20(2), 127–45.

38   Hollebeek, Linda (2011). Demystifying customer brand engagement: exploring the loyalty nexus. *Journal of Marketing Management*, 27(7–8), 785–807.

39   Fleming, J.H. and Asplund, J. (2007). *Human Sigma: managing the employee–customer encounter*. New York: Gallup Press.

40   See these websites for further information: http://www.gamification.co/2013/07/08/earn-your-wings-air-canadas-successful-gamification-venture-into-loyalty/ and http://www.commercelab.ca/air-canada-pilots-gamification-with-earn-your-wings-loyalty-program/ (Accessed 14 February 2014).

41   See Dowling's critique of loyalty for consumer marketing, albeit it should be recognized that this article evaluates CRM as it was in its formative stages and we believe that our understanding of what it can deliver and how it works has advanced substantially. Nonetheless this is a salutary warning that merely creating a CRM programme does not guarantee business success: Dowling, G. (2002). Customer Relationship Management: in B2C markets, often less is more. *California Management Review*, 44, 87–103.

42   Nelson-Horchler, J. (1984). Fighting a boycott: image rebuilding, Swiss style. *Industry Week*, 220, 54–6.

43   http://nypost.com/2010/06/26/stormy-weather-bps-stock-hits-new-low/ (Accessed 14 February 2014).

44   Follows, S.B. and Jobber, D. (2000). Environmentally responsible purchase behaviour: a test of a consumer model. *European Journal of Marketing*, 34(5/6), 723–46.

45   Helyar, J. (2002). Will Harley-Davidson hit the wall? *Fortune*, 146(3), 120–4. See also: http://www.reuters.com/article/2013/06/21/us-harleydavidson-boomers-analysis-idUSBRE95K0GU20130621 (Accessed 17 February 2014).

46   Schell, C. (1996). Corporate banking. In F. Buttle (ed.) *Relationship marketing: theory and practice*. London: Paul Chapman, pp. 91–103.

47   Ahmad, R. and Buttle, F. (2002). Customer retention management: a reflection on theory and practice. *Marketing Intelligence and Planning*, 20(3), 149–61.

48   Keaveney, S.M. (1995). Customer switching behaviour in service industries: an exploratory study. *Journal of Marketing*, 59, 71–82.

49   East, R., Harris, P., Lomax, W., Willson, G. and Hammond, K. (1998). Customer defection from supermarkets. *Advances in Consumer Research*, 25(1), 507–12.

50   Hart, C.W.L., Heskett, J.L. and Sasser, Jr, W.E. (1990). The profitable art of service recovery. *Harvard Business Review*, July–August, 148–56.

51   Leszinski, R., Weber, F.A., Paganoni, R. and Baumgartner, T. (1995). Profits in your backyard. *McKinsey Quarterly*, No. 4, 118.

52   Ahmad, R. and Buttle, F. (2002). Retaining telephone banking customers at Frontier Bank. *International Journal of Bank Marketing*, 20(1), 5–16.

53   Helm, S., Rolfes, L. and Günter. B. (2006). Suppliers' willingness to end unprofitable customer relationships: an exploratory investigation in the German mechanical engineering sector. *European Journal of Marketing*, 40(3/4), 366–83.

Part II

STRATEGIC CRM

Strategic CRM is the core customer-centric business strategy that aims at winning and keeping profitable customers. We address three important strategic CRM issues in the following chapters. Chapter 5 examines the practice of customer portfolio management (CPM). A company's customer portfolio is made up of customers clustered on the basis of one or more strategically important variables. Each customer is assigned to just one cluster in the portfolio, and each cluster is offered a different value proposition. CPM consists of a number of disciplines and allows companies to decide which customers they want to serve, and broadly how to serve them. Chapter 6 explores customer-perceived value. Customers will only be retained if they experience value as a result of their transactions with a company. Chapter 7 investigates customer experience. There is a growing recognition that customer experience throughout the lifecycle and at every touchpoint must meet customer expectations.

CHAPTER 5

CUSTOMER PORTFOLIO MANAGEMENT

CHAPTER OBJECTIVES

By the end of this chapter you will understand:

- The benefits that flow from managing customers as a portfolio.
- A number of disciplines that contribute to customer portfolio management, including market segmentation, sales forecasting, activity-based costing, lifetime value estimation and data mining.
- How customer portfolio management differs between business-to-consumer and business-to-business contexts.
- How to use a number of business-to-business portfolio analysis tools.
- The range of customer management strategies that can be deployed across a customer portfolio.

WHAT IS A PORTFOLIO?

The term portfolio is often used in the context of investments to describe the collection of assets owned by an individual or institution. Each asset is managed differently according to its role in the owner's investment strategy. Portfolio has a parallel meaning in the context of customers. A customer portfolio can be defined as follows:

A customer portfolio is the collection of mutually exclusive customer groups that comprise a business's entire customer base.

In other words, a company's customer portfolio is made up of customers clustered on the basis of one or more strategically important variables. Each customer is assigned to just one cluster in the portfolio. At one extreme, all customers are assigned to a single cluster and offered the same value proposition; at the other, each customer is a unique 'cluster-of-one' and offered a unique value proposition. Most companies are positioned somewhere between these extremes.

Some explanation of the term 'value proposition' may be helpful here. A value proposition is a company's promise that customers will experience a specified bundle of benefits from their use or consumption of a company offering. Value propositions typically vary between different clusters of a company's customer portfolio. It is common practice for differentiated bundles of product features and service standards to be assembled and offered to different clusters of a company's customers. We explore customer value in more depth in the next chapter.

One of strategic CRM's fundamental principles is that not all customers can, or should, be managed in the same way – unless its makes strategic sense to do so. Customers not only have different needs, preferences and expectations, but also different revenue and cost profiles, and therefore should be managed in different ways. For example, in the B2B context, some customers might be offered customized product and face-to-face account management; others might be offered standardized product and web-based self-service. If the second group were to be offered the same product options and service levels as the first, they might end up being unprofitable customers for the company.

Customer Portfolio Management (CPM) aims to optimize business performance – whether that means sales growth, enhanced customer profitability or something else – across the entire customer base. It does this by offering differentiated value propositions to different segments of customers. For example, the UK-based NatWest Bank manages its business customers on a portfolio basis. It has split customers into three segments based upon their size, lifetime value and creditworthiness. As Case study 5.1 shows, each cluster in the portfolio is treated to a different value proposition. When companies deliver tiered service levels such as these, they face a number of questions. Should the tiering be based upon current or future customer value? How should the sales and service support vary across tiers? How can customer expectations be managed to avoid the problem of low tier customers resenting not being offered high tier service? What criteria and rules should be employed when shifting customers up and down the hierarchy? Finally, does the cost of managing this additional

CASE STUDY 5.1

SERVICE LEVELS VARY BY CUSTOMER TIER AT NATWEST BANK

NatWest Bank's Corporate Banking division has three tiers of clients ranked by size, lifetime value and creditworthiness.

1 The top tier numbers some 60 multinational clients. These have at least one *individual relationship manager* attached to them.

2 The second tier, which numbers approximately 150, has *individual client managers* attached to them.

3 The third tier, representing the vast bulk of smaller business clients, has access to a 'Small Business Adviser' at 100 business centres.

complexity pay off in customer outcomes such as enhanced retention levels, or financial outcomes such as additional revenues and profit?

WHO IS THE CUSTOMER?

The customer in a B2B context is different from a customer in the B2C context. The B2C customer is the end consumer – an individual or a household. The B2B customer is an organization – company (producer or reseller) or institution (not-for-profit or government body). CPM practices in the B2B context are very different from those in the B2C context.

The B2B context differs from the B2C context in a number of ways. First, there are fewer customers. In Australia, for example, although there is a population of 24 million people, there are only two million actively trading businesses. Second, business customers are much larger than household customers. Third, relationships between business customers and their suppliers typically tend to be much closer than between household members and their suppliers. Often business relationships feature reciprocal trading. Company A buys from company B, and company B buys from company A – this is particularly common amongst small and medium-sized enterprises. Fourth, the demand for input goods and services by companies is derived from end-user demand. Household demand for bread creates organizational demand for flour. Fifth, organization buying is conducted in a professional way. Unlike household buyers, procurement officers for companies are often professionals with formal training. Buying processes can be rigorously formal, particularly for mission-critical goods and services, where a decision-making unit composed of interested parties may be formed to define requirements, search for suppliers, evaluate proposals and make a sourcing decision. Often, the value of a single organizational purchase is huge – buying an airplane, bridge or power station is a massive purchase few households will ever match. Finally, much B2B trading is direct. In other words, there are no channel intermediaries, and suppliers sell direct to customers.

BASIC DISCIPLINES FOR CPM

In this section, you will read about a number of basic disciplines that can be useful during CPM. These include market segmentation, sales forecasting, activity-based costing (ABC), customer lifetime value estimation and data mining.

Market segmentation

CPM can make use of a discipline that is routinely employed by marketing management – market segmentation. Market segmentation can be defined as follows:

> **Market segmentation is the process of dividing up a market into more-or-less homogenous subsets for which it is possible to create different value propositions.**

At the end of the process the company can decide which segment(s) it wants to serve. If it chooses, each segment can be served with a different value proposition, and managed in different ways. Market segmentation processes can be used during CPM for two main purposes. They can be used to segment *potential* markets to identify which customers to acquire, and to cluster *current* customers with a view to offering differentiated value propositions supported by different relationship management strategies.

In this discussion, we will focus on the application of market segmentation processes to identify which customers to acquire. What distinguishes market segmentation for this CRM purpose is its very clear focus on customer value. The outcome of the process should be the identification of the value potential of each identified segment. Companies will want to identify and target those customers that can generate profit in the future: these will be those customers that the company is better placed to serve and satisfy than competitors.

Market segmentation is increasingly being transformed by information technology, particularly in consumer markets. The dramatic increase in customer-related data is increasingly used by companies to segment customers according to their attributes and behaviour. Regrettably, segmentation remains highly intuitive or habitual in many companies, particularly so in B2B where the expertise and data richness are less. In a CRM context, however, market segmentation is highly data-dependent. Internal data from marketing, sales and finance records are often enhanced with additional data from external sources such as marketing research companies, partner organizations in the company's network and data specialists. Increasingly companies are using 'big data' to enhance their segmentation practices. Regardless, either through data and/or intuition, the customer management team will develop profiles of customer groups based upon insight and experience. This is then used to guide the development of marketing strategies across the segments.

The market segmentation process can be broken down into a number of steps:

1 Identify the business you are in.

2 Identify relevant segmentation variables.

3 Analyze the market using these variables.

4 Assess the value of the market segments.

5 Select target market(s) to serve.

Table 5.1 Intuitive and data-based segmentation processes

Intuitive	Data-based

• brain-storm segmentation variables
  – age, gender, lifestyle
  – SIC, size location
• produce word-profiles
• compute sizes of segments
• assess company/segment fit
• make targeting decision
  – one/several/all segments?
	• obtain customer data
	  – Internal and external
	• analyze customer data
	• identify high/medium/low value customer segments
	• profile customers within segments
	  – age, gender, lifestyle
	  – SIC, size location
	• assess company/segment fit
	• make targeting decision
	  – one/several/all segments?

Identify the business you are in

'What business are you in?' is an important strategic question to which many, but not all, companies have an answer. Ted Levitt's classic article, 'Marketing Myopia', warned companies of the dangers of thinking only in terms of product-oriented answers.[1] He wrote of a nineteenth-century company that defined itself as being in the buggy-whip industry. It has not survived. It is important to consider the answer from the customer point of view. For example, is Blockbuster in the video rental business, or some other business, perhaps home entertainment or retailing? Is a manufacturer of kitchen cabinets in the timber processing industry, or the home improvement business?

A customer-oriented answer to the question will enable companies to move through the market segmentation process because it helps identify the boundaries of the market served, it defines the benefits customers seek and it picks out the company's competitors.

Let's assume that the kitchen furniture company has defined its business from the customer's perspective. It believes it is in the home value improvement business. It knows from research that customers buy its products for one major reason: they are homeowners who want to enhance the value of their properties. The company is now in a position to identify its markets and competitors at three levels:

1   *Benefit competitors*: other companies delivering the same benefit to customers. These might include window replacement companies, heating and air-conditioning companies and bathroom renovation companies.

2   *Product competitors*: other companies marketing kitchens to customers seeking the same benefits.

3   *Geographic competitors*: these are benefit and product competitors operating in the same geographic territory.

Identify relevant segmentation variables and analyze the market

There are many variables that are used to segment consumer and organizational markets. Companies can enjoy competitive advantage through innovations in market segmentation. For example, before Häagen-Dazs, it was known that ice cream was a seasonally sold product aimed primarily at children. Häagen-Dazs innovated by targeting adults with a different, luxurious and adult product that had all-year-round purchasing potential. We will look at consumer markets first.

Consumer markets

Consumers can be clustered according to a number of shared characteristics. These can be grouped into *user* attributes and *usage* attributes, as summarized in Table 5.2

In recent years there has been a trend away from simply using demographic attributes to segment consumer markets. The concern has been that there is too much variance within each of the demographic clusters to regard all members of the segment as more-or-less homogenous. For example, some 30–40-year-olds have families and mortgaged homes; others live in rented apartments and go clubbing at weekends. Some members of religious groups are traditionalists; others are progressives.

Table 5.2 Criteria for segmenting consumer markets

User attributes	*Demographic attributes*: age, gender, occupational status, household size, marital status, terminal educational age, household income, stage of family lifecycle, religion, ethnic origin, nationality
	Geographic attributes: country, region, TV region, city, city size, postcode, residential neighbourhood
	Psychographic attributes: lifestyle, personality
Usage attributes	Benefits sought, volume consumed, recency–frequency–monetary value, share of category spend

The family lifecycle (FLC) idea has been particularly threatened. The FLC traces the development of a person's life along a path from young and single, to married with no children, married with young children, married couples with older children, older married couples with no children at home, empty nesters still in employment, retired empty nester couple, sole survivor working or not working. Life for many, if not most, people does not follow this path. It fails to take account of the many and varied life choices that people make – some people never marry, others are late marriers, and there are also childless couples, gay and lesbian partnerships, extended families, single-parent households and divorced couples.

Let's look at some of the variables that can be used to define market segments. Occupational status is widely used to classify people into social grades. Systems vary around the world. In the UK, the Joint Industry Committee for National Readership Surveys (JICNARS) social grading system is employed. This allocates households to one of six categories (A, B, C1, C2, D and E) depending upon the job of the head of household. Higher managerial occupations are ranked A; casual, unskilled workers are ranked E. Media owners often use the JICNARS scale to profile their audiences.

A number of companies have developed geo-demographic classification schemes. CACI, for example, has developed ACORN that segments UK postcodes into six categories, 18 groups and 62 types (Table 5.3). There is an average of 18 households in each postcode. Types are further subdivided into around 300 micro-segments that can be used to add an extra level of precision to segmentation. Most people in the UK live in private households. Five of the ACORN categories, comprising 17 of the groups and 59 of the types, represent the population in private households. The last of the 18 groups is reserved for other kinds of postcode, primarily communal households who live in various kinds of institution rather than in private households, and postcodes with no resident population.

Lifestyle research became popular in the 1980s. Rather than using a single descriptive category to classify customers, as had been the case with demographics, it uses multivariate analysis to cluster customers. Lifestyle analysts collect data about people's activities, interests and opinions. A lifestyle survey instrument may require answers to 400 or 500 questions, taking several hours to complete. Using analytical processes such as factor analysis and cluster analysis, the researchers are able to produce lifestyle or psychographic profiles. The assertion is made that we buy products because of their fit with our chosen lifestyles. Lifestyle studies have been done in many countries, as well as across national boundaries. A number of companies conduct lifestyle research on a commercial basis and sell the results to their clients.

Table 5.3 ACORN geo-demographic household classification (UK)[2]

ACORN categories		% of UK households
1	Affluent achievers	21.3
2	Rising prosperity	9.4
3	Comfortable communities	27.0
4	Financially stretched	24.2
5	Urban adversity	17.9
6	Not private households	0.2

Usage attributes can be particularly useful for CRM purposes. Benefit segmentation has become a standard tool for marketing managers. It is axiomatic that customers buy products for the benefits they deliver, not for the products themselves. Nobody has ever bought a 5mm drill bit because they want a 5mm drill bit. They buy it because of what the drill bit can deliver – a 5mm hole. CRM practitioners need to understand the benefits that are sought by the markets they serve. The market for toothpaste, for example, can be segmented along benefit lines. There are three major benefit segments: white teeth, fresh breath, and healthy teeth and gums. When it comes to creating value propositions for the chosen customers, benefit segmentation becomes very important.

The two other usage attributes – volume consumed and share of category spend – are also useful from a CRM perspective. Many companies classify their customers according to the volume of business they produce. For example, in the B2C context, McDonald's in the USA have found that 77 per cent of their sales are to males aged 18 to 34 who eat at McDonald's three to five times per week, this despite the company's mission to be the world's favourite family restaurant. Assuming that they contribute in equal proportion to the bottom line, these are customers that the company must not lose. The volume they provide allows the company to operate very cost-effectively, keeping unit costs low.

Market segmentation based on recency of purchase, frequency of purchase and the monetary value of purchases (RFM) adds another level of insight to the volume-only variable. Customers can be clustered according to their RFM behaviours. For example, some customers may purchase large volumes but very infrequently, and others may buy smaller quantities but more often. If a consumer falling into this latter group shows no evidence of recent buying, they might be targeted with a win-back campaign. One hotel chain clusters customers into seven groups based on RFM data, and has created a CRM application that helps check-in staff recognize and welcome customers differently based on when they last visited the hotel, the frequency of their bookings and how much they spend.

Companies that rank customers into tiers according to volume, and are then able to identify which customers fall into each tier, may be able to develop customer migration plans to move lower volume customers higher up the ladder from first-time customer to repeat customer, majority customer, loyal customer, and onwards to advocate status. This only makes sense when the lower volume customers present an opportunity. The key question is whether they buy products from other suppliers in the category. For example, customer

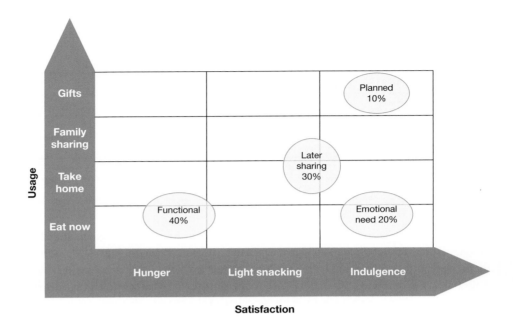

Figure 5.1 Bivariate segmentation of the chocolate market

Jones buys five pairs of shoes a year. She only buys one of those pairs from 'Shoes4less' retail outlets. She therefore presents a greater opportunity than customer Smith who buys two pairs a year, but both of them from Shoes4less. Shoes4less has the opportunity to win four more sales from Jones, but none from Smith. This does not necessarily mean that Jones is more valuable than Smith. That depends on the answers to other questions. First, how much will it cost to switch Jones from her current shoe retailer(s), and what will it cost to retain Smith's business? Second, what are the margins earned from these customers? If Jones is very committed to her other supplier, it may not be worth trying to switch her. If Smith buys high margin fashion and leisure footwear and Jones buys low margin footwear, then Smith might be the better opportunity despite the lower volume of sales.

Most segmentation programmes employ more than one variable. For example, a chain of bars may define its customers on the basis of geography, age and music preference. Figure 5.1 shows how the market for chocolate can be segmented by usage occasion and satisfaction. Four major segments emerge from this bivariate segmentation of the market.

Business markets

Business markets can also be segmented in a number of ways, as shown in Table 5.4.

The basic starting point for most B2B segmentation is the International Standard Industrial Classification (ISIC), which is a property of the United Nations Statistics Division. ISIC classifies businesses according to their dominant economic activity. ISIC consists of a coherent and consistent classification structure of economic activities based on a set of internationally agreed concepts, definitions, principles and classification rules. Whilst this is a standard that is in widespread use, some countries have developed their own schemes.

Table 5.4 How business markets are segmented

Business market segmentation criteria	Illustration
International Standard Industrial Classification	An internationally agreed standard for classifying goods and service producers
Dispersion	Geographically concentrated or dispersed
Size	Large, medium, small businesses: classified by number of employees, number of customers, profit or turnover
Account status	Global account, national account, regional account, A or B or C class accounts
Account value	< $50,000, < $100,000, < $200,000, < $500,000
Buying processes	Open tender, sealed bid, Internet auction, centralized, decentralized
Buying criteria	Continuity of supply (reliability), product quality, price, customization, just-in-time, service support before or after sale
Propensity to switch	Satisfied with current suppliers, dissatisfied
Current share of customer spend in the category	Sole supplier, majority supplier, minority supplier, non-supplier
Geography	City, region, country, trading bloc (ASEAN, EU)
Buying style	Risk averse, innovator

In the USA, Canada and Mexico, there is the North American Industry Classification System (NAICS). In New Zealand and Australia there is the Australia and New Zealand Standard Industrial Classification (ANZSIC).

The ISIC classifies all forms of economic activity. Each business entity is classified according to its principal product or business activity, and is assigned a four-digit code. These are then amalgamated into 99 major divisions. Table 5.5 details several four-digit codes.

Governments and trade associations often collect and publish information that indicates the size of each ISIC code. This can be a useful guide when answering the question, 'Which customers should we acquire?' However, targeting in the B2B context is often conducted not at the aggregated level of the ISIC, but at an individual account level. The question is not so much, 'Do we want to serve this segment?' as, 'Do we want to serve this customer?'

Table 5.5 Examples of ISIC codes

ISIC 4-digit code	Activity
1200	Manufacture of tobacco products
2511	Manufacture of structural metal products
5520	Camping grounds, recreational vehicle parks and trailer parks
8530	Higher education

CASE STUDY 5.2

IBM TARGETS 18 DIFFERENT INDUSTRY SECTORS

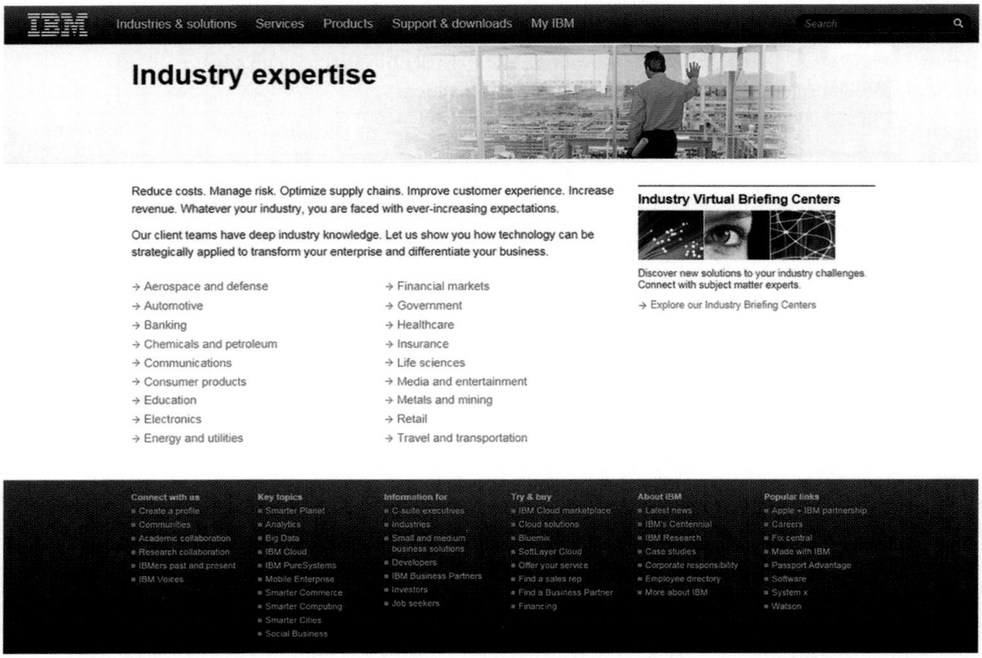

Several of these account-level segmentation variables are specifically important for CRM purposes: account value, share of category (share-of-wallet) spend and propensity-to-switch.

- *Account value*. Most businesses have a scheme for classifying their customers according to their value. The majority of these schemes associate value with some measure of sales revenue or volume. This is not an adequate measure of value, because it takes no account of the costs to win and keep the customer. We address this issue later in this chapter.
- *Share-of-wallet (SOW)*. Share of category spend gives an indication of the future potential that exists within the account. A supplier that only has a 15 per cent share of a customer company's spending on some raw material has, on the face of it, considerable potential.
- *Propensity-to-switch* may be high or low. It is possible to measure propensity-to-switch by assessing satisfaction with the current supplier, and by computing switching costs. Dissatisfaction alone does not indicate a high propensity-to-switch. Switching costs may be so high that even in the face of high levels of dissatisfaction, the customer does not feel able switch. For example, customers may be unhappy with the performance of their telecoms supplier, but not switch because of the disruption that such a change would bring about.

CASE STUDY 5.3

CPM AT SYNGENTA AG

Syngenta AG is a large global Switzerland-based chemicals company that markets seeds and pesticides. Its purpose is 'Bringing plant potential to life'. Syngenta wanted to segment the global market for crop protection products, such as herbicides and pesticides. Using qualitative and quantitative data Syngenta identified four segments amongst farmers.

1 'Professionals'. These are large spenders and keen to trial new technologies.
2 'Progressives'. These have large landholdings and are early adopters of new technologies.
3 'Traditionalists' are older and spend the least on crop protection products.
4 'Operators' are pessimistic about farming and have difficulty in keeping up to date with new technologies and farming practices.

Syngenta now uses these four segments to guide all of its customer management activities. Service levels vary between segments. Face-to-face communications are available to Professionals and Progressives and direct mail used for Traditionalists and Operators.

What is missing from current segmentation practices for B2B customers is an understanding of how they wish to work with suppliers to generate value. Needs-based segmentation would consider the customer's desire for strategic partnerships, the degree to which the customer expects the supplier to co-create solutions and other important issues in the customer's supply chain strategy. As B2B relationships become ever more sophisticated, we expect to see a commensurate increase in the insight suppliers use for market segmentation.

Assessing the value in a market segment and selecting which markets to serve

A number of target market alternatives should emerge from this market segmentation process. The potential of these to generate value for the company will need to be assessed. The potential value of the segmentation opportunities depends upon answers to two questions:

1 How attractive is the opportunity?
2 How well placed is the company and its network to exploit the opportunity?

Table 5.6 identifies a number of the attributes that can be taken into account during this appraisal. The attractiveness of a market segment is related to a number of issues, including its size and growth potential, the number of competitors and the intensity of competition between them, the barriers to entry and the propensity of customers to switch from their existing suppliers. The question of company fit rotates around the issue of the relative competitive competency of the company and its network members – suppliers, partners and distributors in particular – to satisfy the requirements of the segment.

In principle, if the segment is attractive and the company and network competencies indicate a good fit, the opportunity may be worth pursuing. However, because many

Table 5.6 Criteria for appraising segmentation opportunities

Segment value and attractiveness

Size of segment, segment growth rate, price sensitivity of customers, bargaining power of customers, customers' relationships with current suppliers, barriers to segment entry, barriers to segment exit, number and power of competitors, prospect of new entrants, potential for differentiation, propensity for customer switching

Company and network fit

Does the opportunity fit the company's objectives, mission and values? Does the company and its network possess the operational, technological, marketing, people and other competencies, and the liquidity to exploit the opportunity?

companies find that they have several opportunities, some kind of scoring process has to be developed and applied to identify the better opportunities. The matrix in Figure 5.2 can be used for this purpose.[3] To begin, companies need to identify attributes that indicate the attractiveness of a market segment (some are listed in Table 5.6), and the competencies of the company and its network. An importance weight is agreed for each attribute. The segment opportunity is rated against each attribute and a score is computed. The opportunities can then be mapped into Figure 5.2.

Sales forecasting

The second discipline that can be used for CPM is sales forecasting. One major issue commonly facing companies that conduct CPM is that the data available for clustering customers take a historical or, at best, present-day view. The data identify those customers who have been, or presently are, important for sales, profit or other strategic reasons. If management believes the future will be the same as the past, this presents no problem. However, if the business environment is changeable, this presents a problem. Because CPM's

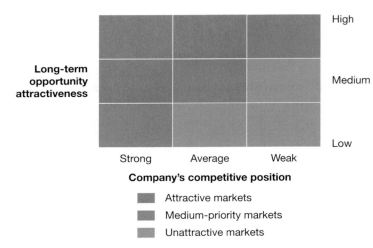

Figure 5.2 McKinsey/GE customer portfolio matrix

goal is to identify those customers that will be strategically important in the future, sales forecasting can be a useful discipline.

Sales forecasting, some pessimists argue, is a waste of time, because the business environment is rapidly changing and unpredictable. Major world events such as terrorist attacks, war, drought and market-based disruptors such as new products from competitors or high visibility promotional campaigns can make any sales forecasts invalid.

There are a number of sales forecasting techniques that can be applied, providing useful information for CPM. These techniques, which fall into three major groups, are appropriate for different circumstances.

- *Qualitative methods*
  - customer surveys
  - sales team estimates
- *Time-series methods*
  - moving average
  - exponential smoothing
  - time-series decomposition
- *Causal methods*
  - leading indicators
  - regression models

Qualitative methods are probably the most widely used forecasting methods. *Customer surveys* ask consumers or purchasing officers to give an opinion on what they are likely to buy in the forecasting period. This makes sense when customers forward plan their purchasing. Data can be obtained by inserting a question into a customer satisfaction survey. For example, 'In the next six months are you likely to buy more, the same or less from us than in the current period?' And, 'If more, or less, what volume do you expect to buy from us?' Sometimes, third-party organizations such as industry associations or trans-industry groups such as the Chamber of Commerce or the Institute of Directors collect data that indicate future buying intentions or proxies for intention, such as business confidence.

Sales team estimates can be useful when salespeople have built close relationships with their customers. A key account management team might be well placed to generate several individual forecasts from the team membership. These can be averaged or weighted in some way that reflects the estimator's closeness to the customer. Account managers for Dyno Nobel, a supplier of commercial explosives for the mining and quarrying industries, are so close to their customers that they are able to forecast sales two to three years ahead.

Operational CRM systems support the qualitative sales forecasting methods, in particular sales team estimates. The CRM system takes into account the value of the sale, the probability of closing the sale and the anticipated period to closure. Many CRM applications also allow management to adjust the estimates of their sales team members, to allow for overly optimistic or pessimistic sales people.

Time-series approaches take historical data and extrapolate them forward in a linear or curvilinear trend. This approach makes sense when there are historical sales data, and the

Table 5.7 Sales forecasting using moving averages

Year	Sales volumes	2-year moving average	4-year moving average
2013	4,830		
2014	4,930		
2015	4,870	4,880	
2016	5,210	4,900	
2017	5,330	5,040	4,960
2018	5,660	5,270	5,085
2019	5,440	5,495	5,267
2020		5,550	5,410

assumption can be safely made that the future will reflect the past. The *moving average* method is the simplest of these. This takes sales in a number of previous periods and averages them. The averaging process reduces or eliminates random variation. The moving average is computed on successive periods of data, moving on one period at a time, as in Table 5.7.

Moving averages based on different periods can be calculated on historic data to generate an accurate method. A variation is to weight the more recent periods more heavily. The rationale is that more recent periods are better predictors. In producing an estimate for year 2020 in Table 5.7, you could weight the previous four years' sales performance by 0.4, 0.3, 0.2 and 0.1 respectively to reach an estimate. This would generate a forecast of 5,461. This approach is called *exponential smoothing*.

The *decomposition* method is applied when there is evidence of cyclical or seasonal patterns in the historical data. The method attempts to separate out four components of the time series: trend factor, cyclical factor, seasonal factor and random factor. The trend factor is the long-term direction of the trend after the other three elements are removed. The cyclical factor represents regular long-term recurrent influences on sales; seasonal influences generally occur within annual cycles.

It is sometimes possible to predict sales using *leading indicators*. A leading indicator is some contemporary activity or event that indicates that another activity or event will happen in the future. At a macro-level, for example, housing starts are good predictors of future sales of kitchen furniture. At a micro-level, when a credit card customer calls into a contact centre to ask about the current rate of interest, this is a strong indicator that the customer will switch to another supplier in the future.

Regression models work by employing data on a number of predictor variables to estimate future demand. The variable being predicted is called the dependent variable; the variables being used as predictors are called independent variables. For example, if you wanted to predict demand for cars (the dependent variable) you might use data on population size, average disposable income, average car price for the category being predicted and average fuel price (the independent variables). The regression equation can be tested and validated on historical data before being adopted. New predictor variables can be substituted or added to see if they improve the accuracy of the forecast. This can be a useful approach for predicting demand from a segment.

Activity-based costing

The third discipline that is useful for CPM is activity-based costing. Many companies, particularly those in a B2B context, can trace revenues to customers. In a B2C environment, it is usually only possible to trace revenues to identifiable customers if the company operates a billing system requiring customer details, or a membership scheme such as a customer club, store card or a loyalty programme.

In a B2B context, revenues can be tracked in the sales and accounts databases. Costs are an entirely different matter. Because the goal of CPM is to cluster customers according to their strategic value, it is desirable to be able to identify which customers are, or will be, profitable. Clearly, if a company is to understand customer profitability, it has to be able to trace costs as well as revenues to customers.

Costs do vary from customer to customer. Some customers are very costly to acquire and serve, others are not. There can be considerable variance across the customer base within several categories of cost:

- *Customer acquisition costs.* Some customers require considerable sales effort to shift them from prospect to first-time customer status: more sales calls, visits to reference customer sites, free samples, engineering advice, guarantees that switching costs will be met by the vendor.

- *Terms of trade.* Price discounts, advertising and promotion support, slotting allowances (cash paid to retailers for shelf space), extended invoice due dates.

- *Customer service costs.* Handling queries, claims and complaints, demands on salesperson and contact centre, small order sizes, high order frequency, just-in-time delivery, part-load shipments, breaking bulk for delivery to multiple sites.

- *Working capital costs.* Carrying inventory for the customer, cost of credit.

Traditional product-based or general ledger costing systems do not provide this type of detail, and do not enable companies to estimate customer profitability. Product costing systems track material, labour and energy costs to products, often comparing actual to standard costs. They do not, however, cover the customer-facing activities of marketing, sales and service. General ledger costing systems do track costs across all parts of the business but are normally too highly aggregated to establish which customers or segments are responsible for generating those costs.

Activity-based costing is an approach to costing that splits costs into two groups: volume-based costs and order-related costs. Volume-related (product-related) costs are variable against the size of the order, but fixed per unit for any order and any customer. Material and direct-labour costs are examples. Order-related (customer-related) costs vary according to the product and process requirements of each particular customer.

Imagine two retail customers, each purchasing the same volumes of product from a manufacturer. Customer 1 makes no product or process demands. The sales revenue is $5,000;

the gross margin for the vendor is $1,000. Customer 2 is a different story: customized product, special overprinted outer packaging, just-in-time delivery to three sites, provision of point-of-sale material, sale or return conditions and discounted price. Not only that, but customer 2 spends a lot of time agreeing these terms and conditions with a salesperson who has had to call into the account three times before closing the sale. The sales revenue is $5,000, but after accounting for product and process costs to meet the demands of this particular customer, the margin retained by the vendor is $250. Other things being equal, customer 1 is four times as valuable as customer 2.

Whereas conventional cost accounting practices report what was spent, ABC reports what the money was spent *doing*. Whereas the conventional general ledger approach to costing identifies resource costs such as payroll, equipment and materials, the ABC approach shows what was being done when those costs were incurred. Figure 5.3 shows how an ABC view of costs in an insurance company's claims processing department gives an entirely different picture to the traditional view.[4]

General ledger: claims processing dept.				ABC view: claims processing dept.	
	$ Actual	$ Plan	$ Variance		$
				Key/scan claims	31,500
				Analyze claims	121,000
Salaries	620,400	600,000	(21,400)	Suspend claims	32,500
				Receive provider enquiries	101,500
Equipment	161,200	150,000	(11,200)	Resolve member problems	83,400
				Process batches	45,000
Travel expenses	58,000	60,000	2,000	Determine eligibility	119,000
				Make copies	145,500
Supplies	43,900	40,000	(3,900)	Write correspondence	77,100
				Attend training	158,000
Use and occupancy	30,000	30,000	_____	Total	914,500
Total	914,500	880,000	(34,500)		

Figure 5.3 Activity-based costing in a claims processing department

ABC gives the manager of the claims processing department a much clearer idea of what activities create cost. The next question from a CPM perspective is 'Which customers create the activity?' Put another way, which customers are the cost drivers? If you were to examine the activity cost item 'Analyze claims: $121,000', and find that 80 per cent of the claims were made by drivers under the age of 20, you would have a clear understanding of the customer group that was creating that activity cost for the business.

CRM needs ABC, because of its overriding goal of generating profitable relationships with customers. Unless there is a costing system in place to trace costs to customers, CRM will find it very difficult to deliver on a promise of improved customer profitability.

Overall, ABC serves customer portfolio management in a number of ways:

1   When combined with revenue figures, ABC tells you the absolute and relative levels of profit generated by each customer, segment or cohort.

2   ABC guides you towards actions that can be taken to return customers to profit.

3   ABC helps prioritize and direct customer acquisition, retention and development strategies.

4   ABC helps establish whether customization, and other forms of value creation for customers, pays off.

ABC sometimes justifies management's confidence in the Pareto principle, otherwise known as the 80:20 rule. This rule suggests that 80 per cent of profits come from 20 per cent of customers. ABC tells you which customers fall into the important 20 per cent. Research offers some support for the 80:20 rule. For example, one report from Coopers and Lybrand found that in the retail industry the top 4 per cent of customers account for 29 per cent of profits, the next 26 per cent of customers account for 55 per cent of profits and the remaining 70 per cent account for only 16 per cent of profits.

Lifetime value estimation

The fourth discipline that can be used for CPM is customer lifetime value (CLV) estimation, which was first introduced in Chapter 2. CLV is measured by computing the present-day value of all net margins (gross margins less cost-to-serve) earned from a relationship with a customer, segment or cohort. CLV estimates provide important insights that guide companies in their customer management strategies. Clearly, companies want to protect and ring-fence their relationships with customers, segments or cohorts that will generate significant amounts of profit.

Sunil Gupta and Donald Lehmann suggest that customer lifetime value can be computed as follows:

$$CLV = m \left[\frac{r}{1+i-r} \right]$$

where

CLV = lifetime value
m   = margin or profit from a customer per period (e.g. per year)
r   = retention rate (e.g. 0.8 or 80 per cent)
i   = discount rate (e.g. 0.12 or 12 per cent)[5]

This means that CLV is equal to the margin (m) multiplied by the factor $r/(1 + i - r)$. This factor is referred to as the *margin multiple*, and is determined by both the customer retention rate (r) and the discount rate (i). For most companies the retention rate is in the region of 60 per cent to 90 per cent. The weighted average cost of capital (WACC), which was discussed in Chapter 2, is generally used to determine the discount rate. The discount rate is applied to bring future margins back to today's value. Table 5.8 presents some sample margin multiples based on the two variables – customer retention rate and discount rate. For example, at a 12 per cent discount rate and 80 per cent retention the margin multiple is

Table 5.8 Margin multiples

Retention rate	Discount rate			
	10%	12%	14%	16%
60%	1.20	1.15	1.11	1.07
70%	1.75	1.67	1.59	1.52
80%	2.67	2.50	2.35	2.22
90%	4.50	4.09	3.75	3.46

2.5. From this table, you can see that margin multiples for most companies, given a WACC of 10 per cent to 16 per cent and retention rates between 60 per cent and 90 per cent, lie between 1.07x and 4.5x. When the discount rate is high, the margin multiple is lower. When customer retention rates are higher, margin multiples are higher.

Table 5.8 can be used to compute customer value in the following way. If you have a customer retention rate of 80 per cent and your WACC is 12 per cent, and your customer generates $100 margin in a year, the CLV of the customer is about $400, or $409 to be precise (i.e. 4.09 times $100). The same mathematics can be applied to segments or cohorts of customers. Your company may serve two clusters of customers, A and B. Customers from cluster A each generate an annual margin of $400; cluster B customers each generate $200 margin. Retention rates vary between clusters. Cluster A has a retention rate of 80 per cent; cluster B customers have a retention rate of 90 per cent. If the same WACC of 12 per cent is applied to both clusters, then the CLV of a customer from cohort A is $1,000 ($400 x 2.50), and the CLV of a cohort B customer is $818 ($200 x 4.09). If you have 500 customers in cluster A, and 1,000 customers in cohort B, the CLV of your customer base is $1,318,000, computed thus: ((500 x $1,000) + (1,000 x $818)).

Application of this formula means that you do not have to estimate customer tenure. As customer retention rate rises there is an automatic lift in customer tenure, as shown in Table 2.2 in Chapter 2. This formula can be adjusted to consider change in both future margins and retention rates, either up or down, as described in Gupta and Lehmann's book *Managing Customers as Investments.*[6]

Table 5.8 can be used to assess the impact of a number of customer management strategies: What would be the impact of reducing cost-to-serve by shifting customers to low-cost self-serve channels? What would be the result of cross-selling higher margin products? What would be the outcome of a loyalty programme designed to increase retention rate from 80 per cent to 82 per cent?

An important additional benefit of this CLV calculation is that it enables you to estimate a company's value. For example, it has been computed that the CLV of the average US-based American Airlines customer is $166.94. AA has 43.7 million such customers, yielding an estimated company value of $7.3 billion. Roland Rust and his co-researchers noted that given the absence of international passengers and freight considerations from this computation, it was remarkably close to the company's market capitalization at the time their research was undertaken.[7]

Data mining

The fifth discipline that can be used for CPM is data mining. It has particular value when you are trying to find patterns or relationships in large volumes of data, as found in B2C contexts such as retailing, mobile telephony, financial services and Internet-based activities.

Tesco, for example, has about 16 million Clubcard members in the UK alone. Not only does the company have the demographic data that the customer provided on becoming a club member, but also the customer's transactional data. If ten million club members use Tesco in a week and buy an average basket of 30 items, Tesco's database grows by 300 million pieces of data per week. This is certainly a huge cost, but potentially a major benefit.

Data mining can be thought of as the creation of intelligence from large quantities of data.

Customer portfolio management needs intelligent answers to questions such as these:

1   How can we segment the market to identify potential customers?

2   How can we cluster our current customers?

3   Which customers offer the greatest potential for the future?

Data mining can involve the use of statistically advanced techniques, but fortunately managers do not need to be technocrats. It is generally sufficient to understand what the tools can do, how to interpret the results and how to perform data mining.

Two of the major vendors of data mining tools are SAS and SPSS, the latter owned by IBM. SAS promotes a five-step data mining process called SEMMA (Sample, Explore, Modify, Model, Assess).

Before any analysis starts, the first step is to define the business problem you are trying to solve (such as the three examples listed above). Then you have to create a database that can be subjected to data mining. Best practice involves extracting historical data from the data warehouse, creating a special data mart, and exploring that dataset for the patterns and relationships that can solve your business problem. Trying to conduct analysis on operational databases can be very troublesome – hence the advice to create a special dataset for mining. The problem-solving step involves an iterative process of developing a hypothetical solution to the problem (also known as model building), testing and refinement. Once a model is developed that appears to solve the business problem it can be applied by management. As new data are loaded into the data warehouse, further subsets can be extracted to the data mining mart and the model can be subjected to further refinement.

A number of different data mining tools are applicable to CPM problems – clustering, decision trees and neural networks.

Clustering techniques are used to find naturally occurring groupings within a dataset. As applied to customer data, these techniques generally function as follows:

1   Each customer is allocated to just one group. The customer possesses attributes or behaves in ways that are more closely associated with that group than any other group.

2   Each group is relatively homogenous.

3   Each group is significantly different from others.

In other words, clustering techniques generally try to maximize both within-group homogeneity and between-group heterogeneity. There are a number of clustering techniques, including CART (Classification and Regression Trees) and CHAID (Chi-square Automatic Interaction Detection).[8] Once statistically homogenous clusters have been formed they need to be interpreted.

CRM practitioners are often interested in the future behaviours of customers – segment, cohort or individual. Customers' potential value is determined by their propensity to buy products in the future. Data miners can build predictive models by examining patterns and relationships within historic data. Predictive models can be generated to identify:

1   Which customer, segment or cohort is most likely to buy a given product.

2   Which customers are likely to default on payment.

3   Which customers are most likely to churn.

Data analysts scour historic data looking for predictor and outcome variables. Then a model is built and validated on these historic data. When the model seems to work well on the historic data, it is run on contemporary data, where the predictor data are known but the outcome data are not. This is known as 'scoring'. Scores are answers to questions such as the propensity to buy, default and churn questions listed above.

Predictive modelling is based on three assumptions, each of which may be true to a greater or lesser extent:[9]

1   The past is a good predictor of the future – BUT, this may not be true. Sales of many products are cyclical or seasonal. Others have fashion or fad lifecycles.

2   The data are available – BUT, this may not be true. Data used to develop the model may no longer be collected. Data may be too costly to collect, or may be in the wrong format.

3   Customer-related databases contain what you want to predict – BUT, this may not be true. The data may not be available. If you want to predict which customers are most likely to buy mortgage protection insurance, and you only have data on life policies, you will not be able to answer the question.

Two tools that are used for predicting future behaviours are decision trees and neural networks.

Decision trees are so called because the graphical model output has the appearance of a branch structure. Decision trees work by analyzing a dataset to find the independent variable that, when used to split the population, results in nodes that are most different from each other with respect to the variable you are tying to predict. Table 5.9 contains a set of data about five customers and their credit risk profile.[10] We want to use the data in the first four columns to predict whether a customer is a good or poor risk as shown in the fifth column. A decision tree can be constructed for this purpose.

In the decision tree analysis, Risk is in the 'dependent' column. This is also known as the target variable. The other four columns are independent columns. It is unlikely that the customer's name is a predictor of Risk, so we will use the three other pieces of data as independent variables – debt, income and marital status. In the example, each of these is a

Table 5.9 Credit risk training set

Name	Debt	Income	Married?	Risk
Joe	High	High	Yes	Good
Sue	Low	High	Yes	Good
John	Low	High	No	Poor
Mary	High	Low	Yes	Poor
Fred	Low	Low	Yes	Poor

simple categorical item, each of which only has two possible values (High or Low; Yes or No). The data from Table 5.9 are represented in different form in Table 5.10 in a way that lets you see which independent variable is best at predicting risk. As you examine the data, you will see that the best split is income. Two of the three high-income customers are good credit risks, but both low-income customers are high credit risks. The risk splits for the other two predictors, debt and marital status, do not produce such a clear differentiation. The diagonal indicated by the double-headed arrow sums to four, which is greater than the diagonals for either of the other two predictor variables. This indicates that income is the best predictor.

Table 5.10 Cross-tabulation of dependent and independent variables

Predicted risk	High debt	Low debt	High income	Low income	Married	Not married
Good	1	1	2	0	2	0
Poor	1	2	1	2	2	1

Once a node is split, the same process is performed on each successive node, either until no further splits are possible or until you have reached a managerially useful model.

The graphical output of this decision tree analysis is shown in Figure 5.4. Each box is a node. Nodes are linked by branches. The top node is the root node. The data from the root node are split into two groups based on income. The right-hand, low-income box, does not split any further because both low-income customers are classified as poor credit risks. The left-hand, high-income box does split further, into married and not-married customers. Neither of these split further because the one unmarried customer is a poor credit risk and the two remaining married customers are good credit risks.

As a result of this process the company knows that customers who have the lowest credit risk will be high income and married. They will also note that debt, one of the variables inserted into the training model, did not perform well. It is not a predictor of creditworthiness. Decision trees that work with categorical data such as these are known as classification trees. When decision trees are applied to continuous data they are known as regression trees.

Neural networks, also known as machine-based learning, are another way of fitting a model to existing data for prediction purposes. The expression 'neural network' has its origins in the work of machine learning and artificial intelligence. Researchers in this field have tried to learn from the natural neural networks of living creatures.

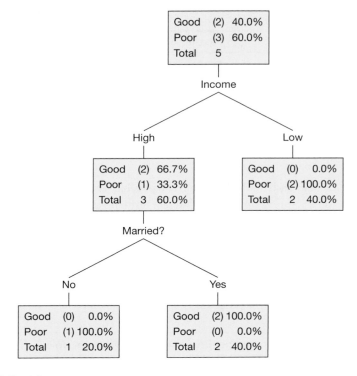

Figure 5.4 Decision tree output

Neural networks can produce excellent predictions from large and complex datasets containing hundreds of interactive predictor variables, but the neural networks are neither easy to understand nor straightforward to use. Neural networks are represented by complex mathematical equations, with many summations, exponential functions and parameters.[11]

CASE STUDY 5.4

CUSTOMER PORTFOLIO ANALYSIS AT TESCO

Tesco, the largest supermarket chain in the UK, has developed a CRM strategy that is the envy of many of its competitors. Principally a food retailer, in a mature market that has grown little in the last 20 years, Tesco realized that the only route to domestic growth was taking market share from competitors. Consequently, the development of a CRM strategy was seen as being imperative.

In developing its CRM strategy, Tesco first undertook Customer Portfolio Analysis (CPA) to examine its customer base. It found that the top 100 customers were worth the same as the bottom 4,000. It also found that the bottom 25 per cent of customers represented only 2 per cent of sales, and that the top 5 per cent of customers were responsible for 20 per cent of sales.

The results of this analysis were used to segment Tesco's customers and to develop its loyalty programmes.

Like decision trees and clustering techniques, neural networks need to be trained to recognize patterns on sample datasets. Once trained, they can be used to predict customer behaviour from new data. They work well when there are many potential predictor variables, some of which are redundant.

CPM IN THE BUSINESS-TO-BUSINESS CONTEXT

Many B2B companies classify their customers into groups based on sales revenue. They believe that their best customers are their biggest customers. Some of these companies consciously apply the Pareto principle, recognizing that 80 per cent of sales are made to 20 per cent of customers, as shown in Figure 5.5.

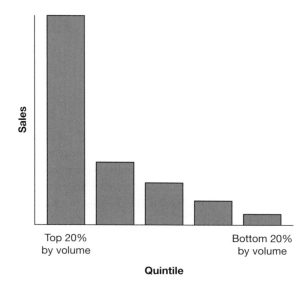

Figure 5.5 The Pareto principle, or 80:20 rule

Having clustered their customers by volume, they may then assign their best representatives, and offer the best service and terms of trade to these, the biggest and best customers. The assumption is often made in B2B contexts that large accounts are profitable accounts. Activity-based costing tells us that this is not necessarily so. It is not uncommon to find that small customers are unprofitable because the process costs they generate are greater than the margins they generate. Similarly, many companies find that their largest accounts are unprofitable too. Why? Large accounts create more work, more activity. The work of managing the account might require the services of a large number of people – sales manager, customer service executive and applications engineer amongst others. The customer might demand customized product, delivery in less-than-container loads, just-in-time, extended due dates for payment and, ultimately, volume discounts on price. Very often it is the mid-range sales volume customers that are the most profitable. Figure 5.6 shows the profitability of customers who have been previously clustered according to volume. The chart

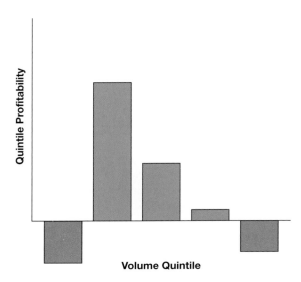

Figure 5.6 Customer profitability by sales volume quintile

shows that the top 20 per cent of customers by volume are unprofitable, just like the bottom 20 per cent by volume.

When Kanthal, a Swedish manufacturer of electrical resistance heating elements, introduced activity-based costing, they found that only 40 per cent of their customers were profitable. Two of their top three sales volume customers were among the most unprofitable. The most profitable 5 per cent of customers generated 150 per cent of profits. The least profitable 10 per cent lost 120 per cent of profit. The challenge for Kanthal was deciding what to do with the unprofitable customers.[12] Their options included implementation of open-book accounting so their customers could see how much it cost to serve them, negotiation of service levels with customers, introducing transparent rules for migrating customers up and down the service level ladder, simplifying and standardizing the order process, introducing a self-service portal, negotiating price increases, sorting product lines into those that could be delivered ex-stock and others for which advance orders were required, and rewarding account managers for customer profitability – both percentage margin and total Krona (Crown) value.

CUSTOMER PORTFOLIO MODELS

Since the early 1980s there have been a number of tools specifically designed for assessing B2B companies' customer portfolios.[13] They generally classify existing customers using a matrix and measurement approach. Many of these contributions have their origins in the work of the IMP (Industrial Marketing and Purchasing) group that you can read about in Chapter 2. CPM in B2B companies uses one or more variables to cluster customers. The most common single-variable approach is to use sales revenue to cluster companies. You know from the discussion immediately above that this does not necessarily deliver a satisfactory profit outcome. We present a review of three customer portfolio models.

Bivariate models

Benson Shapiro and his colleagues developed a customer portfolio model that importantly incorporated the idea of cost-to-serve into the assessment of customer value.[14] Figure 5.7 presents the matrix they developed.

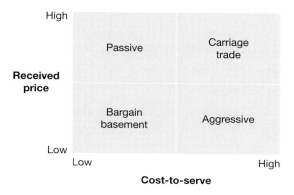

Figure 5.7 Shapiro *et al.*'s customer portfolio matrix

In this model, customers are classified according to the price they pay and the costs incurred by the company to acquire and serve them. Four classes of customer are identified: carriage trade (often newly acquired customers who are costly to serve but pay a relatively high price), passive customers, aggressive customers and bargain basement customers. The important contribution of this customer portfolio model is that it recognizes that costs are not evenly distributed across the customer base. Some customers are more costly to win and serve, and, if this is accompanied by a relatively low received price, the customer may be unprofitable. Table 5.11 shows how costs can vary before the sale, in production, in distribution and after the sale.

Table 5.11 How costs vary between customers

Pre-sale costs	Production costs	Distribution costs	Post-sale costs
Geographic location: close vs distant	Order size	Shipment consolidation	Training
Prospecting	Set-up time	Preferred transportation mode	Installation
Sampling	Scrap rate	Back-haul opportunity	Technical support
Human resource: management vs reps	Customization	Location: close vs distant	Repairs and maintenance
Service: design support, applications engineering	Order timing	Logistics support, e.g. field inventory	

Renato Fiocca improved this customer portfolio modelling by introducing a two-step approach.[15] At the first step customers are classified according to:

1 The strategic importance of the customer.

2 The difficulty of managing the relationship with the customer.

The *strategic importance* of a customer is determined by:

- the value or volume of the customer's purchases
- the potential and prestige of the customer
- customer market leadership
- general desirability in terms of diversification of the supplier's markets, providing access to new markets, improving technological expertise, and the impact on other relationships.

The *difficulty of managing the customer* relationship is related to:

- Product characteristics such as novelty and complexity.
- Account characteristics such as the customer's needs and requirements, customer's buying behaviour, customer's power, customer's technical and commercial competence and the customer's preference to do business with a number of suppliers.
- Competition for the account that is assessed by considering the number of competitors, and the strengths and weaknesses of those competitors.

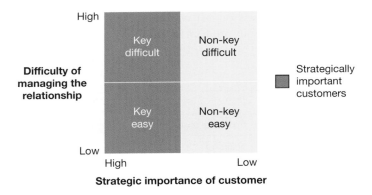

On the basis of this information, it is possible to construct a two-dimensional matrix as in Figure 5.8, the result of which is identification of strategically important key accounts.

The second step involves further analysis of the key accounts (in the left-hand cells of Figure 5.8). They are classified according to:

1 The customer's business attractiveness.

2 The relative strength of the buyer–seller relationship.

Figure 5.8 Fiocca's CPM model: step 1

The attractiveness of the customer's business is strongly influenced by conditions in the customer's served market. Fiocca classifies these as market factors, competition, financial and economic factors, technological factors and socio-political factors, as detailed in Table 5.12.

Table 5.12 Factors influencing the customer's attractiveness (Fiocca's model)

Market factors	Financial and economic factors
• Size of key segments served by customer	• Customer's margins
• Customer's share of key segments	• Customer's scale and experience
• Customer's growth rate	• Barriers to customer's entry or exit
• Customer's influence on the market	• Customer's capacity utilization
Competition in the customer's market	*Technological factors*
• Customer's position and strength	• Customer's ability to cope with change
• Customer's vulnerability to substitutes	• Depth of customer's skills
• Customer's level of integration	• Types of technological know-how
	• Level of customer patent protection
Socio-political factors	
• Customer's ability to adapt and fit	

The relative strength of the customer relationship is determined by:

- the length of relationship
- the volume or dollar value of purchases
- the importance of the customer (customer's purchases as a percentage of the supplier's sales)
- personal friendships
- cooperation in product development
- management distance (language and culture)
- geographical distance.

The data from this second step are then entered into a final nine-cell matrix as shown in Figure 5.9, which points to three core customer management strategies – hold, withdraw or improve. There have been a couple of published validations of this model,[16] but it has been criticized for its failure to consider customer profitability, and its rejection of non-key customers at step 1.

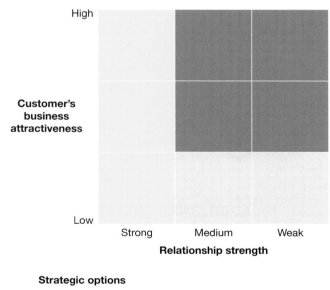

Figure 5.9 Fiocca's CPM model: step 2

Trivariate CPM model

Peter Turnbull and Judy Zolkiewski have developed the three-dimensional CPM framework as shown in Figure 5.10.[17] The dimensions they propose are cost-to-serve, net price and relationship value. The first two variables are adopted from the Shapiro model. Relationship value, the third dimension, allows for other strategic issues to be taken into account. Relationship value is 'softer' or more judgemental than the other two dimensions. Among the questions considered when forming a judgement on relationship value are the following:

- Are the goods or services critical to the customer?
- Is the customer a major generator of volume for the supplier?
- Would the customer be hard to replace if they switched to another supplier?
- Does the customer generate cost savings for the supplier?

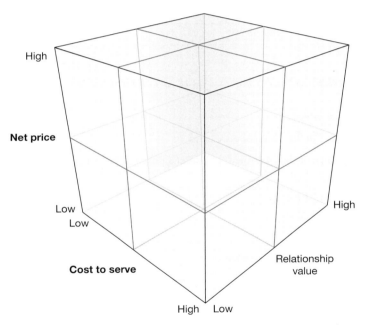

Figure 5.10 Turnbull and Zolkiewski's three-dimensional customer classification matrix

ADDITIONAL CUSTOMER PORTFOLIO MANAGEMENT TOOLS

In addition to the CPM tools described previously, there are a number of other useful tools that are in common use for strategic planning. These tools, however, operate at company-specific level. This means that a CRM strategist could apply these tools to assess a particular customer's attractiveness and to choose between customers for relationship-building investment. We explore two tools: SWOT analysis and BCG matrix analysis.

We will introduce them here briefly. For a fuller report you would be well advised to refer to any basic corporate strategy or marketing strategy book.

SWOT

SWOT is an acronym for Strengths, Weaknesses, Opportunities and Threats. SWOT analysis explores the internal environment (S and W) and the external environment (O and T) of a current or potential business customer. Properly done, SWOT helps firms identify opportunities in the environment best suited to their competitive advantages and threats in the environment that potentially exploit their weaknesses. The internal (SW) audit looks for that customer's strengths and weaknesses relative to competitors in the business functions of sales, marketing, manufacturing or operations, finance and people management. It then looks cross-functionally for strengths and weaknesses in, for example, cross-functional processes (such as new product development) and organizational culture. It is essential that strengths and weaknesses are always expressed comparative to competitors: so a 'good reputation amongst customers' is only a strength if it is a *better* reputation than competitors'.

The external (OT) audit analyses the macro- and micro-environments in which the customer operates. These opportunities or threats are present as market growth or contraction, changes in legislation, new technology, competitive conditions, evolving customer attitudes and so on.

A CRM-oriented SWOT analysis would be searching for customers or potential customers that emerge well from the analysis. These would be customers that:

- possess relevant strengths to exploit the opportunities open to them;
- are overcoming their own weaknesses by partnering with other organizations to take advantage of opportunities;
- are investing to exploit opportunities in their served market;
- are responding to competitive threats by diversification.

The Boston Consulting Group (BCG) matrix

The Boston Consulting Group (BCG) matrix was designed to analyze a company's product portfolio so that companies can develop strategies that enhance their profit and cash flow. The analysis takes into account two criteria – relative market share and market growth rate – to identify where profits and cash flow are earned. Figure 5.11 is a sample BCG matrix. The BCG claims that the best indicator of a market's attractiveness is its growth rate (hence the vertical axis of the matrix) and that the best indicator of competitive strength is market share (the horizontal axis) relative to the strongest competitor in the target market or segment. There are two theories that support the strategy prescriptions. First, the product lifecycle suggests that all high growth markets eventually stop growing or decline. Therefore, over time all company offerings move to the lower quadrants in the BCG grid. Second, in product markets (not necessarily services), the firm with the greatest output enjoys the lowest cost due to economies of scale.

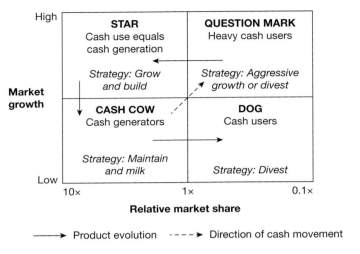

Figure 5.11 Boston Consulting Group matrix

The matrix categorizes products in a portfolio into one of four quadrants and prescribes certain strategies: milk the cows, invest in the stars, ditch the dogs and sort the question marks into those that you want to support as they become stars, and the remainder that you expect to convert into dogs.

A balanced portfolio of products contains question marks, stars and cash cows. Cash cows generate the cash flow that supports the question marks. As the question marks grow their relative market share, and become stars, they are establishing a position in the market that will eventually yield strong positive cash flows. This happens when a leading product maintains that position in a mature market.

From a CRM perspective, a customer with a balanced portfolio of products of its own has greater CLV potential for a supplier than a customer with an unbalanced portfolio. A company with no new products in the pipeline will struggle to remain viable when the existing cash cows dry up. This happens as competitors fight to win market share and substitutes emerge.

STRATEGICALLY SIGNIFICANT CUSTOMERS

The goal of this entire analytical process is to cluster customers into groups so that differentiated value propositions and relationship management strategies can be applied. One outcome will be the identification of customers that will be strategically significant for the company's future. We call these strategically significant customers (SSCs). There are several classes of SSC, as follows:

1   *High future lifetime value customers.* These high CLV customers will contribute significantly to the company's profitability in the future.

2 *High volume customers.* These customers might not generate much profit, but they are strategically significant because of their absorption of fixed costs, and the economies of scale they generate to keep unit costs low.

3 *Benchmark customers.* These are customers that other customers follow. For example, Nippon Conlux supplies the hardware and software for Coca-Cola's vending operation. Whilst they might not make much margin from that relationship, it has allowed them to gain access to many other markets. 'If we are good enough for Coke, we are good enough for you', is the implied promise. Some IT companies create 'reference sites' at some of their more demanding customers.

4 *Inspirations.* These are customers that bring about improvement in the supplier's business. They may identify new applications for a product, product improvements or opportunities for cost reductions. They may complain loudly and make unreasonable demands but, in doing so, force change for the better.

5 *Door openers.* These are customers that allow the supplier to gain access to a new market. This may be done for no initial profit, but with a view to proving credentials for further expansion. This may be particularly important if crossing cultural boundaries, say between West and East.

One company, a Scandinavian processor of timber, has identified five major customer groups that are strategically significant, as in Case study 5.5.

CASE STUDY 5.5

STRATEGICALLY SIGNIFICANT CUSTOMERS AT A SCANDINAVIAN TIMBER PROCESSOR

The forestry industry is extremely important in Scandinavian countries. In Norway, 30,000 people are employed in forestry, and over half the production is exported. One leading Norwegian forestry company uses five criteria to identify customers that are strategically significant.

1 *Economic return.* This considers the gross and net margins currently earned from the relationship.

2 *Future business potential.* Even if the current economic return isn't strong, the forestry company looks to the future, and estimates future sales and margins from the customer.

3 *Learning value.* A customer can be strategically significant if the forestry company can learn from it. For example, product innovation, quality improvement and cost savings.

4 *Reference value.* A customer can be strategically significant if it occupies an established and respected position in its industry. This position can be leveraged by the forestry company to gain access to new customers.

5 *Strategic value.* A customer may be strategically significant for a number of broader strategic reasons, such as:

a providing access to new markets
b strengthening incumbent positions
c building barriers to new entrants.

THE SEVEN CORE CUSTOMER MANAGEMENT STRATEGIES

Customer portfolio analysis pays off when it helps companies develop and implement differentiated CRM strategies for each cluster of customers in the portfolio. There are several core customer management strategies:

1   *Protect the relationship.* This makes sense when the customer is strategically significant and attractive to competitors. We discuss the creation of exit barriers in our review of customer retention strategies in Chapter 4.

2   *Re-engineer the relationship.* This strategy makes sense when the customer is currently unprofitable or less profitable than desired. However, the customer could be converted to greater profit if costs were trimmed from the relationship. This might mean reducing or automating service levels, or servicing customers through lower cost channels.

3   *Grow the relationship.* Like the strategy above, the goal is to migrate the customer up the value ladder. In this case it is done not by re-engineering the relationship, but by increasing your share of customer spend on the category, and by identifying up-selling and cross-selling opportunities.

4   *Harvest the relationship.* When your share-of-wallet is stable, and you do not want to invest more resources in customer development, you may feel that the customer has reached maximum value. Under these conditions you may wish to harvest, that is, optimize cash flow from the customer with a view to using the cash generated to develop other customers. This may be particularly appealing if the customer is in a declining market, has a high cost-to-serve or has a high propensity-to-switch to competitors.

5   *End the relationship.* Sacking customers is generally anathema to sales and marketing people. However, when the customer shows no sign of making a significant contribution in the future it may be the best option. We discuss sacking customers in Chapter 4.

6   *Win-back the customer.* Sometimes customers take some or all of their business to other suppliers. If they are not strategically significant, it may make sense to let them go. However, when the customer is important, companies will want to develop and implement win-back strategies. The starting point must be to understand why they took their business away.

7   *Start a relationship.* This makes sense when a supplier has identified a prospect as having potential strategic significance for the future. The company will need to develop an acquisition plan to recruit the customer onto the value ladder. You can read about customer acquisition strategies in Chapter 3.

SUMMARY

In this chapter you have learned about customer portfolio management. CPM is an essential component of strategic CRM. CPM is underpinned by analysis that clusters customers into groups that can then be treated to differentiated value propositions and customer management strategies. It strives to do this by estimating the current and future value of each group, taking into account the revenues each group will generate and the costs that will be incurred in acquiring and serving those customers. A number of basic disciplines underpin the CPM process – market segmentation, sales forecasting, activity-based costing, customer lifetime value estimation and data mining. Market segmentation, which is widely practised by marketing management, needs to have a clear focus on customer value when used for CPM purposes. A number of sales forecasting techniques can also be used to estimate what customers are likely to buy in the future. Activity-based costing enables companies to understand the costs of marketing, selling and servicing customers and, consequently, customer profitability. Customer lifetime value estimation models can be used to evaluate a customer's future worth to a company, and data mining techniques are particularly useful for detecting patterns and relationships within historic customer data.

The CPM process tends to differ from business-to-consumer to business-to-business contexts. Not only have a number of portfolio analysis tools been developed specifically for B2B contexts, but activity-based costing is more easily applied in B2B contexts, whereas data mining is more visible in B2C contexts.

The purpose of all this analysis is to disaggregate potential and current customers into subsets so that different value propositions and relationship management strategies can be developed for each group. We close the chapter by identifying seven core customer management strategies that can be applied selectively across the customer portfolio.

NOTES AND REFERENCES

1   Levitt, T. (1960). Marketing myopia. *Harvard Business Review*, July–August, 45–56.

2   © CAC Limited 1979–2014.

3   Day, G.S. (1986). *Analysis for strategic market decisions.* St Paul, MN: West Publishing.

4   Cokins, G. (1996). *Activity-based cost management: making it work.* New York: McGraw-Hill.

5   Gupta, S. and Lehmann, D.R. (2005). *Managing customers as investments: the strategic value of customers in the long run.* Upper Saddle River, NJ: Wharton School Publishing.

6   Gupta, S. and Lehmann, D.R. (2005). *Managing customers as investments: the strategic value of customers in the long run.* Upper Saddle River, NJ: Wharton School Publishing.

7   Rust, R.T., Lemon, K.N. and Narayandas, D. (2005). *Customer equity management.* Upper Saddle River, NJ: Pearson Prentice Hall.

8   Saunders, J. (1994). Cluster analysis. In G.J. Hooley and M.K. Hussey (eds). *Quantitative methods in marketing.* London: Dryden Press, pp. 13–28.

9   Berry, M.J.A. and Linoff, G.S. (2000). *Data mining: the art and science of customer relationship management*. New York: John Wiley.

10   The illustration is taken from Brand, E. and Gerritsen, R. Decision trees. Available online at: http://www.dbmsmag.com/9807m05.html.

11   Berry, M.J.A. and Linoff, G.S. (2000). *Data mining: the art and science of customer relationship management*. New York: John Wiley.

12   Kaplan, Robert S. (1989) Kanthal (A). Harvard Business School Case 9–190–002. July. (Revised April 2001). Boston, MA: Harvard Business School Press.

13   Reviewed by Zolkiewski, J. and Turnbull, P. (1999). *A review of customer relationships planning: does customer profitability and portfolio analysis provide the key to successful relationship management?* UMIST, Manchester, UK: MSM Working Paper Series. See also Zolkiewski, J. (2005). Customer portfolios. In Littler, D. (ed.). *Blackwell encyclopedia of management, vol. 9: marketing*. Oxford: Blackwell; and Johnson, M.D. and Selnes, F. (2004). Customer portfolio management: towards a dynamic theory of exchange relationships. *Journal of Marketing*, 68(2), 1–17; Zolkiewski, J. (2014). Recent developments in relationship portfolios: a review of current knowledge. In D. Woodburn and K. Wilson (eds). *The handbook of strategic account management*. Chichester: John Wiley.

14   Shapiro, B.P, Rangan, K.V., Moriarty, R.T. and Ross, E.B. (1987). Manage customers for profits (not just sales). *Harvard Business Review*, September–October, 101–8.

15   Fiocca, R. (1982). Account portfolio analysis for strategy development. *Industrial Marketing Management*, 11, 53–62.

16   Turnbull, P.W. and Topcu, S. (1994). Customers' profitability in relationship life-cycles. *Proceedings of the 10th IMP conference*, Groningen, the Netherlands; Yorke, D.A. and Droussiotis, G. (1994). The use of customer portfolio theory: an empirical survey. *Journal of Business and Industrial Marketing*, 9(3), 6–18.

17   Turnbull, P. and Zolkiewski, J. (1997). Profitability in customer portfolio planning. In D. Ford (ed.). *Understanding business markets*, 2nd edn. London: Dryden Press.

CHAPTER 6

HOW TO DELIVER CUSTOMER-EXPERIENCED VALUE

CHAPTER OBJECTIVES

By the end of this chapter you will understand:

- The meaning of the term 'value'.
- How customers weigh up 'benefits' and 'sacrifices' in the value equation.
- Three major types of value proposition.
- How marketers enable customer-experienced value by deploying a number of variables known as the 7Ps.
- The importance of customization in creating customer-experienced value.
- How the Internet is changing the way that customers receive value from communication and distribution.

INTRODUCTION

This chapter is the second of three on the topic of strategic CRM. A core assumption in CRM is that customers are more likely to experience the value they seek if they build a relationship with a company that has a good understanding of their needs, than if they were to buy transactionally on the open market. In this chapter you will learn about how companies enable and deliver such value to customers. You will find out what customers mean when they talk about value, and the various elements that make up a company's value proposition.

Our definition of CRM, repeated below, stresses the centrality of value creation and delivery.

CRM is the core business strategy that integrates internal processes and functions and external networks, to *create and deliver value to targeted customers at a*

profit. It is grounded on high-quality customer-related data and enabled by information technology.

The task of enabling the creation and delivery of value to targeted customers at a profit is a role for strategic CRM.

UNDERSTANDING VALUE

Although the term 'value' is used in a number of different ways,[1] in a CRM sense it can be thought of as follows:

Value is the customer's perception of the balance between benefits received from a product or service and the sacrifices made to experience those benefits.

It is possible to represent this definition in the form of an equation:

$$Value = \frac{Benefits}{Sacrifices}$$

The equation shows that managers can enhance customer-perceived value in two main ways: increase the benefits they experience, or decrease the sacrifices they make.

Let's first look at sacrifices. Customers make several types of sacrifice.

- *Money*. This is the price of the product or service, which may or may not be the listed price. There may be additional costs such as credit card surcharges, interest charges on extended payments or warranty costs. There may be discounts applied for relationship customers, early payment or volume purchases.

- *Transaction costs*. Oliver Williamson[2] is acknowledged as the creator of Transaction Cost Economics. In addition to money, he proposed that customers incurred transaction costs when searching for solutions, negotiating with suppliers, and receiving and integrating the goods and services. Particularly for B2B, the purchasing process may include exhaustive pre-purchase work in searching for solutions and comparing alternatives. Major tenders for new IT systems or infrastructure may take years to complete and cost the buying organization millions of dollars. Negotiations and performance monitoring can also be complex and costly to conduct and monitor; think of major long-term contracts for building and operating hospitals or power plants. Transaction costs are normally lower when search costs are eliminated, and purchasing processes are routinized. Some suppliers are prepared to take on the costs of managing inventory for important customers, so that they are less tempted to search for alternative solutions. Known as Vendor Managed Inventory (VMI), it reduces search and reorder costs for customers. Building trust is another way of lowering transaction costs; the level of negotiation and monitoring can be substantially reduced. In B2C, transaction costs are also important. You might have a favourite clothing store that reduces your search costs because you trust their fashion sense. Apple users often buy multiple devices for their seamless integration. Reduced transaction costs may explain a buyer's desire to build relationships with suppliers.

- *Psychic costs.* Purchasing can be a very stressful and frustrating experience. Will this new device work? Will I feel foolish for buying now when something much better is coming out in a few months? Will people think me naive for buying that model of car? Is this outfit unflattering? Will this gift be appreciated or cause me shame? Making decisions can be stressful. It demands a cognitive effort that consumers often wish to avoid.[3] Inertia may be a consequence. Famously, people are reluctant to switch between banks even if they are thoroughly dissatisfied with their current bank's performance.

Perceived risk is a consideration in assessing psychic cost. Perceived risk takes a variety of forms – performance, physical, financial, social and psychological. Performance risk occurs when the customer is not fully sure that the product will do what is required. Physical risk is when the customer feels that there may be some bodily harm done by the product. Financial risk is felt when there is danger of economic loss from the purchase. Social risk is felt when customers feel that their social standing or reputation is at risk. Psychological risk is felt when the customer's self-esteem or self-image is endangered by an act of purchase or consumption. When perceived risk is high, psychic cost is correspondingly high. Research suggests that we are not totally rational in our ability to assess perceived risk. We tend to worry too much about potentially bad outcomes, even if their probability of happening is very small, and we assess gains differently than losses.[4] Traditional economic theory suggests that rational decision makers consider the expected utility (risk multiplied by outcome) and therefore treat expected losses and gains in an equivalent manner. Research has called this into question. Kahneman and Tversky[5] find that people feel losses more than they do gains; we are loss averse.

Customers often feel uncomfortable at higher levels of perceived risk, and may try to reduce risk in a number of ways as indicated in Table 6.1. When customers try to reduce perceived risk, they are in effect trying to reduce the denominator of the value equation, thereby improving value. Suppliers can develop ways that help customers reduce their levels of perceived risk in a number of ways. For example, performance risk is reduced by performance guarantees; financial risk is reduced by firm prices and interest-free payment plans.

Clearly there is more to the sacrifice component of the value equation than money alone. This explains why customers buy what appear to be suboptimal solutions to their problems. Why would a customer buy a printer for $300 when an identically specified machine is available for $100? Perhaps the answer lies in transaction and psychic costs.

There is a trend towards considering costs from the perspective of 'total cost of ownership' or TCO. TCO looks not only at the costs of acquiring goods and services, but also the full costs of using and servicing them throughout their life, and ultimately disposing of them. What is thought of as 'consumption' can be broken down into a number of activities or stages, including search, purchase, ownership, use, consumption and disposal. TCO is an attempt to come up with meaningful estimates of lifetime costs across all these stages.

Table 6.1 How customers try to reduce perceived risk

1	Delay purchase
2	Seek word-of-mouth endorsement
3	Negotiate service contracts
4	Seek additional information from advertising copy
5	Buy established brands
6	Build a relationship with a supplier
7	Transact with reputable supplier
8	Seek performance guarantees
9	Buy with credit card (protection if product fails)
10	Negotiate discounts
11	Take out insurance
12	Request pre-purchase trial
13	Read testimonials

When customers take a TCO view of purchasing, suppliers can respond through a form of pricing called Economic Value to the Customer (EVC). In a B2B context, EVC works by proving to customers that the value proposition being presented improves the profitability of the customer, by increasing sales, reducing costs or otherwise improving productivity. EVC computes for customers the value that the solution will deliver over the lifetime of ownership and use. Suppliers can apply EVC thinking to each stage of the 'consumption' process described above. For example, a computer supplier may agree to provide free service, and to collect and dispose of unwanted machines after four years. Customers performing these tasks themselves would incur tangible costs. This is therefore the value that these activities have for customers. EVC encourages suppliers to customize price for customers on the basis of their particular value requirements. In a B2B context, a distinction is sometimes made between economic value (satisfying economic needs at low transaction costs) and social value (satisfaction with the relationship with the supplier).[6]

WHEN DO CUSTOMERS EXPERIENCE VALUE?

Adam Smith, the eighteenth-century father of economics wrote:

The word value, it is to be observed, has two different meanings, and sometimes expresses the utility of some particular object, and sometimes the power of purchasing other goods which the possession of that object conveys. The one may be called 'value-in-use', the other, 'value-in-exchange'.[7]

Value-in-exchange

Value-in-exchange is the exchange of one form of value for another. In developed economies value-in-exchange takes the form of money being exchanged for a good or service at the point of sale. One form of value (the good or service) is exchanged for another (money). In less developed economies, barter is a common non-monetized form of value-in-exchange, goods or services being exchanged for other goods or services.

Value-in-exchange logic suggests that value is created by the firm, embedded in products, distributed to the market and realized when those products are exchanged for money. From this perspective, the roles of producers and consumers are distinct, and value is created when production, marketing, distribution and selling processes are performed by the firm.

Value-in-use

Value-in-use holds that value is realized only when customers possess, use, consume or interact with the good or service. Until consumers perform these actions, goods are simply inert bundles of attributes – they have no value whatsoever. This perspective on value suggests that value is 'not what the producer puts in, but what the customer gets out'.[8] Firms can only create value propositions. Customers co-create value-in-use when they use or otherwise interact with the firm's products. This suggests that value-in-use is context-dependent.[9] Younger consumers attending a birthday party hosted by a fast-food chain may experience considerable value-in-use, but using the same service provider for a wedding celebration may yield considerably less value-in-use for participants.

Value-in-experience

Contextualized value-in-use is consistent with our view of CRM. However, we do not just claim that customers co-create value when they use products and services (or 'dis-value' if their experience is unsatisfactory). We also suggest that customers can experience value as they interact with or are exposed to any marketing, sales or service output of the firm throughout the customer lifecycle. Let's consider marketing first. There is potential value in enjoying the humour in an ad, or learning about a food product's ingredients from its packaging, whether or not purchase takes place. Sales activities can also help a customer experience value, for example when a pitcher demonstrates how a product works in a television infomercial, or when a salesperson skilfully proves that a product can solve a customer problem. Service activities can also enable a customer to experience value. When a customer calls to request service under warranty, a skilled customer service agent can make the customer feel comforted that the issue will be resolved quickly and effectively. Contact centre staff with high emotional intelligence can add considerably to customer perceptions of value.

Managers who design and deliver customer experience throughout the customer life-cycle need to be aware that the customer's interactions with the firm's products, services, people, processes, communications and other outputs, whether from marketing, sales or service departments, can have a significant effect on the customer's value-perceptions.

Value is *not* only experienced when customers *use* products and services. Consequently, we prefer the expression 'value-in-experience' to 'value-in-use'.

MODELLING CUSTOMER-PERCEIVED VALUE

Researchers have developed several typologies of customer-perceived value. Valarie Zeithaml identified four different forms of customer-perceived value: value as low price; value as whatever the customer wants in the product; value as the quality obtained for the price paid; and value as what the customer gets for what the customer sacrifices.[10]

More recently, researchers have come to appreciate that consumers experience hedonic or affective value such as pleasure, fun, amusement and entertainment, as well as functional value. Functional value might take the form of price-savings, service excellence, time-savings and choice, and hedonic value takes the form of entertainment, escape and interaction.[11]

As researchers have developed a deeper understanding of customer-perceived value, a number of multidimensional models have been published. Jag Sheth and colleagues have identified five types of value: functional, social, emotional, epistemic and conditional value.[12] Functional value is the utility associated with an offering's functional, utilitarian or physical performance. Social value is associated with the offering's connectedness to one or more specific social groups. Emotional value is experienced when the offering arouses feelings or emotional states. Epistemic value is the utility acquired from an offering's capacity to arouse curiosity, provide novelty and/or satisfy a desire for knowledge. The conditional value of an offering is experienced as the result of the specific situation or set of circumstances facing the consumer.

Morris Holbrook proposed a typology of consumer value with three dimensions: extrinsic or intrinsic – the consumer perceives value in using or owning a product or service as a means to an end versus an end in itself; self-oriented or other-oriented – consumers perceive value for their own benefit or for the benefit of others; active or reactive – the consumer experiences value through direct use of an offering in contrast to apprehending, appreciating or otherwise responding to it. These three dimensions give rise to eight types of consumer-experienced value: efficiency, excellence, play, aesthetics, status, esteem, ethics and spirituality, as shown in Table 6.2. Holbrook argues that all eight types of value tend to occur together to varying degrees in any given consumption experience.[13]

In a well-regulated, competitive economy, most companies compete by developing offerings that deliver consistently better value than competitors. This means companies have to understand customers' requirements fully, and create and deliver better solutions and experiences than competitors. In order to create better value for the customers, companies have to reinvent the numerator (benefits) and/or denominator (sacrifices) of the value equation. In a B2B context, customized solutions are often created in partnership with customers, on a customer-by-customer basis. In B2C contexts, solutions are more often segment- or niche-specific, and are supported by market intelligence. To win and keep customers, companies have to constantly seek to improve customer-experienced value. Given that this happens in a competitive environment, it is necessary not only to keep current with customer requirements, but also to stay up to date on competitors' efforts to serve these customers.

Table 6.2 Holbrook's typology of consumer value

		Extrinsic	Intrinsic
Self-oriented	Active	Efficiency (output/input, convenience)	Play (fun)
	Reactive	Excellence (quality)	Aesthetics (beauty)
Other-oriented	Active	Status (success, impression management)	Ethics (virtue, justice, morality)
	Reactive	Esteem (reputation, materialism, possessions)	Spirituality (faith, ecstasy, rapture, sacredness, magic)

SOURCES OF CUSTOMER VALUE

It is the job of professional marketers to construct the offers that enable customers to experience value – the so-called value proposition. We can define value proposition as follows:

A value proposition is the explicit or implicit promise made by a company to its customers that it will deliver a particular bundle of value-creating benefits.

Michael Treacey and Fred Wiersema have suggested that successful companies offer one of three value propositions to their customers: low price, innovative products and services, or customized solutions.[14]

- *Low price.* Companies that offer the low price value proposition do a limited number of things very efficiently – at very low cost – and pass on those savings to customers. Companies renowned for this are Wal-Mart, Giordano and McDonald's. Unexpectedly, Toyota might also fit this strategy. If customers take a total cost of ownership view of price, then Toyota, with its reputation for reliability, durability and competitive service costs, fits the operational excellence model well. Companies offering this value proposition tend to operate lean manufacturing and efficient supply chains, have close cooperation with suppliers, rigorous quality and cost controls, process measurement and improvement, and management of customer expectations.

- *Product innovation.* Companies that offer the product innovation value proposition aim to provide the best products, services or solutions to customers. Continuous innovation underpins this strategy. Companies renowned for this are 3M, Intel, GSK, LG and Singapore Airlines. Product innovation is associated with companies that have a culture that encourages innovation, a risk-oriented management style, and investment in research and development.

- *Customized solutions.* Companies that offer this value proposition are able to adapt their offers to meet the needs of individual customers. Customized solutions must be based on customer insight. Companies renowned for customized solutions include Saatchi and Saatchi, McKinsey, and the US department store, Nordstrom.

CUSTOMIZATION

CRM aims to build mutually beneficial relationships with customers, at segment, cohort or individual level. One way of achieving this goal is to customize the value proposition. CRM aims to fit the offer, or some value-delivering parts of it, to the requirements of the customer; it is not a one-size-fits-all approach – unless that is what the customer wants!

Customization means that companies have to be aware of and responsive to customers' differing requirements. Customization has both cost and revenue implications. It may make strategic sense because it generates competitive advantage and is appealing to customers, but there may be reservations because of the costs of customization. Customization may mean the loss of economies of scale, thus increasing unit costs. There may also be additional technology costs, for example purchase of a Product Configurator licence. Product configurators are integrated into some CRM technology solutions. SAP CRM, for example, offers configurator functionality.

Configurator technologies can be quite sophisticated. In their simplest form they contain a set of rules (if the customer chooses the 1.8 litre engine, only allow chassis type A). At the other end of the spectrum are constraint-based optimization technologies. The constraints are applied in a systematic way to ensure the final configuration is optimal, for example in producing least cost products.

Customization has been the norm in B2B markets for many years. Suppliers routinely make adaptations to suit the needs of customers. It is also true that customers make adaptations to suit suppliers. These adaptations serve as investments that make the relationship harder to break. As shown in Table 6.3, suppliers are sometimes able and willing to adapt, or customize, any parts of the offer.

Mass customization

A distinction can be made between 'craft customization' and 'mass customization'. Mass customization means that an organization is able to offer customized value propositions to individual customers on a massive scale. Craft customization also involves customized offers but not at mass-market levels.

Mass customization can be defined as follows:

Mass customization is the use of flexible processes and organizational structures to create varied and even individually tailored value propositions to order. In most cases, this is achieved with only a limited cost or lead-time penalty.

Table 6.3 Customization can be applied to any part of the offer

1	Product	Solvay Interox, a chemicals company, customizes its hydrogen peroxide product for textile industry customers.
2	Price	Dell Computer offers lower prices to its larger relationship customers than its small office/home office (SOHO) customers.
3	Promotion	Ford customizes communications to its dealership network.
4	Place	Procter and Gamble delivers direct to store for its major retail customers but not smaller independents.
5	Process	Xerox customizes its service guarantee and recovery processes for individual customers.
6	People	Hewlett Packard creates dedicated virtual project groups for its IT project clients.
7	Physical evidence	Cosmos and other major tour operators customize point-of-sale material by overprinting with travel agency details.

	Type of mass customization	How it works	Example
Minor	Match-to-order or locate-to-order	Selection of existing standard products or services to match customer requirements	Cars
	Bundle-to-order	Bundling of existing products and services to suit customer requirements	Conferences
	Assemble-to-order	Assembly of products or services from existing standardized components or processes	Insurance
	Make-to-order	Manufacture of customized products including components	Tailored suits
Major	Engineer-to-order	Customer co-designs products or services which are then made-to-order	Aircraft

Figure 6.1 Different forms of mass customization

Mass customization is not the same as offering customers more choice. Customers certainly want their needs to be met. They do not necessarily want choice. Giving customers choice has been the default strategy when companies have been unable to identify or meet customers' precise requirements. Choice means work for the customer in comparing offers. Work adds to the customer's transaction and psychic costs.

A number of different types of mass customization have been identified, as shown in Figure 6.1.[15] A relatively minor form of mass customization involves match-to-order. This simply involves finding a match from a range of standard products to a particular customer's requirements. At the other extreme is engineer-to-order. This involves the co-design, in a joint enterprise between customer and supplier, of a unique solution to that customer's problem.

It is in B2C markets that mass customization has recently become more widespread. Traditionally B2C companies have either mass marketed standardized products or have developed product variants for particular niches. A growing number are now attempting to mass customize their offers. This is enabled by databases that store customer preferences, Internet-enabled interactivity that permits companies to learn about changing customer requirements through improved communication, modular product design, flexible manufacturing operations and supply chains, and mass customization technologies.

Mass customization is widespread in service industries serving end-consumers. This is largely because of the interaction between consumers and service producers during the service encounter that lets customers influence both the service delivery process and the outcome.

Mass customization is becoming more common in manufacturing companies, too. Additive printing, more commonly known as 3D printing, promises to dramatically change mass customization. In just a few years, this technology has evolved from experimental machines that were enormous and expensive, to compact, reliable machines that can fit on desktops at a cost within reach of many people. This 3D printing works by converting 3-dimensional digital designs into solid objects. A software programme slices the design into digital cross-sections so the printer is able to build it layer by layer. There is considerable promise in 3D printing for customization of offerings. Imagine customers co-designing exactly what they want, ordering online and printing the object in their own home or, in the case of a more complex object, at a local high-quality 3D printing shop that uses larger, more sophisticated machines.

Key issues for CRM strategists considering customization are these:

1   Do customers want customized products and services?

2   What degree of customization is desired?

3   Will customers pay a premium for customization?

Frank Piller and Melanie Müller have reviewed the research on these questions, giving particular attention to the shoe manufacturing industry.[16] They found that consumers generally are aware of and value the benefits of mass customization (for shoe customers, better fit is the single most important benefit, followed at some distance by style and functionality), and the majority are willing to pay a premium – particularly women. Willingness to pay more varies across brands and customer segments. Adidas, for example, is able to command a 50 per cent price premium for customized sports shoes. Customization, however, does not universally mean that customers pay more. Some customized products eliminate features that have no value for customers, resulting in lower costs passed on in reduced price.

Amazon.com has become the world's largest and most successful online retailer diversifying from books and CDs into other areas such as electronics and clothing. Much of Amazon's continued success has been related to its CRM strategy of retaining customers and growing share-of-wallet. Amazon utilizes CRM software to customize offerings to each customer. Based on information such as your previous purchases, products that you have recently browsed and the purchasing behaviours of other customers, Amazon's CRM software can predict a range of other products you are likely to be interested in. For example, a customer who purchases an Ernest Hemingway novel may receive a recommendation to purchase another novel by the author or a DVD documentary of Hemingway's life. Netflix, the US-based online provider of streamed media including TV shows and film, does much the same. It records customers' viewing behaviour (titles, time, date and device) and online searches. The data are analyzed so that Netflix can recommend the next film or TV series that you might wish to view. Amazon and Netflix learn from their customers' behaviour on their sites and use that information to direct customers to the most appropriate items in their vast catalogues. The more customers do on the site, the better the recommendations they get. Amazon and Netflix have invested significantly in training the recommendation engines, and as a consequence customers are less likely to defect.[17]

VALUE THROUGH THE MARKETING MIX

As mentioned earlier in this chapter, it is the responsibility of marketing people to develop value propositions. They use a toolkit known as the marketing mix. The term 'marketing mix' is really a metaphor to describe the process of combining together various components that contribute to the value experienced by customers. Eugene McCarthy grouped these components into a classification known as the 4Ps – product, price, promotion and place.[18] This is widely applied by goods manufacturers.

Services marketing experts in both B2B and B2C contexts have found this 4P taxonomy inadequate because it fails to take account of the special attributes of services. Services are, for the most part, intangible (they can't be seen or touched), inseparable (produced at the same time and place they are consumed), heterogeneous (of variable quality) and perishable.

Service marketers' response to these special characteristics has been to develop a new toolkit for creating value propositions. It contains another set of 3Ps, making 7Ps in total.[19] The additional 3Ps are people, physical evidence and process, as shown in Figure 6.2. As we now explain, the 7Ps provide a useful framework for goods manufacturers too.

Over the next few paragraphs we will look at how customer-perceived value can be enabled by astute management of the marketing mix variables.

Figure 6.2 The marketing mix

Value from products (and services)

Companies may make products, but customers do not buy products. Customers buy solutions to their problems. They buy benefits, or, better said, they buy the expectation of benefits. Nobody ever buys a lawnmower because they want a lawnmower; people want attractive lawns. Products are means to ends. Products that offer improved solutions to problems create more value for customers. A better solution is one in which the balance between benefits and sacrifices of the value equation is enhanced for the customer.

Marketers often distinguish between different levels of the product, sometimes known as a customer value hierarchy.[20] The *core* product is the basic benefit that customers buy. Companies competing for customer demand must be able to meet the core benefit requirements. Let's consider the market for MBA-level education. MBA students typically are buying one or more of three basic benefits: salary enhancement, career development or personal growth. A second level is the *enabling* product. This consists of the physical goods and service that are necessary for the core benefit to be delivered. In the MBA case, this would comprise the buildings, classroom fixtures, faculty and educational technology. A third level, the *augmented* product consists of the factors that position and differentiate one competitor from another. In the MBA illustration this might be teaching method, for example, learning through real-life projects, or an extensive international exchange programme, or a leafy out-of-town location.

Companies offering the same core benefit have to compete to deliver value to customers through the enablers and the augmentations. As Ted Levitt noted,

> Competition is not between what companies produce in their factories, but between what they add to their factory output in the form of packaging, services, advertising, customer advice, financing, delivery arrangements, warehousing, and other things that people value.[21]

Product-based value is experienced by customers when they benefit from product innovation, incremental benefits, product-service bundling and branding. We explore these below.

Product innovation

Most 'new' products are, in fact, modifications of existing products, cost reductions or line extensions. Very few products are 'new-to-the-world' or create new product categories. New products in all of these categories can improve customer value perceptions, but it is the dramatic ground-breaking inventions that create leaps in customer value. History is littered with them – Stephenson's locomotive, Edison's incandescent light bulb, Hargreaves's spinning jenny, Newcomen's steam engine and Robert Noyce's silicon microchip. Friends Reunited, founded in 1999, pioneered social media. It was established to help old school friends find each other online. Facebook may be remembered as the first major social media success story, but it was a me-too follower, established in 2004. Facebook did not create the category. That honour goes to Friends Reunited.

Occasionally, old technologies provide a platform for value-delivering modern-day solutions. Trevor Bayliss invented the wind-up radio after seeing a programme about the spread of AIDS in Africa. The programme highlighted the difficulty that health professionals faced getting safe sex messages to rural and poor areas where there were no power sources for conventional radios. Large-scale manufacturing of the Freeplay® wind up radio began in 1995. The product has created value for all concerned: the manufacturers, investors, resellers, employees, Bayliss and, of course, radio audiences.

Incremental benefits

Companies can generate customer-perceived value by claiming additional benefits for their products. A lawnmower does not just cut grass beautifully, but operates more quietly. A car comes with a five-year unlimited mileage warranty. Hedonic value can be added to already satisfactory functional value. Apple has done this through the excellent design of its MacBook Pro computer, iPhone and iPad products. Sometimes additional benefits are accompanied by repositioning the product in a different segment of the market. Lucozade had originally been a glucose drink (originally named Glucozade) for older people, and was widely associated with illness. Lucozade is now repositioned in the rapidly growing sports drink market, where it has enjoyed considerable success (see Figure 6.3).

Low involvement product categories have low personal significance or relevance to customers. Customers feel very little sense of engagement with any brand and are therefore

Figure 6.3 Repositioning Lucozade as a sports drink

Reproduced with the permission of Lucozade Ribena Suntory Ltd. All rights reserved.

easily switched to competitors. Adding additional benefits helps brand owners to increase the level of customer involvement. There are two main approaches: product modification and product association. Product modification means changing the product in some way so that it ties in more closely to the customer's needs, values and interests. Detergent manufacturers, for example, have reformulated their brands so that they are more environmentally friendly. Product association means linking the brand to some issue or context that is of high importance to customers. PlayStation, for example, associates its soccer simulation with the FIFA world cup.

Product-service bundling

Product-service bundling is the practice of offering customers a package of goods and services at a single price. Tour operators routinely bundle several elements of a vacation together – flights, transfers, accommodation and meal plan, for example. For the customer, bundling can reduce money, transaction and psychic costs. For the company, there are economies in selling and marketing.

Changing the composition of a bundle can have the impact of increasing customer-perceived value. Adding or removing elements from the bundle can both have this effect. Adding elements to the bundle increases the benefits side of the value equation. In a B2C context, for example, supermarket operators can offer a bagging service at checkout at no extra cost to the customer. If the people performing this task are diverted from other tasks, then there may be no additional costs for the operator. Removing elements from a bundle enables the company to establish a new price point, therefore adjusting the value equation for customers. In a B2B context, companies often ask for elements to be removed from a bundle in return for a lower price. For example, a training college with its own IT department may ask the supplier of its IT equipment for a lower price in return for not using the supplier's help desk and IT support facilities. If the price is reduced by $5,000 and the saving to the supplier is $6,000 then both parties win.

Branding

A brand can be defined as follows:

A brand is any name, design, style, words or symbols that distinguish a product from its competitors.

Brands create value for customers in a number of ways, on both sides of the value equation. Brands reduce transaction costs by clearly identifying the product as different from others. Brands can also reduce psychic costs. Over time, customers assign meanings to brands. If you buy a Mercedes vehicle, it may be because you understand that the brand attributes are excellence in engineering, assured quality build and high resale value. A customer who understands what the brand means experiences less risk than the customer who does not understand. Brand knowledge like this is acquired from experience, word-of-mouth, online brand communities or social media and marketer-controlled communication. Brands also offer an implicit assurance of a particular customer experience. When you buy any of the products carrying the Virgin brand it may be because you believe that Virgin's brand values are service excellence, innovation and good value.

Value from service

A service is a performance or act performed for a customer. Service is an important part of many companies' value propositions. In most developed economies, about 70 per cent of gross domestic product is created by services organizations. For these organizations, service is the core product. Some manufacturing firms have also come to recognize that service is their core product. An engineering company that designs and makes computer-controlled lathes knows that its customers are buying expectations that a particular service will be performed: precise replication of an engineered object. For most manufacturers, service is an important part of the enabling and augmented product. For example, carpet manufacturers make floor coverings to international standards. Whilst there is some potential to compete through product innovation, many manufacturers believe the best way to compete is through offering better service to their distributors, and corporate and domestic customers. Typical services include stockholding, design, measurement, cutting to order, delivery and fitting. Some manufacturing firms offer Product-Service Systems (PSSs), integrated bundles of products and services, to their customers. Both GE and Rolls-Royce have developed PSSs for their airline customers. These airlines no longer buy Rolls-Royce jet engines. Rather, they buy a managed service contract wherein they pay the engine manufacturer a fee based on the hours the engine is in service.[22]

Companies wishing to enhance customer-perceived value through service improvement need to understand that their efforts should be focused on the service elements that are important to customers and where current service performance is poor. If the customer's biggest problem is your failure to deliver on time, in full and with no error, it makes little sense to invest in updating the livery of your vehicles and drivers.

In this section we look at a number of service-related methods for enhancing customer-perceived value – improving service quality, service guarantees, service level agreements and service recovery programmes.

Service quality

There are two major perspectives on service quality:

1   Quality is *conformance to specification*. This is consistent with Philip Crosby's view of quality.[23] The business specifies what counts as quality, and measures its performance to that standard. Conformance to specification might mean producing error-free invoices, delivering on time and in full as promised to customers, or acknowledging a customer complaint within 24 hours.

2   Quality is *fitness for purpose*. Joseph M. Juran claimed that quality means creating products that meet customer expectations. It is the customer, not the company, who decides whether quality is right.[24] If you are a farmer, a Land Rover is the right quality vehicle. If you are an executive limousine company, a Mercedes is the right quality vehicle. In a services environment, fitness for purpose might mean offering savings plans that help first-time home buyers, recruiting customer contact staff who are highly empathic and responsive, or customizing service delivery for customers.

These perspectives on quality can happily coexist. Specifications for service performance can be based on customer expectations. If customers determine the standards, there need be no conflict between these two approaches.

Service quality theories

Two service quality theories have dominated management practice as companies try to improve their service performance: the Nordic model and the SERVQUAL model.

The *Nordic* model, originated by Christian Grönroos and developed by others, identifies three components of service quality: technical, functional and reputational (Table 6.4).[25]

Table 6.4 Grönroos model of service quality[26]

Technical	The quality of the outcome of a service performance
Functional	The quality of the performance of a service
Reputational	The quality of the service organization's image

Technical quality can be thought of as the 'what' of service quality. Was the floor vacuumed thoroughly and surfaces dusted meticulously by the office-cleaning contractor? Did the specialist audit firm finish the stock-check within one day? Functional quality can be thought of as the 'how' of service quality. Was the cleaner courteous? Was the stock-check team responsive? Reputational quality is not only an outcome of technical and functional quality, in that reputation derives from performance, but it also produces a halo effect that can influence customer perceptions of quality, for better or worse. If I'm attending an opera at Teatro alla Scala (La Scala) in Milano then it must be good! If I'm receiving service from a state monopoly then it must be bad!

The significance of the Grönroos model is that it stresses the importance of understanding customer expectations and of developing a service delivery system that performs well at meeting customers' technical and functional service quality expectations.

The *SERVQUAL* model, developed by A. 'Parsu' Parasuraman and colleagues in North America, identifies five core components of service quality: reliability, assurance, tangibles, empathy and responsiveness, defined as in Table 6.5.[27] You can remember them through the mnemonic RATER.

The SERVQUAL authors have also developed a measurement and management model to accompany the conceptual model. The measurement model uses a 44-item questionnaire

Table 6.5 SERVQUAL components[28]

Reliability	Ability to perform the promised service dependably and accurately
Assurance	Knowledge and courtesy of employees and their ability to convey trust and confidence
Tangibles	Appearance of physical facilities, equipment, personnel and communication materials
Empathy	Provision of caring, individualized attention to customers
Responsiveness	Willingness to help customers and to provide prompt service

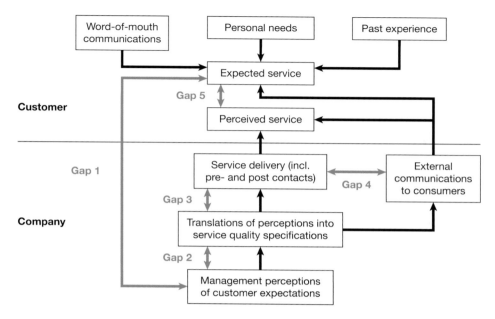

Figure 6.4 The SERVQUAL gaps model

to measure customers' expectations and perceptions of the RATER variables.[29] The relative importance of these variables is also measured. This enables users to compute the relative importance of any gaps between expectation and perceptions. Management can then focus on strategies and tactics to close the important gaps.

The management model, reproduced in Figure 6.4, identifies the reasons for any gaps between customer expectations and perceptions (gap 5). Gap 5 is the product of gaps 1, 2, 3 and 4. If these four gaps, all of which are located below the line that separates the customer from the company, are closed then gap 5 will close. The gaps are as follows:

1   Gap 1 is the gap between what the customer expects and what the company's management think customers expect.

2   Gap 2 occurs when management fails to design service quality specifications based on customer expectations.

3   Gap 3 occurs when the company's service delivery systems – people, processes and technologies – fail to deliver to the specified standard.

4   Gap 4 occurs when the company's communications with customers promise a level of service performance that the service delivery system cannot deliver.

The importance of SERVQUAL is that is offers managers a systematic approach to measuring and managing service quality. It emphasizes the importance of understanding customer expectations, and of developing service quality standards and service delivery systems that meet customer expectations. Among the strategies and tactics that might be employed to close gaps 1–4 are the following:

1   To close gap 1 (between what customers expect and what managers think customers expect): conduct primary research into customers' service quality expectations; learn from front-line customer contact staff; flatten the hierarchical structure; include expectations data in customer records.

2   To close gap 2 (between what managers think customers expect and service quality specifications): commit to the development of service standards wherever possible; assess the feasibility of meeting customer expectations; develop a standards documentation process; automate processes where possible and desirable; outsource activities where you lack the competencies; develop service quality goals.

3   To close gap 3 (between service quality specifications and actual service delivery): invest in people: recruitment, training and retention; invest in technology; redesign workflow; encourage self-organized teams; improve internal communication; write clear job specifications; reward service excellence.

4   To close gap 4 (between actual service delivery and the promises communicated to customers): brief communications teams and advertising agency on customer service expectations; train employees not to over-promise; penalize employees who over-promise; encourage customers to sample the service experience; excel at service recovery; encourage and manage customer complaints.

There is growing evidence that investment in service quality improvements pays off in enhanced customer satisfaction and customer retention, although, like other investments, there does appear to be a point at which diminishing returns set in.[30]

The SERVQUAL model has been subject to much criticism[31] but it is still in widespread use in original and customized forms.[32] One criticism is that customers often do not have clearly formed expectations, and therefore that the expectations–disconfirmation approach is inappropriate. Some of these critics have developed an alternative, perceptions-only, model of service quality that they have dubbed SERVPERF.[33]

Figure 6.5 Scandinavian Airline's understanding of customer expectations

It is worth noting that some experts criticize service quality theory for its bias towards assessing single episodes or customer encounters. They suggest that customers assess the quality of their customer experiences over an extended time period, through repeated interactions with a supplier (pre, during and post-purchase), across multiple channels and they form emotional responses as well as a cognitive appreciation of service delivery.[34] We will cover the concept of customer experience in depth in the next chapter.

Service guarantees

From the customer's perspective, guarantees can be an effective way to reduce risk, and thereby increase customer-perceived value. Service guarantee can be defined as follows:

> A service guarantee is an explicit promise to the customer that a prescribed level of service will be delivered.

Service guarantees can be either specific or general. Specific service guarantees apply to particular parts of the customer experience. For example:

> Friendly service, clean rooms and comfortable surroundings every time. If you're not satisfied we don't expect you to pay. (First Hampton Inns)

General service guarantees apply to the entire customer experience. For example:

> We guarantee to give perfect satisfaction in every way. (L.L.Bean)

CASE STUDY 6.1

ADT MONEY-BACK SERVICE GUARANTEE

ADT Money-Back Service Guarantee

If within six months you are not satisfied,
ADT will give you a full refund of your installation price and any monitoring fees paid. See back for details.

Customer_____ Account #_____

Signature _____
Mike Snyder, President

ADT
Always There.

©2002 ADT Security Services, Inc. • www.adt.com

Although these examples are of guarantees offered to external customers, they can also be designed for internal customers. For example, the housekeeping supplies department at Embassy Suites guarantees that its internal customer, the housekeeping department, will get supplies on the day requested. If not, the department pays $5 to the housekeeper.

Service guarantees can be customized for individual customers or segments. An IT service centre guarantees a 3-hour service to priority-1 customers, and 48-hour service to all others. Should the company fail to honour these guarantees, it 'fines' itself by issuing a credit note to the customers.

Some guarantees, such as the L.L.Bean example cited above, are unconditional. Others are conditional.

Service level agreements

Service level agreement (SLA) can be defined as follows:

> **A service level agreement is a contractual commitment between a service provider and customer that specifies the mutual responsibilities of both parties with respect to the services that will be provided and the standards at which they will be performed.**

SLAs can apply to both internal and external customer relationships. For example, it is not uncommon for utility companies to outsource their customer contact function to a contracted call centre or contact centre service provider. An external SLA is negotiated that carefully defines both parties' expectations of the services to be performed, the service processes to be followed, the service standards to be achieved and the price to be paid. The SLA may well form part of an enforceable legal contract. A number of metrics are used to measure performance of the supplier and compliance with SLA service standards. These may include:

- *Availability.* The percentage of time that the service is available over an agreed time period.
- *Usage.* The number of service users that can be served simultaneously.
- *Reliability.* The percentage of time that the service is withdrawn or fails in the time period.

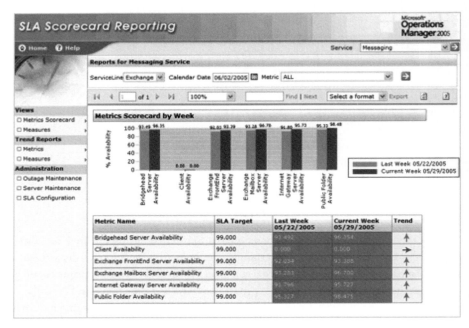

Figure 6.6 Service level agreement scorecard[35]

Used with permission from Microsoft.

- *Responsiveness.* The speed with which a demand for service is fulfilled. This can be measured using turn-around time or cycle-time.

- *User satisfaction.* This can be measured at the time the service is delivered or periodically throughout the agreed service period.

Many companies also have internal SLAs between service departments and their internal customers. An IT services department, for example, may establish a number of different SLAs with different customer groups. For example, it might undertake to process payroll for the human resource department, or to maintain and service desktop devices for a contact centre. Internal SLAs are unlikely to be formalized in a contract.

SLAs create customer-perceived value by reducing uncertainty about the services that will be delivered, their standards and costs. A successful SLA clarifies the boundaries and relative roles of customer and supplier. Each knows the other's responsibility. Service automation technologies discussed in Chapter 10 allow companies to manage service levels.

Service recovery programmes

Service recovery can be defined as follows:

Service recovery includes all the actions taken by a company to resolve a service failure.

Services fail for many different reasons.[36] Sometimes technical service quality fails; other times the failure is in functional service quality. Sometimes the fault lies with the company, sometimes with the customer and sometimes with a business partner. Typically customers are not concerned with who is to blame; they just want the situation resolved.

Research shows that when companies resolve problems quickly and effectively there are positive consequences for customer satisfaction, customer retention and word-of-mouth.[37] It has even been found that customers who have been let down, then well recovered, are more satisfied than customers who have not been let down at all.[38] This can perhaps be explained in terms of the RATER dimensions of service quality. Getting service right first time demonstrates reliability, but recovering well after service failure shows empathy and responsiveness. Reliability can be programmed into a company's service production and delivery processes. Empathy and responsiveness demonstrate the human attributes of concern for others and flexibility. Conversely, customers who have been let down once, only to experience unsatisfactory recovery, can turn into 'terrorists' who actively look for opportunities to spread bad word-of-mouth.[39]

When customers experience service failure, they have the choice of doing nothing or voicing their displeasure. Customers who choose to voice can complain to the service provider, complain to friends and others in their personal network, or complain to a third party such as a consumer affairs organization or industry ombudsman.

Equity theory suggests that customers who complain are seeking justice and fairness. Equity theory explains that customers compare the sacrifices they make to the benefits they experience (as in the value equation) to other customers' sacrifices and benefits. When customers pay the same price but experience an unsatisfactory level of service compared to other customers, they feel a sense of inequity or unfairness. When they complain, they want the company to fix the imbalance. They want justice.

Research suggests that there are different types of justice. Table 6.6 highlights the three forms of justice that complainants seek: distributive justice, procedural justice and interactional justice.[40] Distributive justice is achieved if the customer gets the material outcome they want. Customers might be satisfied with an apology, or a credit note against future purchases. Alternatively, a customer may want the service to be re-performed. If distributive justice is concerned with *what* is received, procedural justice is concerned with the customers' evaluation of the *processes and systems* that they encounter during the service recovery process. Customers generally do not want to complete forms, provide difficult-to-find proofs of purchase, or write formal letters confirming their issue. These requirements do not suggest that a company is organized and willing to resolve the problem quickly. Interactional justice is achieved if the customer judges that service recovery-related interactions with the provider's *people* have been satisfactory. They want employees to be responsive and empathic.

Table 6.6 What customers want from service recovery

Distributive justice	What the firm offers by way of recovery and whether this offsets the costs incurred by the customer from service failure.
	Distributive outcomes include compensation, re-performance, apologies.
Procedural justice	The customer's perception of the process they went through to get satisfaction following service failure.
	Some service recovery processes deliver prompt recovery, others delayed; some require complaints to be justified and proofs provided.
Interactional justice	The customer's perception of the performance of the people they encounter during the service recovery process.
	Customers generally expect the people they encounter to show empathy, politeness, courtesy, expertise and effort.

Value from processes

In the previous section we have described some business processes that help create customer-perceived value – the service quality management process and the service recovery process. Elsewhere in the book we touch on additional processes that impact on customers: the selling process, the campaign management process, the database development process and the innovation process, for example.

We define a business process as:

a set of activities performed by people and/or technology in order to achieve a desired outcome.

Business processes are how companies get things done. Companies are comprised of very large processes. IBM, for example, identified 18 critical processes, Xerox 14 and Dow Chemical 9.[41] These big processes in turn are composed of smaller processes. For example, the manufacturing process takes a number of inputs – materials, technology, labour – and converts them into products. This big process is composed of several smaller processes such as machining, assembly and packing processes. Companies have thousands of processes. But processes are more than simply workflow; they are also resources that can be used to compete more effectively, to create more value for both customers and company.[42] Xerox's 14 key business processes appear in Table 6.7. Many of these macro-processes have an impact upon customer experience or value perceptions, including the customer engagement, market management, product maintenance, and product design and engineering processes.

Process innovation can enhance customer-experienced value significantly. For example, First Direct started out as a telephone bank with no branch network. Customer management was entirely IT-enabled, with customer service being delivered from a number of call centres. The bank's customer satisfaction ratings have been consistently higher than competitors who have branch operations. Customer experience at First Direct was under better control and costs were lower. EasyJet speeded up customer service by improving plane turnaround times from 50 minutes to 33, through improved teamwork.

In this section, we examine one additional process that impacts on the external customer's perception of value: the complaints management process.

Table 6.7 Xerox's 14 key business processes

1.	Customer engagement
2.	Inventory management and logistics
3.	Product design and engineering
4.	Product maintenance
5.	Technology management
6.	Production and operations management
7.	Market management
8.	Supplier management
9.	Information management
10.	Business management
11.	Human resource management
12.	Leased and capital asset management
13.	Legal
14.	Financial management

The complaints management process

Customers complain when they experience one of two conditions: their expectations are underperformed to a degree that falls outside their zone of tolerance; or they sense they have been treated unfairly. Equity theory, described above, explains the customer's response to being treated unfairly. Customers also have a zone of tolerance for service and product performance. The range of tolerable performance will depend upon the importance of the product, or the particular product attribute that is giving cause for complaint. Tolerances will be stricter for more important products and attributes. For unimportant products and attributes, customers tend to be less demanding. Where customer experience falls outside the zone of tolerance, there is cause for complaint.

No one likes receiving complaints, but they are unavoidable. Even the best companies sometimes fail customers and give cause for complaint. Therefore, it makes sense to implement a policy and process to receive, handle and resolve customer complaints. Customers who complain are giving the firm a chance to win them back and retain their future value. Not only that but complaints provide information that can help companies identify, and correct, root causes of problems. Furthermore, the presence of a documented complaints-handling process has been shown to be strongly associated with excellent customer retention.[43] Worryingly, customers who don't complain may already have taken their business elsewhere.

CASE STUDY 6.2

PROCESS INNOVATION AT SECOM

SECOM is the largest supplier of security services in Japan. Historically service was very labour intensive, as security guards were located to client sites. SECOM automated the detection of security breaches, by combining crime detection sensors and telecommunications technology, and moving its guards to a central location from where they were despatched to deal with incidents. The business experienced high growth as a result. Subsequently, new technologies were added – remote sensing, image enhancement, geographical information systems and automated payment systems for clients.

A successful complaints-handling process enables companies to capture customer complaints before customers start spreading negative word-of-mouth or take their business elsewhere. Research suggests that negative word-of-mouth can be very influential.[44] Up to two-thirds of customers who are dissatisfied do not complain to the organization.[45] They may, however, complain to their social networks. Unhappy customers are likely to tell twice as many people about their experience than customers with a positive experience.[46]

Many customers who are unhappy don't complain. Why? There are a number of possible reasons:

- They feel the company doesn't care. Perhaps the company or the industry has a reputation for treating customers poorly.
- It takes too much time and effort.
- They fear retribution. Many people are reluctant to complain about the police, for example.
- They don't know how to complain.

Companies can address all of these issues by making their customers aware of their complaints policy and processes. A complaints management process that is simple and easy to access should facilitate the capture of complaints. Some companies use dedicated free-phones and web forms to encourage complaints. Some reward complainants. Stew Leonard's, the Connecticut retailer, rewards in-store complainants with an ice cream.

Complaints enter companies at many different customer touchpoints – accounts receivable, order processing, sales engineering, logistics, customer contact centre – and so on. A well-designed complaints-handling process will capture complaints from various touchpoints, then aggregate and analyze them to identify root causes. Ultimately this should enable the company to achieve a higher level of first-time reliability, reduce the amount of rework, and lift levels of customer satisfaction and retention. An international standard – ISO 10002 – has been released to help companies identify and implement best practices in complaints policy and process. Software is available to help companies improve their complaints-handling expertise.[47]

Table 6.8 lists some ideas for improving complaints management processes.

Table 6.8 How to improve complaints management processes

1	Make the complaints-handling policy and processes visible and accessible to customers and employees
2	Design your complaints-handling policy and processes to ISO 10002 standards
3	Enable web-based complaints capture
4	Empower employees to resolve complaints
5	Install a dedicated free-phone line to receive complaints
6	Link complaints to customer satisfaction and retention goals
7	Appoint a complaints management executive
8	Teach customers how to complain; publish your process
9	Ensure all employees understand the complaints management process
10	Reward customers who complain
11	Collect complaints data and analyze root causes
12	Use technology to support complaints-handling and deliver useful management reports.

Value from people

Many companies claim that people are their key differentiators, and a major source of customer value. This is especially so in professional services such as counselling, consulting and coaching where people *are* the product. The UK-based home improvement retailer, B&Q, has also added value to the shopping experience by recruiting former building tradesmen such as carpenters, electricians and plumbers to help customers diagnose their problems and choose the right products in-store.

One of the more important jobs in CRM is the customer contact role. The customer contact role is a boundary-spanning role. That is, the role occupant sits in the space between an organization and its external customers. They are paid by the company, but work closely with customers. Boundary spanners have two fundamental and interdependent roles: information management and relationship management. Boundary spanners are accountable for collecting information about customers. What are the customer's requirements, expectations and preferences? What are the customer's future plans? Who is involved in the customer's buying decisions? The boundary spanner may have responsibility for maintaining the currency of the customer data record. This information enables the role occupant to perform the second role, managing the customer relationship. This might involve winning, growing and maintaining the customer's business, handling customer queries and complaints, representing the customer's interests to their employer, and ensuring the customer's satisfaction.

There is a trend towards key account management (KAM) that is driven by a number of trends: global customers, consolidated purchasing, vendor reduction programmes and customers who want better service and closer relationships with their suppliers. The role of key account manager, national account manager or global account manager is extremely important. Occupants needs an advanced, and rare, skill set including selling skills, negotiating skills, communication skills, analytical skills, problem-solving skills, customer knowledge, market knowledge, competitor knowledge, customer orientation, as well as a detailed understanding of what their own company can deliver. We explore KAM in more detail in Chapter 13.

Value from physical evidence

Some companies enable customers to experience value by their management of physical evidence. This is especially important for service companies with intangible-dominant outputs. In the absence of physical evidence, customers may find it very hard to determine whether they are experiencing value or not. Physical evidence can be defined as follows:

Physical evidence consists of the tangible facilities, equipment and materials that companies use to communicate value to customers.

Physical evidence includes a company's premises, and their internal and external environments, print materials, websites, corporate uniforms and vehicle livery.

Banks traditionally have occupied buildings with columns, portico, steps and large, heavy doors. This is designed to communicate conservative values, security and probity. McDonald's uses primary colours, bright lights and the ubiquitous golden arches in the form of the letter M. Hospitals convey impressions of hygiene and care through white uniforms, immaculately clean premises and well-maintained gardens. You only need to reflect on the traditional clothing, livery and appearance of funeral services to understand the significance of physical evidence.

Online presence is also a form of physical evidence. Remotely located customers who don't receive visits from sales reps might only transact through a company's online channel that consequently can become very influential in their perception of value. Many companies have developed online channels for their customers and partners. Managers can push information out to users, on a segment or individual basis. Users can transact, communicate and enquire online in a secure environment.

In addition to company-owned online channels, many customers interact through portals that we define as:

A web portal is a website that serves as a gateway to a range of subject-related resources.

There are two types of portal: public and enterprise. A public portal is a website or service that gives users access to a broad range of resources and services, such as email, search engines, directories and online shopping malls. Search engines such as Google, Yahoo! and MSN have transformed into public portals. Enterprise portals are organization-specific web-based gateways to enterprise applications, databases and systems. Enterprise portal users generally obtain access through a secure sign-on procedure and then have access to information relevant to their own role, for example as customer, or partner. Enterprise portals are sometimes specifically developed for CRM purposes. For example, a manufacturer may establish a portal so that business partners such as resellers, distributors and wholesalers can update their own details, access product information, spec sheets, price lists, relevant customer records, download collateral materials, manage cooperative advertising arrangements, place orders, track order progress, pay, submit a service request and so on.

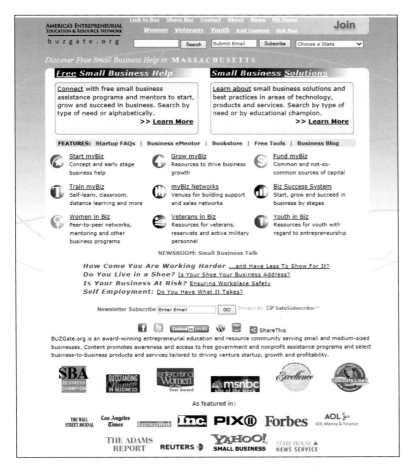

Figure 6.7 Information availability online at www.buzgate.org[48]

Some public portals appeal to niche user groups. There are niche portals for special interest groups such as gardeners (www.garden.com), cricket fans (www.cricinfo.com), investors (www.fool.com) and chief executives (www.ceoexpress.com).

Public portals enable customer-experienced value by bringing together related content from different sources, and providing convenient access for users. For example, the website www.buzgate.org (see Figure 6.7) is a portal that provides access to a comprehensive array of online public and private sector resources for small and medium-sized businesses. Portals like these function in much the same way as a high-street retailer, in that they act as points of display and sale for many different products.

Value from customer communication

Companies are now in a position to enable customer-experienced value from communication practices that were impossible only ten years ago.

A significant change is that companies are now able to facilitate multilateral communication: company-to-customer, customer-to-company and even customer-to-customer.

Traditionally customer communication has been one way – from companies to customers. The conventional tools for company-to-customer communication are unilateral: advertising, sales promotion, publicity, public relations and personal selling. With the exception of selling, these communication channels are non-interactive. Customer–company communication is enabled through email, web-forms, instant messaging, phone, fax, web collaboration, as well as old-fashioned correspondence. Companies can also facilitate customer-to customer (peer-to-peer) communication by web-logs (better known as blogs), chat-rooms, newsgroups, online communities and, increasingly, by using social media such as Facebook and Twitter. Collectively, these are known as customer-generated media (CGM). Southwest Airline, for example, has established a blog intended to 'build a personal relationship between our Team and you, and we need your participation' (see Figure 6.8), and many universities, from the Agricultural University of Athens to the University of Zimbabwe, have Facebook pages.

Social media are becoming more important elements of the communications mix for many companies. They are used for marketing, advertising, selling and service purposes. Twitter is increasingly a platform for service improvement and recovery. Airlines have adopted Twitter to respond quickly, and sometimes in real time, to customer complaints. JetBlue, an American carrier, initially used Twitter to get a better understanding of customer experience of its service, then as an outbound communication channel and most recently as a vehicle for service improvement. Many variables outside the control of the carrier impact on customer experience: air traffic control delays, severe weather, problems with connecting flights, staff shortages, mechanical failure and so on. The airline needs to be able to resolve

Figure 6.8 Southwest Airline's blog[49]

problems quickly in order to create a good customer experience. When the company sees a tweet from a disgruntled passenger, made in the moment the customer faces the problem, JetBlue can respond in real time, perhaps thereby stopping the spread of the message into the Twittersphere. RyanAir is another carrier that has invited its customers to contact it through Twitter with ideas for improving customer service.[50]

As companies use social media for customer management purposes, they will need to invest in people, processes and technology in order to respond to potentially thousands of messages in real time.

Three processes are responsible for the enhanced power of communication to create value for customers: disintermediation, personalization and interactivity.

Disintermediation

Disintermediation refers to the removal of intermediaries such as broadcast and print media from the company's communication channels with customers. Today, new technologies have led to the emergence of many direct-to-customer (DTC) communication tools including email, direct mail, and SMS and MMS messaging to cell phones. Companies are now able to get their message direct to customers. Equally, customers can get their messages direct to companies, and to other customers in the ways described above.

Personalization

High-quality customer-related data, CRM technologies and DTC channels in combination enable companies to tailor offers and communications to individual customers. This is what Don Peppers and Martha Rogers have called one-to-one marketing.[51] Data on customers' buying history and propensities-to-buy can be used to develop offers that meet with a much higher response rate and conversion rate than conventional mailings. The content, timing and delivery channels for communications can be based on customer preferences.

CRM technologies allow customers to personalize their own corporate web pages. Customers of www.lastminute.com can personalize their home page using technology that stores their preferences. This enables the company to refine its messaging. It claims to achieve click-through rates that are 30 per cent higher than non-targeted messaging.[52] You can also create you own daily newspaper (at www.ft.com) based on your personal interests and preferences. This can then be used as your homepage.

CRM technologies used in call and contact centres allow for personalized interactions between customers and customer service agents. For example, scripts can be tailored to enable agents unfamiliar with a product or customer segment to perform competently in telephone interactions.

Interactivity

Interactive technologies have been around since the advent of the telephone. However, the Internet has revolutionized the scope for interactivity through three major technologies: email, instant messaging and the World Wide Web (WWW). Email enables customers and company to interact effectively though not necessarily in real time. For example, customers can email for information that is unavailable on the Frequently Asked Questions (FAQ) pages of corporate websites. Email gives customers access to a specific named person or work group such as help@ or info@. Contact with a name gives customers the sense that there is an

PERSONALIZED COMMUNICATIONS AT WESTPAC[53]

Westpac is one of the big four banks operating in Australia. The bank's 'Know Me' programme uses customer data to improve interactions on a one-to-one basis through the bank's online and offline customer touchpoints. Two Westpac customer data sources support 'Know Me'. First, the bank has experienced massive growth in data available about customers, including contributions to social media, online click-stream information and customer notes. Second, the bank has massive data from customer interactions with online and mobile banking take-up, reaching 60 million online interactions with customers per month.

Westpac uses this information to provide a range of personalized communications to customers including reminders of when credit card payments are due, notifications around topping up superannuation funds before the end of the financial year, offering travel insurance when someone is transacting overseas and congratulating customers on paying off a home loan.

The data also support the bank's 'next best offer' programme. This integrates all the data sources listed above to deliver real-time communication and offers that are based on what the customer wants to buy, rather than what the bank wants to sell. The bank calls this 'service led communication'. The next best offer programme is run across the branch network branches, call centres, the online portal, social media and Westpac's online banking facilities. In the nine months since the programme's launch, Westpac chalked up 812,000 next best offer conversations with customers in branches, leading to 37 per cent new product uptake. In the call centre, 490,000 customers were contacted, achieving 60 per cent new product uptake. Targeted online communications, which appeared in 80 per cent of customer online banking profiles, also generated $7.8 million in incremental revenue. In total, next best offers delivered $22 million in annualized revenue, double the target set at the start of the programme.

individual who is taking care of them. Instant messaging enables communications to take place in real time, which is not always possible in email.

The WWW allows computer users globally to communicate with each other. A company can upload a website or create a Facebook page anticipating huge reach. Websites come in a variety of forms. Some are simply electronic brochures. Others enable transactions to be made. Another group of sites are highly interactive. Some excellent websites offer an experience similar to human dialogue. Configuration engines allow the most appropriate products to be offered based on an analysis of the customer's specific needs, problem resolution logic allows customers to find the best solution to a problem and web-chat windows allow human dialogue over the Web if all else fails.

Value from channels

The traditional task of distribution is to provide time and place utilities to customers. This means getting products and services to customers when and where they want. Consumer goods companies have usually constructed channels using intermediaries such as wholesalers and retailers. B2B companies usually sell direct or employ industrial distributors. The location of service providers may be critical or irrelevant to the creation of value for customers. Customers want their grocery retailers to be conveniently located, but don't care where their Internet service provider is located.

An emerging task for intermediaries in the B2B environment is value augmentation. Channel partners in technology industries add services and complementary products that are not available from the technology manufacturer. The purchase of an enterprise resource planning (ERP) system, for example, may require implementation services, technical services, business process re-engineering, change management, customization of software and specialized hardware such as radio frequency (RF) handheld units in the warehouse. Channel partners not only distribute the ERP product, they also provide or coordinate others to provide these additional products and services.

Internet-enabled disintermediation has allowed companies to replace or supplement their traditional bricks-and-mortar channels. Many companies have elected to develop transactional websites so that they can sell direct. Others have developed brochure-ware sites that direct interested prospects to traditional channel members. One major benefit attached to this latter option is that it reduces the level of channel conflict that can be extremely high if an intermediary believes that a supplier is attempting to sell direct to the intermediaries' customers. Additional routes to market include:

- social media platforms such as Facebook
- search engines such as Google
- public or enterprise portals such as www.eMall.sg
- virtual resellers such as Amazon.[54]

Customers may find that it is too costly and inefficient to deal with a large number of disintermediated suppliers. This has created opportunities for reintermediation. Reintermediation adds an electronic intermediary to the distribution channel. These intermediaries act as electronic store-fronts. Examples include:

- www.comparethemarket.com – for household insurance products
- www.lastminute.com – for holidays, flights, accommodation, car hire and gifts
- www.laterooms.com – for discounted hotel rooms
- www.moneyworld.com – for mortgages, credit cards, bank loans, insurances and pensions.

Until recently, businesses thought of the online world in terms of electronic routes-to-market, with participation being optional, depending on company strategy.[55] This now seems unrealistic. Every organization, of any size, needs an online presence in some form. Customers expect this.

SUMMARY

This chapter has stressed the importance of customer-experienced value. One of the major issues for strategic CRM is to enable customers to experience value. Value can be thought of as the relationship between the benefits experienced from a product or service and the sacrifices made to enjoy those benefits. Value is therefore enhanced when sacrifices are reduced or benefits increased. Three major types of sacrifice have been identified – money, transaction and psychic costs. Companies can offer improved value to customers by creating and delivering better solutions to customers' problems.

There are three explanations of when customers experience value. These are known as the value-in-exchange, value-in-use and value-in-experience explanations. Our position is that customers can experience value throughout the customer lifecycle, not only from use of the product or service but also from any interactions with the marketing, selling and service outputs of the firm. A number of multidimensional models of customer-perceived value have been proposed, the dominant ones being developed by Sheth *et al.*, and Holbrook. We suggest that companies cannot create value; they can only create value propositions. Researchers have identified three major types of value proposition: low price, product innovation and customized solutions. Marketers are generally responsible for designing value propositions. Value propositions are constructed by mixing together a number of variables that will appeal to customers. These variables are known as the marketing mix. For goods manufacturers they comprise the 4Ps: product, price, promotion and place. For service industries, 7Ps have been identified; the 4Ps are supplemented by process, physical evidence and people. In the B2B environment, value propositions have long been customized. Customization is now emerging as a powerful force in the B2C environment too. Any of the 7Ps can be customized.

Management can create opportunities for customers to experience value by their management of the 7Ps. For example, product innovation, branding and product-service bundling are ways to create additional value. Similarly, service quality improvement programmes, service guarantees, service level agreements and service recovery programmes may be seen as value adding.

The Internet, customer-related databases and CRM technologies are allowing companies to tailor their customer communication strategies at segment or, often, unique customer level. Messages can be communicated directly to customers, side-stepping the media long used for broadcast advertising. They can also be personalized not only in form of address but also in content and timing. Unlike traditional media, the newer channels, including the Internet, are interactive. Companies are increasingly using social media for customer management purposes.

NOTES AND REFERENCES

1 Zeithaml, V.A. (1988). Consumer perceptions of price, quality and value: a means–end model and synthesis of evidence. *Journal of Marketing*, 52 (July), 2–22.

2 Williamson, O. (1981). The economics of organization: the transaction cost approach. *American Journal of Sociology*, 87(3), 548–77; Williamson, O. (1985). *The economic institutions of capitalism*. New York: Free Press. Williamson, O. and Ghani, T. (2012). Transaction cost economics and its uses in marketing. *Journal of the Academy of Marketing Science*, 40, 74–85.

3 Argyriou, E. and Melewar, T.C. (2011). Consumer attitudes revisited: a review of attitude theory in marketing research. *International Journal of Management Reviews*, 13(4), 431–51.

4 This assertion is based on the widely cited work from Tversky and Kahneman under 'Prospect Theory': this is first discussed in their article: Kahneman, D. and Tversky, A. (1979). Prospect theory: an analysis of decision under risk. *Econometrica: Journal of the Econometric Society*, 47(2), 263–91. There are numerous further publications from the authors. Tversky, A. and Kahneman, D. (1992). Advances in prospect theory: cumulative representation of uncertainty. *Journal of Risk and Uncertainty*, 5(4), 297–323.

5 Loss aversion is one of many major contributions of Nobel prize-winning psychologists Kahneman and Tversky. Their work is instrumental in understanding choice and decision making and underpins much of what is now known as Behavioural Economics. For an excellent overview of their work, we recommend a bestselling textbook: Kahneman, D. (2012). *Thinking, fast and slow*. London: Penguin.

6 Gassenheimer, J.B., Houston, F.S. and Davis, J.C. (1998). The role of economic value, social value, and perceptions of fairness in inter-organizational relationship retention decisions. *Journal of the Academy of Marketing Science*, 26 (Fall), 322–37.

7 Smith, Adam (1776). *An inquiry into the nature and causes of the wealth of nations*. New York: Bantam Classics, republished 2009.

8 Doyle, P. (1989). Building successful brands: the strategic objectives. *Journal of Marketing Management*, 5(1), 77–95.

9 Chandler, J.D. and Vargo, S.L. (2011). Contextualization and value-in-context: how context frames exchange. *Marketing Theory*, 11(1), 35–49.

10 Zeithaml, V.A. (1988). Consumer perceptions of price, quality and value: a means–end model and synthesis of evidence. *Journal of Marketing*, 52 (July), 2–22.

11 Lee, E.J. and Overby, J.W. (2004). Creating value for online shoppers: implications for satisfaction and loyalty. *Journal of Customer Satisfaction, Dissatisfaction and Complaining Behavior*, 17, 54–67.

12 Sheth, J.N., Newman, B.I. and Gross, B.L. (1991). *Consumption values and market choices: theory and applications*. Cincinnati, OH: South-Western Publishing.

13 Holbrook, Morris (1996). *Consumer value: a framework for analysis and research*. London: Routledge.

14 Treacey, M. and Wiersema, F. (1995). *The discipline of market leaders*. London: Harper Collins.

15 Figure 6.1 is based on Piller, F.T., Moeslein, K. and Stotko, C.M. (2004). Does mass customization pay? An economic approach to evaluate customer integration. *Production Planning and Control*, 15(4), 435–44.

16 Piller, F.T. and Müller, M. (2004) A new marketing approach to mass customisation. *International Journal of Computer Integrated Manufacturing*, 17(7), 583–93.

17 http://www.wired.com/2013/08/qq_netflix-algorithm/ (Accessed 10 May 2014).

18 McCarthy, E.J. (1996). *Basic marketing*, 12th edn. Homewood, IL: R.D. Irwin.

19 Booms, B.H. and Bitner, M-J. (1981). Marketing strategies and organizational structures for service firms. In J. Donnelly and W.R. George (eds). *Marketing of services*. Chicago, IL: American Marketing Association, pp. 47–51.

20 See, for example, Kotler, P. (2000). *Marketing management: the millennium edition*. Upper Saddle River, NJ: Prentice Hall; and Levitt, T. (1980). Marketing success – through differentiation of anything. *Harvard Business Review*, January–February, 83–91.

21 Levitt, T. (1969). *The marketing mode*. New York: McGraw Hill, p. 2.

22 Macdonald, E., Martinez, V. and Wilson, H. (2009). Towards the assessment of the value-in-use of product-service systems: a review. In Performance Management Association Conference, Dunedin, New Zealand. Baines, T.S., Lightfoot, H.W., Evans, S., Neely, A., Greenough, R., Peppard, J., *et al.* (2007). State-of-the-art in product-service systems. *Proceedings of the Institution of Mechanical Engineers – Part B – Engineering Manufacture (Professional Engineering Publishing)*, 221(10), 1543–52.

23 Crosby, P.B. (1979). *Quality is free*. New York: McGraw Hill.

24 Juran, J.M. (1964). *Managerial breakthrough*. New York: McGraw Hill.

25 Grönroos, C. (1984). A service quality model and its marketing implications. *European Journal of Marketing*, 18, 36–44.

26 Grönroos, C. (1984). *Strategic management & marketing in the service sector*. Bromley: Chartwell-Bratt.

27 Parasuraman, A., Zeithaml, V.A. and Berry, L.L. (1985). A conceptual model of service quality and its implications for future research. *Journal of Marketing*, 49 (Fall), 41–50; Parasuraman, A., Zeithaml, V.A. and Berry, L.L. (1988). SERVQUAL: a multiple-item scale for measuring consumers' perceptions of service quality. *Journal of Retailing*, 64(1), 22–37; Parasuraman, A., Zeithaml, V.A. and Berry, L.L. (1991). Refinement and reassessment of the SERVQUAL scale. *Journal of Retailing*, 64, 12–40. Parasuraman, A., Zeithaml, V.A. and Berry, L.L. (1994). Reassessment of expectations as a comparison standard in measuring service quality: implications for future research. *Journal of Marketing*, 58(1), 111–32.

28 Parasuraman, A., Zeithaml, V.A. and Berry, L.L. (1988). SERVQUAL: a multi-item scale for measuring consumer perceptions of service quality. *Journal of Retailing*, 64(1), 22–37.

29 Parasuraman, A., Zeithaml, V.A. and Berry, L.L. (1988). SERVQUAL: a multiple-item scale for measuring consumers' perceptions of service quality. *Journal of Retailing*, 64(1), 22–37; Parasuraman, A., Zeithaml, V.A. and Berry, L.L. (1991). Refinement and reassessment of the SERVQUAL scale. *Journal of Retailing*, 64, 12–40.

30 Buttle, F. (1996). SERVQUAL: review, critique and research agenda. *European Journal of Marketing*, 30(1), 8–32. Rust, R.T. (1995). Return on quality (ROQ): making service quality financially accountable. *Journal of Marketing*, 59(2),58–71.

31 Buttle, F. (1996). SERVQUAL: review, critique, research agenda. *European Journal of Marketing*, 30(1), 8–32.

32 Buttle, F. (1996). SERVQUAL: review, critique and research agenda. *European Journal of Marketing*, 30(1), 8–32; Robinson, S. (1999). Measuring service quality: current thinking and future requirements. *Marketing Intelligence & Planning*, 17(1), 21–32.

33 Cronin, J.J. and Taylor, S.A. (1992). Measuring service quality: a re-examination and extension. *Journal of Marketing*, 56 (July), 55–68; Cronin, J.J and Taylor, S.A. (1994). SERVPERF versus SERVQUAL: reconciling performance-based and perceptions-minus expectations measurement of service quality. *Journal of Marketing*, 58 (January), 125–31.

34 Customer experience is a growing field in service marketing. One of the authors has been involved in an attempt to measure IT analogous to SERVQUAL but for the context of experience: Klaus, P. and Maklan, S. (2012). EXQ: a multi-item scale for assessing service experience. *Journal of Service Management*, 23(1), 5–33. The concept has been explored empirically by: Lemke, F., Clark, M. and Wilson, H. (2011). Customer experience quality: an exploration in business and consumer contexts using repertory grid technique. *Journal of the Academy of Marketing Science*, 39(6), 846–69.

35 http://technet.microsoft.com/en-us/library/Aa996021.67ad4a0d-8784–4988-be36–70b3a8a3dce2 (en-us,TechNet.10).gif (Accessed 21 January 2008).

36   Keaveney, S.M. (1995). Customer switching behaviour in service industries: an exploratory study. *Journal of Marketing*, 59 (April), 71–82.

37   Tax, S.W., Brown, S.W. and Chandrashekaran, M. (1998). Customer evaluations of service complaint experiences: implications for relationship marketing. *Journal of Marketing*, 62 (April), 60–76.

38   Hart, C.W., Heskett, J.L. and Sasser, Jr, W.E. (1990). The profitable art of service recovery. *Harvard Business Review*, 68 (July–August), 148–56.

39   Tax, S.S. and Brown, S.W. (1998). Recovering and learning from service failure. *Sloan Management Review*, Fall, 75–88.

40   Sparks, B. and McColl-Kennedy, J.R. (2001). Justice strategy options for increased customer satisfaction in a service recovery setting. *Journal of Business Research*, 54, 209–18.

41   Davenport, T.H. (1993). *Process innovation: reengineering work through information technology.* Boston, MA: Harvard Business School Press.

42   Process engineering is a complex topic that is beyond the scope of this book. Interested readers can find out more in Hammer, M. and Champy, J. (1993). *Re-engineering the corporation.* New York: Harper Business; Davenport, T.H. (1993). *Process innovation: reengineering work through information technology.* Boston, MA: Harvard Business School Press; Keen, P.G.W. (1997). *The process edge: creating value where it counts.* Boston, MA: Harvard Business School Press.

43   Buttle, F. and Ang, L. (2006). Customer retention management processes: a quantitative study. *European Journal of Marketing*, 40(1/2), 83–99.

44   Buttle, F.A. (1998). Word-of-mouth: understanding and managing referral marketing. *Journal of Strategic Marketing*, 6, 241–54.

45   Richins, M. (1983). Negative word-of-mouth by dissatisfied customers: a pilot study. *Journal of Marketing*, 68, 105–11.

46   TARP (1995). American Express – SOCAP study of complaint handling in Australia. Society of Consumer Affairs Professionals.

47   http://www.listeningpost.com.au/Services/LPReviewcheckyour10002conformance/tabid/57/Default.aspx (Accessed 11 October 2007).

48   www.buzzgate.org (Accessed 6 March 2014).

49   http://www.blogsouthwest.com/ (Accessed 6 March 2014).

50   http://www.irishtimes.com/news/consumer/o-leary-makes-youtube-pledge-to-significantly-improve-service-1.1640935 (Accessed 27 December 2013).

51   Peppers, D. and Rogers, M. (1993). *The one-to-one future.* London: Piatkus; Peppers, D. and Rogers, M. (1997). *Enterprise one-to-one.* London: Piatkus; Peppers, D., Rogers, M. and Dorf, B. (1999). *The one-to-one fieldbook.* Oxford: Capstone; Peppers, D. and Rogers, M. (2000). *The one-to-one manager.* Oxford: Capstone.

52   Lastminute.com. (2001). Annual report.

53   http://www.cmo.com.au/article/538956/customer-led_big_data_programs_deliver_millions_westpac_bottom_line/ (Accessed 4 February 2014).

54   Sarkar, M., Butler, B. and Steinfeld, C. (1996). Exploiting the virtual value chain. *Journal of Computer Mediated Communication*, 1(3).

55   Kumar, N. (1999). Internet distribution strategies: dilemmas for the incumbent. *Financial Times*, Special issue on mastering information management, no. 7. www.ftmastering.com.

CHAPTER 7

MANAGING CUSTOMER EXPERIENCE

CHAPTER OBJECTIVES

By the end of this chapter you will be aware of:

- A definition of customer experience.
- The emergence and importance of the experience economy.
- The differences between goods, services and experiences.
- Three key concepts in customer experience management – touchpoint, moment of truth and engagement.
- A number of methods for better understanding customer experience.
- The similarities and differences between customer experience management and CRM.
- How customer experience is changed by CRM strategy and technology, sometimes for the better and sometimes for the worse.
- Four features of CRM applications that have an impact on customer experience.

INTRODUCTION

This is the final of three chapters on strategic CRM. Strategic CRM is the core customer-centric business strategy that aims at winning and keeping profitable customers. This chapter investigates customer experience. There is a growing recognition that customer experience throughout the lifecycle and at every touchpoint must meet customer expectations. Indeed, in the last chapter we introduced the idea of value-in-experience that explicitly acknowledges that customers can experience value throughout the customer journey. If customers' expectations of their experiences are underperformed they may defect to competitors that provide a better experience. Implementation of CRM technology may have major consequences for customer experience. In this chapter you will find out more about customer experience and how CRM can change it – often for the better, but sometimes for the worse.

WHAT IS CUSTOMER EXPERIENCE?

These days, companies are becoming more interested in managing and improving customer experience. McDonald's, for example, is 'committed to continuously improving our operations and enhancing our customers' experience'.

Customer experience has been described as 'the next competitive battleground'.[1]

In general terms, an experience is an intrapersonal response to, or interpretation of, an external stimulus. But, what about *customer* experience? If you were to ask your customers, 'What is it like doing business with us?' their answers would be descriptions of their customer experience (CX). More formally customer experience can be defined as follows:

Customer experience is the cognitive and affective outcome of the customer's exposure to, or interaction with, a company's people, processes, technologies, products, services and other outputs.

Let's pick apart this definition. When customers do business with a company, they not only buy products but they also experience or interact with other types of company output. They might be exposed to your company's TV commercials, they might interact with a customer service agent in a call centre or they might conduct product research at your company's sales portal. All these contribute to customer experience.

Fred Lemke and co-authors share our perspective on CX, defining it as follows: CX is 'the customer's subjective response to the holistic direct and indirect encounter with the firm, including but not necessarily limited to the communication encounter, the service encounter and the consumption encounter'.[2]

Customer experience consists of both cognitive impressions (beliefs, thoughts) and affective impressions (feelings, attitudes) about a range of issues including value and quality, which in turn influence the customer's future buying and word-of-mouth intentions. As noted by Marian Petre and her colleagues: 'It is the "total customer experience" (TCE) that influences customers' perceptions of value and service quality, and which consequently affects customer loyalty.'[3] One study in the hospitality industry, for example, found that 75 per cent of restaurant customers tell others about poor service experiences, but only 38 per cent tell others about excellent experience. Improving customer experience may therefore produce two benefits for companies. It can reduce negative word-of-mouth (WOM); it can also increase positive WOM.

Joseph Pine and James Gilmore[4] suggested that economies shift through four stages of economic development: extraction of commodities, manufacture of goods, delivery of services and staging of experiences, as in Figure 7.1. Customers have always had experiences, but Pine and Gilmore recognized a new form of value-adding economic activity that had previously been hidden or embedded in the service economy, and they named this the experience economy. Pine and Gilmore's work is important because they were the first to clearly articulate the idea that experience has real value to customers. They suggested that differences

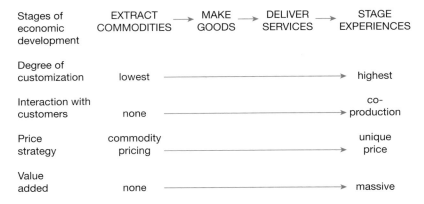

Figure 7.1 Evolution towards the experience economy

between competitors' products and service performance evaporate quickly and that customers end up making choices based on the totality of their experiences of searching, acquiring and using an offering. In the terms that we are using in this book, customer experience occurs throughout the customer lifecycle and as customers interact with all of the marketing, sales and service outputs of the firm.

Many CRM technology firms and consultancies now recognize that CX is significantly influenced by customer interactions with companies' people (e.g. sales reps), processes (e.g. issue resolution) and technologies (e.g. call centre). These three components – people, process and technology – are the core elements of CRM strategy, as we have noted in previous chapters. Major IT vendors are now using the terminology of CX when promoting their CRM solutions. There is a considerable overlap between the two concepts, but businesses can implement a CX strategy without developing a CRM strategy and vice versa, as we outline later.

Companies' efforts to manage CX have their origins in the convergence of service marketing and total quality management (TQM).

Service marketing

Services management experts have identified a number of special attributes that characterize services. Services are performances or acts that are:

- *Intangible-dominant*. Services cannot be seen, tasted or sensed in other ways before consumption. A customer buying an office-cleaning service cannot see the service outcome before it has been performed. Services are high in experience and credence attributes but low on search attributes. Experience attributes are those attributes that can only be experienced by trying out an offer. Your last vacation was high in experience attributes. You weren't able to judge fully what it would be like before you took the trip. Services like healthcare, insurance and investment advice are high in credence attributes. Even when you have consumed these services you cannot be sure of the quality of the service delivered. How confident are you that your car is well serviced by your service station? Search attributes are attributes that can be checked out in advance of a purchase. Services are low in these because of their intangible-dominant character. Buyers therefore look for tangible clues to help them make sensible choices. Perhaps a buyer will look at the appearance of the equipment and personnel, and view testimonials in a 'brag-book'. Service marketers therefore need to manage tangible evidence by 'tangibilizing the intangible'.

- *Inseparable.* Unlike goods that can be manufactured in one time and location and consumed at a later time in another location, services are produced at the same time and place they are consumed. Your dentist produces service at the same time you consume it. This means that service customers are involved in and sometimes co-produce the service (see also Figure 7.1). This co-production means that quality is more difficult to control and service outcomes harder to guarantee. For example, a correct diagnosis by a doctor depends in large measure upon the ability of the patient to recognize and describe symptoms. Sometimes service providers' best intentions can be undone by customer behaviour. Promoters of rock concerts where there have been riots know only too well that customer behaviour can change the fundamental character of a concert experience. Sometimes other customers' participation in the service experience make it more, and sometimes less, satisfying. In a bar, other customers create atmosphere, adding to the value of the experience. In a cinema, ringing cell phones and talkative patrons can spoil an otherwise excellent movie experience.

- *Heterogeneous.* Unlike goods that can be robotically reproduced to exact specifications and tolerances, services cannot. This is particularly true of services produced by people, because people do not always behave as scripted or trained. A band can perform brilliantly one weekend but 'die' the next. Sometimes the service is co-produced by customer and service provider. All of these factors make it hard for companies to guarantee the content and quality of a service encounter. Many services, for example in the financial services sector, are becoming increasingly automated in order to reduce the unacceptable level of quality variance that is associated with human interaction. Many customer service centres now script their interactions with customers to eliminate unacceptable customer experience.

- *Perishable.* Services, unlike goods, cannot be held in inventory for sale at a later time. A hotel room that is unoccupied on Monday night cannot be added to the inventory for Tuesday night. The opportunity to provide service and make a sale is gone for ever. This presents marketers with the challenge of matching supply and demand.

You can remember these attributes using the mnemonic HIPI – heterogeneity, intangibility, perishability and inseparability.

Service marketers use the expressions 'service encounter' and 'service experience' to describe customer-service provider interactions at the moment of service delivery. Customers have always had service experiences, in the sense that they co-create service encounters in interaction with service providers, but Pine and Gilmore suggest that the *planned* customer experience differs because management tries to engage the customer in a positive and memorable way. Using stage performance as their metaphor, they write: 'experiences occur whenever a company intentionally uses services as the stage and goods as props to engage a [customer]'.[5] This distinction points us towards two perspectives on customer experience – normative and positive. *Positive* customer experience describes customer experience as it is. It is a value-free and objective statement of what it is like to be a customer. *Normative* customer experience describes customer experience as management or customers believe it ought to be. It is a value-based judgement of what the experience should be like for a customer.

The planned customer experience

As noted above, customers have always undergone an experience whenever a service is performed, whether that is viewing a movie, going to a supermarket or undergoing a government tax audit. They also experience goods as they are consumed or used – driving a car, wearing a suit or operating a flight simulator.

Some customer experiences are commodity-like and purchased frequently; others are one-off or 'peak' experiences never to be experienced again and highly memorable. One experience of travelling to work on London Underground is much like another, but co-piloting a jet fighter to celebrate an important birthday would be, for most of us, a unique experience.

Customer experience may be the core product that customers buy, or a differentiating value-add. Some companies are now in the business of staging and selling customer experiences as a core product.[6] You can buy experiences such as white-water rafting, swimming with dolphins, feeding elephants, paragliding, bungee jumping, driving a racing car, going on safari or climbing Sydney Harbour Bridge. Customers buy the experience – the bundle of cognitive and affective impressions that the purchase delivers (see Case study 7.1).

However, many marketers try to add value to, and differentiate, their service by enhancing customer experience. You can see this when the variety of experiences in a service category varies substantially. Your experience on a charter flight differs from your experience on a scheduled flight; your experience at the Hard Rock café differs from your experience at McCafé.

Sometimes, these differentiated experiences are so singular that they become the embodiment of the brand. Branded customer experiences such as the IKEA shopping

---

CASE STUDY 7.1

THE KIWI EXPERIENCE[7]

The Kiwi Experience is a company that takes customers, mostly backpackers, on bus tours around New Zealand. Unlike most bus tours, customers can join, leave and rejoin the tour whenever they want. Kiwi Experience customers aren't buying a ticket from A to B; they buy an entire experience that incorporates accommodation, travel, entry to attractions, the company of other travellers and the leadership of the driver. Each customer's experience has the potential to be unique, even amongst those travelling on the same tour.

CASE STUDY 7.2

THE IKEA SHOPPING EXPERIENCE

IKEA is a global home furnishings retailer with a distinctive blue and yellow livery. Most IKEA stores offer free parking. The in-store experience directs shoppers on a one-way route through room set-ups that allow IKEA merchandise to be displayed as if in use. On arrival at a store entrance customers can pick up pencils, paper, tape measures, store layout guides, catalogues, shopping carts, shopping bags and baby strollers. Shoppers can try out merchandise without being bothered by IKEA sales people. Price tags contain details including item name, colours, materials and sizes. Shoppers note the items they want and either collect them from the self-serve area or have a staff member arrange for it to be available at the furniture pick-up point. Since most IKEA furniture is flat-packed, shoppers can take purchases home immediately, or IKEA will arrange home delivery. There are in-store restaurants. IKEA accepts cash, credit cards, debit cards and IKEA gift cards. IKEA offers a return and exchange solution to customers who are not fully satisfied. The entire in-store experience is very carefully planned, and periodically reviewed and improved.

experience (Case study 7.2) are very distinctive. When companies plan customer experience, they are attempting to influence the cognitive, affective, behavioural and social responses of customers, by carefully designing the elements that influence these responses.

Total quality management

Pine and Gilmore's thinking about the 'experience economy' came hard on the heels of the business world's wide-scale adoption of total quality management (TQM). TQM is a structured approach to business management that aims to improve the quality of products and processes by learning from the objective and systematic feedback of important stake-holders, including customers. TQM promoted the objective of 'zero defects' in manufacturing, where it proved successful in reducing costs and improving quality. Management theorists then began to consider quality improvement in the service sector. In a famous article, Frederick Reichheld and W. Earl Sasser announced, 'Quality Comes to Services'.[8] This promoted the objective of 'zero defections', that is the loss of no customers to competitors because of poor-quality service experiences. A number of service quality theories were developed, including the Grönroos and the Parasuraman, Zeithaml and Berry (PZB) models we introduced in the previous chapter. The most widely deployed of these has been the SERVQUAL model developed by PZB.[9] SERVQUAL identifies five dimensions of service quality: reliability, assurance, tangibles, empathy and responsiveness, which you can remember using the mnemonic RATER. Research has established a clear link between service quality perceptions, customer retention and business performance.[10]

Service quality is important for our understanding of CX. Why? It is important because customers experience quality, or lack of it, in their interactions with service providers. Consider, for example, an encounter with a technician from an IT help desk. The technician turns up late, has not been properly briefed about the issue, does not have the experience or access to a knowledge base to help him resolve the issue and, even if he did, does not carry the necessary parts to resolve it. Poor service quality pervades the entire experience.

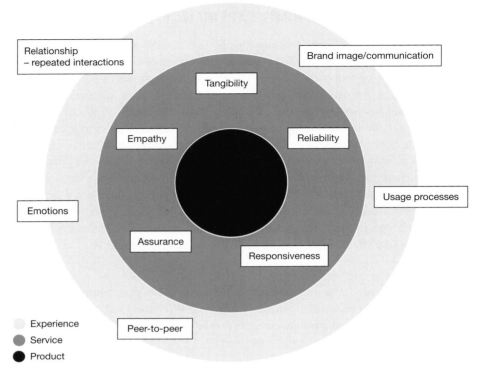

Figure 7.2 Layered model of customer experience[12]

Recently, CX has been conceptualized as 'SERVQUAL *plus*'.[11] In addition to the SERVQUAL RATER dimensions described above, 'SERVQUAL *plus*' also considers emotions, peer-to-peer interactions, the way the customer uses the product, the relationship between supplier and buyer, and brand communication and image, as shown in Figure 7.2. SERVQUAL itself considers only whether customer expectations of the RATER dimensions have been met during service performance. The 'SERVQUAL *plus*' approach goes further, and considers CX as something bigger than mere cognitive evaluations of service quality (as is SERVQUAL) and which is high in emotional content and felt over a longer period of time.

In a study of customer experience in the UK property lending market, Klaus and Maklan created the first multidimensional scale for measuring the quality of customer experience (dubbed EXQ).[13] The authors agreed that CX is a holistic concept that includes search, purchase, consumption and use phases of the customer lifecycle, and that it is a composite outcome of some elements within management's control (the marketing mix, service quality) and some outside management control (customers' objectives, the social context).[14]

CUSTOMER EXPERIENCE CONCEPTS

There are a number of core concepts that are associated with customer experience management. These include touchpoints, moments of truth and customer engagement.

Touchpoints are found wherever your customer comes into virtual or concrete contact with your company's products, services, communications, places, people, processes or technologies. Touchpoints include websites, Facebook and other social media, service centres, warehouses, call and contact centres, events, exhibitions, trade shows, seminars, webinars, direct mail, email, advertising, sales calls and retail stores. The variety and number of customer touchpoints varies across industry and between companies, but with the advent of social media they are increasing. The National Australia Bank, for example, has ten customer touchpoints: branch, email, NAB website, social media, ATM, financial planner, Internet banking, personal banker, mobile mortgage specialist and customer contact centre. If you were undergoing hospital treatment, your 'customer' experience would be made up of experiences at a number of touchpoints: during admission, in the ward, in the theatre, after surgery and during discharge.

The expression *moment of truth* (MOT) was first introduced by Richard Normann, and popularized by Jan Carlzon, former president of the airline SAS.[15] Carlzon described a MOT as follows: 'Last year, each of our 10 million customers came in contact with approximately five SAS employees, and this contact lasted an average of 15 seconds each time. Thus SAS is created 50 million times year, 15 seconds at a time. These 50 million "moments of truth" are the moments that ultimately determine whether SAS will succeed or fail as a business.' Extending the metaphor beyond the importance of people, Carlzon's original focus, we can identify a MOT as any occasion the customer interacts with, or is exposed to, any organizational output that leads to the formation of an impression of the organization. Moments of truth occur during customer interactions at touchpoints. These are the moments when customers form evaluative judgements, positive or negative, about their experience. For example, when a customer calls a contact centre and interacts with an IVR (interactive voice response) robot, receives a visit from an account executive or enters a branch office, these are moments of truth. If a service technician turns up late for an appointment, this negative moment of truth might taint the entire experience, even though the service job was well performed. Customers generally have expectations of what should happen during moments of truth, and if those expectations are underperformed, dissatisfaction will result.

Customer engagement is an expression that we first introduced in Chapter 4. Engaged consumers tend to have a higher intensity of participation in and connection to a brand or organization.[16] They feel a strong sense of identification, based on their experiences of the firm's offerings, activities and reputation. Engaged customers are more committed to the brand or firm than customers who are just satisfied. Traditional measures of satisfaction do not perform well as measures of engagement, so managers need to develop new metrics.[17] A comprehensive set of measures would provide insights into all four dimensions of customer engagement: cognitive, emotional, behavioural and social. Examples of measures include the following:

- *Cognitive*: Does the customer know our brand values? Does the customer know about our sustainability awards? Does the customer know the name of our local sales rep?

- *Emotional*: Does the customer like the experience offered by our firm? Does the customer prefer our offerings to our major competitors'? Is the customer excited about our new product launch?

- *Behavioural*: How often does the customer visit our website? How long does the customer dwell on the website? Does the customer click through to our newsletter?

- *Social*: Has the customer used our Recommend-a-Friend programme? Does the customer 'like' our Facebook page? Does the customer join our Twitter conversation?

Customers who are engaged might express a sense of confidence, integrity, pride, delight or passion in the brand.[18] Forrester Inc., the technology and market research organization, defines customer engagement as 'the level of involvement, interaction, intimacy, and influence that an individual has with a brand over time'.[19] These have become known as the 4Is. *Involvement* is indicated when a customer presents at a touchpoint. *Interaction* focuses on what the customer does at the touchpoint. *Intimacy* is the emotional sentiment of the customer towards touchpoint experiences. *Influence* focuses on the advocacy behaviours of the customer. Forrester recommends that management develop a set of relevant indicators for the 4Is, a number of which appear in Table 7.1

Table 7.1 The 4Is of customer engagement

Metric category	Examples of measures
Involvement	Unique site visitors, advertising impressions, website page views, time spent per session, time spent per page, in-store visits, newsletter subscriptions
Interaction	First-time purchases, videos played, community contributions, warranty registrations, loyalty card registrations, requests for free samples, comments in social media, click-throughs on banner ads, photos uploaded
Intimacy	Satisfaction scores, sentiment in blog and social media posts, call centre feedback, focus group contributions
Influence	Content forwarded, friends invited to join online communities, word-of-mouth, creation of user-generated content, invitations to join member-get-member programme, content embedded in blogs

Clearly, from these measures, customers who are engaged do more than just buy.

Companies that consciously design customer experience want to evoke strong, positive engagement. They do this by carefully designing what happens during moments of truth at customer touchpoints and providing both functional and emotional clues with which the customer can engage.[20] One of the challenges to delivery of consistent customer experience is variance between channels. What the customer experiences from interaction with people, process and technology at a retail point-of-sale may differ significantly from the experience at the same company's website. Companies generally try to configure all the company channels, for example stores, social media and catalogues, to deliver a consistent customer experience. Often this is the objective of a strategic CRM project. Customer experience can become stale over time, and stale experiences are not engaging. Repeat business from customers at Planet Hollywood and Rainforest café is poor for this reason. It is therefore necessary to constantly refresh the customer experience.

HOW TO MANAGE CUSTOMER EXPERIENCE

Companies aiming to improve customer experience need to understand the customer's current experience before they redesign what happens at touchpoints.

Companies can use a number of methods for improving their insight into customer experience, including mystery shopping, experience mapping, customer ethnography, and participant and non-participant observation.

- *Mystery shopping* involves the recruitment of paid shoppers to report on their customer experience. Usually they report on their experiences of the company sponsoring the research, but they might also compare the sponsor's performance with competitors. A number of market research companies offer mystery shopping services. Mystery shopping is widely used in B2C environments such as retailing, banks, service stations, bars, restaurants and hotels. It is sometimes used in B2B environments. For example, an insurance company might use mystery shopping to assess the performance of its broker network.

- *Experience mapping* is a process that strives to understand, chart and improve what happens at customer touchpoints. Focus groups, face-to-face interviews or telephone interviews are conducted with a sample of customers who describe their experience at these touchpoints. The focus is on two important questions. What is the experience like? How can it be improved? The objective is to identify the gaps between actual experience and desired experience. Then the company can begin to focus on strategies to close the gaps. These strategies typically involve improvements to people and processes. Outcomes might be better training and reward schemes for people, or investment in IT to support process improvements. Figure 7.3 illustrates a hotel guest's experience map.

The map shows that the customer's experience occurs over four time periods. 'Arrival at hotel' is decomposed into three secondary episodes – parking the car, checking-in and taking bags to the room. The check-in episode is again decomposed, this time into six main components. It is at this level that the customer experiences the hotel's people and processes. This is where opportunities for improving people and processes can focus. Every customer experience can be decomposed and redesigned in this way. However, not all customer encounters contribute equally to the overall assessment of experience. For example, hospital patients are often prepared to tolerate food quality of a standard that would be utterly unacceptable for a surgical procedure. Companies are well advised to focus on the critical episodes and encounters that make up customer experience.

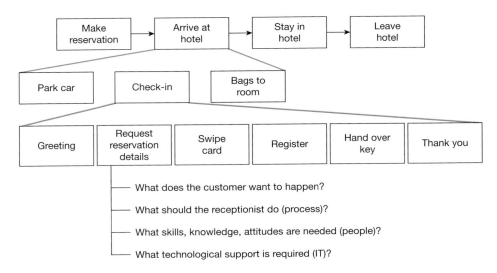

Figure 7.3 Experience map of a hotel guest

Ethnographic methods can be used to gain a better understanding of the socio-cultural context of customer experience. Martyn Hammersley characterizes ethnography as participation, either overt or covert, in people's daily lives over a prolonged period of time, watching what happens, listening to what is said and asking questions.[21] Consumers may be able to conduct their own ethnographies without the intervention of a researcher, using apps that allow them to record their activities using the video, audio, photo, text and barcode-reading functionality of their mobile phones. Ethnography is a naturalistic form of investigation that reveals customer experience as it occurs in everyday life. Even mundane goods can be

CASE STUDY 7.3

OBSERVATIONAL RESEARCH HELPS IMPROVE 3 MOBILE'S CUSTOMER EXPERIENCE[22]

3 Mobile is a leading provider of mobile broadband in the UK. Setting up mobile broadband requires customers to insert a subscriber identity module or SIM card into a 'dongle' and then install software on their computer. 3 knew from calls to their customer service centre that some customers had difficulty setting up the service. 3 decided it needed to better understand customer experience so that it could offer improved support and reduce the costs of handling customer queries. 3's research company New Experience observed eight prospective customers setting up mobile broadband for the first time. They were given a dongle pack, a SIM pack and a PC, and asked to set it up. Members of 3's user experience team also watched what happened. It became apparent that potential customers had a limited understanding of how the service worked. All but two were surprised to find a SIM card and didn't understand what it was for. Also, the design of the dongle made it hard for people to see how to insert the SIM while the user guide indicated that all users needed to do was plug and play. These findings helped 3 improve its customer experience.

experienced in emotionally charged ways. Eric Arnould, for example, shows how a table can be much more than just a piece of furniture. 'The table has become the "heart of the home" where meals, crafts, and study occur under mother's watchful eye.'[23] It has been well established that customers appropriate the values of up-market brands such as Rolex or Chanel when they consume, but Jennifer Coupland's ethnography also shows how low-involvement, 'invisible', everyday products can serve an important social purpose, allowing families to create meanings that transcend the values that are usually associated with the brand name. She notes how families 'strive to erase brands . . . and create their own product value as if the brand never existed in the first place. Brands get in the way.'[24]

Participant observation. Companies can develop a better understanding of customer experience by participating in the customer experience at various touchpoints. Some companies require their senior management to learn about customer experience by providing front-line customer service. This ensures that executives who are several hierarchical levels removed from customers understand what it is like to be a customer. For example, McDonald's periodically requires its senior managers to work as crew-members in restaurants.

CASE STUDY 7.4

REINVENTING CUSTOMER EXPERIENCE AT ROYAL BANK OF SCOTLAND[25]

Following the 2008 near collapse of its parent bank (Royal Bank of Scotland – RBS), the head of NatWest Bank surprised even his own management team with a public announcement that NatWest was to be 'the helpful bank' and that it would publish its performance against a customer charter. A centralized team took on the challenge of mapping, evaluating and redesigning the experience of retail customers. The team deconstructed customer experience into a limited number of episodes, each focused on a single service that the bank provided, such as opening (or closing) an account, issuing a credit card or processing a mortgage application. The service became the unit of analysis. For each service, the team calculated how much it cost to deliver, how well it performed (using operational quality measures, such as elapsed time) and how it was perceived by customers. Customer evaluations of their experience were measured by a combination of customer effort score, customer satisfaction and Net Promoter Score. Building this dataset was challenging, but once generated, the bank had a systematic and evidence-based means of assessing its activities with respect to quality, customer appreciation and cost. Working with these three dimensions, the bank continues to improve the services that matter most to customers, where it performs poorly and or where customers are least satisfied. The data also allow the bank to reduce costs by eliminating over-delivery on services that do not matter much to customers. The programme generated immediate and large cost savings, effectiveness improvements and improved customer satisfaction. It is now being rolled out in other RBS divisions. This programme has deployed process, tools and measures for systematically improving customer experience in a large and complex organization.

Non-participant observation. Some companies require their senior managers to observe customer interactions at customer touchpoints. This is particularly suitable when the primary customer touchpoint is a call centre or contact centre. Managers can listen to customer calls to obtain a better understanding of customer experience, but not actually make or receive calls.[26]

Britain's Royal Bank of Scotland provides an example of the re-engineering of customer experience. It marries experience mapping with customer satisfaction, service quality and cost data in order to improve customer experience and profitability. See Case Study 7.4.

WHAT DISTINGUISHES CUSTOMER EXPERIENCE MANAGEMENT FROM CUSTOMER RELATIONSHIP MANAGEMENT?

Customer experience management or CXM is the practice of designing, implementing and improving customer experiences at organizational touchpoints. Although CRM and CXM generally go hand in hand, and aim to achieve the same goals, it is possible to conceive of one without the other. They are similar in the following respects:

- CRM and CXM strategies may pursue the same objectives, including customer retention, customer satisfaction and CLV. Increasingly, both CXM and CRM projects measure customer effort or 'pain' as customers interact with business processes and systems.

- Both stress the integration of customer touchpoints, channels and communication to provide coherence and identity. For large-scale organizations this often requires major investment in IT infrastructure and business processes able to track individual customers as they make their journey from prospect, to customer, through sales service, into repeat purchase and advocate status.

- Both require customer-focused behaviours of customer-facing employees at all touchpoints. CXM and CRM projects both consider how to motivate employees to provide better customer experience, which in turn drives business performance.[27]

- Segmentation, targeting and creating segment-specific offers (experiences) is evident in both CRM and CXM programmes. Not all customers want the same package of benefits or experiences, not all customers buy and use goods and services identically, and not all customers are equally adept at extracting value from their purchases.

To some extent a turf war is fought over language and concepts but, at their core, most CRM strategies focus on providing enhanced CX and most CXM strategies are implemented using CRM tools and technologies.

CRM's influence on CX

The implementation of a CRM strategy, and the deployment of CRM technologies, can have a significant impact on customer experience.

Strategic CRM's goal of winning and keeping profitable customers through a customer-centric organizational culture implies that there will be a dedicated focus on meeting the requirements of targeted customer groups. Customer experience should therefore satisfy the expectations of these particular customers, whilst other potential customers or market segments may not be served. The principles of customer portfolio management discussed in Chapter 5 suggest that companies offer different value propositions (including service levels) to different clusters of customers. There will therefore be differentiated customer experiences across the portfolio.

However, not every company that has a well-executed CX strategy uses the CRM toolkit we describe in this book. The technology and lifestyle brand, Apple, has a highly developed CX strategy, carefully managing customer experience at every touchpoint with a laser-like focus on customers' value-in-use, that is, the ability to use Apple devices to their full extent, easily. However, Apple, to the best of our knowledge, does not have a highly developed CRM programme. They do not differentiate their product offer or experience for different customers based on customer preferences or CLV. The Apple experience does not change over time, as customers become loyal advocates. Apple does not mine its customer database to make targeted and specific offers. Everyone is treated the same in-store or on the phone. Its customer management is undifferentiated, albeit at a very high quality, and there are no tiered loyalty and management structures.

Operational CRM involves the application of technology in the customer-facing functions of sales, marketing and service. Operational CRM can influence customer experience in a number of positive ways: customers will be recognized, their needs better understood, order fulfilment and billing will be more accurate, communications will be more relevant and timely, and service will be more responsive and reliable. However, CRM technology implementations are often motivated by efficiency measures, rather than a drive to improve CX. For example, the implementation of interactive voice response (IVR) technologies in call centres has allowed routine customer interactions to be automated, reducing transaction costs by up to 60 per cent, and service agent numbers to be downsized to those required for more complex calls. Customer response to IVR implementations is not always positive, particularly in more conservative segments of the customer base. That said, customers may not even be aware of several improvements that IVR can bring to customer experience – more accurate information (less human error), 24/7 access to information, and enhanced data security and privacy.

Analytical CRM is the process through which organizations transform customer-related data into actionable insight for either strategic or tactical purposes. When analytical CRM works well, customers receive timely, relevant communications and offers. CRM practitioners are able to predict propensities to buy and detect opportune times to make offers, therefore ensuring that customers are not burdened with irrelevant communications. Analytical CRM can also be used to help customers in unexpected ways – bank customers can be alerted when approaching a credit limit thereby avoiding unwelcome fees, or telco customers can be migrated to a more suitable telephone contract thereby reducing their operating costs. The CEO of CRM technology vendor RightNow Technologies uses a mining metaphor to describe how analytical CRM has been deployed historically.[28] He suggests that sales-focused CRM implementations have conventionally been used to strip-mine customers, rather than understand and meet their needs better. Strip-mining has compromised many efforts to deliver excellent customer experience. Rather than strip-mining, he suggests that it makes better sense to nurture customers as if they were renewable resources.

HOW CRM SOFTWARE APPLICATIONS INFLUENCE CUSTOMER EXPERIENCE

There is very little research evidence of how CRM technologies influence customer experience.[29] The Meta Group reports:

> Business customers want to be identified for their appropriate requirements (e.g., resupply of goods and services that they already purchase), so that they can save time. Many consumers fall into a similar camp. But in exchange for being identified (e.g., providing information about themselves, or having it collected), customers/consumers expect to be treated as 'special.' This means free products, better service, useful information, and so on. They also do not want to be bothered by endless phone calls or e-mails to sell them more 'stuff.'[30]

As customers surrender data about themselves to suppliers, they expect that information to be used wisely to communicate relevant and timely offers.

Such comments imply that CX, following a CRM technology implementation, is not necessarily positive. Customers who are accustomed to receiving face-to-face calls from sales reps might find they are expected to place orders and pay through a sales portal. Self-service through portals delivers a completely different customer experience. Resistance, resentment and churn may result. Weary workers arriving home after a hard day's labour are confronted with cold calls selling products that aren't of the slightest interest. Customers of a multi-channel retailing firm find they receive conflicting or duplicated offers from different channels – a clear indication that customer data are held in silos. The avoidance of negative customer experience from ineptly implemented CRM is an important reason for ensuring the voice-of-the-customer is heard during CRM project planning and implementation. It also signals the importance of monitoring customer response after a CRM implementation.

Despite these cautions, technology can fundamentally change CX for the better because it reinvents what happens at customer touchpoints. Imagine a sales rep who has always carried hard-copy brochures. He is sitting in front of a qualified prospect with a product-related query, and who is ready to buy. The rep goes to his briefcase. The brochure he needs is missing, and he cannot answer the query. 'I'll get back to you,' he says. But he doesn't. He forgets and the opportunity is lost. Equipped with CRM, the interaction is very different. The rep carries a laptop with a current, searchable, product database, and the customer's record. He answers the query successfully. The prospect asks for a firm quote. The rep activates the quotation engine. A quote is prepared and discussed. The rep requests the order. He wins the order. The rep converts the quote to an order by checking a box on a quotation engine screen. The rep shares the screen information with the customer. An electronic signature is obtained. Order confirmation is sent to the buyer's email address immediately. That night the rep keys in his call report, synchronizes his laptop with the company's main computer and the order fulfilment process begins.

Features of CRM applications that improve customer experience

CRM software applications that are difficult to navigate or configure, or that are slow to respond, leave the customer painfully aware of the limitations of a company's customer management expertise. Furthermore, once a CRM application is published on the Web for customers and channel partners to use, performance and usability issues are experienced first-hand. Usability, flexibility, performance and scalability are key features of CRM solutions that deliver a favourable customer experience.[31]

Usability

Usability refers to the ease with which a CRM application can be navigated or used. High usability applications are intuitive, and require very little effort to perform the required task, whether that is updating customer contact details, making an offer or resolving a complaint. High usability applications require minimal user training prior to, or at, deployment, and are experienced as highly responsive by the customer. A highly responsive application is a necessary ingredient in delivering a highly responsive experience for the customer.

Older-style CRM applications traditionally used menu systems and function keys for navigation. Function keys can be very fast to use once the user has learned the keystrokes. However they can only take the user through a flow that was originally conceived during system design. These approaches can be cumbersome in the front office, and take time to arrive at the customer's desired outcome. Web technologies, on the other hand, incorporate hyperlinks and drill-downs that support an intuitive, 'go where the customer wants' approach. If you want more information on something, you can click on the link. For this reason, a web-style interface has become the norm for CRM applications. The only caveat to this is in the call centre, where high volumes of calls take place in a largely predictable manner. In these situations, basic web-style technologies are not adequate, and must be augmented by scripting or applets in order to deliver the required level of interactivity and performance.

Flexibility

Responsiveness can be 'hard-wired' by pre-empting all of the processes that a customer may require, and implementing these in the application in advance. The difficulty with this approach is that customers don't always follow the system engineer's or workflow designer's script. An application's flexibility determines how many alternatives are available to the user at any given time; these alternatives are often implemented through hyperlinks, buttons or screen tabs. A highly flexible application will have many such links, and will not require specific processes to be followed. The customer does not want to be told 'I'm sorry, but I can't do B until I've done A'.

High performance

The performance of a CRM system is often determined by its weakest link. All technologies must be in alignment in order to create a high performance system. A CRM application running on an extremely fast network will still be slow if the database is overloaded. Even the best software application will be unresponsive if network performance, database performance or server performance are substandard. Most CRM applications separate the application server from the database server in order to improve performance.

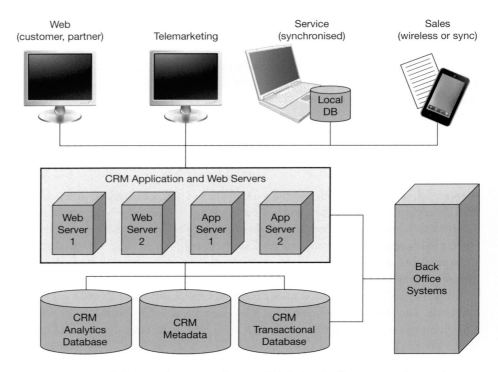

Figure 7.4 Typical CRM architecture, showing Web, back-office integration and mobile. Note the database tier (bottom), the application server tier (middle) and the user interface tier (top).

Performance is also determined by integration and synchronization technologies. A CRM application will appear slow if the user has to wait for an automatic email to be created and sent via the email interface. Remote users such as field service engineers will perceive the system as slow if they have to wait more than a few minutes for their daily synchronization to their laptop. The speed of these processes can have a dramatic effect on system acceptance and uptake.

An important characteristic of a high performing CRM system architecture is not only this ability to separate high load areas such as the database and application servers, but also the ability to expand the application and web server tier by adding more servers as required. This is shown in the Figure 7.4.

Scalability

As the CRM system grows, and is used by more internal and external people, the scalability of the system becomes important. Acceptable performance with 100 call-centre users may become inadequate once the customers are online and hitting the website, or field sales reps start synchronizing across all territories at the same time. CRM applications should be evaluated based on proven numbers of users, and types of users (concurrent on the Web, synchronization, full load call centre, etc.) in order to assess their ability to scale. A system that is unable to scale will deliver inadequate customer experience as user numbers grow.

Finally, it should be recognized that high performance CRM systems require investment to keep up with changing customer expectations. It is most important that the CRM application be constantly monitored against predefined performance targets to ensure performance remains acceptable. This is particularly the case in high turnaround areas where the customer is involved, such as the call centre and website, and where high loads take place at the same time, such as the afternoon synchronization run or back-office integration run.

SUMMARY

In this chapter you have read about the links between CRM and customer experience. We defined customer experience as the cognitive and affective outcome of the customer's exposure to, or interaction with, a company's people, processes, technologies, products, services and other outputs. Customer experience is important because it influences future buying behaviour and word-of-mouth. Although customers have always had experiences in the purchase and consumption of goods and services, we have recently seen the emergence of the experience economy, in which companies have brought to market experiences such as open-garden weekends, team-building exercises and white-water rafting.

Three key concepts capture the essence of customer experience management – touchpoint, moment of truth and engagement. Customers are exposed to or interact with companies' people, processes and technologies at touchpoints such as call centres, websites, shop fronts or automated kiosks. Some of these exposures or interactions are more significant than others and become moments of truth that are important in the building of customer experience. Managers are keen to promote engagement with the company, brand or offer by delivering experiences that meet or exceed customer expectations.

In order to improve customer experience it is important to understand current customer experience. A number of techniques are available to management for this purpose, including mystery shopping, experience mapping, ethnographic research, and participant and non-participant observation. Measures of customer experience, including involvement, interaction, intimacy and influence (the 4Is), help companies determine whether customer experience objectives are being achieved. CRM practitioners want technology implementations to influence customer experience in a number of positive ways such as more relevant and timely communications, and more responsive and reliable service, but customers do not always respond positively to change. Features of CRM solutions that influence customer experience include usability, flexibility, high performance and scalability.

NOTES AND REFERENCES

1   Shaw, C. and Ivens, J. (2002). *Building great customer experiences*. Basingstoke: Palgrave Macmillan.

2   Lemke, F., Clark, M. and Wilson, H. (2011). Customer experience quality: an exploration in business and consumer contexts using repertory grid technique. *Journal of the Academy of Marketing Science*, 39(6), 846–69.

3   Petre, M., Minocha, S. and Roberts, D. (2006). Usability beyond the website: an empirically grounded e-commerce evaluation instrument for the total customer experience. *Behaviour and Information Technology*, 25(2), 189–203.

4   Pine, B.J. and Gilmore, J.H. (1998). Welcome to the experience economy. *Harvard Business Review*, July–August, 97–105.

5   Pine II, B. Joseph and Gilmore, J. (1999). *The experience economy*. Boston, MA: Harvard Business School Press.

6   See for example: http://www.redballoondays.com.au/.

7   http://www.kiwiexperience.com/ (Accessed 20 January 2008).

8   Reichheld, F.F. and Sasser, W. Earl (1990). Zero defections: quality comes to services. *Harvard Business Review*, 68(5), 105.

9   Parasuraman, A., Zeithaml, V. and Berry, L. (1988). SERVQUAL: a multiple-item scale for measuring consumer perceptions of service quality. *Journal of Retailing*, 64(1), 12–40.

10   Some of the studies include: Al-Hawari, M., Ward, T. and Newby, L. (2009). The relationship between service quality and retention within the automated and traditional contexts of retail banking. *Journal of Service Management*, 20(4), 455–72; Dagger, T., Sweeney, J. and Johnson, L. (2007). A hierarchical model of health service quality: scale development and investigation of an integrated model. *Journal of Service Research*, 10(2), 123–42; Falk, T., Hammerschmidt, M. and Schepers, J. (2010). The service quality–satisfaction link revisited: exploring asymmetries and dynamics. *Journal of the Academy of Marketing Science*, 38, 288–302; Richard, M. and Allaway, A. (1993). Service quality attributes and choice behavior. *Journal of Services Marketing*, 7(1), 59.

11   Lemke, F., Clark, M. and Wilson, H. (2011). Customer experience quality: an exploration in business and consumer contexts using repertory grid technique. *Journal of the Academy of Marketing Science*, 39(6), 846–69.

12   Lemke, F., Clark, M. and Wilson, H. (2011). Customer experience quality: an exploration in business and consumer contexts using repertory grid technique. *Journal of the Academy of Marketing Science*, 39(6), 846–69.

13   Klaus, P. and Maklan, S. (2012). EXQ: a multiple-item scale for assessing service experience. *Journal of Service Management*, 23(1), 5–33.

14   Verhoef, P., Lemon, K.N., Parasuraman, A., Roggeveen, A., Tsiros, M. and Schlesinger, L.A. (2009). Customer experience creation: determinants, dynamics and management strategies. *Journal of Retailing*, 85(1), 31–41.

15   Normann, Richard (2002). *Service management: strategy and leadership in service business*, 3rd edn. New York: John Wiley.

16   Vivek, S.D., Beatty, S.E. and Morgan, R.M. (2012). Customer engagement: exploring customer relationships beyond purchase. *Journal of Marketing Theory and Practice*, 20(2), 127–45.

17   For more information refer to Bowden, J. (2007). The process of customer engagement: an examination of segment specific differences. *Proceedings of the Academy of Marketing Conference*, Kingston Business School, Egham, Surrey, July, CD-ROM.

18   McEwen, W. (2004). Why satisfaction isn't satisfying. *Gallup Management Journal Online*, November, 1–4.

19   Haven, B. and Vittal, S. (2008). Measuring engagement: four steps to making engagement measurement a reality. Forrester Inc. www.forrester.com

20 Juttner, U., Schaffner, D., Windler, K. and Maklan, S. (2013). Customer service experiences: applying a sequential incident laddering technique. *European Journal of Marketing*, 47(5/6), 738–69.

21 Hammersley, M. and Ackersley, P. (1995). *Ethnography: principles in practice*, 2nd edn. London: Routledge.

22 http://www.new-experience.com/_downloads/3%20Mobile%20Broadband%20set-up%20case%20study.pdf (Accessed 17 March 2014).

23 Arnould, E. and Proce L. (2006). Market-oriented ethnography revisited. *Journal of Advertising Research*, September, 251–62.

24 Coupland, J.C. (2005). Invisible brands: an ethnography of households and the brands in their kitchen pantries. *Journal of Consumer Research*, 32, 106–18.

25 Maklan, S. and Antonetti, P. (2014). Customer experience management at the Royal Bank of Scotland RBS: delivering helpful banking, Case Clearing House Reference no. 513–122–1.

26 For an analysis of the listening tools that companies are using, see McGuire, S., Koh, S.C.L. and Huang, C. (2007). Identifying the range of customer listening tools: a logical precursor to CRM? *Industrial Management and Data Systems*, 107(4), 567–86.

27 Heskett, J., Jones, T.O., Loveman, G.W., Earl Sasser, W. and Schlesinger, L.A. (1994). Putting the service-profit chain to work. *Harvard Business Review*, 72(2), 164–75.

28 http://www.mycustomer.com/cgi-bin/item.cgi?id=132411 (Accessed 27 September 2007).

29 Verhoef, P., Lemon, K.N., Parasuraman, A., Roggeveen, A., Tsiros, M. and Schlesinger, L.A. (2009). Customer experience creation: determinants, dynamics and management strategies. *Journal of Retailing*, 85(1), 31–41.

30 http://www.ctiforum.com/technology/CRM/wp01/download/meta_tocrm.pdf (Accessed 28 September 2007).

31 This section is based on John Turnbull's contribution in Chapter 6 in Buttle, F. (2009). *Customer relationship management: concepts and technologies*. Oxford: Elsevier.

OPERATIONAL CRM

Part III explores operational CRM. Operational CRM involves the application of technologies to support customer-facing processes in selling, marketing and customer service operations. This part consists of three chapters. Chapter 8 explores sales force automation. Chapter 9 looks at marketing automation and Chapter 10 surveys service automation.

SALES FORCE AUTOMATION

CHAPTER OBJECTIVES

By the end of this chapter you will understand:

- What is meant by sales force automation (SFA).
- The members of the SFA eco-system.
- The benefits derived from SFA.
- The functionality that is available in SFA software applications.
- Why companies choose to adopt SFA.
- What can be done to encourage salespeople to use SFA.

INTRODUCTION

Operational benefits are normally the first returns from IT-enabled CRM programmes.[1] Customer-facing processes in selling, marketing and customer service areas become more efficient because they are formalized and standardized, generating operational cost savings.

It is important to realize that an organization's CRM strategy options are limited by its operational capabilities.[2] Typically, a firm moving towards a customer-centric strategy invests first in building a single view of the customer (SVOC). The SVOC integrates data from all operational units that touch customers, including sales, marketing, customer service and accounts, to create a coherent picture of the customer's interactions with the business. Once the SVOC is created CRM users can interact with customers on a one-to-one basis, in full knowledge of their history with the business, thereby enhancing customer experience throughout the customer's relationship with the firm. Once the customer-related data are of sufficiently high quality, firms are then able to buy analytical software and develop the capabilities to mine the data in order to generate actionable insights, such as 'next best offer'.

Appropriate customer management actions can only be taken if the insight is delivered to the customer-facing employees who use the firm's selling, marketing and service operational processes. Without well-designed and applied operational processes, there is little possibility of implementing the CRM strategy. This capability almost always requires IT investment in the following solutions: sales force automation, marketing automation and service automation. Many firms stop their CRM drive once technology-supported operational capability is in place, such as call centre operations and online self-service. Hence, CRM is often misconstrued in organizations as a 'technology solution' rather than a strategic initiative.

This is the first of three chapters on CRM operational solutions. This chapter is about technologies used by salespeople and their managers. Subsequent chapters review marketing automation and service automation.

Sales force automation (SFA) has offered technological support to salespeople and managers since the beginning of the 1990s. SFA is now so widely adopted in business-to-business environments that it is seen as a 'competitive imperative'[3] that offers 'competitive parity'.[4] In other words, SFA is just a regular feature of the selling landscape.

Salespeople are found in a wide variety of contexts – in the field calling on business and institutional customers, in offices, contact centres and call centres receiving incoming orders and making outbound sales calls, in retail business-to-customer settings, in the street selling door-to-door, and even in the home, where party planners sell a variety of merchandise ranging from adult sex aids to cleaning products. All these sales contexts deploy SFA in some form or other.

We start by defining sales force automation, and identifying members of the SFA eco-system.

WHAT IS SFA?

Sales force automation (SFA) can be defined as follows:

Sales force automation is the application of computerized technologies to support salespeople and sales management in the achievement of their work-related objectives.

Hardware and software are the key technological elements of SFA. Hardware includes desktop, laptop and handheld devices such as tablets and smart phones, and contact/call centre technology. Software comprises both 'point' solutions that are designed to assist in a single area of selling or sales management, and integrated solutions that offer a range of functionality. Integrated packages are offered as SFA-specific packages only or can be incorporated into more comprehensive CRM suites that operate over the three front-office areas of marketing, service and sales.

All SFA software is designed so that companies can collect, store, analyze, distribute and use customer-related data for sales purposes. Customer-related data are key to customer orientation[5] and the development of long-term mutually beneficial relationships with customers.[6] SFA software enables reps and their managers to manage sales pipelines, track contacts and configure products, amongst many other things. SFA software also provides reports for sales reps and managers. In short, SFA enables salespeople and sales managers to become more effective or efficient in the pursuit of their objectives.

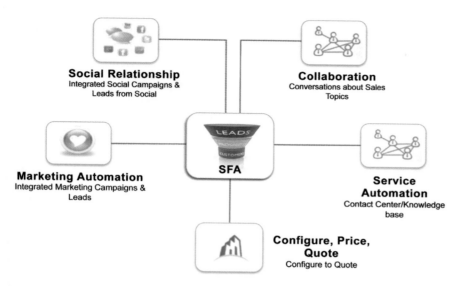

Figure 8.1 Components of Oracle's SFA solution[7]

THE SFA ECO-SYSTEM

The SFA eco-system is made up of three components: SFA solutions providers, hardware and infrastructure vendors, and associated service providers.

SFA solutions providers

SFA solutions providers can be classified in a number of ways. Some are SFA specialists. They compete against enterprise and mid-market CRM suites that include SFA modules, and enterprise suite vendors that offer a full range of IT solutions to support business, including supply chain management (SCM), enterprise resource planning (ERP) and customer relationship management (CRM). A number of illustrative examples are given in Table 8.1.

SFA solutions, like other CRM technologies, are accessed in one of two ways. The solution can either be installed on the user company's own servers or it can be accessed on another party's servers via the Internet. The former is known as on-premise, offline or installed SFA. The latter is known as hosted, online or on-demand SFA, web-service, the ASP (Application Service Provider) model, or the Software as a Service (SaaS) model.

Table 8.1 Classification of SFA vendors (sample only)

SFA specialists	SFA as part of CRM suite	SFA as part of enterprise suite
CyberForms	Microsoft Dynamics	IBM
Salesnet	salesforce.com	Oracle
Selectica	SalesLogix	SAP

Figure 8.2 Customer overview configured for iPad[8]

© 2014 SAP AG or an SAP affiliate company. All rights reserved. Used with permission of SAP AG or an SAP affiliate company.

Salesforce.com was the early leader in offering SaaS, and other major CRM solutions providers have since responded with their own SaaS offers. Access for SaaS users is on a pay-as-you-go (price per seat per month) or subscription basis. We explore the issues around how organizations choose between these two modes of delivery in Chapter 14.

Some SFA specialists focus on particular areas of functionality within SFA. Selectica, for example, builds customized configurators. A configurator is a rule-based engine that allows companies to configure complex products and services for clients. Sometimes, customers interact directly with configurators rather than collaborating with a sales rep who has access to the technology.

Hardware and infrastructure

The performance requirements of SFA applications can create significant challenges for both hardware and technology infrastructure. Whereas office-bound salespeople and sales managers might be happy to use desktops or laptops, field sales staff mostly prefer to use mobile data devices: smart phones or tablets. Where companies have geographically dispersed external salespeople, SFA systems have to operate 24/7 in real time, allowing organizations to manage opportunities as quickly as possible. SFA applications often need to integrate with back-office systems so that field sales has visibility of, for example, outstanding service issues or order progress in advance of a client meeting.

Services

The services component of the SFA ecosystem is very diverse. When a SFA project is undertaken, service costs may add significantly to overall project expenditure. In addition to paying for software and hardware, SFA project leaders might buy services from providers that re-engineer selling processes, manage projects, train salespeople, consult on sales force organizational structure or conduct customer portfolio analysis. Service providers can contribute significantly both to SFA project costs and the probability of success.

The hardware and software for a SFA project may account for between 10 per cent and 50 per cent of overall costs. The balance is made up of service costs. Although some software vendor case studies suggest that payback is achievable within days, many projects take between 12 months and 24 months to implement, let alone yield a return. It has been suggested that the average implementation period is 21 months[9] and that users need over 100 hours experience with new technologies before they could claim to have mastered it.[10] During the implementation period, salespeople will need to populate the SFA system with data from operational databases and then learn how to analyze and leverage the data. This can take much longer than the purely technical implementation of a software system.

SFA SOFTWARE FUNCTIONALITY

SFA applications offer a range of functionality, as listed in Table 8.2. Not all solutions provide the full complement of sales-related functionality.

In the next few paragraphs, we will describe this functionality in more detail, in alphabetical order.

- *Account management* offers sales reps and managers a complete view of the customer relationship including contacts, contact history, completed transactions, current orders, shipments, enquiries, service history, opportunities and quotations. This allows sales reps and account managers to keep track of all their obligations in respect of every account

Table 8.2 Functionality offered by SFA software

• Account management	• Pipeline management
• Activity management	• Product encyclopedias
• Contact management	• Product configuration
• Contract management	• Product visualization
• Document management	• Proposal generation
• Event management	• Quotation management
• Incentive management	• Sales forecasting
• Lead management	• Sales management reporting
• Opportunity management	• Territory management
• Order management	• Workflow development

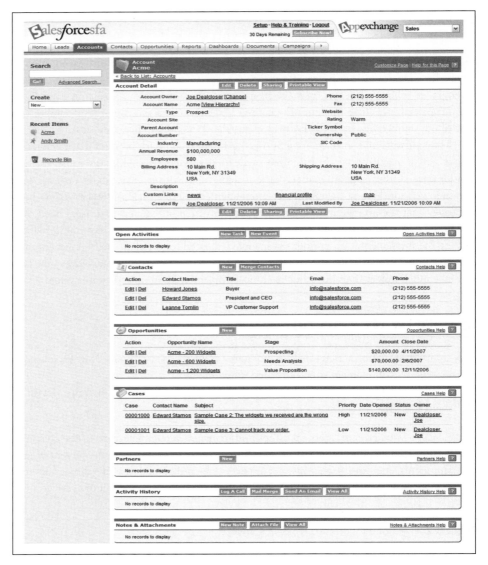

Figure 8.3 Account management screenshot[11]

for which they are responsible, whether this is an opportunity to be closed, an order or a service enquiry. Figure 8.3 is an account management screenshot from CRM SaaS company salesforce.com. You will see that it shows account details, contacts, opportunities, activities and service cases that are unresolved. Account management functionality allows sales reps and managers to stay on top of their obligations in respect of the accounts for which they are responsible.

- *Activity management* keeps sales reps and managers aware of all activities, whether complete or pending, related to an account, contact or opportunity, by establishing to-do lists, setting priorities, monitoring progress and programming alerts. Activities include preparation of quotations, scheduling of sales calls and following up enquiries, for example.

- *Contact management* functionality includes tools for building, sharing and updating contact lists, making appointments, time setting, and task, event and contact tracking. Contact list data include names, phone numbers, addresses, images, preference data and email addresses for people and companies, as well as a history of in-bound and out-bound communications. Contact management functionality is a cornerstone of most SFA applications. When contact management functionality supports the goal of having a single view of the customer, customer-facing staff in all parts of the business – sales, marketing, service, customer accounts – can see the history of communications with the customer. It means that a late-paying customer can be speaking to an accounts receivable team member who will know that the customer is in negotiations with a sales team member for a large contract. Rather than demand payment, the clerk may take a more judicious approach that does not put the opportunity at risk. Figure 8.4 is a contact summary screenshot from Oracle.

Figure 8.4 Contact management screenshot[12]

- *Contract management* functionality enables reps and managers to create, track, progress, accelerate, monitor and control contracts with customers. Contract management applications manage a contract's lifespan by shortening approval cycles for contracts, renewing contracts sooner and reducing administrative costs. The software may use security controls to ensure only approved people have access to contracts.

- *Document management* software allows companies to manage sales-related documents, keep them current and ensure that they are always available to reps, managers and partners when needed. Companies generate and use many documents to support the sales process – brochures, product specifications, installation instructions, user manuals, case studies, white papers, price lists, warranties, competitive comparisons, spreadsheets, email templates and templates for preparing quotations, for example. External agencies, including government departments, may require companies to maintain records of compliance with standards or regulations relevant to the products and services they sell. These documents can be stored securely online, versioned to ensure they remain traceable and current, and downloaded on-demand. Metadata, that is, data about data, can be applied to documents so that the correct materials can be found quickly.

- *Event management* enables sales reps, managers and others to plan, implement, control and evaluate events such as conferences, seminars, trade shows, exhibitions and webinars, whether run solo or jointly with customers or other partners. Some events, such as conferences, can be very complex and involve many stakeholders such as sponsors, exhibitors, security partners, police, accommodation partners, travel partners, catering partners, lighting and sound contractors, guest speakers, invitees and the general public. Indeed, some major events are planned many years in advance – you only need to consider the Olympics or FIFA World Cup to appreciate the grand scale of some major events. Sales-related events don't reach a comparable level of complexity, but events to which customers and key partners are invited must run smoothly, or the company risks being regarded as unprofessional.

  Event management software offers a range of functionality that can be used by event organizers across the event cycle, from initial event development and marketing to attendee registration and event operations, evaluation and reporting. The tools include event calendaring, event website design, event marketing, integration with social media, online registration, contact management, online payment and refund, partner management tools, event reports and analytics, attendee communications and management tools, badge and event documentation creation and venue management tools.

- *Incentive management* is an issue for sales managers who use commissions and other incentives to lift and direct sale reps' efforts, and to reward performance. In many companies, commissions are calculated using stand-alone spreadsheets. When part of a sales force automation solution, incentive management eliminates the need to re-enter or transfer data from spreadsheets, leading to better visibility, accuracy and higher efficiency. With incentive management models that consider quotas, sales volumes, customer profitability, customer satisfaction, customer retention, Net Promoter Scores and other performance criteria can be created. Sales team members can be given complete visibility into the sources and components of their commission. Incentive management applications can be linked into back-office payroll applications that automate payment.

- *Lead management* allows companies to capture, score, assign, nurture and track sales leads. Effective lead management processes are important because a significant proportion of leads, estimated at between 40 per cent and 80 per cent, are lost before the sales cycle is completed.[14] Leads can be captured from various touchpoints – web form or registration page on a company website, or a Facebook page for example – and automatically fed into the lead management system. Some SFA systems are integrated

EVENT MANAGEMENT AT KELLER AND HECKMAN[13]

Keller and Heckman is a US-based legal firm. Seminars are a key component of Keller and Heckman's brand development, lead generation and client-retention strategies. The seminar team, consisting of two full-time and one part-time employees, conducts approximately ten events each year for a total of 350 attendees drawn from both existing and potential clients.

The seminar team was tasked with growing seminar attendance, but was using manual systems for event planning, marketing, registration and payment. Some 40 per cent of event coordinator time was spent registering attendees for events alone, and, given the team's inability to process credit card payments, they decided to invest in technology to support the event calendar.

Having chosen an event management solution, Keller and Heckman first redesigned its event websites. Each event website and registration page is now paired with a custom event header, complete with the firm's logo. The seminar team began to promote early bird and last chance specials with customized emails, encourage attendees to share events with their contacts, and send automated invitation reminders. Event-specific websites provide details such as event fees and discounts, the agenda and hotel/room block information. The event management application enables the team to take credit card payments and make automated refunds if necessary. This has improved the registrant and attendee experience and freed the events team from fielding repetitive questions and manual fee processing, so they can focus on other key event deliverables and business development.

The software application has halved the time it takes to manage registrations, and the application's budget module makes the costing process easier. The event management functionality has resulted in significant lifts in attendance due to the team's ability to reach more people and the easy registration process.

CASE STUDY 8.1

with external databases that can be searched for relevant leads. Lead management software enables leads to be scored against a set of criteria established by sales management, so that the company can focus its limited sales resources where they are likely to generate most return. Scoring criteria might include consideration of bad data in the database record (e.g. a digit appears in the 'name' field), source of contact (referrals might be preferred to leads generated by cold-calling), and whether a personal or a corporate email is recorded in the email address field.

User-defined rules allow leads to be allocated or routed to reps and account managers on the basis of role, territory, product expertise or other variables. Lead nurturing is the practice of maintaining a healthy bilateral relationship with the lead until ready to buy. This can be achieved by delivering relevant, useful and personalized content through the channels preferred by the lead. This may mean email, but there may also be a role for events and pre-sales consulting. Essentially, lead nurturing is a demonstration of the seller's commitment to the lead. Interactivity between lead and supplier is an indicator that the lead is being successfully nurtured. Lead management software allows for more equitable workload distribution across a sales team, and implements security controls to ensure that reps can only access their own leads.

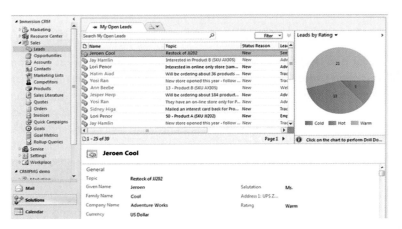

Figure 8.5 Lead management screenshot[15]

Used with permission from Microsoft.

- *Opportunity management* software enables reps and managers to monitor progress of an opportunity against a predefined selling methodology, ensuring that opportunities are advanced towards closure. An opportunity is a record of a potential sale or any other type of revenue generation. There are a number of selling methodologies all of which identify a number of stages such as lead qualification, initial approach, understanding the customer's requirements, developing a solution, crafting a proposal and closing the sale. Salespeople follow the steps of the methodology as if following a checklist, ensuring that all opportunities are handled consistently. Sales reps can associate their own opportunities with additional information such as contacts, activities, pricing rules, products, proposals, projects, presentations, quotations, competitors, estimated revenue, cost-of-sales, probability of closure, sales stage and so on. Managers can receive reports on the progress of opportunities as they move towards closure, broken down by salesperson, territory, type, date or other criteria. Figure 8.6 shows an opportunity management report. Note the selling model in the window on the left at the bottom of the screen, and the probability of closing the opportunity at the top of the screen.

- *Order management* functionality allows reps to convert quotations and estimates into orders once a customer has made the decision to buy. Order management software may include a quotation engine, a pricing module and a product configurator. Order management functionality accelerates the order-to-cash cycle by eliminating manual processing and errors and by quickly advancing the status of a sales quotation to approved order. The order management process can be integrated with back-office fulfilment, invoicing and payment processes, thereby accelerating cash flow for the seller. If order management functionality is used in front of a customer, the order can be loaded into production or picked from a warehouse more quickly. With visibility through a portal, the customer, rep and manager have access to the same, up-to-date order information. Some order management systems allow customers to manage their bills and other information online, thereby reducing account management costs for the seller.

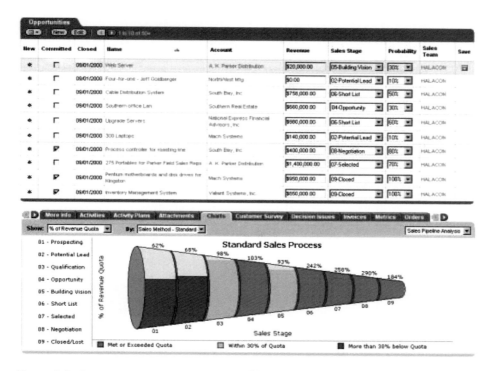

Figure 8.6 Opportunity management report[16]

- *Pipeline management* is the process of managing the entire sales cycle, from identifying prospects, estimating sales potential, managing leads, forecasting sales, initiating and maintaining customer relationships, right through to closure. A well-defined sales pipeline helps minimize lost opportunities and breakdowns in the sales process. Sales pipelines typically have between five and seven defined stages such as lead generation, lead qualification, initial meeting, submit quotation, sales presentation and closure. As opportunities move through the pipeline the probability of making the sale increases. For example, a sales rep might assign a 5 per cent probability of closing the sale to an opportunity that reaches 'initial meeting' stage, but a 60 per cent probability to an opportunity at the 'sales presentation' stage. Because these probabilities indicate that not all opportunities will progress down the pipeline, sales reps know that they have to have three to four times the value of their target or quota in the sales pipeline.

- A *product encyclopedia* is a searchable electronic product catalogue that generally contains product names, stock numbers, images and specifications. These can be stored on reps' computers, smart phones and tablets and/or made available to customers and partners online.

- *Product configuration* applications enable salespeople, or customer themselves, automatically to design and price customized products, services or solutions. Configurators

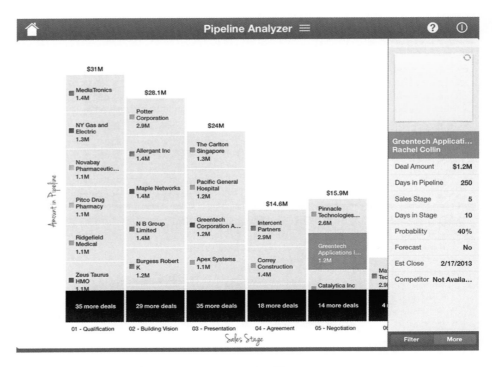

Figure 8.7 Oracle pipeline overview screenshot[17]

are useful when the product is particularly complex or when customization is an important part of the value proposition. Configurators guide users through the buying and specification process, offering only valid options and features at each step. This can deliver benefits to customers, salespeople and management. Customers can define and build their preferred customized solutions, reducing cost and meeting specifications. Salespeople no longer need master comprehensive product or service technical data, because these are built into the engine. Training costs for salespeople are therefore reduced. The potential for incorrectly specifying a solution for a customer is decreased. Configurators enable mass customization. Case study 8.2 shows how customers can build and price their own Jeep® brand vehicle online. Customers select a model and a colour. Next they browse and select interior, exterior and powertrain options. A customized price is computed and payment options offered. The customer is immediately presented with a list of nearby dealers carrying inventory that matches the specification, and the customer can then jump on the dealer's website and place the order. More advanced configurators enable customers to approach configuration from any starting point and in any sequence. For example, a buyer might make engine capacity the entry point, not the model.

- *Product visualization* software enables sales reps and customers to produce realistic computer-generated images or animations of products before they are manufactured. This is a useful application when linked to a product configurator. Static images can take the form of a simulated photograph, 3-D model or technical drawing. Some applications

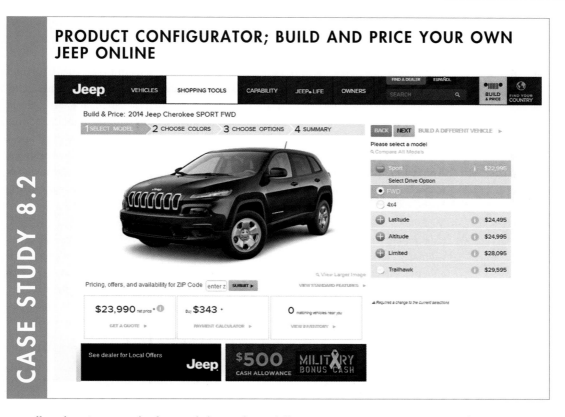

allow these images to be drag-and-dropped into different settings or contexts. Animated visualizations can be rendered in different ways to show how products are built, installed or used. Visualization software often allows users to change certain parameters, for example models, colours, fabrics and sizes, as in the Jeep example. Visualizations can be augmented by other information such as specifications or prices.

- *Proposal generation* software allows users to create customized branded proposals for customers. Users draw on information held in one or more databases to create proposals which, typically, are composed of several parts, some of which are customized: cover page and letter, introduction, objectives, products, product features, services, benefits, prices, specifications, pictures, drawings, embedded video, people, experience, résumés, references, approach, schedule, organization, scope of work and appendices. Proposal templates can speed up the creation of proposals that can then be delivered to customers whilst they are in buying mode. Templates exist for different types of proposals such as Statements of Work, Grant Applications and Service Level Agreements. Some can even be co-created on the fly in real time as customer and salesperson talk through what is required. One survey suggests that proposals produced with software have a much higher win rate (46 per cent) than proposals produced manually (26 per cent).[18]

- *Quotation management* software allows reps and managers to prepare costed proposals – quotes – for opportunities. The software allows users to create, edit, approve and produce costed, customized proposals quickly and reliably. Some software enables users to create multimedia quotations with audio, animation and video.

- *Sales forecasting* applications offer sales reps and managers a number of qualitative and quantitative processes to help forecast sales revenues and close rates. Among the qualitative methods are sales team estimates that can be created collaboratively, and among the quantitative methods are time-series analysis and regression models. Some sales forecasting methods project historical sales into the future. Other methods draw on and interpret the sales opportunity and pipeline data maintained in CRM systems. Another method is to import data from external sources and apply quantitative methods to forecast sales. Accurate sales forecasts help resource allocation throughout the business.

- *Sales management reporting* functionality is integrated into all SFA systems. This offers users a number of standardized reports that can help sales managers evaluate and enhance the effectiveness and efficiency of their sales team. In addition managers can create ad hoc reports on any variable or mix of variables maintained in the sales database – this can include reports on all the issues we are discussing here: contacts, contracts, orders, opportunities, proposals, sales pipeline and so on. See Table 8.3 for a selection of reports that sales managers can request.

Table 8.3 Examples of reports available from SFA software

• cost-to-serve	• sales cycles
• customer profitability	• share of market
• lead conversion	• share-of-wallet
• pipeline progress	• salesperson productivity
• quotation performance	• win–loss rates

Salesforce.com, for example, offers over 50 standard reports, and enables users to construct their own customized reports using wizards. These deliver charts, tables, text and other graphics to receivers' devices. Dashboards deliver real-time sales data to executives that can be refreshed at a single click. Customized dashboards ensure that people receive reports matched to their roles and responsibilities. Drill-down capabilities mean that users can thoroughly investigate the reasons behind results in dashboard reports. Furthermore, dashboards can be integrated with third-party analytics to deliver deeper analysis of sales performance and problems. Figure 8.8 is a sample sales manager's dashboard.

- *Territory management* applications allow sales managers to create, adjust and balance sales territories, so that sales reps have equivalent workloads and/or opportunities. Territory management applications usually come with a territory management methodology that users can follow when establishing sales territories.[20] Some applications

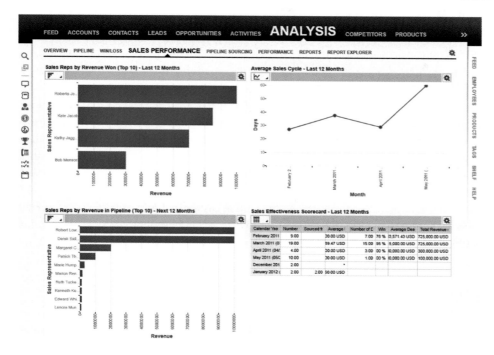

Figure 8.8 Sales management report[19]

© 2014 SAP AG or an SAP affiliate company. All rights reserved. Used with permission of SAP AG or an SAP affiliate company.

integrate geographic mapping or geo-demographic data into the application. Applications generally enable companies to match sales coverage to market opportunity, create sales territory hierarchies (cities, states, regions) and reduce the cost of selling by reducing travel time. Call cycle scheduling, calendaring and lead management is often enabled by the software. Eligibility and exception rules can be established in and monitored by the software. A sales rep might be eligible to sell some products but not others, to service all customers in her territory with the exception of certain named accounts, or to sell into certain accounts in another territory because she has a well-established customer relationship.

- *Workflow development* software is used to design sales-related processes including the lead management process and the event management process. A simple automated workflow spells out the actions that are taken when a web-form enquiry is received by the business. A more complex project is to automate the workflow in the selling process itself – the series of steps that a sales rep must follow in shifting a prospect from initial awareness to the close. Some leading SFA applications contain modules where selling workflow follows established published methodologies. For example, Microsoft Dynamics CRM has a module for Solution Selling® and Oracle CRM for Target Account Selling®. Workflow applications automate business processes, so that process owners know what to do, the order in which actions should be performed and who is responsible for each action. Automated processes are much easier to monitor for process failure. When a process fails, often this can be an indication that the process needs to be simplified, user training needs to be refreshed or technological support for the process needs to be upgraded.

Although we have thus far discussed a generic set of sales-related functionality, SFA software is also designed for context-specific applications. For example, sales reps selling liquor to a retail store might employ software that recommends planograms, optimizes the allocation of retail display space, audits inventory levels, recommends prices and controls cooperative promotional support. In some contexts, graphics, video and sound support are important. Leading SFA vendors offer functionality designed for salespeople in particular industries. SAP CRM and Oracle CRM, for example, both offer customized SFA solutions for over 20 different industries ranging from aerospace and defence to wholesaling. These solutions come with industry-specific database models.

SFA ADOPTION

Generally, a company's decision to adopt SFA follows a two-step process. First, senior management decides to invest in SFA, and second, sales reps and their managers decide to use SFA. Both groups – senior management and users – will anticipate benefits from SFA, and unless those benefits are delivered SFA may be abandoned.[21]

Benefits from SFA

Vendors and consultants claim a number of benefits from SFA implementation, including accelerated cash flow, shorter sales cycles leading to faster inventory turnover, improved customer relationships, improved salesperson productivity, accurate management reports, increased sales revenue, market share growth, higher win rates, reduced cost-of-sales, more closing opportunities and improved profitability. These benefits appeal to differing SFA stakeholders:

- *Salespeople*: shorter sales cycles, more closing opportunities, higher win rates.
- *Sales managers*: improved salesperson productivity, improved customer relationships, accurate reporting, reduced cost-of-sales.
- *Senior management*: improved visibility of the sales pipeline, reduced risk of unexpected variations from sales forecasts, accelerated cash flow, increased sales revenue, market share growth, improved profitability.

In addition to these hard outcomes, there may be additional softer benefits such as less rework, more timely information and better quality management reports. Software vendor case histories of SFA implementations offer testimonials to SFA's impacts (see Case study 8.3: Freight Traders).

CASE STUDY 8.3

FREIGHT TRADERS ENJOYS BENEFITS FROM SFA[22]

Freight Traders, a subsidiary of global food manufacturer Mars, Incorporated, is a Web-based logistics consultancy that connects shippers to carriers. The company facilitates the transit of cargo between the two parties. Customers include Kellogg's, Lever Fabergé and Sainsbury's supermarket group. Garry Mansell is managing director.

'We had the system up and running in three days,' says Mansell. 'Within eight days the whole company was using it across multiple countries. Ease of use and speed of implementation were everything I expected of a Web-based solution.' Major benefits include far greater customer, lead and prospect visibility. 'We operate dispersed account teams and they now have a single view of customers and prospects.' Another major benefit is accessibility. 'Regardless of where I am in the world, I only have to log on to see how our business is doing,' says Mansell.

'The reporting tools are really useful to our business,' continues Mansell. 'We don't need to waste time chasing sales teams for reports. Once we put in the information, reports are automated and can be tailored to our requirements.' Mansell finds these reports a valuable tool to the running of the business. It helps the company focus on maximizing resources, by identifying where and when the best sales opportunities arise and responding to them.

Freight Traders uses salesforce.com to communicate best practices across the organization. 'Because the system is so transparent we can show clearly what works best with a particular company, country or industry and share that vital intelligence across the organization. All the information is contained in our salesforce.com account.'

Independent research, summarized in Table 8.4, suggests that the primary motivation for senior management's investment in SFA solutions is improved efficiency, although not every SFA implementation has specified formal goals.[23]

HOW SFA CHANGES SALES PERFORMANCE

There have been a number of independent assessments of the effects of SFA on sales performance.[25] One empirical investigation of a pharmaceutical company's operations in three countries finds a clear relationship between SFA adoption and salesperson performance. The researchers conclude that 16.4 per cent of the variance in sales is explained by the use of the SFA solution.[26] Another investigation found that use of SFA was associated with improvements in sales reps' targeting and selling skills, market and technical knowledge, call productivity and sales performance. Essentially these sales reps' use of SFA accounted for a small, yet significant portion (7 per cent) of their sales performance.[27] However, not all research indicates positive outcomes from the implementation of SFA.[28]

Table 8.4 Motivations for implementing SFA[24]

Motivation	% of sample reporting
Improve efficiencies	72
Improve customer contact	44
Increase sales	33
Reduce costs	26
Improve accuracy	21

It seems likely that SFA will have more impact on sales performance when a number of conditions are met.[29] These include:

1 Salespeople find that the SFA application is easy to use.

2 Salespeople find the technology useful because it fits their roles well.

3 Availability of appropriate-to-task SFA training.

4 Users have accurate expectations about what SFA will deliver.

5 Users have a positive attitude towards innovation.

6 Users have a positive attitude towards technology.

7 Availability of user support after roll-out, for example, a help desk.

8 Involvement of user groups including sales reps and managers during SFA project planning and technology selection.

9 Deployment of a multidisciplinary team in the SFA project planning phases.

10 Senior management support for SFA.

Some ease-of-use considerations include screen design, the use of a graphical user interface, system navigation, online help, user documentation, data synchronization and system support. Screen layouts that are clean and bright appear uncluttered and are easier to read. System navigation is good if users can move from field to field, tab to tab, screen to screen, module to module and function to function with no difficulty. The basic components of a device's graphical user interface (GUI, pronounced goo-ee) are a pointing device and graphical icons. The pointing device can be a mouse or, on touch-sensitive screens, a finger. Before GUIs were introduced SFA users had to remember commands that involved using ctrl, alt, del and other keys in various combinations. Online help means users can resolve questions quickly. User documentation that includes screenshots, text or instructional video clips is appreciated, as is simple, fast, data synchronization and general system support through training and a help desk.

SUMMARY

Sales force automation is a competitive necessity which involves the application of technology to support salespeople and their managers. Broadly, SFA enables members of sales teams to become more efficient and effective in their job roles. The SFA eco-system includes a wide range of software, hardware, infrastructure and service organizations. SFA software offers an enormous range of functionality including account management, activity management, contact management, contract management, document management, event management, incentive management, lead management, opportunity management, order management, pipeline management, product encyclopedias, product configuration, product visualization, proposal generation, quotation management, sales forecasting, sales management reporting, territory management and workflow development.

Three stakeholder groups – salespeople, sales managers and senior management – have a particular interest in generating benefits from SFA adoption, and each may have a different perspective on what counts as success. For a salesperson, success might mean 'increased commission' or 'more time released from administrative tasks for selling'. For a sales manager, success might be 'better management of underperforming reps'. For senior management, success might be 'improved market share and reduced cost-to-serve'.

None of these benefits are likely to be delivered if salespeople fail to adopt the technology. Adoption is more likely if salespeople find the technology is useful and easy to use, and they receive training.

NOTES AND REFERENCES

1   Peppard, J., Ward, J. and Daniel, E. (2007). Managing the realization of business benefits from IT investments. *MIS Quarterly Executive*, 6(1), 1–17.

2   This argument about the relationship between strategy and the competencies or 'dynamic capabilities' of organizations is a foundation of 'The Resource Based View' of the firm, perhaps the dominant academic discourse on strategy over the past 20 years. This view is held widely by IS scholars and marketing researchers looking at the relationship between CRM and business performance.

3   Morgan, A. and Inks, S.A. (2001). Technology and the sales force. *Industrial Marketing Management*, 30(5), 463–72.

4   Engle, R.L. and Barnes, M.L. (2000). Sales force automation usage, effectiveness, and cost-benefit in Germany, England and the United States. *Journal of Business and Industrial Marketing*, 15(4), 216–42.

5   Lambe, C.J. and Spekman, R. (1997). National account management: large account selling or buyer–seller alliance? *Journal of Personal Selling and Sales Management*, 17(4), 61–74.

6   Grönroos, C. (2000). *Service marketing and management: a customer relationship management approach*, 2nd edn. Chichester: John Wiley.

7   Courtesy Oracle.com. Used with permission.

8   Courtesy SAP.com. Used with permission.

9   Taylor, T.C. (1994). Valuable insights on sales automation progress. *Sales Process Engineering and Automation Review*, December, 19–21.

10 Conner, K.R. and Rumelt, R.P. (1991). Software piracy: an analysis of protection strategies. *Management Science*, 37(2), 125–39.

11 Courtesy salesforce.com www.salesforce.com

12 Courtesy of Oracle. Used with permission.

13 http://www.cvent.com/en/pdf/keller-heckman-success-story.pdf (Accessed 24 March 2014).

14 http://www.yankeegroup.com/ResearchDocument.do?id=13970 (Accessed 24 March 2014).

15 Courtesy Microsoft Dynamics www.microsoft.com/en-au/dynamics/crm.aspx.

16 Courtesy Siebel Systems. http://www.oracle.com/applications/crm/siebel/resources/siebel-salesforce-sales-data-sheet.pdf (Accessed 25 January 2008).

17 Courtesy Oracle.com. Used with permission.

18 http://www.realmarket.com/news/pragmatech121102.html (Accessed 21 November 2007).

19 Courtesy SAP.com. Used with permission.

20 http://download-uk.oracle.com/docs/cd/B11454_01/11.5.9/acrobat/jty115ig.pdf.

21 Speier, C. and Venkatash, V. (2002). The hidden minefields in the adoption of sales force automation technologies. *Journal of Marketing*, 66(3), 98–111.

22 http://www.salesforce.com/customers/casestudy.jsp?customer=ft (Accessed 26 August 2005).

23 Erffmeyer, R.C. and Johnson, D.A. (2001). An exploratory study of sales force automation practices: expectations and realities. *Journal of Personal Selling and Sales Management*, 21(2), 167–75; Ingram, T.N., LaForge, R.W. and Leigh, T.W. (2002). Selling in the new millennium: a joint agenda. *Industrial Marketing Management*, 31(7), 559–67.

24 Erffmeyer, R.C. and Johnson, D.A. (2001). An exploratory study of sales force automation practices: expectations and realities. *Journal of Personal Selling and Sales Management*, 21(2), 167–75.

25 Erffmeyer, R.C. and Johnson, D.A. (2001). An exploratory study of sales force automation practices: expectations and realities. *Journal of Personal Selling and Sales Management*, 21(2), 167–75; Engle, R.L. and Barnes, M.L. (2000). Sales force automation usage, effectiveness, and cost-benefit in Germany, England and the United States. *Journal of Business and Industrial Marketing*, 15(4), 216–42; Ahearne, M. and Schillewaert, N. (2001). *The acceptance of information technology in the sales force*. eBusiness Research Center, Working paper 10–2000. Penn State University.

26 Engle, R.L. and Barnes, M.L. (2000). Sales force automation usage, effectiveness, and cost-benefit in Germany, England and the United States. *Journal of Business and Industrial Marketing*, 15(4), 216–42.

27 Ahearne, M. and Schillewaert, N. (2001). *The acceptance of information technology in the sales force*. eBusiness Research Center, Working paper 10–2000. Penn State University.

28 See review of SFA research in Buttle, F., Ang, L. and Iriana, R. (2006). Sales force automation: review, critique research agenda. *International Journal of Management Reviews*, 8(4), 213–31.

29 This section draws on Buttle, F., Ang, L. and Iriana, R. (2006). Sales force automation: review, critique research agenda. *International Journal of Management Reviews*, 8(4), 213–31.

CHAPTER 9

MARKETING AUTOMATION

CHAPTER OBJECTIVES

By the end of this chapter you will understand:

- What is meant by marketing automation (MA).
- The benefits that MA can deliver to organizations.
- The functionality available within MA software.

INTRODUCTION

This is the second of the three chapters in Part III that survey operational CRM. This chapter is about technologies used by marketers. The preceding chapter reviewed sales force automation and the next examines service automation. The chapter starts with a definition of marketing automation (MA) and then describes some of the functionality that is available in MA software.

WHAT IS MARKETING AUTOMATION?

Marketing practices have historically been very ad hoc. Some of the major companies, particularly fast-moving consumer goods companies such as Unilever and Procter and Gamble, have bucked the trend and developed marketing processes that brand managers, segment managers, market managers and marketing managers are obliged to follow. However, they are the exception. In general, marketers have not been structured in the way that they plan, implement, evaluate and control their marketing strategies and tactics. Marketing automation has brought increased rigour to marketing processes. Moreover, gone are the days when an organization might run a handful of campaigns every year. The modern, information-enabled marketer can run thousands of highly targeted campaigns based on complex data mining and predictive analytics. CRM technologies enable marketing campaigns to be created for individual customers. MA has now reached such a level of

MARKETING AUTOMATION AT STAPLES[1]

Staples is a US-based multinational retailer of office supplies. It is a worldwide category leader which innovated the 'big box' retailing format. As a 'category killer' it services customers both online and in-store. It implemented SAS marketing automation and analytics to manage 1,500 separate campaigns across 25 million customer records. The improved number and targeting of the campaigns is reported to have generated a 137 per cent return on investment. In addition, the CRM systems monitor the behaviour of regular customers and can intervene with bespoke offers when their spending drops. The tools permit different ways of monitoring customer retention and identify those most at risk of defection through models of customers' purchasing behaviour.

sophistication that the whole process of marketing from customer selection to offer presentation can be directed by business rules and fuelled by data. Contemporary marketing managers need the ability to adapt and scale up their operational processes to handle the increased complexity facing them.

The term marketing automation can be defined as follows:

Marketing automation is the application of computerized technologies to support marketers and marketing management in the achievement of their work-related objectives.

A very wide range of marketing positions can make use of MA including marketing manager, campaign manager, market analyst, market manager, promotions manager, database marketer and direct marketing manager.

Hardware and software are the key technological elements of MA. Hardware includes desktop, laptop and handheld devices such as tablets and smart phones. Software comprises both 'point' solutions that are designed to assist in a single area of marketing or marketing management, and integrated solutions that offer a range of functionality. Some integrated packages are dedicated to marketing applications only; others are incorporated into broader CRM solutions that operate over the three front-office areas of marketing, service and sales.

BENEFITS OF MARKETING AUTOMATION

Marketing automation can deliver several benefits. These include the following:

- *Enhanced marketing efficiency.* The replication of marketing processes delivers greater control over costs. When marketers use manual systems and ad hoc processes, there can be considerable inefficiencies. MA enables companies to develop more streamlined, cost-efficient processes, that can be operated by any marketing incumbent, whether experienced or new-to-role.

- *Greater marketing productivity.* In the days before MA, marketers might be expected to run a modest number of advertising campaigns and sales promotions in a single year. MA enables companies to run dozens, even thousands of campaigns and events through multiple channels simultaneously without a commensurate increase in the cost and complexity of running the business.

- *More effective marketing.* MA allows marketers to employ what is known as closed-loop marketing (CLM). CLM is based on a Plan–Do–Measure–Learn cycle, as illustrated in Figure 9.1. Marketers plan a campaign or event, implement the plan, measure the outcomes, learn from the outcomes and subsequently modify the next campaign or event. CLM ensures that companies learn continuously from their marketing activities, achieving higher levels of marketing effectiveness. Companies can also identify and abandon failing marketing initiatives before they drain financial resources.

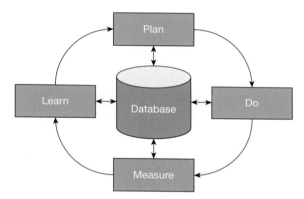

Figure 9.1 Closed-loop marketing

- *Improved accountability* for marketing expenditure. MA provides better data and analysis on which to judge the commercial return from marketing activities, improved transparency and faster (almost real-time) information for management.

- *Enhanced responsiveness.* Marketers have traditionally created and implemented annual marketing plans with campaigns and promotions planned and scheduled many months ahead. MA allows marketers to respond instantly to opportunities, even if not part of a plan. MA functionality enables companies to engage in real-time marketing, responding immediately to an identified opportunity. For example when a female customer buys baby clothes from a catalogue for the first time, marketers can send an automated offer inviting the customer to join a mother-and-baby club which offers additional customer benefits to new mothers.

- *Improved marketing intelligence.* MA's embedded reporting and analytics functionality provides valuable management insights into markets, customers, campaigns, events and so on, leading to both enhanced efficiency and effectiveness.

- *Improved customer experience.* Customers receive personalized, relevant communications and offers at appropriate times. MA means less Spam, from the customer's perspective.

- *Improved customer engagement.* Customers develop a stronger sense of emotional and behavioural identification with the firm when they experience offers and communications that are based on deep understanding of their needs and preferences.

SOFTWARE APPLICATIONS FOR MARKETING

MA applications offer a range of functionality, which can be grouped into applications that support marketing campaigns, those that support digital and online marketing, and those that support strategic and broader marketing management matters, as listed in Table 9.1. The table lists both macro-MA solutions that offer a wide range of functionality, and micro-MA solutions that offer a narrow range of functionality. The macro-solutions, such as Integrated Marketing Management, deliver much of the functionality present in the micro-solutions.

We will now describe this functionality in more detail: first, we will review the functionality for campaign management; second we will report on functionality for online and digital marketing; then we will turn to functionality for strategic and other marketing issues.

Table 9.1 Functionality offered by MA software

Marketing campaigns	Digital and online marketing	Strategic and other marketing
Campaign management	Online marketing	Integrated marketing management
Direct mail campaign management	Content management	Marketing performance management
Email campaign management	Keyword marketing	Marketing resource management
Event-based marketing	Search engine optimization	Loyalty management
Trigger marketing	Social media marketing	Partner marketing
Marketing optimization	Digital analytics	Market segmentation
Telemarketing		Customer segmentation and selection
Lead generation		Product lifecycle management
		Asset management
		Document management
		Marketing analytics
		Workflow development

Campaigning

Campaign management

Campaign management can be defined as follows:

Campaign management is the technology-enabled application of data-driven strategies to select customers or prospects for customized communications and offers that vary at every stage of the customer lifecycle and buyer readiness.

Campaign management automates the processes involved in planning, implementing, measuring and learning from communication programmes targeted at prospects or customers. Campaigns may be used to raise awareness, influence emotions or motivate behaviours such as buying a product or visiting a website. The key elements of campaign management software are workflow, segmentation and targeting, personalization, execution, measurement, modelling and reporting.

- *Workflow*. Before any campaign is run, the overall campaign development and implementation process has to be designed. Workflow establishes the order in which tasks have to be performed. The tasks may include setting measurable objectives, setting a budget, getting approvals, creating a database of contacts, selecting contacts, creating a core message, testing the core message, customizing the message for individual recipients, selecting communication channels, executing the campaign, measuring response, reporting outcomes, and reviewing and learning from the campaign. Workflow functionality allows managers to plan, design, manage and monitor and report specific marketing campaigns, which are often complex and follow event-based next-step rules (if this–then that).

- *Segmentation and targeting*. The customer base or source list can be divided into subsets so that one or more subsets can be treated to a customized campaign. Segmentation is the process of identifying subsets, and targeting is the selection of the subset(s) that will receive the content. A common approach to segmentation is to partition customers based on recency of purchase, frequency of purchase and monetary value, targeting different offers at different subsets. As customer insight increases over time companies may find they are able to target individual customers with uniquely structured messages and offers. Customer targeting is based on customer data from operational systems, channels and social media.

- *Personalization*. Messaging and offers are tailored for individual recipients at each stage of the customer lifecycle and buyer readiness. MA, when supported by customer insight, means that customers are known as individuals rather than demographic stereotypes. Personalization can happen in real time contingent upon the individual's revealed preferences or behaviours.

- *Execution*. Campaign execution happens when the message is delivered through the selected communication channels. Campaigns can be run in many channels, independently, consecutively or simultaneously: direct mail, email, social media, website, outbound or inbound telephone, text message or multimedia message. Campaign management solutions can be integrated with sales and distribution for the fulfilment of orders.

- *Measurement*. The results from the campaign are assessed at segment and individual recipient level. Measures focus on the objectives originally set.

- *Modelling*. Modelling is the process of interpreting campaign results statistically, so that future campaigns can be based on statistical insight into what works and what doesn't.

- *Reporting*. Campaign results are computed and delivered in standard or customized management reports to relevant parties. Reports enable companies to enjoy the benefits of closed-loop marketing, through cycles of learning and improvement.

The ability to run integrated marketing campaigns over multiple channels, optimize campaigns, and integrate with sales and service applications are important considerations for large-enterprise users of campaign management.

According to independent analysts, Gartner Inc., leading solutions for multi-channel campaign management include SAS, Teradata, IBM and Oracle (Siebel).[2] There are many other challenger and niche campaign management software offerings. Multi-channel campaign management (MCCM) processes enable companies to construct and communicate

CASE STUDY 9.2

DIAL ECO-SMART MULTI-CHANNEL MARKETING[3]

Dial Eco-Smart aims to replace the typical hotel amenity bottles with tamper-proof, refillable dispensers. While this new programme guarantees the hotel a minimum of 50 per cent savings, it is a radical departure from the established industry norm of the iconic little shampoo bottles. Eco-Smart's year one launch used traditional push marketing targeting mid-level hotels. The campaign cost $90,000 budget and used advertisements placed in hospitality trade magazines. The ads gave contact information and a call to action that invited people to email for more information. The results from the entire first year were just five total requests for further information.

Given this failed year one campaign, Dial implemented a multi-channel campaign management strategy in year two. This consisted of a direct mail campaign linked to a PURL (personalized landing page) that communicated with a call centre and a sales team. This campaign was targeted at the same audience as the previous year. This multi-channel campaign took two months to build including design, gathering data and doing some on-site photography of Eco-Smart products. The initial direct mail portion of the marketing campaign went to 940 prospects and invited each of them to visit a personalized landing page with more information on the product. From the PURL, the prospects could request samples to pilot-test at their hotel.

When a specific PURL was visited by a prospect, the call centre was notified and the prospect received an outbound call from an agent in as little as five minutes. This multi-channel marketing campaign cost just over $6,000. One month after the multi-channel marketing campaign rolled out, Dial had received 53 responses asking for a sales representative to call them. This compares well to the five they received the previous year.

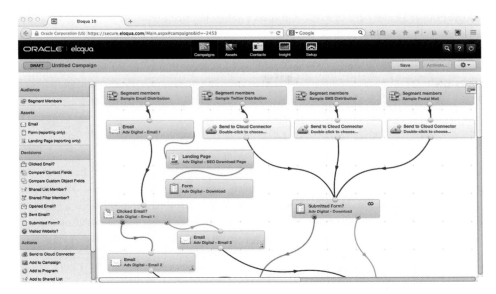

Figure 9.2 Oracle (Eloqua) multi-channel campaign management application[4]

offers to individual customers or customer segments across multi-channel environments. Sometimes MCCM campaigns are integrated with sales for execution. The most basic campaign management functionality enables campaign workflow, audience segmentation and targeting, and campaign execution. Some campaign management applications include powerful analytics and campaign optimization. Advanced execution functionality integrates campaigns with loyalty programmes, and is supported by content management, event triggering and real-time offer management in inbound and outbound environments. These issues are discussed in more detail below.

Direct mail campaign management

Direct mail campaign management is a specific form of campaign management in which the communication medium is direct mail. About 75 per cent of direct mail targets consumer audiences, the balance being sent to business audiences. In most developed markets, direct mail volumes have been stabilizing or declining as marketers opt for digital media. Direct mail has many applications including lead generation, lead nurturing, building awareness, sales, customer service, customer retention, database building or reputation enhancement. Important contributors to direct mail success are list quality, the creative execution, the offer and the timing. Making the right offer to the right person at the right time in a creatively compelling way will produce greater success. Automated processes can help deliver all these outcomes. A high-quality list that is clean and contemporary, a creative execution that catches the eye and promotes action, an offer that is determined by the list member's propensity-to-buy and that is personalized will achieve greater success that the conventional mass mail-outs that have been marketing's tradition.

Consumer preferences also figure in the decision to use direct mail. Consumers typically prefer to receive offers from local stores and suppliers by direct mail, but prefer email for competitions. The old cry that 'it's a numbers game' has been replaced by a clear focus on customized, personalized offers. The average response rate for both business and consumer mailings is around 4 per cent; about 1 in 25 recipients does what the mailer wants them to do, whether that is register for an event, redeem a coupon or call a toll-free number. Response rates range from below 1 per cent to over 30 per cent (for government mailings).[5] Many companies elect to outsource direct mail campaigns to third-party service providers that are themselves big users of marketing automation.

Email campaign management

Email campaign management is a specific form of campaign management in which the communication medium is email. Email is cheap, easy to use and ubiquitous. Over 90 per cent of Internet users have one or more email addresses.[6] Email marketing is a massive industry. In the USA alone, Forrester Research estimates that spending on email marketing is showing compound growth of 10 per cent a year, to reach $2.5 billion in 2016.[7] Legitimate email marketing is tainted by the widespread use of email Spam; that is, unsolicited bulk email. Up to 50 per cent of email messages are Spam.

The typical legitimate opt-in (or permission-based) email marketing message contains text and a link through to a website. Open and click-through rates, the most commonly used email marketing metrics, provide marketers with some insight into how an email message has performed. These metrics can be combined into a click-to-open rate (CTOR) that measures click-through rates as a percentage of messages opened, instead of messages delivered. UK research reports average open rates of 22.87 per cent, average click-through rates of 3.26 per cent and average CTOR of 14.25 per cent.[8] As with all customer communications it is very important to specify clear objectives. If the objective is to sell 100 products, reporting success in terms of CTOR makes little sense.

There is a significant and growing volume of research into the effectiveness of email marketing. The Email Experience Council (www.emailexperience.org) and the Email Statistics Center (www.emailstatcenter.com) act as gateways to many of these resources. Among the statistics they cite are the following, which collectively indicate the potential and challenges of email:

- Global spending on email marketing is forecast to reach US$15.7 billion by 2017.[9]
- The Direct Marketing Association reports that email marketing has a return on investment of $57.25 for every dollar spent.
- It is estimated that there will be over 2.7 billion email users in 2016.
- The total worldwide email traffic including both business and consumer emails will grow to over 192 billion emails/day by 2016.
- Customer acquisition (32 per cent) and lead nurturing (27 per cent) are the two primary goals of business-to-business email campaigns.
- 38 per cent of people have two personal email accounts; 21 per cent have three accounts; 57 per cent have one business email account.
- 49 per cent of people have email accounts for messages they rarely intend to open.
- 91 per cent of consumers check their email at least once a day.

- 91 per cent of people use their smart phone to check their personal email.

- 32 per cent of marketers do not have a strategy in place to optimize emails for mobile devices. Email is easy to read on large-screen devices but can be problematic on smart phones, where messages and links to websites are rendered in very small text.

- The top three marketing channels that organizations are integrating into their email programmes are: website (75 per cent), social media (56 per cent) and events such as tradeshows, webinars, etc. (40 per cent).

- Nearly all adult Internet users, or 78.4 per cent of the US adult population, will send an email via any device at least once per month.

- 69 per cent of companies use email marketing to build customer loyalty and retention, 50 per cent to build awareness, 45 per cent to drive revenue.

- Permission email marketing accounts for 27 per cent of the email that consumers receive in their primary personal inboxes.

- One in five emails is invisible and ineffective due to blocked images.

- 45 per cent of click-through landing pages do not repeat the promotional copy found in the email, thus failing to reinforce the call-to-action that prompted the email recipient to click a link in the first place.

- Only 10 per cent of email campaigns are fully individualized in terms of salutation, images, timing and promotion.

There are many email campaign management software packages, either stand-alone or integrated into more comprehensive campaign management or MA offerings. Basic functionality available in these packages includes campaign workflow, implementation, tracking and reporting, and a user interface suitable for marketers. Advanced functionality includes predictive analytics and event triggering. Predictive analytics give users the ability to predict a customer's next most likely purchase and propensity to buy. Email campaigns can also be trained to respond to a significant event in the customer relationship. See the following two sections on event-based marketing and trigger marketing for more information. Figure 9.3 is an example of email campaign management workflow in LISTSERV Maestro.

Event-based marketing

Event-based marketing (also called event marketing) occurs when an event triggers a communication or offer. Event-based campaigns are usually initiated by customer behaviours or contextual conditions. Here are some examples of customer behaviours (events) that trigger marketing responses:

- A customer who uses a credit card less than six times in a three-month period receives an invitation to participate in a frequency reward programme designed to encourage repeated use.

- A bank customer who deposits $50,000 or more into a savings account receives an offer of investment advice from a licensed financial planner.

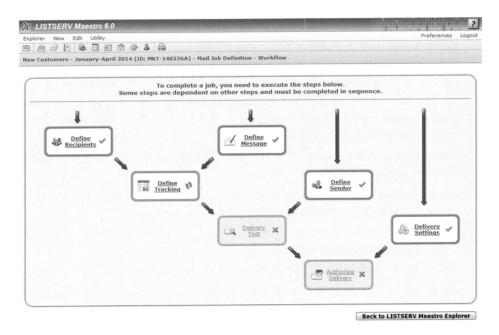

Figure 9.3 Email campaign management workflow[10]

Copyright © 2013. SAS Institute Inc. All rights reserved. Reproduced with permission of SAS Institute Inc., Cary, NC, USA.

- A customer buys gardening gloves online. This triggers an automated email confirming purchase, providing tracking information and offering a related product purchase – gardening tools.
- An online shopper abandons a shopping cart before payment. This triggers a follow-up reminder email aimed at converting the lapsed browser into a purchaser.

Here are some examples of contextual conditions that trigger a marketing response:

- A customer's birthday triggers a congratulatory message containing a customized offer.
- A change of address triggers an approach to update other contact details.
- Religious festivals such as Eid, Christmas and Hanukkah trigger marketing campaigns.

Trigger marketing

Trigger marketing is the practice of responding to some event in a way that is designed to achieve some marketing goal such as make a sale, identify a cross-sell opportunity, prevent negative word-of-mouth or promote positive word-of-mouth. The event triggers the response. As noted in the previous section on event-based marketing, the triggers are usually customer behaviours or contextual conditions. Trigger marketing software can be trained to identify events, and either to send an automated response such as an email, digitally personalized direct mail piece or text message, or to feed the information through to a sales person or customer service agent for follow-up. Trigger marketing ensures that the communication is

TRIGGER-BASED MARKETING AT HPES[11]

HPES provides education and training products and services to Hewlett Packard's (HP) clients. The offering includes partner training, virtual classrooms and a number of distance learning solutions, along with accreditation programmes. HP noticed that attaching HPES products and services to hardware sales enabled their customers to gain more from their purchase, whilst the customer in turn became far more loyal and profitable to HP.

HP created a pilot study to assess whether or not trigger-based marketing could be used to identify opportunities to attach HPES products and services to existing sales opportunities.

HP sales teams had been reluctant to sell HPES products and services, so the pilot study set out to identify the correct points in the sales cycle to send sales reps an appropriate trigger-based communication to encourage them, and provide them with the information, to make incremental HPES sales.

The HP CRM team collaborated with an external consultancy to explore the customer and sales data that resided in the CRM system. The result was a bespoke set of event-based rules that would trigger a personalized communication from HPES to the rep.

The email contained information to assist in the conversion of the sale whilst attaching a relevant HPES solution. The resultant communication was tracked and the results fed back into Oracle (Siebel) CRM to determine sales value and ROI measure. The 12-week pilot generated $450,000 of incremental revenue. An extended (Europe, the Middle East and Africa – EMEA) pilot generated additional revenue of $2 million and a projected sales uplift across EMEA of $8.2 million. The pilot achieved a 60 per cent response rate by HP sales reps to the personalized automated communication, and lifted the perception of HPES within the HP sales team.

relevant to the recipient, because it is a contextualized response to a customer event. For example, when a customer is approaching their credit limit you might send an email notifying them so they can avoid fees and charges. This would surely be welcomed.

Marketing optimization

Campaign management solutions are very popular but most cannot handle a complex environment in which a fixed number of campaign dollars have to be distributed over many offers in many channels to many customer segments with a view to achieving some overarching commercial goal such as maximum sales or contribution to profit. Marketing optimization provides a mathematics-based solution to this problem. Users of marketing optimization software do not need to understand the complex optimization algorithm that underpins this application.

Marketing optimization software allows you to select an overall goal, such as sales or profit margin maximization, and specify all of the constraints of your marketing campaign strategy, such as budget, customer contact policy (e.g. no more than three offers per customer per year), channels available (e.g. direct mail, email, branch, mobile, call centre), minimal cell size per offer (e.g. target customer segment size of at least 250 persons), product-specific volume requirements (e.g. must sell 10,000 Gizmos this quarter), customer segments' propensities-to-buy different products, and channel constraints (e.g. call centre can only make

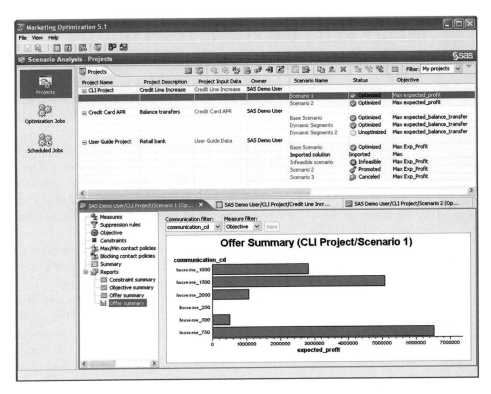

Figure 9.4 Marketing optimization: scenario testing[12]

200 outbound calls per week), to name but a few. The software then determines which customers should get which offer through which channel to ensure your campaign objectives are met.

Marketing optimization software also lets you explore any number of 'what-if' scenarios (see Figure 9.4), changing constraints and objectives, and compare the results, before committing any marketing resources. The more advanced marketing optimization technology operates in real-time, allowing a company website to present the right offer and call centre agents to promote the right promotion during each customer interaction.

In short, marketing optimization enables marketers to extract the best return – however defined – from their campaign dollar whilst taking account of a range of constraints such as budgets, customer segments, propensities-to-buy, contact policies, channel availability and channel capacity.

Telemarketing

Telemarketing can be defined as follows:

Telemarketing is the use of the telephone to identify and qualify prospects, and to sell and service the needs of customers.

Telemarketing takes two forms: inbound (calls from customers) and outbound (calls to customers). Some call centres perform a blended function with agents both making and receiving calls. Telemarketing is widely employed in both B2C and B2B environments, but can be subject to legislative control due to its intrusive nature. For example, both the USA and Australia operate a Do Not Call register on which telephone account holders can list their numbers. With a few exceptions – charities, political organizations, research firms – marketers are not allowed to call listed numbers, and penalties apply.

Telemarketing software applications offer a wide range of functionality over landlines, mobile networks and VoIP (Voice over Internet Protocol):

- auto-dialling
- predictive dialling
- automated voice-messaging
- contact list management
- agent management
- Do Not Call compliance
- screen pop with caller ID
- scripting, including objection response
- Computer Aided Telephone Interviewing (CATI)
- Interactive Voice Response (IVR).

Auto-diallers queue a list of calls and automatically dial the next number either when the current call is finished or the agent presses a hot key. Predictive diallers predict when an agent is about to conclude a call, and auto-dials the next call in anticipation. Automated voice-messagers will make telephone calls automatically to a contact list and convey a message to them. This is used for lead generation, debt collection, political canvassing and reminding customers about appointments. Telemarketing software that integrates with campaign management and event-based marketing applications enables agents to make real-time offers to customers. In-call online access to a searchable knowledge base enables agents to resolve issues and enquiries quickly. IVR systems allow customers to interact with a company's host system by voice or telephone keypad, giving them the opportunity to service their own enquiry by following the IVR dialogue. IVR technology is useful if an interaction can be broken down into a series of simple questions and answers. We discuss this further in the next chapter.

Lead generation

Lead generation is an important objective of marketing campaigns, particularly in business-to-business contexts. Sales people challenged to grow the numbers of customers served need to be presented with high-quality leads for follow-up. Marketers can deploy email, direct mail and telemarketing campaigns, events, seminars, webinars and other tactics to generate the leads.

Online and digital marketing

Online marketing

Online marketing can be defined as follows:

Online marketing is the process of creating value by building and maintaining online customer relationships.

Online marketing is also known as Internet marketing. There are many online marketing practices that grow in number year-on-year. Online marketing applications enable users to perform a wide range of online activities designed to generate and monetize website and mobile traffic. Users can do the following: develop and manage online content, create a social media presence in platforms like Facebook and YouTube, establish a blog, create an engaging online customer experience, develop and promote apps, obtain search engine listings, perform search engine optimization, implement keyword marketing, generate customer reviews, obtain and verify customer information, customize web pages (known as dynamic web pages) and site visitor communications, run online advertising campaigns using the likes of Google Adwords, manage pay-per-click programmes, operate or join affiliate marketing programmes, run mobile and email campaigns, and perform web analytics.

Content management

Content management applications allow marketers to manage digital content throughout its lifecycle, including creation, editing, approval, storage, publishing, versioning (updating) and deletion. Marketers deploy content in many different environments, including advertising, corporate website, blogs, social media, user manuals and print materials for example. Content management systems, of which there are hundreds, offer marketers a number of benefits: conformance of content with brand values, consistency of appearance and messaging across all customer touchpoints, asset security (see asset management later in this chapter), reduced duplication of effort in content creation, streamlined production and approval processes, better control of versioning and updates thereby ensuring content is always current, and creation of content in appropriate formats, for example HTML for Web applications. Consumers rely increasingly on digital content to inform their buying decision, and it is therefore critical that marketers maintain the quality of that content.

Keyword marketing

Keyword marketing is the practice of generating website traffic from Internet users who have entered keywords (search terms) into search engines such as Google and AOL. A company that is interested in improving its complaint management processes might use the keywords 'complaint-handling' and 'ISO10002' to search the Web for useful information. The keywords will lead to millions of listings. Marketers generally want their website to appear on the first or second page of listings. Keyword marketing software applications enable companies to feature early in these listings. Some keyword marketing involves purchasing advertising space, typically banners and text links, on the search results page. The other major form of keyword marketing is search engine optimization (SEO), which aims to get unpaid listings on the early search results pages. Google pages feature both. Ads that have been bought appear on the right-hand side of the search results page, and SEO listings appear on the left. We cover SEO next. Successful keyword marketing starts by understanding the terms that prospective customers use to search for potential suppliers. These terms can then be embedded in the text of a company's website, and on the site's page titles, URLs and metadata.

Search engine optimization

Search engine optimization can be defined as follows:

> **Search engine optimization (SEO) is the practice of improving the quantity and quality of website traffic generated by search engines.**

Whereas companies can pay for their web page to appear on the first page of a listing generated by a browser's keyword search, SEO aims to get high organic (unpaid or free) visibility. Higher ranking results that appear earlier in the listings are more visible and therefore generate more click-through visitors. SEO aims to get web pages listed on the first or second pages. The major search engines use web crawlers, also known as web spiders or web robots, to browse the World Wide Web methodically. Crawlers such as Google's Googlebot visit websites, read the site's text, images and meta tags, and visit linked sites, reading content and meta tags there too. The crawler dumps all the data into a central depository, where they are indexed. The crawler returns to the sites to check for any changed information at periods that are determined by the search engine's management. Unlike visible content, meta tags provide information about who created the page, the freshness of its content, what the page is about and the keywords that describe the page's content. A website's position on a results page is determined by that search engine's ranking algorithm. Algorithms are formulae composed of a set of weighted criteria – Google's algorithm considers over 200 variables. These criteria are periodically reviewed. Each search engine has its own algorithm that is a trade secret.

CASE STUDY 9.41

FILTREX IMPLEMENTS SEARCH ENGINE OPTIMIZATION[13]

Filtrex (name disguised) is a commercial reseller of industrial air filters that had invested in e-commerce to generate incremental sales of their products. Sales were poor and there was little return on the initial investment. The reseller hired an SEO consulting firm to develop the online sales channel. The goals were to increase order volume, and change the product mix to increase sales of higher margin items. The online air filter market is very competitive, and Filtrex's major competitors were already using a combination of search engine optimization (SEO) and pay-per-click (PPC) marketing to generate traffic and sales.

The consultant researched, developed and implemented a plan to increase Filtrex's sales using a combination of creative website design and the application of advanced SEO techniques. Within three months the results were as follows: order numbers increased by 525 per cent; average dollar order size increased by over 50 per cent; number of unique visitors to the website increased by over 100 per cent; the conversion rate from website visitor to customer increased from 1.3 per cent to over 10 per cent.

SEO software can help users tailor their website so that it meets the criteria that the search engine algorithms employ, therefore giving the site a high ranking. Successful websites employ methods such as the following: strategic keywords that are well matched to the content of the site, strategic meta tags, website structure (each page having its own keyword/s), continually refreshed content, removal of dead links, search engine placement and link relevance. Web masters need to understand the site's marketing goals, the products that are being sold on site, the geographies being served and the keywords employed by users of search engines. They can then ensure that the right keywords and meta tags are used, the right links are embedded in the site and that the site is submitted to search engines that do not use web crawlers.

Social media marketing

Social media marketing can be defined as follows:

Social media marketing is the practice of using social media for customer management purposes.

Social media are 'a group of Internet-based applications that build on the ideological and technological foundations of Web 2.0 and that allow the creation and exchange of user-generated content'.[14] Social media include collaborative communities (Wikipedia), blogs and micro-blogs (Twitter), content-sharing communities (YouTube) and social networking communities (Facebook). Social media users create, share, discuss and modify user-generated content using Web-based and mobile technologies. Major social media platforms include Facebook, YouTube, flikr, Tumblr, Twitter, Pinterest, Wikipedia and LinkedIn. The social media landscape changes at a remarkable pace. A few years ago MySpace was a major social media platform. As this is written, MySpace has about 35 million users and is in decline, whereas Facebook claims over 1 billion users, or 1/7th of the world's population. Social media are disruptive technologies that are responsible for significant and pervasive changes to communication between organizations, communities and individuals. Marketers no longer control brand-related communication. Communication is now multilateral, not unilateral. Consumers use social media to communicate with each other and organizations, and organizations in turn are beginning to use social media to help them initiate, nurture, maintain and monetize relationships with customers.

Gartner Inc. has developed a multi-stage model that visualizes the anticipation, disillusionment and achieved reality of new technologies. They call this the Technology Hype Cycle, a phenomenon they have observed over 100 technology fields, including social media (see Figure 9.5). Hype Cycles offer a snapshot of the relative maturity of technologies. They highlight overhyped areas and show how far newer technologies are from maturity. As we write, technology firms are investing millions in developing tools to help companies to manage customer relationships though social media, and expectations are rising rapidly. Tools that are currently at the peak of expectation include gamification, crowdsourcing and social media analytics. Technologies that are more mature include mobile social networks and internal peer-to-peer communities. There is a pipeline of emergent, as yet unproven, social media technologies climbing the curve towards the peak of inflated expectations. Gartner's review of over 2,000 Hype Cycles shows that the technology firms continue to innovate and

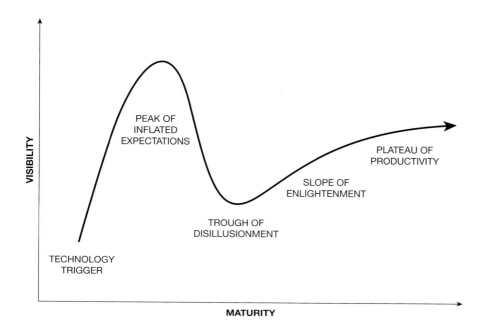

Figure 9.5 Technology Hype Cycle[16]

that after the hype, few technologies really die. Many emerge from the trough of disillusionment only to find narrow, niche markets. Whilst that might disappoint fans and investors who got overexcited early on, nearly every technology eventually finds some use.[15]

We observe that some leading companies are currently exploring ways to improve their management of customer relationships through social media. Companies appear to progress through a social media evolutionary cycle. We can identify five stages:

1   Companies start by tracking consumer sentiment in social media with a view to preventing negative news stories from finding traction. They may use technologies such as text analytics to help them identify issues and trends, and empower public relations departments to respond.

2   The second stage is the active exploitation of social media by marketers to communicate with consumers, promote brands, make offers, run competitions, conduct marketing research and track competitor activity. In this stage marketers might buy advertising space in social media, or create a Facebook page to try to build a brand community. This becomes a location for consumers to communicate with each other and the business about their customer experiences.

3   The third stage is the integration of social media into customer service functions. Consumers report their customer experiences in social media. Issues and complaints are identified by technologies that trawl the social media. Customer service agents resolve individual issues; analytics report trends in the causes of customer complaint relative to competitor brands; companies change processes and product to fix the root causes. Crowdsourced customer service is implemented.

4   The fourth stage is the creation of a social media team across all customer touchpoints – marketing, service, sales and accounts – to share best practices.

5   The fifth stage is the development of an integrated company-wide social media strategy that not only focuses on customers but on other stakeholder groups such as suppliers, employees, investors and partners.

CASE STUDY 9.5

JUST EAT'S BLENDED SOCIAL MEDIA CAMPAIGN[17]

JUST EAT has created an online marketplace for takeaway food that connects over 36,000 local independent restaurants to more than five million local consumers. Positioned as an alternative to preparing food at home, JUST EAT developed an online campaign themed 'Don't Cook, JUST EAT'. This starred a band of rebel takeaway chefs, led by Mr Mozzarella, The Mozz.

The campaign aimed to change the way people thought about takeaway food. JUST EAT rejected the notion – fed by TV cooking shows – that hard-working consumers should be expected to prepare cordon bleu meals at home. This iconoclastic positioning gave JUST EAT plenty of opportunity to create fun, cheeky, irreverent, engaging social media content to amplify their 'Don't Cook' message.

JUST EAT launched a multi-channel campaign with a single 90-second TV ad spot in a high rating Saturday night show, in which Mozz and his associates kidnapped TV chef Antony Worrall Thompson (AWT). JUST EAT then used social media to advance the storyline, ramping up consumer engagement as fans followed AWT's plight via Facebook, Twitter and the campaign's dedicated micro-site.

The campaign, which lasted just one week, had AWT being jokily 'punished' for trying to make people cook cordon bleu meals at home. Fans could participate in an online game to teach AWT the error of his ways by slapping him across the face with a fish. Being sharable on Facebook and Twitter, the joke reached out to many more potential customers of JUST EAT. The online community responded well to the kidnap campaign and JUST EAT was able to strengthen its positioning and increase awareness. Entertaining, sharable content was the key to the campaign's success.

AWT was slapped 850,000 times and the #JUSTEATkidnap hashtag was used nearly 1,400 times during the campaign. The campaign was supported by salesforce.com's ExactTarget marketing solution.

Digital analytics

Digital analytics explore data generated by customer behaviour in interactive channels including online, mobile and social media. Web analytics, a major component of digital analytics, focuses on the behaviour of website visitors. Web analytics report audience size, where the visitors come from (referrals) and what they do on the website. Routine reports generally detail Web traffic data, but may also include performance data from campaigns and events that involve the website, for example the number of click-throughs from a web-link inserted in a campaign email. Two main technologies collect website data: logfile analysis and page-tagging. Web servers record all website activity in a logfile, which can be read by web log analysis software. Logfile analysis can deliver inaccurate readings of human website visitors because of caching and visits by web spiders from search engines. This prompted the introduction of page-tagging as an alternative form of generating website data. Page-tagging requires webmasters to insert some extra Javascript or HTML code onto web pages, so that analytics software can identify how many visitors originate from search engines, the search terms used and whether they arrived from paid-for or free listings.

Three different types of statistics provide insight into a website's performance: frequency counts (e.g. the number of visitors), ratios (e.g. page views per visit) and key performance indicators (KPIs, which can either be a frequency count or ratio). There are a number of important terms that are used by web analytics vendors. These include:

- *Building block terms*: page, page view, visit/session, unique visitor, new visitor, repeat visitor, return visitor.

- *Visit characterization terms*: entry page, landing page, exit page, visit duration, referrer, internal referrer, external referrer, search referrer, visit referrer, original referrer, click-through, click-through rate/ratio, page views per visit.

- *Content characterization terms*: page exit ratio, single-page visit, single-page view visits (bounces), bounce rate.

- *Conversion metrics terms*: event, conversion.

Vendors of web analytics services and software make widespread use of the following measures.

- *Hit*. A request for a file from the web server. This information is only available in log analysis. You should be aware that the number of hits is a misleading measure of a site's popularity, because most web pages are made up of many files, each of which is counted as a hit as the page is downloaded. Most web analytics tools allow users to specify the file types that count as a page (known as analyst-definable content), and to request reports accordingly.

- *Page view*. The number of times a page (as defined by the analyst) is viewed.

- *Visit or session*. An interaction by an individual with a website, consisting of one or more requests for analyst-definable content. A visit usually contains multiple hits (in log analysis) and page views.

- *Visit duration*. The amount of time a visitor spends on a site.

- *Engagement time*. The amount of time a visitor is interacting with the site, for example by moving the cursor, clicking, hovering and scrolling.

- *Event*. The number of times a discrete action occurs on a website. Events include clicks, page views, video plays, downloads and other user actions.

- *First visit or first session*. A visit from a user who has not made any previous visits.

- *Unique visitor*. The number of individuals who make one or more visits to a site within a defined reporting period (e.g. day or month), making requests on the web server (log analysis) or viewing pages (page-tagging). Because most sites do not require log-in, cookies are generally used instead. A cookie is a small file of information (normally less than 1k) that a website places on a visitor's computer hard drive so that it can recognize the visitor on subsequent visits. There are two kinds of cookies: session cookies and persistent cookies. Session cookies are erased when the user goes offline. Web analysis, however, relies on persistent cookies that are stored on the visitor's hard drive until they expire (persistent cookies have expiry dates) or until the user deletes the cookie.

- *Repeat visitor*. A visitor who has made at least two visits to the website in a reporting period.

- *New visitor*. A visitor who has not made any previous visits to the website.

- *Impression*. When a page loads onto a visitor's screen. Advertisers measure the reach of their online ads by tracking ad impressions, or the number of times their ads are loaded onto a visitor's screen.

- *Singleton*. A visit when only a single page is viewed.

- *Bounce rate*. The percentage of visits that enter and exit on the same page, without browsing other pages.

- *Exit rate*. The percentage of visits that end on a particular page.

Google Analytics is the best known service provider in this market, providing a wide range of analytics on digital advertising and campaign performance, audience characteristics and behaviour on corporate websites and social media, audience use of mobile devices and tablets, mobile apps and website performance. The Digital Analytics Association (DAA) is the peak organization for digital analytics. The DAA aims to advance best practice in the use of digital analytics.[18]

Social media analytics are an emergent discipline. Many of the major CRM brands, including SAS, Adobe, Oracle and IBM, offer social media analytics solutions, and there are scores of smaller players specializing in social analytics. One of the major roles of social media analytics is to capture and interpret user-generated social media content, and feed that analysis to brand owners for action. Technology can be used to capture and analyze social network posts, blogs, micro-blogs, chat room and discussion board content so that marketers can develop appropriate responses including media advertising, social media campaigns, event-based marketing actions, public relations interventions and contact centre support. Content and messaging can be adapted accordingly. Another form of social media analytics seeks to identify which social media channels and campaigns have been successful in driving traffic to other customer touchpoints such as stores and corporate websites for fulfilment. Routine digital analytics such as page views, CTOR and conversion rates are useful here. Social media analytics can be integrated with predictive analytics. For example, if historical data show that customers who complain on Twitter have a 60 per cent probability of switching suppliers, marketers can initiate automated event-based next best offers (NBO) whenever that type of sentiment is posted. NBO refers to the process whereby a customer event prompts the marketing automation solution to generate an offer with the highest probability of interesting the customer in real time. Equally, when sentiment is positive marketers can develop strategies and campaigns that build the brand's reputation and promote advocacy.

Figure 9.6 Google Analytics dashboard report[19]

Strategic and other marketing management

Integrated marketing management

Integrated marketing management (IMM) applications offer wide-ranging functionality to support large organizations with 50 or more marketing practitioners. The main role of IMM solutions is to help marketers align their analysis, planning, implementation and control activities so that they can become more effective, efficient and accountable. According to Gartner Inc. IMM includes:

> the marketing strategy, process automation and technologies required to integrate people, processes, campaigns, channels, resources and technologies across the marketing ecosystem. IMM supports closed-loop marketing by integrating operational, executional and analytical marketing processes.[20]

IMM functionality includes campaign management, lead management, marketing resource management, analytics and much more. However, vendors of these comprehensive IMM applications, such as IBM, SAS, SAP and Teradata, not only deliver marketing functionality, but also offer the architectures and platforms necessary for the role-based distribution of information, content and functionality. IMM provides an integrated set of marketing functionality that supports CRM objectives.

Marketing performance management

Marketing performance management (MPM) software enables companies to measure their marketing performance though analysis and reports, and improve outcomes over time through closed-loop marketing.

Gartner Inc. describes MPM as encompassing the technologies and services

> **that support marketing's ability to gain access to insights, analyze data, make predictions, and optimize marketing programmes, campaigns and resources. At the foundational level, MPM includes a data repository, business intelligence tools and analytical workbenches. At the strategic level, MPM provides role-based access to information and KPIs through dashboards, visualization, point-and-click analysis, modelling, simulation and optimization.[21]**

Essentially, MPM helps management assess the effectiveness and the efficiency of marketing strategies and tactics. Senior management is progressively demanding that marketers be accountable for their expenditure, and MPM helps marketers meet that expectation. MPM is routinely built into most MA applications. It enables marketers to:

- assess the effectiveness of marketing campaigns and events, by measuring expenditure and response rates; reporting variance between planned and achieved campaign/event responses and expenditure; tracking cost per lead, cost per sale and revenue per lead;
- evaluate the effectiveness of different offers, channels and creative executions, thereby enabling marketers to identify the most successful strategies and continually fine-tune their programmes;
- forecast ROI from current and future campaigns/events based on the performance of past campaigns/events.

Some of the more advanced MPM applications focus on more strategic aspects of marketing performance measurement. For example, SAS's MPM product is able to deliver a range of reports against a number of KPIs, including:

- Marketing programme metrics that report on the efficiency and effectiveness of marketing tactics.
- Customer metrics including customer satisfaction, Net Promoter Scores, value, churn, migration, etc.
- Business/financial metrics (sales, profitability, cost, etc.) that give senior managers a better insight into marketing's financial impact.
- Marketing process metrics that focus on process efficiency to identify best practices and areas for improvement.

The core components of MPM software are analytics (already discussed) and a reporting process. Reports are typically delivered online in charts, tables, dashboard and text.

Marketing resource management

Marketing resource management applications consist of a range of automated tools that enable marketers to manage their marketing processes and assets more effectively, and to work at greater speed and with improved control. According to Gartner Inc. MRM:

> **applications enable strategic planning and budgeting, programme management, creative development and distribution, content management, media planning and execution, event coordination, and resource measurement.**[22]

MRM toolkits therefore include modules that help CRM practitioners do the following:

- Plan and budget marketing activities and programmes.
- Create and develop marketing programmes and content.
- Collect and manage digital content and knowledge.
- Fulfil and distribute marketing assets, content and collateral.
- Measure, analyze and optimize marketing resources (MRM analytics).

These tools, like other CRM applications, can be accessed on demand or licensed for installation on a company's own hardware. Investment in MRM is more justified if marketing budgets are high; if you need to align implementation across several branches or offices; if collateral material is subject to frequent change; if brands, trademarks and logos are highly valued assets that need to be protected; if you run more than one event simultaneously; if you run more than six campaigns in a year; if you launch more than one new product a year; if you need to facilitate collaboration across departments on projects, events and campaigns. Major suppliers of MRM are Teradata, Infor, IBM, SAP and SAS.

Loyalty management

Customer loyalty is a goal of many CRM programmes. The availability of loyalty management applications is a direct response to this need. Loyalty, or frequency, programmes are important to several constituencies – the business that operates the programme, the member who collects and redeems credits and the channel partner who transacts with the member.

Many loyalty programmes are very simple, particularly when the brand owner has a single retail site, hands a rewards card to the customer and stamps the card when a purchase is made – 'Buy five cups of coffee, get the next one free'. However, there are other programmes that are operationally and technologically complex. Consider the Nectar loyalty programme. Nectar is the UK's largest coalition loyalty programme with half of all UK households owning a Nectar card. Over 19 million collectors earn Nectar points when shopping at over 6,000 retail outlets for groceries, doing DIY, booking a holiday, paying household bills, buying petrol or getting their car serviced. Collectors can also earn Nectar points every time they

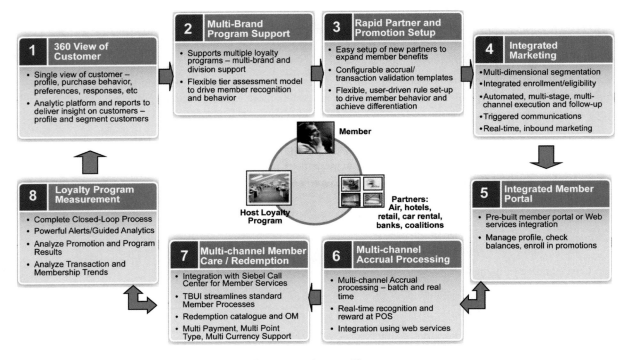

Figure 9.7 Oracle's Loyalty Management software application[23]

shop online via nectar.com at over 500 leading online retailers. Consumers can spend their points on treats including spa days, movie and theatre tickets and luxurious holiday breaks. Dozens of Nectar cards are swiped every second of the day. The technology challenge is massive, and ranges across many of the issues in Figure 9.7.

Leading loyalty management applications enable business users to create, operate and evaluate loyalty and membership schemes, and perform the following tasks:

- Set-up one or more loyalty programmes.

- Manage multiple targeted membership schemes.

- Manage multiple-tier models and classes and control all the aspects of tier management from the number of tiers and tier rewards to point expiration rules.

- Set up partners, products and services offered for accrual and redemptions including product catalogues.

- Create and deploy targeted loyalty promotions.

- Set up and manage simple to complex accrual rules and promotions.

- Define and manage redemption models using multiple payment modes and currencies.

- Perform membership and partner administration tasks.

- Run statements and manage member communications.

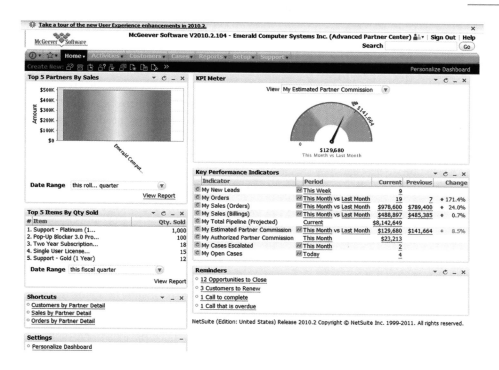

Figure 9.8 NetSuite partner management screenshot[24]

Partner marketing

Partner marketing solutions enable companies to coordinate and work collaboratively with channel partners and others. Many companies market and sell to and through channel members such as travel agents or value-added resellers, or service end-users through specialist partners such as third-party contact centres. Partner marketing solutions allow companies to synchronize the planning and execution of local, regional or global marketing activities by providing partners with controlled access to brand and marketing resources through a portal.

Partner marketing solutions are used to manage processes such as partner qualification, recruitment, on-boarding, development of joint business plans and objectives, cooperative advertising and promotions, lead management, co-branding of collateral and point-of-sale materials, measuring partner performance, partner training and support, administration of marketing funds and specialist partner incentive schemes. Microsoft Canada, for example, describes the value of partnering with this message to their partners: 'Your goals: Increase profitability. Decrease business costs. Our goal: To provide the resources to reach yours.'

Market segmentation

Market segmentation is the practice of partitioning markets into homogenous subsets so that each subset can be addressed as a unique marketing opportunity. MA, when supported by customer-specific data and analytics, can mean that each customer is treated as a unique segment. The same principles discussed in the context of customer segmentation and earlier in Chapter 3 apply here.

Customer segmentation and selection

Customer segmentation and selection is the practice of partitioning customers into homogenous subsets so that each subset can be addressed as a unique marketing audience. The smallest customer segment is the individual customer. Some CRM strategies are focused on understanding, servicing and retaining individual customers; others focus on very large clusters of customers. Historically, segmentation by marketers has been very intuitive. However, as explained in Chapter 3, when customer segmentation is performed from a CRM perspective, it is much more data based. Both consumers and organizational customers can be grouped into clusters based on a wide range of user attributes and usage attributes. In the data-driven world of CRM, marketers often need to use statistical processes to help them identify clusters of customers. Among the widely employed statistical processes are cluster analysis, discriminant analysis, Classification and Regression Trees (CART) and Chi-Square Automatic Interaction Detection (CHAID).[25] We discuss some of these in more detail in chapters 11 and 12.

Product lifecycle management

Products, like people, have lifecycles. The product lifecycle traces the phases of a product's life from initial development and market introduction to withdrawal. Product lifecycle management (PLM) applications help marketers manage lifecycle stages effectively and profitably. PLM applications aim to accelerate time-to-market, ensure that development and engineering processes are optimal and lift the probability of the product being successful. PLM software solutions facilitate collaborative intra- and extra-enterprise engineering, product development, and improved management of projects, product portfolios, documents and quality. PLM applications can provide a single source of all product-related information to use in the innovation, design, engineering, feasibility, launch, market development and market withdrawal processes. PLM applications offer a wide range of functionality, including the following:

- concept evaluation process
- new product development and approval process
- new product launch process
- product costing process
- product sourcing process
- product compliance process (compliance with legal, regulatory and voluntary standards)
- quality assurance process
- quality function deployment (QFD) process
- channel member qualification and recruitment process
- collaborative extra-enterprise product development and engineering processes
- environmental impact management
- computer-aided design (CAD)
- computer-aided engineering (CAE)

- computer-aided manufacturing (CAM)
- product portfolio management
- engineering data management
- product withdrawal process
- workflow management
- project management and scheduling
- action item management
- document management
- product record.

Management of the product lifecycle is aided by PLM analytics. For example, analytics help managers identify bottlenecks in the product approval process that slow down time-to-market, or detect components or sub-assemblies with high cost, quality or compliance risks that adversely impact new product success. 'With the right PLM solution in place, a company is in the best position to create and manage product design ideas, oversee the production pipeline, maximize collaboration efforts across the physical and global borders of the enterprise, and significantly reduce the cost associated with regulatory compliance.'[26]

Companies such as SAP, Infor, Sopheon and Kalypso operate in this field.

Asset management

Asset management enables companies to identify, manage, track and control the assets that customers purchase, license, use, install or download. Assets can be tangible, intangible or blended, as shown in the following examples. The pallet hire company, CHEP, uses asset management to track where its tangible assets – pallets – are in their network, whether at customer sites, depots or in transit, and to ensure that customers are only billed for the periods when the pallets are in use by that customer. Beam Inc. uses asset management to track the use of its intangible asset – the Jim Beam brand – by other manufacturers. Dolby Laboratories uses asset management to track the licensed use of its blended tangible and intangible assets – manufacturing processes and technologies – by other companies that want to exploit Dolby's audio, image and voice capabilities.

Document management

Companies generate and use many documents in their marketing activities. These include brochures, product specifications, price lists and competitive comparisons. Document management software allows companies to manage these documents, keep them current and ensure that they are available to marketing people when needed. Typically, these documents are held in a central repository and made available to users in their browsers. Document management software applications generally deliver similar functionality to content management applications (as considered earlier in the chapter). However, document management systems focus on text documents rather than digital content such as images and movie files, and stress versioning, storage, search and retrieval rather than publishing to the Web.

Marketing analytics

Marketing analytics is the application of mathematical and statistical processes to marketing problems. Marketing analytics can be used to describe, explore and explain. A *descriptive* application of marketing analytics would involve the depiction of some marketing phenomenon such as a customer group, sales territory, market segment, campaign or product category. Descriptive applications focus on who, what, where and when. Some descriptive analyses are cross-sectional and others longitudinal. A cross-sectional analysis involves description at a single point in time. Longitudinal analysis involves repeated data collection about the same variables over time, so that you can get a better sense of change.

Exploratory applications of marketing analytics provide insights into and understanding about issues and problems. For example, you might want to explore the issue of customer defection rates – do some sales territories, customer groups or products experience higher levels than normal? You would want to dig around in customer-related data to get a better understanding of the issue. This might lead you towards defining a problem more precisely, identifying alternative courses of action, developing hypotheses to test, or identifying key variables or relationships to explore further.

An *explanatory* application of marketing analytics would seek to obtain evidence of a cause–effect relationship. Analytics are used to explain why something has happened or to predict what might happen.

There are three types of analytics: standard reports, online analytical processing (OLAP) and data mining. The standardized reports integrated into most MA packages are grounded on relatively simple analytics. Typically these reports provide basic descriptive data such as aggregates, averages, proportions and other simple univariate or bivariate statistics. Figure 9.9 is a standardized report for an email campaign. It reports deliverability, open rate, click-through rate, conversion rate and sales revenues generated.

Standardized reports may meet some managerial needs, but exploratory or explanatory questions usually require the greater analytical power of the two other forms of marketing analytics, OLAP and data mining. OLAP transforms customer-related data into strategic information. An OLAP solution extracts and displays customer data from any angle. For example, an OLAP user can see how many customers purchased lathes in London during October and compare that with the numbers bought in New York in the same month. OLAP organizes data in a series of hierarchies or dimensions such as products, channels, territories, customer segments and time periods. OLAP software locates the intersection of dimensions (for example, the quantity of lathes sold in London during October) and displays the results. Users can choose different display formats including pie charts, bar graphs or worksheets. At its simplest OLAP allows users to 'slice and dice' data; more complex applications include time series modelling. OLAP thus allows data to be viewed from different perspectives and manipulated and analyzed in real time to provide insights not available in packaged reports. Relatively few CRM vendors offer OLAP capability. Cognos, Microsoft and Oracle are important OLAP vendors. We discuss OLAP in more detail in chapters 11 and 12.

Data mining offers the most powerful statistical routines including descriptive statistics (frequency, mean, median, mode, variance, standard deviation), data reduction, bivariate statistical analysis (cross-tabulation, correlation), multivariate statistical analysis (multiple regression, factor analysis, discriminant analysis, cluster analysis, multidimensional scaling, conjoint analysis), decision trees and neural networks, and data visualization.

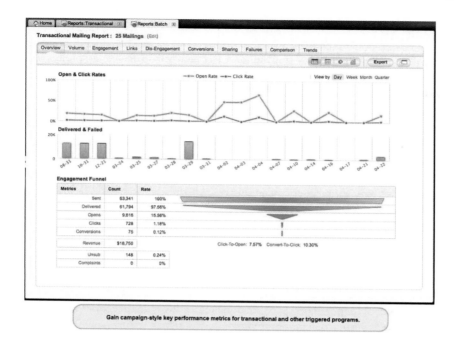

Figure 9.9 Email campaign report

Data mining is used to produce:

- *Scores.* The likelihood a customer will purchase a product; which customer to target for a particular offer.

- *Predictions.* How much a customer will spend in the coming year; the probability of a customer defecting.

- *Descriptions.* The characteristics define profitable customers; the multidimensional profile of a customer segment.

- *Profiles.* The common characteristics of each customer segment; the lifetime value of a customer.[27]

Data mining functionality is integrated into comprehensive CRM and MA suites from vendors like SAP and Oracle. Specialist organizations like SAS and Teradata also operate in this segment.

Workflow development

Workflow development software is useful for designing marketing-related processes, such as the campaigning process, event-based marketing process or the marketing planning process.

SUMMARY

Marketing automation is the application of computerized technologies to support marketers and marketing management in the achievement of their work-related objectives. Many marketing positions can make use of MA including marketing manager, campaign manager, market analyst, market manager, promotions manager, database marketer and direct marketing manager. Hardware and software are the key technological elements of MA. Hardware includes desktop, laptop, tablets and smart phones. Software comprises both 'point' solutions that are designed to assist in a single area of marketing or marketing management, and integrated solutions that offer a range of functionality.

Marketing automation can deliver several benefits, including enhanced marketing efficiency, greater marketing productivity, more effective marketing, enhanced responsiveness, improved marketing intelligence, a better customer experience and higher levels of customer engagement.

MA software applications can be classified into three main groups: applications that support marketing campaigns, applications used in digital marketing and applications that support marketing management. Software applications are available in asset management, campaign management, customer segmentation, direct mail campaign management, digital analytics, document management, email campaign management, event-based marketing, integrated marketing management, keyword marketing, lead generation, loyalty management, market segmentation, marketing analytics, marketing optimization, marketing performance management, marketing resource management, online marketing, partner marketing, product lifecycle management, search engine optimization, telemarketing, trigger marketing and workflow development.

NOTES AND REFERENCES

1 http://www.sas.com/en_us/customers/staples-marketing-automation.html (Accessed 14 April 2014).

2 Gartner Inc. (2013). Magic quadrant for multi-channel campaign management. http://www.gartner.com/technology/reprints.do?id=1–1FUOVTO&ct = 130531&st = sg (Accessed 7 April 2014).

3 http://www.firstedgesolutions.com/dialmarketinglaunch/ (Accessed 10 April 2014).

4 Courtesy Oracle.com Used with permission.

5 http://www.dmis.co.uk/pdfs/Response_Rates_Survey_2006.pdf (Accessed 13 December 2007).

6 http://www.emaillabs.com/tools/email-marketing-statistics.html#emailusage (Accessed 13 December 2007).

7 http://adage.com/article/digital/interactive-marketing-spend-hit-76–6b-2016/229444/ (Accessed 8 April 2014).

8 http://www.smartinsights.com/email-marketing/email-communications-strategy/statistics-sources-for-email-marketing/ (Accessed 9 April 2014).

9   http://www.prweb.com/releases/e_mail_marketing/online_direct_marketing/prweb8257790.htm (Accessed 9 April 2014).

10 http://www.lsoft.com/products/maestro.asp (Accessed 9 April 2014).

11 TW Connect Ltd. http://www.twconnect.co.uk/upload/file/158/79244/FILENAME/HP_Education.pdf (Accessed 26 January 2008).

12 http://www.sas.com/en_us/software/customer-intelligence/marketing-optimization.html (Accessed 12 April 2014).

13 Braveheart Design Inc. http://www.braveheartdesign.com/casestudies/filters.htm (Accessed 17 December 2007).

14 Kaplan, A.M. and Haenline, M. (2101), Users of the world unite! The challenges and opportunities of social media. *Business Horizons*, 53(1), 61.

15 http://blogs.gartner.com/mark_raskino/2014/02/17/hype-cycle-visualization-reveals-some-insights-on-the-state-of-technology/?fnl = search&srcId = 1–3478922254 (Accessed 25 May 2014).

16 Hype Cycles are widely deployed by Gartner Inc. See for example: http://www.gartner.com/technology/research/hype-cycles/

17 http://www.salesforcemarketingcloud.com/wp-content/uploads/2013/07/Just-Eat.pdf?03a0bd (Accessed 14 April 2014).

18 http://www.digitalanalyticsassociation.org/ (Accessed 14 April 2014).

19 http://www.londes.com/analytics (Accessed 14 April 2014).

20 http://www.gartner.com/technology/reprints.do?id=1–1MH4HLT&ct = 131101&st = sb (Accessed 10 April 2014).

21 http://www.gartner.com/it-glossary/marketing-performance-management-mpm (Accessed 14 April 2014).

22 http://www.gartner.com/it-glossary/marketing-resource-management (Accessed 14 April 2014).

23 Courtesy Oracle.com Used with permission.

24 www.netsuite.com.au (Accessed 14 April 2014).

25 Saunders, J. (1994). Cluster analysis. In G.J. Hooley and M.K. Hussey (eds). *Quantitative methods in marketing*. London: Dryden Press, pp. 13–28.

26 http://ptccreo.files.wordpress.com/2013/10/top_10_plm_report.pdf (Accessed 14 April 2014).

27 http://www.teradata.com/t/pdf.aspx?a=83673&b=84891 (Accessed 17 December 2007).

CHAPTER 10

SERVICE AUTOMATION

CHAPTER OBJECTIVES

By the end of this chapter you will understand:

- What is meant by customer service.
- What is meant by service automation (SA).
- The benefits that SA can deliver to organizations.
- The functionality available within SA software.

INTRODUCTION

This is the last of three chapters that look at CRM technologies. This chapter is about the technologies used in customer service departments or by service staff. The preceding two chapters reviewed sales force automation and marketing automation. This chapter starts by defining customer service and service automation (SA), before describing some of the functionality that is available in SA software.

WHAT IS CUSTOMER SERVICE?

As customers, we all understand and appreciate when we have experienced excellent customer service. The people who serve us are friendly, responsive, empathic, and they do the right things well, whether that is answering a question, offering advice or accepting the return of faulty merchandise. If we rely on self-service technology, excellent service is experienced when the technology works as expected – for example, the bank's automatic tellers are operational, and the website provides all necessary help and information in a couple of clicks. Equally we can all recognize poor customer service, delivered by surly, unapproachable, peremptory, inflexible staff working with poor information and hampered by outdated technology.

Customer service has always been a necessary preoccupation of service-producing organizations, because they have understood that customers are responsive to the quality of the service they experience. However, the quality of customer service is just as important for agriculturalists, miners and goods manufacturers. This is particularly so when there is product parity, and customers are unable to discern meaningful differences between alternative suppliers, products or brands. For most customers, one brand of carpet is much like another. Carpet manufacturers and retailers find it hard to differentiate in terms of meaningful product-related variables; they therefore use service-related variables such as pre-purchase advice, measurement, delivery, removal of old floor coverings and fitting of new carpet, to win business from customers.

Customer service can be experienced at any stage of the customer purchase cycle: before, during or after purchase. For example, in a B2B context, a company purchasing new manufacturing equipment might need pre-purchase engineering advice, assistance during purchase with drawing up precise specifications for the equipment and post-purchase assistance with operator training. Customers can also assess service standards during service delivery as well as afterwards. The service experience as perceived from the dentist's chair during service delivery might be very different from the assessment a few days later!

MODELLING SERVICE QUALITY

Academics and practitioners have attempted to unpack what is meant by 'service quality'. Two academic models are particularly influential (as introduced in Chapter 6). The *Nordic* model, originated by Christian Grönroos, and developed by others, identifies three components of service quality: technical, functional and reputational.[1] Technical quality can be thought of as the 'what' of service quality. Did the technician fix the water leak from the dishwasher? Functional quality can be thought of as the 'how' of service quality. Did the technician turn up on time and act courteously? Reputational quality is a product of technical and functional quality, in that reputation derives from service performance. However, reputation can also predispose customers towards forming particular perceptions of quality, for better or worse. High quality is experienced when all three forms are excellent. The second service quality model, *SERVQUAL*, was developed by A. 'Parsu' Parasuraman and colleagues in North America and claims there are five core components of service quality: reliability, assurance, tangibles, empathy and responsiveness.[2] These vary in importance across contexts. In banking, reliability – the delivery of the promised service dependably and accurately – is important. Responsiveness becomes very important if you have to call out a technician to fix a water or gas leak.

Customers who receive service from companies that have successfully implemented CRM technology experience a further form of quality – integrative quality. High integrative quality means that a business's processes, people and technology complement each other, working efficiently and effectively to deliver excellent customer service. When customers make a purchase in response to a marketing campaign, they expect the order to be fulfilled rapidly. This requires the company to integrate its marketing automation to back-office payment and fulfilment processes. When these work harmoniously, the customer experiences high integrative quality. Good people either working with ill-defined processes or supported by dated or siloed technologies find it very difficult to deliver excellent customer service. Customer service is a key component of customer experience. Customers rarely report excellent experience if customer service encounters fail to meet their expectations.

Fred Wiersema, a noted practitioner authority on customer service, has researched the attributes that companies renowned for excellent customer service have in common. He identifies six common attributes.[3]

1   Customer service is pervasive. It is everyone's responsibility; it is neither delegated nor relegated to a single department or function.

2   Their operations run smoothly with minimal product and service defect rates, allowing them to focus on pleasing customers.

3   They are always looking for ways to improve.

4   Customer service lies at the heart of the value proposition. Customer service is the main selling point.

5   They build personal relationships with customers.

6   They employ the latest technologies that allow their customers to interact with them more conveniently, help them develop a profound understanding of what customers need and want, and enable them to track activities and processes that influence customer experience.

From a CRM perspective, these are all important, but particularly the last three. Customer service is the key element of these renowned companies' value propositions – an important component of strategic CRM. They understand that customers are responsive to excellent customer service, whatever the basic product or service they offer. They also build personal relationships with customers. They understand the needs and requirements of customers at an individual level, and they recognize and respond to events in the customer's life – delivered by analytical CRM. Finally, they employ the latest information technology that allows customers to interact with them whenever they want through multiple channels – an important component of operational CRM. IT also enables them to learn about and respond to customer requirements, and to track interactions and processes that connect them to their customers.

CUSTOMER SERVICE EXCELLENCE CERTIFICATION

The Customer Service Excellence® standard has been developed by the UK government with a view to providing guidance to public and private sector organizations that want to make a significant difference to the quality of their customer service. The standard identifies five criteria that need to be satisfied for excellent customer service to be delivered. The standard's criteria, and their relevant elements, are detailed in the published standard, and summarized below.[4]

- *Customer insight.* Effectively identifying customers, consulting them in a meaningful way and efficiently measuring customer service outcomes are vital. It's not just about being able to collect information; it's about having the ability to use that information to improve service delivery.

- *The culture of the organization.* It is challenging for any organization to build and foster a truly customer focused culture. To cultivate and embed this there must be a commitment to it throughout an organization, from the strategic leader to the front-line staff.

- *Information and access.* Customers value accurate and comprehensive information that is delivered or available through the most appropriate channel for them. Putting the customer first can be an important step towards providing effective communications.

- *Delivery.* How a business achieves its business aims, the outcomes for customers and how problems are managed can determine the organization's success. Listening to customers' views about their service experiences can be just as important as achieving key performance targets. Comments, feedback and complaints from customers can help make vital adjustments to the way the organization runs and support better delivery.

- *Timeliness and quality of service.* The promptness of initial contact and keeping to agreed timescales is crucial to customer satisfaction. However, speed can be achieved at the expense of quality, therefore the issue of timeliness has to be combined with quality of service to ensure the best possible result for customers.

Much of the language in this standard is compatible with CRM principles – using customer insight to improve customer experience, applying that insight to build a customer-focused organization, putting the customer first (as in strategic CRM), learning from customer feedback (as in closed-loop marketing) and focusing on customer satisfaction. In order to be recognized as having achieved Customer Service Excellence® an organization must

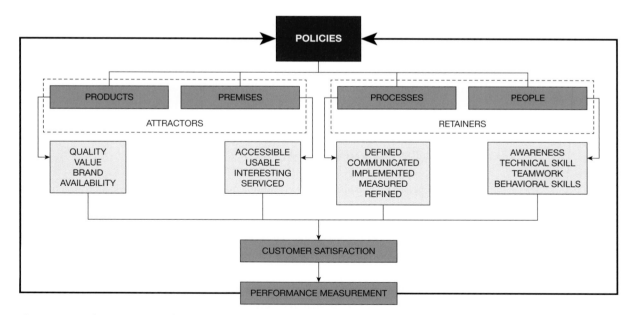

Figure 10.1 The International Customer Service Standard[5]

be successfully assessed against the criteria of the standard by a number of licensed certification bodies.

In addition to this government-sponsored model, the International Customer Service Institute has also developed its own customer service standard, dubbed The International Standard for Service Excellence (TISSE). This aims to become a global standard for customer service practitioners.

The model, shown in Figure 10.1, distinguishes five main components of customer service excellence. Known as the 5Ps, they influence customer acquisition, retention and satisfaction. The 5Ps are: policies, products, premises, processes and people. A company's policies about the allocation of resources to customer service act as an enabler of the other 4Ps. The other Ps are split into two groups – products/services and premises help attract customers; processes and people are key to retaining customers. From a CRM perspective, where the goal is to retain the most valued customers, people and processes are clearly important.

WHAT IS SERVICE AUTOMATION?

The term, service automation (SA), can be defined as follows:

Service automation is the application of computerized technologies to support service staff and management in the achievement of their work-related objectives.

Companies deliver customer service across multiple channels – face-to-face, over the phone, via email, mail, SMS, multimedia messaging (MMS), social media, web chat or fax, through the corporate website and automated self-service channels. In a connected world, however, it is not only companies that deliver customer service; other customers who report their product experiences in social media and on company websites are also providing service to potential or current customers. Some companies are trying to harness this type of customer-to-customer, or peer-to-peer, customer service for corporate ends.

Customer service departments are responsible for managing inbound call centre operations, complaint handling and resolution, order entry and processing, providing field sales support, managing outbound call centre operations and acting as liaison to other departments. It is in these and related activities that SA is deployed.

Service automation is used in four major contexts: contact centres, call centres, at the help desk and in field service.

- *Contact centres* are configured to communicate with customers across multiple channels including voice telephony, the Web, mail, email, SMS, multimedia messaging, instant messaging, web chat, social media and fax. In addition to people-assisted interactions, contact centres deliver automated self-service, using interactive voice response (IVR) and speech recognition technologies, for example. Contact centre technologies are used by customer and employee service and support centres, inbound and outbound telemarketing services, help-desk services and government-operated support centres. Service agents need to be able to access and update an entire communication history regardless of channel, when communicating with customers about service issues.

Channel integration is therefore an important feature of contact centre technologies. Contact centre staff may be called on to handle inbound service-related calls, participate in outbound marketing campaigns and respond to service enquiries in multiple channels. As contact centres spend more time and resources on interactions with customers in social media, some leading firms are beginning to reimagine their contact centres as *customer engagement centres*. This repositioning clearly emphasizes their objective of building closer, interactive and enduring relationships with customers.

- *Call centres* are generally dedicated to voice telephony communications, whether through a public switched telephone network, cell-phone network or Voice over Internet Protocol (VoIP). Agents operating in call centres require a different skill set from those operating in multi-channel contact centres. There is a less compelling need for excellent literacy skills such as reading and writing; they do, however, need excellent listening and responding skills. Access to a searchable knowledge base helps agents deliver excellent service.

- *Help desks* are usually associated with IT environments where assistance is offered to IT users. SA applications such as case management, job management and service level management are used in this setting. Help-desk solutions often comply with, and support, third-party standards such as ITIL (Information Technology Infrastructure Library)[6] and the ITSM (Information Technology Service Management)[7] reference model.

- *Field service* is widespread in both B2C and B2B environments. Service engineers for white goods such as dishwashers and washing machines, or brown goods such as televisions and hi-fi, visit consumers' homes to install, maintain or repair products. In the B2B context, technicians and engineers visit factories, depots, warehouses, workshops, offices and other workplaces before, during and after purchase to help customers specify, select, procure, install, service and decommission a wide range of machines and systems, ranging from machine tools to fork-lifts to IT infrastructure. Field service applications allow users to achieve a number of objectives:

1 Receive requests for a field service technician from the Internet, by telephone, by manual entry or through remote monitoring.

2 Assign a service technician – with long, mid-range, weekly and intra-day optimization of work orders, factoring in constraints (for example, assets, skills and so on) and service-level-agreement compliance.

3 Make the technician completely mobile to perform end-to-end service tasks, including the ability to look up inventory status in real time or cached on a wireless device.

4 Integrate with GPS and geographic information system (GIS) capabilities.

5 Provide field service functionality that supports a continuum of field service models, from reactive to preventive service.[8]

Unlike their office-bound colleagues, field service staff must have access to SA applications and data on their laptops, tablets and smart phones. Technology firms such as ClickSoftware, TOA Technologies, SAP, Oracle, ServiceMax and Astea operate in this space.

In addition to engineers and technicians, others may also be involved in providing customer service aided by service automation: customer service agents, sales reps, sales administration and marketers, for example.

Infrastructure, data, devices and software are the key technological elements of service automation. Infrastructure plays an important role in enabling service to be delivered. When service is delivered through a central call centre or contact centre, in a multi-channel environment there needs to be tight integration between various communication systems, including telephony, email, and the Web. A customer may browse the Web to find out how to obtain service, before communicating the service request by voice telephony into a call centre. However, the customer may expect to receive the initial notification of service appointment time by email, and any change to that time by text message. Call centres need integration between the software on the customer service agent's desktop and the automated call distributor (ACD) or switch hardware, so that calls are prioritized and routed appropriately.

Access to the right customer-related data, to enable the service agent to identify and fix the issue promptly, is critical to the delivery of responsive customer service. Customer-related data include both structured data such as contact history, account balances and agreed service levels, and unstructured data such as emails and agent notes about telephone conversations. Being able to draw on a searchable database of service issues and fixes allows the agent to resolve problems quickly and completely.

Where service is delivered by a distributed workforce, smaller, lighter devices such as laptops, tablets and smart phones tend to be employed; these are typically not found in call and contact centres. Synchronization is also an issue for a distributed service team. Synchronization with the central CRM database enables service engineers and others to ensure that they are fully apprised of their daily scheduled appointments, and the associated contact history.

BENEFITS FROM SERVICE AUTOMATION

Service automation has an important role to play in allowing companies to deliver excellent customer service. SA can deliver several benefits, including the following:

- *Enhanced service effectiveness.* Service requests can be completed more quickly to the customer's satisfaction by ensuring that requests are handled at the first point of contact or routed to the right service engineer or customer service agent, who is able to draw on an up-to-date knowledge base to resolve the issue.

- *Enhanced service efficiency.* Costs are taken out of service delivery when customers use self-service instead of interacting with an agent. High levels of first contact resolution mean that companies only deal once with a customer issue. Right first time means reduced levels of rework.

- *Greater service agent productivity.* Call and contact centre management systems ensure that the optimal number of agents is scheduled and that their time is used productively. Skills-based routing ensures that service enquiries are routed to the most appropriate

Figure 10.2 Full visibility into customer service history (Oracle RightNow screenshot)[9]

available agent. Field service applications ensure that workload is equitably and optimally distributed.

- *Better agent work experience.* Agents have the right tools to do their jobs well, leading to more enjoyable work experience.

- *Improved customer experience.* Agents have full visibility into the customer history and service requests and can therefore ensure that service delivery is appropriate to customer status or agreed service levels, and satisfies the customer. Customers experience more consistent service as business rules are followed and service standards are implemented. Customers who prefer to self-serve online can do so.

- *Improved customer engagement.* Rather than sending or receiving one-way communications, customer contact centres are now repositioning themselves as customer engagement centres, particularly if they participate in a lot of interactive communications with customers in social media.

- *Improved customer retention.* Higher quality service and better customer experience means that customers are less likely to churn to alternative suppliers. Service quality drives customer retention.

SERVICE AUTOMATION AT ICEE[10]

The ICEE Company is a division of J&J Snack Foods and is located in Ontario, California. Its flagship product is the ICEE, a flavoured frozen ice beverage that is carbonated and comes in various flavors. ICEE also produces other slushies, beverages and ice pops under both the ICEE and Slush Puppie brands. The company serves over 300 million ICEEs per year.

ICEE employs 800 people with 400 field technicians who service 30,000 ICEE machines across the USA. ICEE began to scrutinize the inefficiencies they found in the ICEE machine repair process. The company's existing process was very inefficient and error-prone. The challenges were to transform the inefficient paper-based machine repair processes, shorten billing cycles, capture accurate inventory and customer data electronically and transmit in real time, respond to customer requests more quickly, eliminate an ineffective paper-based parts inventory system and reallocate dispatchers' time.

After researching several alternatives, ICEE concluded that a real-time wireless data solution would provide them with many more benefits than a batch system, which would require that technicians connect to a landline and synchronize data at the beginning and end of each day. The final solution comprised a wireless handheld device from Symbol Technologies, coupled with Countermind's Mobile Intelligence Field Service Automation Solution, which was tailored to reflect ICEE's business process. This application runs on AT&T's GSM/GPRS network.

Now, all repair data are captured electronically on handheld devices. Billing cycles are reduced because manual data entry is eliminated. Complete job information is available to field technicians in real time. Field technicians can complete more work orders in a day, improving productivity and customer satisfaction. Parts inventory is managed more effectively and accurately.

SOFTWARE APPLICATIONS FOR SERVICE

Service automation applications offer a range of functionality, as listed in Table 10.1. Note that different SA vendors use the terms issue, case, incident, trouble ticket and service request synonymously to describe the different customer problems that service agents are called on to fix. Table 10.1 lists both macro-SA solutions that offer a wide range of functionality, and micro-SA solutions that offer a narrow range of functionality. The macro-solutions, such as case management and customer communications management, deliver much of the functionality present in the micro-solutions.

In the next few paragraphs, we will describe this functionality in more detail.

Activity management enables service staff to review their workload, to-do list and priorities as directed by their manager or scheduler, to coordinate activities with other service staff, and to report back on progress, results and issue resolution. Some applications allow activities to be updated in real time by dispatchers and routed to the technician, so that work can be reprioritized. Alerts can be set so that appointments are not missed, or to notify agents and their managers that issues are unresolved or service levels are about to be, or have been,

Table 10.1 Functionality offered by service automation software

• Activity management	• Knowledge-base self-service
• Agent management	• Mapping and driving directions
• Case assignment	• Outbound communications management
• Case management	• Predictive dialling
• Contract management	• Queuing and routing
• Customer communications management	• Scheduling
• Customer self-service	• Scripting
• Email response management	• Service analytics
• Escalation	• Service level management
• Inbound communications management	• Spare parts management
• Interactive voice response	• Voice biometrics
• Invoicing	• Web collaboration
• Job management	• Workflow development

violated. Activity management applications usually integrate with Outlook and other calendaring and communications applications. Data in activity management apps need to be synchronized with the CRM database either in real time or periodically, and attached to an account, contact or opportunity so that other customer contact staff have a complete view of customer interactions, and billable hours are recorded.

Agent management is a high priority for call and contact centre managers. Managers want to employ the lowest head-count compatible with the desired level of customer service. Too few agents and customers will be dissatisfied with wait-times; too many agents and payroll costs will be unnecessarily high. Customers and managers both want issues to be resolved quickly by agents. Technologies that contribute to this outcome include queuing, scripting and knowledge management, which are discussed in more detail below. Agent managers may be faced with the challenge of managing globally dispersed service agents, employed both in-house and outsourced, operating in different times zones, languages and currencies. Dashboards provide managers with visibility into the performance of both contact centres and individual agents. A large number of key performance indicators are used in call and contact centre environments. Among them are the following:

- *Volumes received.* The total number of inbound contacts across all channels.
- *Average queuing time.* The average amount of time a customer is held in a queue awaiting agent response.
- *Average handle time (AHT).* The average amount of time it takes to complete a call or other customer interaction, measured from the customer's initiation of the contact/call, including hold time, talk time and related record-keeping tasks that follow the transaction. AHT is the major consideration when deciding agent numbers.

- *Abandon rate.* The percentage of calls in which the caller hangs up before agent response.

- *Average speed of answer.* Measured as the percentage of calls answered within a given number of seconds or rings of reception into the contact centre. For example, 80 per cent of calls answered in 20 seconds. This is sometimes known as service level.

- *Response time.* The amount of agent time that is consumed in responding to 100 per cent of inbound contacts. This metric is often specific to each channel and associated with a given objective, for example, 'all customer email enquiries will be handled within eight hours'.

- *First call (or contact) resolution (FCR).* Customers want to have their question answered at their first contact with the service provider. They do not want to have to call back. SQM Group's research indicates that on average only 68 per cent of first-time calls result in the issue being resolved to the satisfaction of the customer. According to the SQM Group 'FCR is the highest correlated metric to customer satisfaction of all the call centre metrics. Absence of FCR is the biggest driver of customer dissatisfaction'.[11] FCR also leads to a better work experience for agents. Unsurprisingly, agent efforts to cross-sell during calls that do not achieve FCR are largely unsuccessful.

- *Self-service issue resolution.* Many call centre managers want to deflect as many calls as possible from the agent queue to self-service systems – mainly IVR and interactive Web applications. This not only cuts costs, but also frees up agents to handle more complex issues. However, there may be a cost to the business in terms of reduced customer satisfaction and subsequent churn.

Case assignment applications ensure that each enquiry or issue gets routed to the right agent or technician for resolution. Customer service agents might, for example, be organized according to language skills. When an email enquiry is received in Urdu it is assigned to the agent competent in that language. Field technicians might be organized according to product category. When a service request is received to fix a printer, it is assigned to a technician who is knowledgeable about that product class, not to a more expensive expert in photocopiers. Assignment rules may consider a wide range of other criteria including customer value, sale territory, issue complexity and technician availability.

Case management covers the full cycle of activities involved, from receiving initial notification of a matter of concern to a customer to its final resolution and the case file being closed. Case management is also known as incident management and issue management. Case management applications enable case handlers to manage simple incidents, customer complaints and complex cases and investigations. Case management processes are typically designed using workflow applications within SA software. Workflow depicts the activities that must be performed, the sequence in which they occur, and sometimes include the standards to which the activities must comply. Workflow ensures that business rules are followed by case handlers. Cases, incidents or issues are initiated by the creation of a trouble ticket. Customers may be able to do this by web form, or by emailing or calling a service or contact centre, or at retail point-of-sale. Companies may also initiate a trouble ticket if they find that an incident is reported in social media. The ticket is assigned to a service engineer. The software automatically communicates with the customer at different trigger events such as

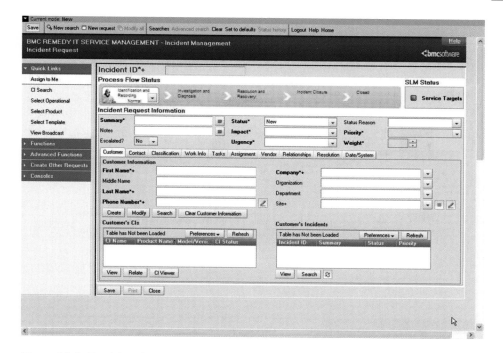

Figure 10.3 Trouble-ticket screenshot[12]

scheduling of appointments, or follow-up after the case is closed. Case management software is often integrated with a service knowledge base that enables technicians to diagnose and fix problems quickly, document management, billing systems and a reporting engine.

Contract management functionality enables service engineers and managers to create, track, progress, accelerate, monitor and control service contracts with customers. Many companies now sell extended service contracts to customers when warranty periods have expired. Contract management software offers a range of functionalities: document management, contract authoring, workflow, email or SMS alerts (about contract expiry, for example), contract approval processes, contract security, collaborative contract development, licensing, electronic signatures, calendaring and to-do lists, for example.

Customer communications management (CCM) applications aim to 'improve an organization's creation, delivery, storage, and retrieval of outbound and interactive communications with its customers'.[13] CCM applications enable customer interactions through a wide range of communication media, including email, SMS, websites, social media, print and customer self-service. CCM applications help users compose, personalize, format and deliver content acquired from various sources in the form of targeted electronic and physical communications. Core elements of these applications are a design tool, a composition engine, a workflow/rule engine, multi-channel delivery and reporting capabilities. Additional functionality may include digital rights management, electronic signatures, content development and approval processes, integration to social media and mobile apps, and content creation

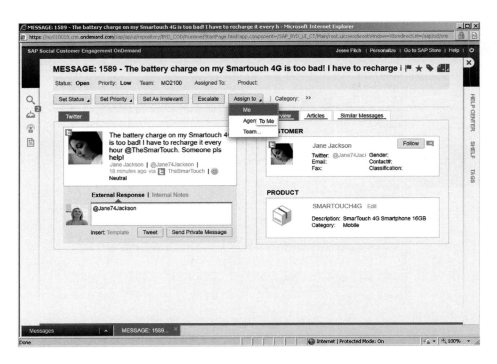

Figure 10.4 Agent response to Twitter feed[14]

© 2014 SAP AG or an SAP affiliate company. All rights reserved. Used with permission of SAP AG or an SAP affiliate company.

in multiple languages. Demand for CCM applications is driven by users wanting to reduce the costs of print, and improve communications and engagement with their customers.

As companies interact more frequently with customers in social media, they have begun to appreciate the importance of customer engagement; that is, the development in the customer of a strong emotional and behavioural identification with the firm. CCM applications that offer social media functionality enable companies to build improved levels of customer engagement. Hence, some multi-channel customer communication applications are now repositioning as customer engagement applications. According to Gartner Inc. 'At their most basic level, these applications handle a wide range of tasks, including engaging customers and prospects across multiple channels, and handling trouble ticketing, order management, case management, advisory services, problem diagnostics and resolution, account management, and returns management. This may also involve knowledge-enabled resolution (such as advanced search tools), process-centric/enabled service resolution, community management, and management and service analytics dashboards.'[15] Figure 10.4 is an example of a trouble ticket raised following a Twitter post.

Customer self-service (CSS) is an attractive option for companies because it transfers the responsibility and cost for service to the customer. Oracle reports that self-service provides significant savings in staffing costs. For simple customer transactions such as notifying changes to contact details, companies that offer self-service deflect a significant number of contact centre calls to the Web. More broadly, by improving systems and online content, companies can reduce call volumes by 20 per cent or more, which results in substantial savings. Average call centre costs are $5.50 per call, whereas the average cost per Web self-service transaction is $0.10. Even in small call centres annual self-service savings quickly reach the six-figure mark and many enterprises can realize cost reductions in the multi-millions.[16] Customers are typically more competent at self-serving when transactions are involved (for example online banking or music downloads); however, they are less competent when problem resolution is concerned. CSS technologies have been around for a long time – automated teller machines (ATMs) were introduced in 1967! Today CSS technologies include:

- *Web self-service*. Customers can perform routine transactions online, and access information by searching a knowledge base or reviewing a frequently asked questions (FAQ) page. In some sectors, it is commonplace to be able to place orders online and track the progress of the order. For example, customers can track-and-trace the location of packages they have sent or are expecting to receive. One website (www.track-trace.com) serves as a central track-and-trace clearing house for couriers DHL, UPS, TNT, FedEx and dozens of other market participants.

- *Interactive voice response (IVR)*. Customers can interact with an automated telephony system to perform tasks that follow step-like procedures.

- *Kiosks* enable customers to perform specific tasks such as checking in at an airport.

- *Self-checkout* is available in supermarkets and hotels. In the supermarket customers can scan, bag and pay for purchases at checkout. Theft of goods at self-service is an issue for supermarket operators. They need to assess whether the costs of customer theft are greater than the cost savings from self-service.

- *Apps*. Many companies have developed apps that are loaded onto smart phones, tablets or laptops, allowing customers to perform simple tasks like checking an account balance, checking weekly specials at local stores or finding out the time of the next bus.

Portals are widely used to enable customers to self-serve. Customers use portals to place orders, pay and check order and shipment progress, any day, any time. Searchable online knowledge bases also facilitate problem resolution by customers. Customers can browse for answers to their queries or solutions to their problems. In the event that this is unsuccessful, companies can allow customers to use an online web form to create a case or an issue for the company to follow up and resolve, or offer Web collaboration (see below). Many companies have policies about what sorts of customer self-service are allowed. For example, cable network customers can upgrade their package online but have to call a contact centre to downgrade or cancel their package. These calls are directed to a 'saves' team who try to persuade the customer not to reduce their expenditure. Some companies support peer-to-peer self-service (P2PSS). P2PSS is evident when customers report their experiences, issues and solutions in chat rooms, forums and social media, and offer assistance to each other. Companies can support this effort with content from their knowledge base.

Forrester Research Inc. reports that 72 per cent of customers attempt to self-resolve their service query online initially instead of making contact with a human service agent.[17] Companies that introduce self-service technologies need to understand that this fundamentally alters customer experience, and may have consequences for customer satisfaction and retention. Some customers love self-service because they are in control, can get the service they need at any time, and there is no agent attempting to sell them something. Other customers prefer human interaction.

Email response management systems (ERMS) are an increasingly important part of the service automation landscape. Email is widely used for both inter-personal and inter-company communications. According to the Radicati Group there were over 4.1 billion email accounts in 2014 with the number expected to rise to 5.2 billion by 2018. Email remains the most common communication channel used by businesses. Business email volumes are growing at 7 per cent per annum, and by 2018, over 139 billion emails will be sent each day. Consumer email traffic, however, is slowing down. While there is a growing number of consumer email accounts and users, many consumers are opting for other forms of communication such as social networking sites, instant messaging and SMS/text messaging.[18] Low-cost or free VoIP calls may further inhibit consumer use of email.[19] Company collateral, packaging and websites often list email addresses for individuals and departments. Up to 90 per cent of company websites provide email contacts for customer service.[20] In addition, many companies have generic email addresses such as info@, sales@ and support@. Customers increasingly expect companies to offer an email communication channel, not just for general communications but also for service-related issues. They also expect companies to respond promptly to incoming emails. One survey indicates room for improvement in this regard, with 37 per cent of Fortune 100 companies failing to offer any response to inbound customer emails.[21] As individuals, many of us use Outlook, Gmail or Lotus Notes for email. Whilst these may be suitable for small volumes of email, they lack functionality that is useful for higher volume, business-related purposes, such as queuing, routing, intelligent auto-responders, personalization, knowledge-base integration, productivity tools such as templates and multi-language spellcheckers, and email analytics. These are typically part of commercial ERMS.

ERMS are designed to manage the reception, acknowledgement, interpretation, routing, response, storage and analysis of incoming email securely and effectively. Rather than using generic email boxes, many companies have opted to receive customer service requests using pre-configured web forms. These require customers to select responses to a number of predetermined questions using drop-down menus, check boxes and radio buttons. Space may also be provided for customers to key in free-text. Log-in data or cookies allow companies to respond to web form service requests according to customer-related metrics such as customer value and purchase history. Where companies choose to receive customer emails into generic email boxes, there needs to be a manual or automated system for reading and responding to them, and routing them to responsible individuals where necessary. First-generation automated readers typically were trained to recognize keywords and respond accordingly. Second-generation readers recognize patterns across the entire email text rather than simply recognizing keywords. Pattern recognition has the added advantage of being able to detect the emotional tone of an email, so that a particularly angry customer might be identified and receive an immediate response. ERMS also have specialized Spam recognition and filtering features, and anti-virus tools. According to Kaspersky Lab, the email and Internet security firm, about 68 per cent of all email is Spam.[22]

Routing rules in ERMS allow incoming emails to be routed into queues for particular agents or departments. Most ERMS allow clients to configure routing rules using an administrative interface that can only be accessed by authorized administrators. Routing rules can push emails to particular queues based on agent workload, agent language skills, agent product knowledge, subject matter expertise, customer value or other variable. This speeds up resolution times, and helps meet service levels. Routing also allows more important service requests, perhaps from more valued customers, to be escalated for resolution by higher authorities.

Effective deployment of an ERMS is often accompanied by the publication of service levels. Published service levels such as 'We respond to all emails within 8 hours' help to manage customers' service expectations and motivate employees to act accordingly. Service levels can vary between customer segments and product categories. For example, service issues raised by more valued customers, or related to newly launched products, might receive a faster response.

Response time and response content are two important issues that customers consider in assessing service quality. ERMS can be set up to issue an immediate, personalized acknowledgment and case (tracking) number on receipt of a service-related email. These auto-responses can also be used to set out the service promise, for example, that the issue will be resolved within seven days. Many ERMS also contain response libraries for contact centre staff to browse if standard automated responses are inadequate. Other functionality in ERMS includes source filtering (only accepting emails from recognized sources), multiple email format compatibility (text only or HTML), ability to send and receive attachments, content filtering (filters out Spam, duplicates and other nuisance emails), source blocking, auto-forwarding, grammar and spellchecks, auto-translation, blind carbon copy (BCC) and management reporting. ERMS can also be configured to keep the customer informed of progress in the resolution of the service request and in marketing campaigns to deliver outbound emails and SMS messages.

From the company's point of view, a number of service metrics shed light on the effectiveness of their email management processes: numbers of emails in queues, average response time, service level compliance and agent productivity. From a service delivery perspective the most important measure is customer satisfaction with response time and content.

Escalation ensures that issues get escalated according to internally determined rules. Higher levels of authority typically have greater discretion to resolve issues. For example, a front-line customer service agent might be required to escalate to higher levels of management issues that have a potentially high cost or reputational consequence. A health insurance specialist escalates issues based on their cost implications as follows:

Level	Limit
Customer service agent	< $50
Team leader	< $100
Business unit manager	< $500
Executive manager	> $2,000

Agents in the front-line are trained to recognize issues that fall outside of the normal rules for health insurance provision and to escalate those issues accordingly. Escalation rules are typically built into case management applications.

Inbound communications (or call) management (ICM) applications are widely deployed in contact (or call) centre contexts. The technology allows companies to receive, acknowledge, route, queue and distribute incoming communications from any channel – voice telephony, email, chat, instant message, SMS, fax, social media, web form – to agents in any location including contact centre, in the field or at home. A unified queue, issue/content recognition, intelligent routing and knowledge-base integration allow agents to deliver a consistent customer experience and to respond effectively to service requests whatever the communication channel. Additional technologies that support service delivery in this multi-channel environment include CTI (computer telephony integration), ACD (automated call distribution), IVR (interactive voice response), scripting, call recording, problem diagnostics and service analytics. As with other CRM applications, ICM is available on demand (hosted) or on premise (installed on the user's hardware). We have more to say about IVR and scripting later in this chapter.

Automatic (or automated) call distribution (ACD) is a technology that recognizes, answers and distributes incoming calls. When the ACD system receives an incoming call it follows instructions as to how the call is to be handled. It can route the call to an agent, place it on hold or route it to an IVR message. ACD allows calls to be automatically routed to the most appropriate agent based upon criteria such as the number from which the call was made, customer identification number, language spoken by caller, agent expertise, product category, loyalty scheme membership tier and so on.

When contact centres use a distributed workforce, some agents may be working from home, some from a company site. Cloud-based ICM applications allow users to browse to the application's functionality from wherever they are located.

Interactive voice response (IVR) uses voice or touch-tone keypad input from callers to guide them through a tiered menu structure to the information they require as quickly as possible.

Invoicing is a useful application for service technicians who are called to site to provide out-of-warranty service. Having completed the job to the customer's satisfaction, and captured the customer's signature electronically, the invoice can be raised on the spot, thereby accelerating cash flow. Billing functionality is often integrated into other service automation applications such as case management and job management.

Job management applications offer a range of functionality that is useful to service managers and technicians when planning and performing field service repairs, preventive maintenance, meter readings, inspections, installations, upgrades and other service tasks. Functionality ranges over cost estimation, quotation generation, creation of trouble tickets, job planning, project management, travel time and distance calculation, GPS mapping, job clustering (to reduce travel time), calendaring, scheduling, spare parts management, job progress tracking, invoicing, service level management, technician despatch, time management and product configuration. Jobs are associated with accounts, contacts, contracts or opportunities so that technicians can have access to all relevant customer information on site. Job

SERVICE CENTRE AUTOMATION AT COCA-COLA[23]

Coca-Cola Bottling Unit (CCBU), a soft drinks manufacturer and distributor, is based in Lambeg, Northern Ireland. The company employs over 400 people, and has 14,000 customers. The service support team deals with a range of incoming calls that include complaints, orders, enquiries, delivery and pricing.

The decision to install a single customer service touchpoint dates back to 1996 when a customer satisfaction survey indicated that although customers generally felt they were receiving good service, they wanted a single contact point for customer service.

CCBU's lack of a single contact point meant that inbound calls were not logged in a uniform way. This in turn hindered analysis of call content and frequency, and led to variance in the quality and consistency of responses to service queries. In addition the company had no way of tracking if the advice given resolved the problem.

The company resolved these problems by introducing a single touchpoint for all service issues, and implementing the service automation product, HEAT. The support centre is split between customer services and customer complaints. HEAT is used to monitor product codes found on packaging and products, and when the support team finds three or more complaints that refer to any of these items then an alert message is sent direct to the incident team that then investigates.

CCBU installed service level agreements (SLA), scripted responses and screen customization to ensure high levels of customer service. CCBU's implementation of SLAs means that if a call has not been resolved within a specified period of time it is automatically escalated. The system ensures all calls are logged and are therefore measurable. The customer service team underwent intensive training. Every new employee is trained in first level response across the board which enables everyone within the company to close standard queries and improve the service customers receive.

---

management applications provide technicians with the tools to deliver efficient and effective service to customers, thereby enhancing service experience. Management reports generated by these applications enable managers to keep control over costs and optimize technician numbers and workload.

Knowledge-base self-service enables customers to search a database for answers to their service queries. The database may consist of FAQs, articles and videos produced by the company, and content generated by customers or acquired from third parties. In addition, a 'call-me' web-chat button or telephone number can be offered customers who can't find the answer they seek in the knowledge base. A knowledge-base manager is sometimes assigned to ensure that externally provided content is not malicious or inappropriate. Companies make this information available through a portal, thereby reducing their cost-per-service request. Agents in contact centres can also make use of the same knowledge base by inserting links into emailed or texted responses to customer enquiries.

Solutions that provide *mapping and driving directions* are very useful for service engineers who need to visit customers' homes or business premises. Taking into account the

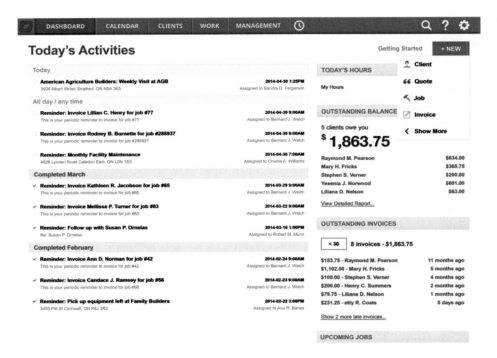

Figure 10.5 Job management application[24]

engineer's point-of-origin, service locations, job priorities, service level agreements and other variables, mapping solutions can minimize travel times and distances to ensure that service tasks are performed optimally.

Outbound communications management software applications are used in a service environment to acknowledge service requests, make and confirm service appointments, advise on the progress of a service task, invoice for out-of-warranty service and follow-up after service to ensure that the customer is satisfied. Customer preferences can be considered when selecting the communication medium, be that telephone, email or SMS. Preferences may be different for the initial scheduling of an appointment (email) and for subsequent changes (text message). The technology firm, KANA, notes that it is possible to convert successful service interactions into up-sell and cross-sell opportunities with follow-up outbound emails and SMS messages.[25]

Predictive dialling is a telephony technology widely used in contact and call centres. It automatically dials groups of telephone numbers, and then passes calls to available agents once the call is connected. The technology quickly terminates calls that are met with no answer, busy signals, answering machines or disconnected numbers while predicting when an agent will be available to take the next call. Predictive diallers measure the number of available agents, available lines, average handling time and other factors to adjust outbound calls accordingly.

Predictive diallers are commonly used for telemarketing, market research surveys, appointment confirmation, payment collection and service follow-ups. Vendors of this technology claim that predictive dialling raises agent productivity. Only calls that are answered by a live person are put through to an agent. Productivity is increased because agents do not make unsuccessful calls; that is left to the technology.

Queuing and routing applications allow issues to be routed to agents with particular expertise and positioned in that agent's queue according to some rule. Universal queuing aggregates all inbound contacts into a single queue regardless of reception channel – voice, email, chat and social media – and applies a common routing rule. This delivers a fairer and more consistent customer experience. Without universal queuing, service performance is likely to vary between channels. Routing is usually determined by case assignment rules (see above) and position in the queue is determined by customer value or some other metric. The objective of queuing and routing is to ensure that every service issue is presented to the most appropriate agent for handling and resolution.

Scheduling involves planning and organizing a service technician's activity plan for a day, week or other period. A technician's schedule contains details on the customer, location, time, product and issue. Some scheduling applications take into account a range of considerations to ensure that the right technician is sent to service the customer. These include travel time and distance, technician availability, technician skills, customer access hours, service level agreement, availability of spare parts and the technician's hourly rates of pay. Optimization engines allow schedules to be changed as new service tickets are created, priorities change and technicians or parts become (un)available. Optimization reduces service costs whilst maintaining service performance levels. Scheduled tasks can be released in batches for days or weeks, or drip-fed to technicians for the coming few hours.

Scripting enables customer service agents to converse intelligently with customers to diagnose and resolve problems, co-creating good customer experience and complying with regulatory requirements, even though they may be untrained as technicians. Scripts are essentially linked screens that the agent talks through with the customer. The 'right script' depends on the purpose of the call. When a customer calls to report a service problem it is critical that the script identifies the caller, clarifies the issue, assesses the significance of the issue (e.g. an electrical appliance malfunction might have life-threatening consequences) and establishes what the customer wants to achieve. In a service encounter, it may be inappropriate to include screens of script that have a selling objective. However, if the service issue is resolved at first contact, up-sell or cross-sell is likely to be more acceptable and productive. Scripts should be designed so that they flex dynamically according to customer response. Inflexible scripts generally deliver poor customer experience. Well-designed scripts deliver customer satisfaction, ensure compliance with any regulatory environment and enhance agent productivity. Scripts reduce agent training costs and time. Scripts are also used in outbound call centre contexts.

Service analytics provide managers with information on how effectively and efficiently customer service generally, and individual agents or technicians specifically, are operating,

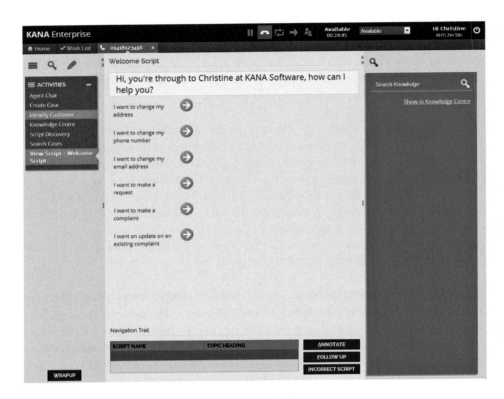

Figure 10.6 Customer service scripting screenshot[26]

and how satisfied customers are with the service they receive. Important metrics for managers of field service operations, for example, include technician utilization, parts inventory, travel time, first-time fix rate (FTFR), mean time to resolve (MTTR) and job backlog. FTFR tells managers how many cases were resolved at the technician's first call. MTTR measures the time elapsed between notification of the service request to the company and its final resolution. With this information, managers can obtain new resources, reassign staff, offer training or recalibrate key performance indicators to enhance service delivery. Service analytics provide insight into the cost-to-serve a customer, and therefore help calculate customer profitability. Many SA applications incorporate embedded analytics that produce standard reports and enable OLAP to be performed. Oracle's Service Analytics product, for example, includes pre-built data models with more than 300 metrics.

Service level management (SLM) applications allow managers to establish, monitor and control the level of service that is offered to customers, and technicians to deliver the level of service agreed. As introduced in Chapter 6, a service level agreement is a contractual commitment between a service provider and customer that specifies the mutual responsibilities of both parties with respect to the services that will be provided and the standards at which they will be performed. Service levels can be agreed for a number of variables including availability (the percentage of time that the service is available over an agreed time period), usage (the number of service users that can be served simultaneously) and responsiveness

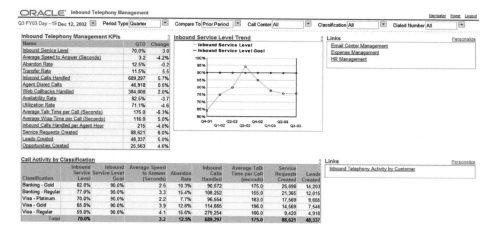

Figure 10.7 Oracle inbound telephony dashboard[27]

(the speed with which a demand for service is fulfilled). SLM applications enable both parties to identify when potential problems, such as service degradation, occur and to respond quickly. Service levels are usually, but not always, subject to negotiation with customers. Instead, many companies simply offer tiered levels of service to customers based on some metric of their own choice, typically customer value as measured by customer profitability or sales.

Technicians who understand the entitlements of customers can service requests to the specified limit, and even up-sell them to a higher level of service.

Spare parts management is an important application for field technicians. They can see what parts they have with them on the road, check the inventory levels held by other technicians and at regional and central warehouses, order new parts, transfer parts from colleagues, manage excess and defective parts, and check on the progress of orders, thereby ensuring that when they turn up at a job they are properly equipped. Managers can use this application to ensure that appropriate levels of parts inventory are maintained and customers are billed correctly. Too few parts and jobs cannot be completed; too many and inventory costs are unnecessarily high.

Voice biometrics or voice recognition has become a reliable technology for authenticating a person's identity. Voice biometrics verifies identity by comparing a person's voice with their voiceprint, a previously recorded representation of their voice. Voice recognition can be used as a standalone authentication protocol, but is more commonly deployed as an additional security layer, especially for organizations targeted by fraudsters – banks, insurance companies and healthcare providers. It provides stronger authentication than a knowledge-based approach by verifying people for who they are, as opposed to what they know, such as a PIN or mother's maiden name. Voice biometrics means customers do not need to answer a set of personal security questions at the start of contact with a call or contact centre. From management's perspective, if voice recognition saves an average of 20 seconds of the agent's time per call there is the prospect of a significant lift in agent productivity, and an improvement in customer experience.

Figure 10.8 Chat window (Oracle Smart technologies) screenshot[28]

Web collaboration is a collective term for the online, social and software tools that enable customers and customer service agents to interact in real time to solve customer problems. These technologies include instant messaging (web chat), web-conferencing, co-browsing of web pages and file-sharing (calendars, to-do lists, videos, documents, presentations and other files). Web collaboration allows the agent to help the customer to resolve the issue in real time. Customer service agents can collaborate with a number of customers simultaneously, or can prioritize based on customer value or some other metric. Transcripts of the chat can be retained and attached to the customer file. Web collaboration is often used as an escalation option for customers who cannot find a solution to their issue through a self-service portal. Web collaboration may reduce online abandonment rates, increase problem resolution and customer satisfaction, and provide up-sell and cross-sell opportunities.

Workflow development software is useful for designing service-related processes, such as problem diagnosis and issue escalation. Workflow for field service operations will define how service requests are validated, how service tickets are issued, how tickets are allocated, how problems will be diagnosed, how parts will be ordered, how problems will be fixed, how customers will be invoiced and so on.

SUMMARY

Service automation is the application of computerized technologies to support service managers, and customer service agents in contact and call centres, help-desk staff and mobile service staff operating in the field, in the achievement of their work-related objectives. Academics, practitioners and government agencies have attempted to understand and characterize customer service and service quality. Companies and their customers can experience many benefits from service automation: enhanced service effectiveness and efficiency, greater service productivity, better agent work experience, and improved customer experience, engagement and retention. Service automation applications offer a range of functionality to service managers and technicians: activity management, agent management, case assignment, case management, contract management, customer communications management, customer self-service, email response management, escalation, inbound communications management, interactive voice response, invoicing, job management, knowledge-base self-service, mapping and driving directions, outbound communications management, predictive dialling, queuing and routing, scheduling, scripting, service analytics, service level management, spare parts management, voice biometrics, Web collaboration and workflow development.

NOTES AND REFERENCES

1   Grönroos, C. (1984). A service quality model and its marketing implications. *European Journal of Marketing*, 18, 36–44.

2   Parasuraman, A., Zeithaml, V.A. and Berry, L.L. (1985). A conceptual model of service quality and its implications for future research. *Journal of Marketing*, 49 (Fall), 41–50; Parasuraman, A., Zeithaml, V.A. and Berry, L.L. (1988). SERVQUAL: a multiple-item scale for measuring consumers' perceptions of service quality. *Journal of Retailing*, 64(1), 22–37; Parasuraman, A., Zeithaml, V.A. and Berry, L.L. (1991). Refinement and reassessment of the SERVQUAL scale. *Journal of Retailing*, 64, 12–40; Parasuraman, A., Zeithaml, V.A. and Berry, L.L. (1994). Reassessment of expectations as a comparison standard in measuring service quality: implications for future research. *Journal of Marketing*, 58(1), 111–32.

3   Wiersema, Fred (1998).*Customer service: extraordinary results at Southwest Airlines, Charles Schwab, Land's End, American Express, Staples and USAA*. New York: Harper Collins.

4   http://www.customerserviceexcellence.uk.com/CSE_Standard.pdf (Accessed 16 April 2014).

5   http://www.ticsi.org/tisse/tisse2012-measurement-model (Accessed 16 April 2012).

6   http://www.itil-officialsite.com/ (Accessed 16 April 2014).

7   www.itsmf.org.au (Accessed 16 April 2014).

8   www.gartner.com. Magic Quadrant for Field Service Management, October 2013 ID: G00252160.

9   Courtesy Oracle.com. Used with permission.

10 www.wireless.att.com/businesscenter/en_US/pdf/ICEECaseStudy.pdf (Accessed 27 January 2008).

11 http://www.sqmgroup.com/fcr-metric-that-matters-most (Accessed 16 April 2014).

12 http://inews.berkeley.edu/articles/Fall2008/remedy-screenshots (Accessed 19 April 2014).

13 http://www.gartner.com/technology/reprints.do?id=1–1NHY9P3&ct = 131127&st = sg (Accessed 18 April 2014).

14 Courtesy SAP.com. Used with permission.

15 http://www.gartner.com/technology/reprints.do?id=1–1FN3JKH&ct = 130514&st = sg (Accessed 18 April 2014).

16 http://www.oracle.com/us/products/applications/siebel/051273.pdf (Accessed 19 April 2014).

17 Forrester Research Inc. (2010). Selecting online customer service channels to satisfy customers and reduce costs. 25 June.

18 http://www.radicati.com/wp/wp-content/uploads/2014/04/Email-Statistics-Report-2014–2018-Executive-Summary.pdf (Accessed 17 April 2014).

19 http://www.idc.com/getdoc.jsp?containerId=prUS20639307&pageType=PRINTFRIENDLY (Accessed 15 January 2008).

20 Talisma Corporation (2007). Winning strategies for email management. White paper.

21 CustomerRespect.com report cited in: http://hd.egain.com/wp-content/uploads/2012/11/egain_whitepaper_erms_10_best_practices.pdf (Accessed 18 April 2014).

22 Kaspersky Lab (2014), cited in: http://www.securelist.com/en/analysis/204792311/Spam_in_Q3_2013 (Accessed 17 April 2014).

23 http://heat.frontrange.co.uk/common/Files/Xtra_Sites/HEAT/casestudy_HEAT_Coca_Cola.pdf (Accessed 28 January 2008).

24 http://www.getjobber.com/?utm_source = getapp&utm_medium = ppc&utm_campaign = get_app (Accessed 19 April 2014).

25 www.kana.com/solutions.php?tid=105 (Accessed 27 December 2007).

26 http://www.kana.com/enterprise/guided-scripting (Accessed 19 April 2014).

27 http://www.dashboardzone.com/inbound-telephony-management-dashboard-call-center-activity-daily-business-intelligence (Accessed 19 April 2014).

28 Courtesy Oracle.com. Used with permission.

ANALYTICAL CRM

Part IV is about analytical CRM, sometimes known as analytic CRM. Analytical CRM is the process through which organizations transform customer-related data into actionable insight for either strategic or tactical purposes. Those strategic purposes might include finding out which customers have the highest lifetime value, so that the business can ring-fence them, or segmenting the customer base so that different value propositions can be created for the identified segments. Tactical uses of analytical CRM might include identifying which customers are at risk of churning so the business can create an offer that encourages them to remain customers, or identifying the next best offer that will cross-sell a customer, and therefore grow customer value.

Analytical CRM relies on customer-related data. Part IV therefore consists of two chapters. Chapter 11 is about customer-related data and database creation, and Chapter 12 is about making use of the data.

DEVELOPING AND MANAGING CUSTOMER-RELATED DATABASES

CHAPTER OBJECTIVES

By the end of this chapter you will understand:

- The central role of customer-related data in the achievement of CRM outcomes.
- The importance of data quality to CRM performance.
- The issues that need to be considered in developing a customer-related database.
- How data integration contributes to CRM performance.
- The purpose of a data warehouse and data mart.
- The uses of knowledge management systems in CRM.

INTRODUCTION

Customer-related databases are the foundation for the execution of CRM strategy. Proficiency at acquiring, enhancing, storing, analyzing, distributing and using customer-related data is critical to CRM performance. Strategic CRM, which focuses on winning and keeping profitable customers, relies on customer-related data to identify which customers to target, win and keep, and which to allow to churn. Operational CRM, which focuses on the automation of selling, marketing and customer service processes, needs customer-related data to be able to deliver excellent service, run successful marketing campaigns and track sales opportunities.

We use the expression 'customer-*related* databases' instead of 'customer databases' deliberately. The data that are employed for CRM purposes are not only *about* customers (i.e. 'customer databases'), but also *for* customers.

Data that are *for* customers include data about products and solutions to service issues. These data are typically stored in a searchable knowledge base and made available to customers and partners through portals. Commercially sensitive or confidential information is usually password protected.

Data *about* customers are not only available in corporate databases maintained in functional areas such as marketing, sales, service, logistics and accounts, but are also available from third parties such as market research firms and credit scoring agencies, and increasingly in social media such as Facebook, Twitter and YouTube.

Our use of the expression 'customer-related' covers data that are both about and for customers.

CORPORATE CUSTOMER-RELATED DATA

Companies typically do not have just one customer database. Instead, they have a number of customer-related databases. These databases capture customer-related data from a number of different functional perspectives – sales, marketing, service, logistics and accounts – each of which serves different operational purposes. These databases might record quite different customer-related data – opportunities, campaigns, enquiries, deliveries and billing, respectively.

Customer-related data might be independently maintained by managers running operations in channels such as company-owned retail stores, third-party retail outlets and online. Similarly, different product managers might maintain their own customer-related data. Customer-related data can have a current, past or future perspective, focusing, for example, upon the current sales pipeline, historic sales or potential opportunities. Customer-related data might be about individual customers, customer cohorts, customer segments, market segments or entire markets. They might also contain product information, competitor information, regulatory data or anything else pertinent to the development and maintenance of customer relationships.

STRUCTURED AND UNSTRUCTURED DATA

Most of the data maintained in corporate databases are structured. Data stored in a fixed and named field in a record or file are called structured data. Structure is provided by a pre-defined data model that specifies the data to be stored in each field, how that data should be recorded (alphanumeric codes or literal text, usually) and how the fields are related to each other. Commercial CRM applications usually come with pre-defined data models. The types of data that are relevant to a banking industry CRM application are quite different from a life sciences CRM application, and the data models are therefore quite different. CRM users within particular industries often customize pre-defined models to make them fit better with their own particular business and customer context.

Structured customer-related data are stored in three different types of database:

- hierarchical
- network
- relational.

Hierarchical and network databases were the most common form between the 1960s and 1980s. The hierarchical database is the oldest form and not well suited to most CRM applications. You can imagine the hierarchical model as an organization chart or family tree, in which a child can have only one parent, but a parent can have many children. The only way to get access to the lower levels is to start at the top and work downwards. When data are stored in hierarchical format, you may end up working through several layers of higher-level data before getting to the data you need. Product databases are generally hierarchical. A major product category will be subdivided repeatedly until all forms of the product have their own record.

To extend the family tree metaphor, the network database allows children to have one parent, more than one parent or no parent. Before the network database had the chance to become popular, the relational database superseded it, eventually becoming an ANSI standard in 1971.[1]

Relational databases are now the standard architecture for CRM applications that use structured data. Relational databases store data in two-dimensional tables comprised of rows and columns, like a spreadsheet. Relational databases have one or more fields that provide a unique form of identification for each record. This is called the primary key. For sales databases, each customer is generally assigned a unique number, which appears in the first column, there being a unique number on each row. Companies that have other databases for marketing, service, inventory, payments and so on, use the customer's unique identifying number to connect the data held in the various databases.

Relational databases share a common structure of files, records and fields (also called tables, rows and columns). Files (tables) hold information on a single topic such as customers, products, transactions or service requests. Each file (table) contains a number of records (rows). Each record (row) contains a number of elements of data. These elements are arranged in a common set of fields (columns) across the table.

Structured data are widely found in corporate databases maintained in sales, marketing, service, logistics and accounts departments. Third-party data sources such as market research firms and credit scoring agencies also provide structured data.

Unstructured data, by comparison, are data that do not fit a pre-defined data model. Unstructured data take the form of textual or non-textual files. Textual corporate unstructured data includes emails, PowerPoint presentations, Word documents, SMS instant messages, PDFs, spreadsheets, faxes and agent notes on a customer's service history. Non-textual data include recorded telephone calls and other MP3 files, images in JPEG and other formats, video in Flash and other

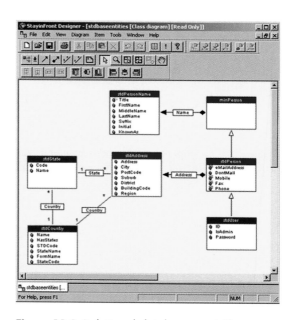

Figure 11.1 Relational database model[2]

formats, and multimedia messages. The massive increase in unstructured corporate data not only creates storage costs, but also presents challenges to privacy and confidentiality. Imagine the consequences of internal emails about product specifications and costs finding their way into competitors' hands.

In addition, there has been a huge lift in the amount of unstructured data produced by users of social media and elsewhere. These data include metering data, climate data, mobile phone GPS signals and stock ticker data. The momentum in the growth of unstructured data is expected to accelerate into the future. This type of data has become known as 'big data'. Big data presents an opportunity for businesses only if the data can be interpreted and acted upon. We first introduced you to Gartner's Hype Cycle in Chapter 9. The Hype Cycle is a visualization of the excitement, disillusionment and achieved reality of new technologies. Gartner's Hype Cycle for big data suggests that many applications of big data are years from being useful, let alone mature. However, some big data technologies useful to CRM practitioners – voice recognition, predictive analytics, social media monitoring and text analytics, for example – are with us today.[3]

DEVELOPING A CUSTOMER-RELATED DATABASE

Whilst unstructured data present some serious challenges and opportunities for CRM practitioners, the 'bread-and-butter' in CRM is still the relational database. We therefore explore in more detail how to develop and manage structured customer-related databases. There are six major steps, as shown in Figure 11.2.

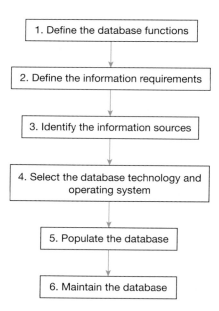

Figure 11.2 Steps in creating a relational database[4]

Define the database functions

The first step is to answer the question 'why do we need customer-related data?' This question means that the business has to revisit to the CRM vision, strategy, goals, objectives and business case, to identify what is expected from CRM. We discuss these issues in more detail in chapters 13 and 14. However, in general, CRM practitioners use databases for all three forms of CRM – strategic, operational and analytical.

Strategic CRM uses customer-related data to identify which customers to target for acquisition, retention and development, and generate insight for the appropriate value propositions and experiences to offer them. Operational CRM uses customer-related data in the everyday selling, marketing and customer service operations of the business. For example:

- A telecommunications company's customer service representative (CSR) needs to access a customer record and check the customer's status so she can prioritize the company's response to a service request.

- A hotel receptionist needs access to a guest's history so that she can reserve the preferred type of room – smoking or non-smoking, standard or deluxe.

- A sales person needs to identify the status of an opportunity and decide on what actions to take before calling on a customer.

Analytical CRM uses customer-related data to support the marketing, sales and service decisions that aim to enhance the value created for and from customers. For example:

- A telecoms company's marketers might want to target a retention offer to customers who are signalling an intention to switch to a different supplier.

- A hotel company's marketers might want to promote a weekend break to customers who have indicated high levels of satisfaction in previous customer surveys.

- Websites direct customers to the 'next best offer' dynamically as they navigate through the site.

Customer-related data are typically organized into two subsets, reflecting these operational and analytical purposes. Operational data reside in an online transaction processing (OLTP) database, and analytical data reside in an online analytical processing (OLAP) database. The information in the OLAP database is normally a summarized extract of the OLTP database, enough to perform the analytical tasks. OLTP data need to be very accurate and up to date. When a customer calls a contact centre to enquire about an invoice, it is no use the agent telling the customer what the average invoice is for a customer in her postcode. The customer wants personal, accurate and contemporary information. OLAP databases, on the other hand, can perform well with less current data.

Define the information requirements

The people best placed to answer the question 'what information is needed?' are those who interact with, or communicate with, customers for sales, marketing and service purposes, and those who have to make strategic CRM decisions.

A direct marketer planning an email campaign might want to know open and click-through rates, and click-to-open rates (CTOR) from previous campaigns, broken down by target audience, offer and execution. She would also want to know email addresses, email preferences (HTML or plain text) and preferred salutation (first name? Mr? Ms?). Operational and analytical needs like these help define the required contents of customer-related databases.

Senior managers reviewing a company's strategic CRM decisions will require a completely different set of information. They may want to know the following. How is the market segmented? Who are our current customers? What do they buy? Who else do they buy from? What is our share-of-wallet? What are our customers' requirements, expectations and preferences across all components of the value proposition, including product, service, channel and communication?

As noted above, packaged CRM applications do much of the database design work for users. The availability of industry-specific CRM applications, with their corresponding industry-specific data models, allows for a much closer fit with a company's data needs. Where there is a good fit out-of-the-box, the database design process for both operational and analytical CRM uses becomes one of implementing exceptions that have been overlooked by the generic industry model. Some CRM vendors have also built in the extract, transform and load processes to move information from OLTP to OLAP databases.

Customer information fields

CRM software is usually modularized. For example, a sales force automation (SFA) application will contain comprehensive information about contacts, opportunities, cases, activities and other issues that are important for the sales rep to work effectively and efficiently on her accounts.

Figure 11.3 SugarCRM screenshot[5]

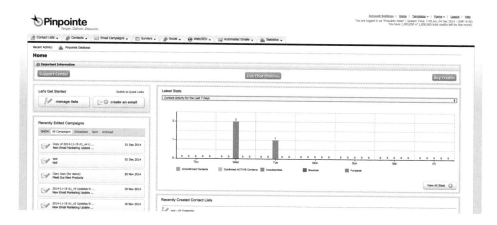

Figure 11.4 Email marketing application[6]

The most comprehensive CRM solutions offer functionality across sales, marketing and service, and will therefore have several modules that relate to each of these functional areas. See, for example, the screenshot from SugarCRM in Figure 11.3, which has modules for accounts, opportunities, quotations, campaigns, knowledge base and cases, amongst others. Each of these modules is associated with a number of fields of data.

Some CRM applications are dedicated to specific purposes, and the fields of data therefore vary accordingly. The email marketing application in Figure 11.4, for example, has modules for contacts, contact lists, email campaigns and reports, amongst others. Each of these modules is associated with a number of pre-defined fields. For example the contacts module will have fields for contact name, email address, salutation, preferred email format (HTML or plain text) and status (whether active or not).

Identify the information sources

Information for customer-related databases can be sourced internally or externally. Internal data are the foundation of most CRM programmes, though the amount of information available about customers depends upon the degree of customer contact that the company has. Some companies sell through partners, agents and distributors and may have little knowledge about the demand chain beyond their immediate contact.

Internal data are found in various functional areas. Marketing might have data on market size, market segmentation, customer profiles, customer acquisition channels, marketing campaigns, product registrations and requests for product information. Sales might have records on customer purchasing history including recency, frequency and monetary value, buyers' names and contact details, account number, Standard Industrial Classification (SIC) code, important buying criteria, terms of trade such as discounts and payment period, potential customers (prospects), responses to proposals, competitor products and pricing, and customer requirements and preferences. Customer service might have records of customers' service histories, service requirements, customer satisfaction levels, customer complaints, resolved and unresolved issues, customer issues raised in social media, enquiries, and loyalty programme membership and status. Finance may have data on credit ratings, accounts receivable and payment histories, and, finally, the webmaster may have click-stream data.

Customer-related data maintained by the functional areas might not be easily captured and migrated to databases used for CRM purposes. Sales reps, for example, might keep customer records in hard copy, spreadsheets or Microsoft Access databases. Marketers might have customer-related data in management reports created in Word. Very often, CRM project leaders find that there is a massive amount of duplication of data. For example, sales, marketing and service records may all have customer email addresses. It is not unusual for the email specifics to be different. Many CRM projects therefore incorporate a data quality phase in which these idiosyncratic records are identified, obtained and qualified. The most accurate and relevant information is then imported into the CRM database.

Enhancing internal data

If internal data are insufficient for CRM purposes, external data can be imported to enhance the customer record. External data can be imported from a number of sources including market research companies and corporate database companies. The business intelligence company Nielsen, for example, sells clients access to their PRIZM, P$YCLE and ConneXions databases. Experian, another business intelligence company, sells geo-demographic data to its clients.

External data can be classified into three groups:

- compiled list data
- census data
- modelled data.[7]

Compiled list data are individual-level data assembled by list bureaux or list vendors. They build their lists from a variety of personal, household and business sources. They might use local or council tax records, questionnaire response data, warranty card registrations or businesses' published annual reports. If you were a retailer considering diversifying from leisurewear into dancewear and had little relevant customer data of your own, you might be interested in buying or renting a compiled list from an external source. The list could be compiled from a variety of sources, such as:

- memberships of dance schools
- student enrolments on dance courses at school and college
- recent purchasers of dance equipment
- lifestyle questionnaire respondents who cite dance as an interest
- subscribers to dance magazines
- purchasers of tickets for dance and musical theatre.

Census data are obtained from government census records. In different parts of the world, different information is available. Some censuses are unreliable; other governments deny third parties, such as companies, access to data for non-governmental use.

In the USA, where the census is conducted every 10 years, you cannot obtain census data at the household level, but you can at a more aggregated geo-demographic level, such as zip code, block group and census tract. Census tracts are subdivisions of counties. Block groups are subdivisions of census tracts, the boundaries of which are generally streets. Census data available at geo-demographic level include:

- median income
- average household size
- average home value
- average monthly mortgage
- percentage ethnic breakdown
- marital status
- percentage college educated.

Individual-level data are better predictors of behaviour than aggregated geo-demographic data. However, in the absence of individual-level data, census data may be the only option for enhancing your internal data. For example, a car reseller could use census data about median income and average household size to predict who might be prospects for a campaign.

Modelled data are generated by third parties from data that they assemble from a variety of sources. You buy processed, rather than raw, data from these sources. Often they have performed clustering routines on the data. For example, Nielsen has a customer classification scheme called PRIZM that helps marketers segment customers and prospects so they can be reached with tailored messages and offers. PRIZM identifies 66 segments that vary according to socio-economic rank, as indicated by characteristics such as income,

CASE STUDY 11.1

PRIZM MARKET SEGMENTATION (US EXAMPLE)[8]

Young Digerati (PRIZM Segment 4) are the nation's tech-savvy singles and couples living in fashionable neighbourhoods on the urban fringe. Affluent, highly educated and ethnically diverse, they live in areas typically filled with trendy apartments and condos, fitness clubs, clothing boutiques, casual restaurants and all types of bars – from juice to coffee to microbrew.

Kids & Cul-de-Sacs (PRIZM Segment 18) are upscale, suburban, married couples with children. Kids & Cul-de-Sacs are a lifestyle group of large families in recently built subdivisions. With a high rate of Hispanic and Asian-Americans, this segment is a refuge for college-educated, white-collar professionals with administrative jobs and upper-middle-class incomes.

Heartlanders (PRIZM Segment 43) consist of older couples with working-class jobs living in sturdy, unpretentious homes. In these communities of small families and empty-nest couples, they pursue a rustic lifestyle where hunting, fishing, camping and boating remain prime leisure activities.

education, occupation and home value, 11 life-stage groups and 14 social groups. The social groups are based on urbanization and socio-economic rank, and the life-stage groups on age, socio-economic rank and the presence of children at home.

Some CRM applications come pre-integrated to external data sources. For example, salesforce.com users can import data from Dun & Bradstreet's corporate information database. Outside of these linkages, if you want to use external data to enhance your internal data, you will most likely have to send a copy of the data that you want to enhance to the external data source. The source will match its files to yours using an algorithm that recognizes equivalence between the files (often using names and addresses). The source then attaches the relevant data to your files and returns them to you.

Secondary and primary data

Customer-related data are either secondary or primary. Secondary data have already been collected, perhaps for a purpose that is very different from your CRM requirement. Primary data are collected for the first time, either for CRM or other purposes.

Primary data collection through traditional means, such as surveys, can be very expensive. Companies have therefore had to find relatively low-cost ways to generate primary customer data for CRM applications. Among the data-building schemes that have been used are the following:

- *Competition entries.* Customers are invited to enter competitions of skill, or lotteries. They surrender personal data on the entry forms.

- *Subscriptions.* Customers are invited to subscribe to a newsletter or magazine, again surrendering personal details.

- *Registrations.* Customers are invited to register their purchase, at which time they also provide additional data such as name, address and contact details.

- *Loyalty programmes.* Many companies run loyalty programmes. These enable companies to link purchasing behaviour to individual customers and segments. When joining a programme, customers complete application forms, providing the company with personal, demographic and even lifestyle data.

Select the database technology and operating system

The database technology and operating system decisions are usually subsumed into the selection of CRM application software. CRM application vendors usually support a specified list of database technologies, for example, Oracle, MySQL, DB2 or SQL Server. It is possible to buy an entire integrated platform, consisting of hardware, operating system (OS), database technology and CRM applications. Leading operating systems include UNIX and Microsoft. A UNIX-based technology 'package' might incorporate a number of hardware/OS/database options such as Hewlett Packard hardware, Digital UNIX operating system and Oracle database. An IBM-based technology 'package' might employ AS/400 hardware, OS/400 operating system and DB2/400 database. CRM project managers and CRM users rarely have to consider database technology and OS issues because modern CRM applications are either bought packaged with database technology and operating system, or support a number of specified database and OS technologies.

If a company were to decide to build its own CRM application it would have to select an operating system (Linux, UNIX, Microsoft, Mac, for example) and a database backend (e.g. SQL Server, MySQL, DB2).

The choice of hardware platform is influenced by several conditions:

- *The size of the databases.* Even standard desktop PCs are capable of storing huge amounts of customer-related data.

- *Existing technology.* Most companies will already have technology that lends itself to database applications.

- *The number and location of users.* Many CRM applications are quite simple, but in an increasingly global marketplace the hardware may need very careful specification and periodic review. For example, hardware might need to enable a geographically dispersed, multi-lingual user group to access real-time data for operational CRM purposes, 24/7.

Populate the database

Having decided what information is needed and the database and hardware requirements, the next task is to obtain the data and enter them onto the database. CRM applications need data that are appropriately accurate. We use the term 'appropriately' because the level of accuracy depends upon the function of the database. As noted earlier, operational CRM applications generally need more accurate and contemporary data than analytical applications. Be aware, though, that the datasets used for analytical purposes are often extracted from operational databases, and therefore high-quality data are often available for analysis.

You may have experienced the results of poor-quality data personally. Perhaps you have received a mailed invitation to become a donor to a charity to which you already donate. This could have happened when a prospecting list that has been bought by the charity was not checked against current donor lists. Perhaps you have been addressed as Mrs although you prefer Ms. This is caused because the company has either not obtained or not acted upon your communication preferences.

Most new CRM projects have a data quality project early on. Operational CRM systems that import poor-quality data from, say, sales reps' handwritten call reports or field service engineers' weekly activity reports, are likely not to create good customer experience in the short term. However, data quality can be built over time by checking with every customer contact that the data on the system are correct.

The main steps in ensuring that the database is populated with appropriately accurate data are as follows:

- verify the data
- validate the data
- de-duplicate the data
- merge and purge data from two or more sources.

Verification. The task of verification is to ensure that the data have been entered exactly as found in the original source. This can be a very labour-intensive process since it generally involves keying the data in twice with the computer programmed to flag mismatches. An alternative is to check visually that the data entered match the data at the primary source.

Validation means that you check the accuracy of the data that are entered. There are a number of common inaccuracies, many associated with name and address fields: misspelt names, incorrect titles and inappropriate salutations. A number of processes can help validate data:

- *Range validation.* Does an entry lie outside the possible range for a field?
- *Missing values.* You can have the computer check for values that are missing in any column.
- *Check against external sources.* You could check postcodes against an authoritative external listing from the mail authorities.

De-duplication is also known as de-duping. Customers become aware that their details appear more than once on a database when they receive identical communications from a company. This might occur when external data are not cross-checked against internal data, when two or more internal lists are used for the mailing or when customers have more than one address on a database. There may be sound cost reasons for this – de-duplication does cost money – but from the customer's perspective it can look wasteful and unprofessional, and it delivers poor customer experience. De-duplication software is available to help in the process.

The de-duplication process needs to be alert to the possibility of two types of error:

- *Removing a record that should be retained.* For example, if a property is divided into unnumbered apartments, and you have transactions with more than one resident, then

DupID	FirstName	LastName	CompanyName	StreetAddress	City	State
483	Stephen	Ayres	US Veterans Affairs Med. Ctr.	1601 SW Archer Rd.	Gainesville	FL
483	Stephen	Aires	US Affairs Medical Center	1601 SW Archer Rd.	Gainesville	FI
573	Karl	Asha	ClearCommerce Corporation	11500 Metric Blvd.	Austen	TX
573	DanieleCarl	Asha	ClearCommerce Corporation	11500 Metric Boulevard	Austen	TX
870	Sherrell	Ballard	Southern Farm Bureau Life Ins.	Box 78	Jackson	MS
870	Cheryl	Ballard	Southern Farm Bur Lf Insur Co	PO Box 78	Jackson	MS
1359	Timothy	Bremere	General Cslty Co of Wisconsin	1 General Dr.	Sun Prairie	WI
1359	Tim	Bremer	General Casualty Companies	One general Drive	Sun Prairie	WI
2101	Mike	Condry	Celina Financial Corp.	One Insurance Sq.	Celina	OH
2101	Mike	Condry	Celina Insurance Group	One Insurance Square	Celina	OH
2800		Carmer	Indiana Lumbermans Insurance	Box 68600	Indianapolis	IN
2800	Patty	Carmer	Indiana Lumbermens Mutl Insur	PO Box 68600	Indianapolis	IN
3363	Robert	Delaney	Principal Mutual Life Insurance	711 High St	Des Moines	IA
3363	B	Delaney	THE PRINCIPAL FINANCIAL GROUP	711 High St	Des Moines	IA
3532	Danny	Teo	Bosley Medical	91 wilsheer	Beverly Hills	CA
3532	Danny	Teo	Bosley	9100 Wilshire	Beverly Hills	CA

Figure 11.5 Output from merge–purge operation[9]

it would be a mistake to assume duplication has occurred and to delete records. Similarly, you may have more than one customer in a household, bearing the same family name or initials, and in this case it would also be wrong to remove one record.

- *Retaining a record that should be removed*. For example, you may have separate records for a customer under different titles such as Mr and Dr.

Merge and purge, also known as merge–purge, is a process that is performed when two or more databases are merged. This might be necessary when an external database is merged to an internal database, when two internal databases are merged (e.g. marketing and customer service databases), or when two external lists are bought and merged for a particular purpose such as a campaign. There can be significant cost savings for marketing campaigns when duplications are purged from the combined lists.

Maintain the database

Customer-related databases need to be updated to keep them useful. Consider these statistics:

- One in five managing directors change jobs in any year.
- Some 8 per cent of businesses relocate in any year.
- In the UK, 5 per cent of postcodes change in an average year.
- In Western economies about 1.2 per cent of the population dies each year.
- In the USA, over 40 million people change addresses each year.

As a result, it does not take long for databases to degrade. Companies can maintain data integrity in a number of ways:

- Ensure that data from all new transactions, campaigns and communications are inserted into the database immediately. Companies may need to develop rules and assign responsibilities to ensure this happens.
- Regularly de-duplicate databases.
- Audit a subset of the files every year. Measure the amount of degradation. Identify the source of degradation: is it a particular data source or field?
- Purge customers who have been inactive for a certain period of time. For frequently bought products, the dormant time period might be six months or less. For products with a longer repeat purchase cycle, the period will be longer. It is not always clear what a suitable dormancy period is. Some credit card users, for example, may have different cards in different currencies. Inactivity for a year only indicates that the owner has not travelled to a country in the previous year. The owner may make several trips the coming year.
- Drip-feed the database. Every time there is a customer contact there is an opportunity to add new or verify existing data.
- Get customers to update their own records. Customers can be given access to some parts of their record, and be allowed to edit the data. When Amazon customers buy online, they need to confirm or update invoice and delivery details.

- Remove customers' records on request.

- Insert decoy records. If the database is managed by an external agency, you might want to check the effectiveness of the agency's performance by inserting a few dummy records into the database. If the agency fails to spot the dummies, you may have a problem with their service standards.

Users with administrative rights can update records. Database updating and maintenance is also enabled by database query language. Common languages are Structured Query Language (SQL) and Query By Example (QBE). Database maintenance actions available in SQL include UPDATE, INSERT and DELETE commands. INSERT, for example, adds a new record to the database.

Desirable data attributes: STARTS

Maintaining customer-related databases means that CRM users will be more likely to have their need for accurate and relevant data met. Accuracy and relevance are two of six desirable data attributes that have been identified – data should be shareable, transportable, accurate, relevant, timely and secure.[10] You can remember these desirable data attributes through the mnemonic STARTS.

- Data need to be *shareable* because several users may require access to the same data at the same time. For example, profile information about customers who have bought annual travel insurance might need to be made available to customer service agents in several geographic locations simultaneously as they deal with customer enquiries in response to an advertising campaign.

- Data need to be *transportable* from storage location to user. Data need to be made available wherever and whenever users require. The user might be a hot-desking customer service representative, a delivery driver en route to a pick-up, an independent mortgage consultant or a salesperson in front of a prospect. Today's international corporations with globally distributed customers, product portfolios across several categories and multiple routes to market face particularly challenging data transportation problems. Electronic customer databases are, of course, essential for today's businesses, together with enabling technologies such as data synchronization, wireless communications and Web browsers to make the data fully transportable.

- Data *accuracy* is a troublesome issue. In an ideal world it would be wonderful to have 100 per cent accurate data. But, data accuracy carries a high level of cost. Data are captured, entered, integrated and analyzed at various moments in time and locations. Any or all of these processes may be the source of inaccuracy. Keystroke mistakes can cause errors at the point of data entry. Inappropriate analytical processes can lead to ill-founded conclusions. In CRM, data inaccuracy can lead to undue waste in marketing campaigns, inappropriate prospecting by salespeople and generally suboptimal customer experience. It also erodes trust in the CRM system, thus reducing usage. This leads to further degradation of data quality. Newsagency and book retailer W.H. Smith attributes the high response rates of CRM-enabled direct marketing to the accuracy of their database. For example, an offer of celebrity chef Delia Smith's book *How to Cook* achieved an 8 per cent response rate after the successful implementation of a data quality project, which was a significant improvement upon W.H. Smith's historic norms.

- *Relevant* data are pertinent for a given purpose. To check a customer's creditworthiness, you need their transaction and payment histories, and their current employment and income status. To flag customers who are hot prospects for a cross-sell campaign, you need their propensity to buy scores.

- *Timely* data are data that are available as and when needed. Data that become available only after a decision is made are unhelpful. Equally, decision makers do not want to be burdened with data before the need is felt. Bank tellers need to have propensity to buy information available to them at the time a customer is being served, not before or after.

- Data *security* is a hugely important issue for most companies. Data, particularly data about customers, are a major resource and a source of competitive advantage. Data provide the foundation for delivery of better solutions to customers, and better customer experience. Companies do need to protect their data against loss, sabotage and theft. Many companies regularly back up their data. Security is enhanced through physical and electronic barriers such as firewalls. Managing data security in a partner environment is particularly challenging, as it is essential that competing partners do not see each other's sales lead and opportunity information, despite being signed into the same CRM system through the same portal.

DATA INTEGRATION

As noted earlier, in most companies there are several customer-related databases, maintained by different functions or channels. Companies often face the challenge of integrating data from several sources into a coherent single view of the customer. Sometimes, this becomes a significant challenge in a CRM project, and a necessary hurdle to cross before implementing operational CRM applications in marketing, sales or service environments. Data integration requires the customer's identity to be traceable in all interactions with the firm, and that any anomalies between the records in various databases are identified and resolved. The major CRM vendors offer solutions to this problem. SAP, for example, offers Master Data Management as part of its business integration platform. This enables companies to capture and consolidate data from different sources into a centralized database.

For companies with older mainframe (legacy) systems, another solution to the problem of database integration is to adopt newer systems with a centralized database that can accept real-time inputs from a number of channels.[11] However, legacy systems are typically batch-processing systems. In other words, they do not accept real-time data. Many technology firms have developed software and systems to allow companies to integrate databases held on different legacy systems. Sometimes, middleware has to be written to integrate data from diverse sources. Middleware is a class of software that connects different parts of a system that would not otherwise be able to communicate with each other. Middleware can be thought of as a kind of 'glue' that holds a network together.

Unless data are integrated, companies cannot create the single view of the customer that provides CRM users with visibility into a customer's history of interactions with the business

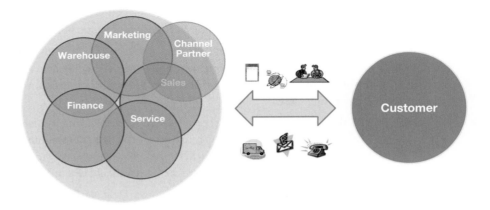

Figure 11.6 Single view of the customer[12]

whether through sales, marketing or service, and across all channels (see Figure 11.6). Failure to integrate data may lead to costly operational inefficiencies, duplication of work, poor customer experience and damaged customer relationships. Customers might experience the effects of poor integration when they have bought an item online only to be later offered the same item through a different channel of the same company.

Customer data integration relies on standardization of data across databases. An indicator of the magnitude of the problem is that when Dun & Bradstreet was integrating data from several sources to create a marketing database it found 113 different entries for the company AT&T alone. These included ATT, A.T.T., AT and T, and so on.

CASE STUDY 11.2

DATA INTEGRATION AT THE AMERICAN HEART ASSOCIATION

The American Heart Association (AHA) is a not-for-profit US health organization dedicated to reducing disability and death from heart attack, stroke and related cardiovascular disorders.

One of the AHA's major goals has been improving its relationships with stakeholders, including many thousands of volunteers conducting unpaid work for the organization, donors, businesses and the media. However, a challenge facing the AHA in achieving this goal was integrating the organization's data, which were previously in over 150 separate databases, often geographically isolated and specific to certain departments within the organization, which provided a limited view of customers' profiles and history of activities.

AHA chose to implement a CRM software system across the organization to integrate all existing databases. Since implementation the AHA has found that its staff are far more productive, it is able to respond to customers more quickly and provide more personalized service. Donations from customers have increased by over 20 per cent using the system to contact potential donors as compared to previous activities.

DATA WAREHOUSING

As companies have grown larger they have become separated both geographically and culturally from the markets and customers they serve. Disney, an American corporation, has operations in Europe, Asia-Pacific and Latin America as well as in the USA. Benetton, the Italy-based fashion brand, has operations across five continents. In retailing alone it operates over 6,000 stores and concessions. Companies like these generate a huge volume of data that needs to be converted into information that can be used for strategic, operational and analytical purposes.

The data warehouse is a solution to that problem. Data warehouses are repositories of large amounts of operational, historical and other customer-related data. Data volume can exceed terabyte levels, i.e. two^{40} bytes of data. Indeed, as we write, the world's largest data warehouse contains over 12.1 petabytes (21,100 terabytes) of raw data.[13] Data warehouses are repositories for data imported from other databases, and typically feature an analytical front-end which enables analysts to deploy a range of statistical processes to make sense out of the data. Retailers, home shopping companies and banks have been enthusiastic adopters of data warehouses.

Watson describes a data warehouse as follows:[14]

- *Subject-oriented*. The warehouse organizes data around the essential subjects of the business – customers and products – rather than around applications such as inventory management or order processing.

- *Integrated*. It is consistent in the way that data from several sources are extracted and transformed. For example, coding conventions are standardized: M = male, F = female.

- *Time-variant*. Data are organized by various time-periods (e.g. months).

- *Non-volatile*. The warehouse's database is not updated in real time. There is periodic bulk uploading of transactional and other data. This makes the data less subject to momentary change.

There are a number of steps and processes in building a data warehouse. First, you must identify where the relevant data are currently stored. This can be a challenge. When the Commonwealth Bank of Australia opted to implement CRM in its retail banking business, it found that relevant customer data were resident on over 80 separate systems. Second, data must be extracted from those systems. It is probable that when these systems were developed they were not expected to align with other systems.

The data then need to be transformed into a standardized and clean format. Data in different systems may have been stored in different forms, as Table 11.1 indicates. Also, the cleanliness of data from different parts of the business may vary. The culture in sales may be very driven by quarterly performance targets, and getting sales reps to maintain their customer files might not be straightforward. Much of their information may be in their heads. On the other hand, direct marketers may be very dedicated to keeping their data in good shape.

After transformation, the data then need to be uploaded into the warehouse. Archival data that have little relevance to today's operations may be set aside, or only uploaded if there

Table 11.1 Data transformation

- Data standardisation
    - Personal data: m/f, M/F, male/female
    - Units of measurement: metric/imperial
    - Field names: sales value, sale$, $val
    - Dates: mm/dd/yy, dd/mm/yyyy, yyyy-mm-dd
- Data cleaning
    - De-duplication
    - Updating and purging
    - Misuse of data entry fields e.g. use phone field to record email address

CASE STUDY 11.3

DATA WAREHOUSING FOR CRM PURPOSES[17]

US Xpress Enterprises is a leading American trucking company with US$1.6 billion in annual revenue. Having grown through acquisition, the company relied on multiple IT systems and lacked visibility into its nationwide operation and affiliate companies. The company lacked control over costs and operations, as many diverse systems and processes were used throughout the business. To solve this, the company built a data warehouse and implemented Microsoft Dynamics CRM to provide the information and process structures for consistent company-wide operations such as strategic planning, bidding, sales and marketing. The data warehouse has delivered a single view of the customer (by integrating data held in the acquired companies' systems), enabled the company to streamline preparation for sales calls, and recover as much as $350,000 a year in lost-opportunity costs. The company has realized improved sales productivity and improved its closure rates on new business.

is sufficient space. Recent operational and transactional data from the various functions, channels and touchpoints will most probably be prioritized for uploading.

Refreshing the data in the warehouse is important. This may be done on a daily or weekly basis depending upon the speed of change in the business and its environment.

Some large data warehousing projects have taken years to implement and yielded few measurable benefits,[15] and according to Sen and co-authors, 50 per cent of data warehousing projects fail to meet their delivery targets.[16]

DATA MARTS

A data mart is a scaled-down version, or subset, of the data warehouse, customized for use in a particular business function or department. Marketing and sales may have their own CRM-related data marts enabling them to conduct separate analyses and make strategic and tactical decisions. Data mart projects are less complex projects – costs are lower because the volume of data stored is reduced, the number of users is capped and the business focus is more precise. Technology requirements are less demanding.

KNOWLEDGE MANAGEMENT

Throughout the book, we have stressed the use of the expression *customer-related* data, not simply customer data. An important contributor to effective CRM is storing and leveraging customer-related knowledge. Knowledge about customers includes not only structured data such as contact history and account balances, but unstructured data such as emails and texts from the customer, and agent notes on telephone conversations. However, *customer-related* data also include a wealth of other types of information useful in marketing, selling and servicing the customer, across all stages of the customer lifecycle. This knowledge ranges across product features and benefits, price lists, competitors' offers, market data, service issues and solutions, business processes, company policies and much more subject matter.

We define knowledge management (KM) from a CRM perspective as follows:

Knowledge management is the practice of consciously gathering, organizing, storing, interpreting, distributing and judiciously applying knowledge to fulfil the customer management goals and objectives of the organization.

When deployed for CRM purposes, most KM systems are IT-based. They feature databases, networks (intranet or extranet) and tools. Databases contain the customer-related information. Intranets allow employees to have access to that knowledge. Extranets give external users, such as customers and partners, access to that knowledge. The tools can include search engines, collaborative platforms (for user input) and content management tools. KM systems aim to give customers, employees and other approved users timely access to the organization's knowledge.

The achievement of CRM goals and objectives, about which we have more to say in chapters 13 and 14, relies in part on how well customer-related knowledge is deployed at customer touchpoints. Those touchpoints include websites, shop-fronts, social media, contact centres, and sales reps and field service technicians. Customers visit these touchpoints in search of information. For example, customers who have problems assembling a piece of self-assembly furniture may visit a company website looking for instructions. If they can't find what they want, they may call a customer service agent. Both the customer and the agent will be searching a customer-related knowledge management system for solutions to the problem. A business partner who is considering buying merchandise from a supplier for the first time may visit the supplier's portal to learn useful information about the item's relative advantages over competitors' price, availability and after-sales support.

Earlier in this chapter, you read about six attributes of good quality data, captured in the mnemonic STARTS: shareable, transportable, accessible, relevant, timely and secure. Knowledge available at the touchpoints needs to satisfy those six same criteria.

Knowledge needs to be shareable if several users require access to the same data at the same time, as might happen in the case of product-specification data. Knowledge also needs to be transportable from storage location to user. Data need to be made available wherever and whenever users require – on the website and on a service engineer's laptop. Knowledge also needs to be appropriately accurate. Price lists and transaction histories need to be absolutely up to date, whereas it might be acceptable for market-related data such as industry sales forecasts to be 12 months out of date. Relevant information needs to be available at the touchpoints. Sales reps do not want to wade through masses of irrelevant information before they find what they need. Timely knowledge is available when needed. Knowledge that is important for competitive advantage needs to be secure.

SUMMARY

This chapter has introduced you to the data foundations of analytical CRM. Analytical CRM is the process through which organizations transform customer-related data into actionable insight for either strategic or tactical purposes. Customer-related data include both data about customers and data for customers. Customer-related data are available in both structured and unstructured forms within and outside organizations. Structured data are typically available in relational databases maintained by operational units including sales, marketing, customer service, logistics and accounts. Companies can use external data sources to enhance their internally available customer-related data. Types of externally available data include compiled list data, census data and modelled data. In recent years there has been a massive increase in the amount of customer-related data – often unstructured – available in social media and other 'big data' sources. We describe a six-step process for developing a customer-related database: define the database functions, define the information requirements, identify the information sources, select the database technology and operating system, populate the database, and maintain the database. Problems at each stage are identified, and solutions proposed. We explain how CRM practitioners attempt to enhance the quality of data by acquiring customer-related data from competition entries, subscriptions, registrations and loyalty programmes. The main processes in ensuring that databases are populated with appropriately accurate data are data verification, data validation, de-duplication and merge–purge. Desirable data attributes include data being shareable, transportable, accurate, relevant, timely and secure. We close with a review of the importance to CRM of data warehouses, data marts and knowledge management.

NOTES AND REFERENCES

1   ANSI is the American National Standards Institute.
2   Courtesy StayinFront Inc. www.stayinfront.com.
3   www.gartner.com/doc/2574616/hype-cycle-big-data (Accessed 8 May 2014).
4   Based on O'Connor, J. and Galvin, E. (2001). *Marketing in the digital age*, 2nd edn. Harlow: Financial Times/Prentice Hall.

5   http://service-push.com/portfolio_item/sugarcrm-6-campaign-screenshot/ (Accessed 9 May 2014).

6   http://www.pinpointe.com/ (Accessed 9 May 2014).

7   Drozdenko, R.G. and Drake, P.D. (2002). *Optimal database marketing: strategy, development and data mining.* Thousand Oaks, CA: Sage.

8   http://www.claritas.com/collateral/segmentation/new_pdf/Nielsen_PRIZM_2013.pdf (Accessed 9 May 2014).

9   Courtesy Intelligent Search Technology Ltd. www.intelligentsearch.com

10 Based on Watson, R.T. (1999). *Data management: databases and organisations.* New York: John Wiley.

11 Drozdenko, R.G. and Drake, P.D. (2002). *Optimal database marketing: strategy, development and data mining.* Thousand Oaks, CA: Sage.

12 Courtesy CustomerConnect Australia, www.customerconnect.com.au. Used with permission.

13 http://www.predictiveanalyticstoday.com/worlds-largest-data-warehouse-record-12–1-pb-from-sap/ (Accessed 26 May 2014).

14 Watson, R.T. (1999). *Data management: databases and organisations.* New York: John Wiley.

15 Gartner says more than 50 percent of data warehouse projects will have limited acceptance or will be failures through 2007 (2005). *Business Wire,* 24 February, p. 1.

16 Sen, A., Ramamurthy, K. (Ram), and Sinha, A.P. (2012). A model of data warehousing process maturity. *IEEE Transactions on Software Engineering,* 38(2), 336–53.

17 http://www.microsoft.com/casestudies/Microsoft-Dynamics-CRM-2011/U.S.-Xpress-Enterprises/Major-Trucker-Moves-to-New-CRM-System-Recovers-Up-to-350–000-in-Lost-Opportunity-Costs/390000000081 (Accessed 25 May 2014).

CHAPTER 12

USING CUSTOMER-RELATED DATA

CHAPTER OBJECTIVES

By the end of this chapter you will understand:

- How analytical CRM supports strategic and operational CRM.

- How analytics support customer management strategy and tactics, throughout the customer lifecycle, in the sales, marketing and customer service functions.

- How standard reports, OLAP and data mining generate insights for CRM users.

- That data mining works in a number of ways: by describing and visualizing, classification, estimation, prediction, affinity grouping and clustering.

- The types of analytics that apply to structured, unstructured and 'big' data.

- The 3Vs of big data.

- Why it is important to understand the differences between nominal, ordinal, interval and ratio data before selected analytical procedures.

- The types of regulatory constraints that regulators impose to ensure the privacy of customer data.

INTRODUCTION

This is the second of two chapters on analytical CRM, sometimes also known as analytic CRM. Analytical CRM is the process through which organizations transform customer-related data into actionable insight for either strategic or tactical purposes. The process is made up of a number of sub-processes including data acquisition (often through operational CRM), data enhancement, data preparation, data analysis and data delivery. CRM analytics has grown in importance over the past 20 years. Organizations have realized that merely streamlining customer-facing operations in sales, marketing and service is not enough. Analytics can provide a deeper insight into the customer, and the cost to serve each customer, enabling organizations to improve key CRM outcomes such as the creation of customer value, improved satisfaction, reduced propensity to churn and lower cost-to-serve.

Analysis of customer-related data supports strategic and operational CRM. Strategic CRM focuses on the development of a customer-centric business dedicated to winning and keeping (potentially) profitable customers by creating and delivering value better than competitors cost-effectively. Analysis of customer-related data can help answer crucial strategic CRM questions such as: Which customers should we serve? What is our share of customer spending on our category? What do our customers think and feel about their experience of doing business with us? What parts of our value proposition are superior or inferior to competitors? Who are our major competitors and what are their strengths and weaknesses?

Operational CRM is also supported by analysis of customer-related data. Operational CRM involves deployment of automated solutions in the sales, marketing and service areas. Analysis of customer-related data can help answer crucial operational CRM questions such as: Which channels should we use to communicate with our customers? What offers should we make, and when should we make them? How does our sales performance differ across territories and product ranges, and how can we fix any problems? How well do we manage

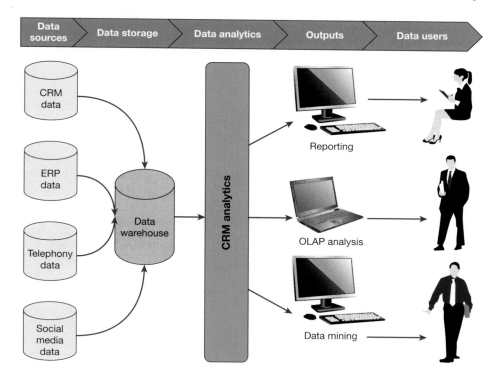

Figure 12.1 Basic data configuration for CRM analytics

our opportunity pipeline? How satisfied are customers with the service we provide and what can be done to improve it?

CRM software applications generally allow users to produce simple descriptive reports, but for deeper insights other forms of analysis are often needed. Figure 12.1 shows how this is usually structured. Data from various sources including the CRM system, the Enterprise Resource System (ERP) system and elsewhere are deposited into a data warehouse. An analytics software package is added to the configuration so that users, whether in sales, marketing, service or management, can interrogate and make sense out of the warehoused data. Insights are delivered to these users through their devices in the form of reports, which can be standardized or ad hoc, Online Analytical Processing (OLAP) outputs or data mining reports. We have more to say about each of these forms of output later in the chapter.

In Chapter 11, we reviewed the development of customer-related databases; in this chapter we explain how organizations can make use of these data to achieve their CRM goals and objectives throughout the customer lifecycle. We start by reviewing the strategic and tactical uses of customer-related data.

ANALYTICS FOR CRM STRATEGY AND TACTICS

Time frame is the key differentiator between strategy and tactics. The word 'strategy' is derived from the Greek *stratégia* (generalship) and has come to mean a plan of action to achieve a long-term goal. Tactics are the particular manoeuvres that are carried out to achieve the goal. CRM programmes typically pursue one or more of three broad strategic goals: building revenues, reducing costs or enhancing customer loyalty/satisfaction.

For example, a company using CRM to build revenues would develop and execute cross-sell and up-sell marketing campaigns aimed at current customers, build strong bonds to ring-fence relationships with the most valued customers, generate more sales leads, acquire more new customers and close more opportunities. The tactics for building loyalty/satisfaction or cutting costs might be quite different, as illustrated in Table 12.1.

The types of analysis that are needed for each of these strategic and tactical uses of CRM would also be different. We will illustrate this with one example. Imagine a marketer charged with growing revenues from current customers by running cross-sell campaigns. She'd want

Table 12.1 CRM strategic goals (bold) and related tactics (not bold)

Build revenues	Reduce costs	Enhance loyalty/satisfaction
Cross-sell campaigns	Automate selling processes	Enhance complaints resolution
Up-sell campaigns	Service customers online	Improve customer service
Protect valued relationships	Improve customer self-service	Improve fulfilment process
Generate sales leads	Sack unprofitable customers	Improve online experience
Acquire new customers	Improve sales rep productivity	Improve value proposition
Close more opportunities	Improve data quality	Introduce CSat measures

to conduct analysis and obtain reports about a number of important issues before deciding on the communication medium and offer. If considering using either direct mail or email as the communication medium (channel) she'd want answers to questions like these:

- How many of our customer records contain a current, accurate postal address and email address?
- What is the preferred communications medium of customers for reception of marketing offers?
- What is the relative effectiveness of each channel at generating incremental sales historically?
- What are the fixed and variable costs of campaign execution in each channel?

To decide 'what should we offer?' the marketer would want answers to questions like these:

- What types of offer have been successful in the past?
- What forms of campaign execution have been successful in the past?
- Should we launch a 'next best offer' campaign customized for each customer?
- What are organizational constraints around the offer, for example, availability of stock, customer contact policy (e.g. no more than one campaign per month per customer) and incremental sales required?

The answers to these questions will draw on different forms of customer-related data and involve different types of analysis. For example, it is a relatively simple matter to create a report on the numbers of customers having data in the 'email address' and 'home address' fields of their record. A review of bounce-backs and open-rates for the listed emails would give a good insight into whether they are currently active or not, as would an appraisal of undelivered mail. However, the question of whether to create 'next best offers' for each customer would involve an assessment of the modelling competences of the business and the availability of appropriate historical data to build, test and apply predictive models at the level of the unique customer.

ANALYTICS THROUGHOUT THE CUSTOMER LIFECYCLE

We have presented the customer lifecycle as an evolution through three phases: customer acquisition, customer retention and customer development. The types of analysis that support a company's customer acquisition, retention and development strategies will be quite different. Customer acquisition strategies need to identify potential new customers and qualify them. The qualification process normally involves scoring, which is an output of data analysis. Higher scores are better prospects. Lead scoring might take account of a wide range of market, organizational, personal, relational and behavioural attributes, as indicated in Table 12.2. Although leads can be scored manually, many lead management applications automate the scoring process, allowing sales managers to create score reports and ensure sales reps are following up the best leads.

Table 12.2 Sample criteria used in prospect scoring

Market	Organizational	Personal	Relational	Behavioural
Market size	Revenues	Seniority	Ex-customer	Website visitor?
Market growth	Profits	Decision role	Lost opportunity	Registrations?
Market segmentation	Spending on category	Budget owner	Lead source – website or ad	Contracted to current supplier?
New entrants	Certifications	Influence	Referral?	Video viewed?
Number of competitors	Social network participation	Years' experience	New to database?	Research participant?

The customer retention stage of the lifecycle demands analysis to answer a different set of questions, such as: Which customers have highest future potential lifetime value? How can we cluster customers so as to develop appropriate customer management strategies (see Chapter 5 for a discussion of the seven core customer management strategies)? Which customers are candidates for termination? What is the cost-to-serve each customer? What is the cost–benefit of our customer loyalty programme?

CRM analytics can contribute significantly to these questions, providing, of course, the right data are available for analysis. One of the main strategies for driving up profitability is to retain those customers who have the greatest future lifetime value. We previously defined customer lifetime value (CLV) as the present-day value of all net margins earned from a relationship with a customer, customer segment or cohort. The data challenges in computing CLV can be great, as described in Chapter 2. Companies need to know the probability that a customer will buy in the future, the gross margins earned on those sales and the cost-to-serve the customer. Cost-to-serve is subtracted from gross margin to compute net margin, which is discounted to produce present value.

Let's consider just one of the analytic tasks involved in computing CLV: forecasting future sales. Depending on the business context and data availability, analysts could use a number of data sources and analytical procedures: analysis of *qualitative* data such as sales team estimates, *quantitative* analysis of customer 'intention-to-buy' surveys, *time-series* analysis of historical sales data using moving average, exponential smoothing and time-series decomposition methods, and *causal* analyses based on leading indicators or regression modelling.

Customer development is the third stage of the customer lifecycle. The goal of customer development is to increase the value to the business of retained customers, by cross-selling and up-selling, or adjusting service levels to improve customer profitability. In the business-to-business context, account managers have the responsibility for identifying opportunities and advancing them towards closure according to pre-defined business processes with the support of CRM tools. Senior managers will usually determine what service levels to provide a customer. Many CRM strategies introduce tiered levels of service for customers, with more personalized and frequent service and better terms being offered to higher value customers. In the business-to-consumer environment, where datasets are larger, CRM analytics must answer questions such as these: What offer should we next make to the customer? What events can we identify to trigger communication with the customer?

Next best action (NBA) is growing in popularity in the business-to-consumer context. NBA merges customer insight (predictive analytics particularly) and context to deliver recommendations for action. The action that companies are particularly interested in is making an up-sell or cross-sell offer that enhances the value of the customer to the business. However, context determines whether or not an offer should be made, what that offer should be and even when it should be made. Contextual conditions act as events that trigger certain types of organizational response (see coverage of event-based marketing in Chapter 9 for more information). If the customer currently has an unresolved complaint then making an offer would simply show a lack of awareness of, and concern for, the customer's experience.

CASE STUDY 12.1

NEXT BEST ACTION AT ING BANK[1]

As one of the largest financial services firms in Europe, ING had a high-volume direct marketing operation, sending out around 60 million pieces of direct mail each year. The bank realized that its campaigns were losing effectiveness because its campaign programme – originally built for direct mail – was not meeting the needs of what was now a multi-channel bank with a strong focus on the online channel.

ING went through a 15-month project that involved a budget of more than €5 million and around 50 full-time employees from marketing, IT, customer intelligence and the different channels to build a state-of-the-art direct marketing programme to overcome the old programme's challenges.

ING's new *klantdifferentiatie* direct marketing programme produces marketing messages that are personalized and delivered through different channels in real time. The programme allows ING to do the following:

- *Run campaigns via multiple channels.* Whereas ING's old campaign management programme was exclusively based on outbound channels like direct mail, email and outbound call centre calls, the new programme supports marketing on inbound channels like branches, the bank's secure website and inbound calls to the call centre.

- *Synchronize marketing across channels.* As campaign management is centralized, campaigns run as a concerted effort across channels – both inbound and outbound. For example, a customer can receive the same savings account offer through email, on the website or both in succession. ING has set norms to ensure that offers are communicated through channels achieving specified response rates.

- *Personalize marketing messages.* Each customer receives an individual product offer based on what's already known about him and what's been learned during the recent interactions. Branch employees can now see what the next best action (NBA) for each individual customer is and suggest a product during a client interaction in a branch.

- *Run as a continuous dialogue.* Instead of focusing entirely on ad hoc campaigns, ING's new campaign management programme runs on a continuous basis. By collecting customer responses from different channels and feeding them back into the data ware-house daily, the bank can constantly optimize the offers made to customers. If an offer is shown several times and the customer does not respond, another offer will be shown.

Perhaps a preferable NBA would be to make an outbound customer service call to establish what the customer expects by way of complaint resolution, to fix the customer's problem or to offer compensation for the unsatisfactory customer experience. If a customer's interaction with a business has been positive, for example because a customer service agent has provided helpful assistance or a complaint has been resolved to the satisfaction of the customer, an offer would usually make more sense. An offer could be based on shopping basket analysis (people who have bought product A also buy product B) or sequential patterns (40 per cent of people buying product X in January buy product Y the following July). However, context-sensitive management might prefer not to make an offer, even if business rules say it can or should be done. There may be a number of contextual conditions that shape the NBA of the firm, which if considered independently would trigger conflicting organizational action. Consider a customer who has failed to pay an invoice on time, but who has also placed an order worth several thousand dollars. On the one hand, the triggered response would be a formal notification that the debt must be paid – or else – and the other triggered response might be a personal call from the store manager thanking the customer for the business. Simple rules-based recommendation engines that rely only on predictive analytics and fail to take account of context can make things worse for the company, not better.

'Next best offer' (NBO) is a subset of NBA. The early groundwork for NBO was laid by Amazon.com who messaged their online customers with 'people who bought this also bought that' recommendations based on simple correlations. Today's modelling is more sophisticated and based on more complex, context-sensitive, predictive analytics that enable the right offer to be made at the right time and in the right channel. The tools that support NBO are known as recommendation engines. They work by identifying and statistically quantifying relationships in historical transactional and demographic data – this is called model development. These models are used to predict future behaviour, a practice known as predictive analytics. Predictions usually take the form of probabilities or scores, providing marketers or agents with a list of ranked offers for the customer. The results of the offers, whether accepted or rejected, become additional data that can be further used to refine the model. Dynamic next best offers can be made to customers in real time as they interact at a business's touchpoints, including website and contact centre.

ANALYTICS FOR STRUCTURED AND UNSTRUCTURED DATA

CRM analytics for structured data are well developed. Simple statistical procedures such as computing totals, averages, modes, medians and ranges are the foundation of many of the descriptive standard reports generated by CRM users. As questions become more complex and shift from mere description to explanation or prediction, the analytical procedures required to generate answers also become more complex. In Figure 12.1 we identify OLAP and data mining as two ways of interrogating warehoused data to deliver answers to these more complex questions. Whereas OLAP queries allow CRM users to drill down into the reasons why a particular piece of data – say a salesperson's exceptional performance – is as it is, data mining tools draw on a well-established array of statistical procedures, such as correlation, regression, decision-tree and clustering routines to produce insights for users.

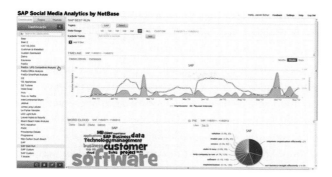

Figure 12.2 Social media sentiment analytics[2]

© 2014 SAP AG or an SAP affiliate company. All rights reserved. Used with permission of SAP AG or an SAP affiliate company.

This book is not the place for a full coverage of these statistical procedures, though we do give a brief introduction to the CRM application of some of these techniques later in the chapter.

Unstructured data, as explained in Chapter 11, are data that do not fit a pre-defined data model: textual and non-textual files including spreadsheets, documents, PDFs, handwritten notes, and image, audio, video and multimedia data are unstructured. Unstructured data often reside outside the business in social media data repositories, which can be huge, hence the term 'big data'. Analytics for these types of data are still evolving.

The most advanced form of unstructured data analytics currently is text analytics. Text analytics extracts relevant information from unstructured text files, and transforms it into structured information that can then be leveraged in various ways. Unstructured textual data is found in call centre agent notes, emails, documents on the Web, instant messages, blogs, tweets, customer comments, customer reviews, questionnaire free-response boxes, social media posts, transcripts of telephone calls and interviews and so on. When we write or speak in natural language, we use slang, dialect, jargon, misspellings, anachronisms, short forms, acronyms, colloquialisms, metaphors, grammatical idiosyncrasies and even multiple languages in the same stream. This presents challenges to analysts but there are a number of text mining tools that can help. SAS Text Miner®, for example, enables users to convert text, audio and other files into a format from which it is possible to extract information by revealing the themes and concepts that are concealed in them.[3] Goutam Chakraborty explains that text analytics has a number of potential uses in CRM:

- Unstructured data specific to the individual customers may be useful in improving the accuracy of the predictive models. These unstructured data can be a customer survey response to a specific product or service. The basic premise for using text data in predictive models is that the terms contained within the text data represent the customer's experiences (bad or good), which may explain the customer's decision to continue with the business or churn.

- Text analytics is widely used for automated routing. Well-known applications of automated routing are email forwarding and spam detection.

- Root cause analysis (RCA) is a method of problem solving that tries to identify the root causes of faults or problems. Text analytics of customer service or complaint records may reveal issues that lie at the root of the problem.

- Trend analysis is a method of understanding how certain entities change over a period of time. Examples of such entities are part numbers of an appliance reported in a failure, serial numbers of a device being serviced, types of customer service request and technical support required. The standard method of analyzing trends is to chart and compare the most frequent entity surfaced in the document collection for a specific duration of time (a minute, an hour, a day or a month) compared to a longer period of time (a day, a week, a month or a year).

- Sentiment analysis. An important goal of analyzing textual data is to get an insight into what customers (or former customers, potential customers, competitors or partners) feel and think about a company, brand, product, service, person or group. Are consumers'

CASE STUDY 12.2

TEXT ANALYTICS IN THE AUTO INDUSTRY[4]

Warranties cost US automotive companies an estimated $35 billion annually. Optimizing warranty cost is a very important lever in the cost equation for automobile manufacturers. One of the underused methods for optimizing warranty cost is learning from service technicians' comments. Text mining these comments can surface component defect insights enabling auto manufacturers to prevent them in the future. Key business questions that can be answered by mining technician comments include:

- What are the main problems encountered by dealers?
- What are the five components mentioned as problems most frequently?
- Is there any seasonal pattern to component failure?
- Is there any association between component failure and the component's warranty cost?
- Which faulty parts receive frequent comment during a car's warranty period?

The text mining solution to answer these questions incorporated four kinds of unstructured data: technician comments on the dealer management system, customer comments on the CRM system, user-generated comments on social media and vehicle reviews in trade journals. The text was input to the application producing three outputs: a list of keywords, a higher level abstraction of these keywords into key vehicle defect themes and a list of high-risk keywords such as 'oil leakage'.

The results allow automobile companies to take a number of actions to reduce warranty-related cost erosion:

- *Auto component sourcing decisions.* Auto manufacturers can share the results with product suppliers and undertake joint initiatives to reduce defect rates.
- *Re-engineer internal manufacturing processes.* If the component is manufactured internally, then the manufacturing process can be re-examined/re-engineered to eliminate reoccurrence.
- *Inventory optimization.* The frequency of occurrence of failed auto parts can be used to forecast demand for parts.

perceptions good, bad or neutral? What attributes (features) of the product or service do they feel good or bad about? What do the customers think of the various attributes of a company's product such as quality, price, durability, safety, ease of use? Typically, if a customer feels good towards an entity, it is classified as a positive sentiment. If the perception is bad, it can be considered as a negative sentiment. Alternatively, if the customer has neither good nor bad opinion sentiment is neutral.[5]

BIG DATA ANALYTICS

Big data is characterized by 3Vs

- *Volume.* Whilst some big data assets do include structured data (for example, sensor data), much big data are unstructured. The massive scale and growth of unstructured data have outpaced traditional storage and analytical solutions. The volume of data is set to increase dramatically with the advent of the 'Internet of Things' – the online linking of traditionally 'dumb' products into an intelligent system.

- *Variety.* Big data are collected from new sources that have not been mined for insight in the past. Traditional analytical processes applied to structured data cannot cope with the heterogeneity of big data, which includes email, social media posts, video, images, blogs, location and sensor data.

- *Velocity.* Big data are not just batched data, but also streamed and produced in real time. Streamed data do not reside quietly in back-office relational databases ready to be analyzed periodically. Streamed data update continually.[6]

Customer managers are migrating from periodic research and a narrow range of transactional data to a socially connected, multi-channel environment in which the volume of consumer-

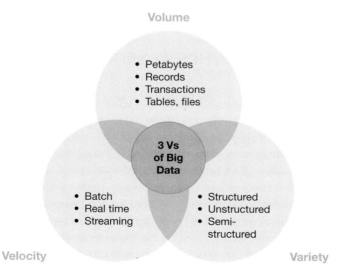

Figure 12.3 The 3Vs of big data[7]

generated data has increased exponentially. Data volume will likely continue to grow with additional data generated by, amongst other technologies, smart phones and the Internet of Things.[8] In 2013 Apple introduced iBeacon which allows retailers to track customers in-store in real time. iBeacon data streams can identify in-store traffic patterns, points of interest where consumers spend time, as well as act as a front end for real-time promotions depending on what the customer has just bought, seen or visited. The Internet of Things describes the linking together of 'dumb' objects to make smart solutions. For example, ever-decreasing prices for chips with radio transmitters (RFID) allow logistics firms to label each item in their system so that the firm knows where each item is in real time, thus reducing errors, increasing accuracy and avoiding lost items. Once the data stream is live and stable, these firms will allow their customers to access the feed and avoid costly service calls (e.g. Where is my parcel?). Some big data enthusiasts are already criticizing marketers for using expert judgement, rather than creating better simulations and trusting the models to make decisions![9]

Not only do companies and their data scientists face the problem of how to interpret and use unstructured data, but also how to integrate and then benefit from structured and unstructured data in combination. This presents a bigger challenge than the analysis of unstructured data alone. Rising to the challenge are some of the biggest names in IT and business intelligence: IBM, SAS and Oracle amongst others are making major investments in both the software and the know-how to help firms extract value from big data. IBM claims to have spent over $14 billion on acquiring analytics companies such as SPSS and Cognos.[10]

Analysis of big data can help managers distinguish important signals, or portents of trends and changes, from a storm of noisy data. eBay Inc. used a big data solution to identify a trend of people buying men's collectable basketball shoes. The trend was picked out from analysis of listings of tens of thousands of shoes sold daily, and other social media data. This information was then communicated immediately to potential sellers, who made additional listings, generating additional revenues for eBay.[11] Conventional research might have taken a month to deliver the same insight. The big data solution allowed the identification of this signal in a single day, making the insight far more actionable and relevant.

CASE STUDY 12.3

BIG DATA ANALYTICS AT BRITISH AIRWAYS[12]

British Airways (BA) enhanced its CRM programme with a big data solution it calls 'Know Me'. This integrates data from its loyalty programme, members' online behaviour, operational data and buying history. The programme allows BA's best customers to be welcomed by name by cabin crew, or to receive a personal apology on a return flight if their outbound leg had been delayed. Managed properly, such applications can personalize service and differentiate the carrier amongst its most profitable customers, a goal of many loyalty/ CRM initiatives.

Emerging big data solutions will enable companies to analyze customer service data streams, such as transcripts of call centre enquiries, blogs, tweets and discussion boards to identify critical service problems in real time, or close to real time, and respond speedily. For example, imagine a firm releasing new software that, despite extensive testing, creates problems for some users' computing infrastructure. Instead of waiting perhaps weeks, if not months, for feedback from sales, summarized reports from customer service centres and analysis of incoming emails, big data analytics can identify the signal-in-the-noise, highlighting the unforeseen problems in hours, allowing the firm to respond with a timely fix. This improves customer experience, promotes loyalty and reduces service costs by resolving problems more quickly.

Many companies deploy various social media analytics to understand what is being said about them, by whom and to what effect. By combining social media data with transcripts from service call centres with sales data, companies can determine with greater effect the value of positive social media publicity, or the damage caused by excessive and strong customer complaints.

The technology essentials

Big data solutions are built upon storing vast amounts of data cheaply, learning patterns, and building and testing models. The backbone of most big data solutions is Hadoop,[13] an open-source framework or computing environment that distributes data across a large number of computers, each of which processes a portion of the data, to permit fast computing of these extremely large big data databases. Commercial software-solution vendors add further management and decision support tools, frameworks and solutions to make it easier for organizations to install, configure and integrate unstructured data with relational databases, and for analysts to use and prepare visual presentations of the data. As we write, a few point technologies are well developed, for example the text analytics described above, but many big data solutions are complex to install, manage and use. Organizations will either have substantial in-house resources to assist CRM practitioners or, more likely, use third parties as partners. Customer-facing managers will, for at least the short term, need to engage actively with other functions and IT vendors in order to provide some strategic guidance for their use of big data.

ANALYTICS FOR STRUCTURED DATA

There are several different types of data kept in relational databases. Managers who act on the outputs of CRM analytics need to have a broad appreciation of these types of data so that they can question whether appropriate statistical procedures have been used in the analysis.

A fundamental distinction is made between *categorical* and *continuous* data. Categorical data, also known as discrete data, are data about entities that can be sorted into groups or categories, for example product types, gender or country. Categorical data that are unordered are called nominal data (e.g. customer name). Categorical data that are ordered are called ordinal data (e.g. a list of customers ordered by sales revenues). Continuous data are data that can take on any value within a finite or infinite range. Continuous data can be either interval data or ratio data. Interval data are measured along a continuum that has no fixed and non-arbitrary zero point. Temperature scales are interval scales. Zero degrees Fahrenheit does not mean there is no temperature! Ratio data are also interval data, but with the added condition that the data point 0 (zero) means there is none of that variable. Height is an example of ratio data.

Nominal, ordinal, interval and ratio scales

Stanley Stevens developed our understanding of the hierarchy of four different data types: nominal, ordinal, interval and ratio.[14] Managers and their data analysts need to understand this hierarchy because it determines the types of analysis that can be performed on the data. Being a hierarchy of data types, each successive level has all the properties of the previous level and some additional properties of its own. We discuss some of the analytical procedures in coming pages, but at this time we want you to understand more about how data differs.

- *Nominal* data are the most rudimentary, and are used only to classify, identify or categorize. A lot of customer-related data is nominal. Unique Customer Numbers, gender classification (M/F) and email addresses are examples of nominal data. Even though a database may choose to record that a customer owns a car with a numeric label '1' in the relevant field (with a non-owner being labelled '0') this does not mean there is any rank order, that $1 > 0$.

- *Ordinal* data rank the variable being measured. Ordinal data tell you that an observed case has more or less of some characteristic than another observed case. They do not, however, indicate the order of magnitude of difference. We would know from an ordinal scale that the first ranked object had more of the measured characteristic than the second ranked, but we would not know whether the latter ranked a close or distant second. A list of customers ranked from 1 to n based on their sales revenues is ordinal data; you would know that the number one ranked customer generates most sales, but the size of the gap between first and second could not be known from the rank order.

- *Interval* data solve the 'order of magnitude' problem associated with ordinal measures. Not only do interval data identify rank orders, but the distance between the rankings is also known. Many survey instruments use interval scales to measure attitudes and opinions. Interval scales have no fixed zero point. The Celsius and Fahrenheit temperature scales are examples of measures that use interval data but have arbitrary zero points. Differences between interval data make sense but the ratios do not. For example, the difference between 20° and 10° is the same as the difference between 60° and 50°, but we could not say that 60° is three times as hot at 20°.

- *Ratio* data, unlike interval data, have a fixed and absolute zero point. Ratio measures also have all the properties of nominal, ordinal and interval measures. Ratio data allow you to classify objects, rank them and compare differences. Customer expenditure is measured on a ratio scale, as is age, weight and height. Whereas addition and subtraction are the only possible operations on interval data, multiplication and division become possible on ratio data. Ratio data, for example, would enable you to claim that a customer paying $150 for a room spent twice as much as a customer paying $75.

The reason we should distinguish between these data types is that analytical procedures differ according to the type of data. Categorical data use nonparametric procedures such as logistic regression. Continuous data use parametric procedures such as linear regression. The methods that are used to correlate sets of ordinal data differ from those used to correlate interval data. Marketing researchers often use ordinal measurement scales, but analyze the data as if they were continuous. A Likert scale that measures customer satisfaction against five scale points – very satisfied, satisfied, neither satisfied nor dissatisfied, dissatisfied, very dissatisfied – is actually an ordinal scale. However, analysts routinely use analytical procedures developed for interval (continuous) data to make sense of the data. Whether they should do so is a source of dispute!

We review a number of statistical procedures later in the chapter's upcoming review of data mining.

THREE WAYS TO GENERATE ANALYTICAL INSIGHT

CRM users who want to interrogate customer-related data for analytical purposes, or receive management reports, have three main ways of doing this: standard reports, online analytical processing (OLAP) and data mining, as illustrated in Figure 12.1.[15]

Standard reports

Reporting is an essential element of an effective CRM system. The foundation of CRM is an understanding and differentiation of customers – something that depends on good customer-related information. Reporting can take the form of simple lists of information such as key accounts and annual revenues, to more sophisticated reports on certain performance metrics. Most CRM technologies enable the automated creation of periodic reports. Examples include monthly reports to sales management about sales rep activity and performance against quota, and daily reports of call centre activity.

Reporting can be standardized (pre-defined) or query-based (ad hoc). Standardized reports are typically integrated into CRM software applications, but often need customization to suit the needs of the organization. Some customization of the report can be done when it is run, for example in selecting options or filtering criteria, but the end result is limited to what the report designers envisaged. Figure 12.4 is a standard report listing Active Accounts of a sales rep.

Query-based reporting, on the other hand, presents the user with a selection of tools, which can then be used to construct a specific report relevant to the user's role. This is far more flexible. This is a powerful tool in the right hands, as it allows specific reports to be requested, for example: 'show me all of the customers that have expired on their maintenance agreement, in my territory, with annual revenues above $50,000'.

Standard reports are often delivered to users in an array of visualization tools such as tables, charts, graphs, plots, maps, dashboards, hierarchies and networks. Reports can be output to other applications such as Excel for further analysis.

As the requirement for analysis grows, the information in customer-related databases may not be structured to deliver the best results; for this reason, online analytical processing (OLAP) has become an essential part of CRM.

Figure 12.4 Standard report example[16]

Online analytical processing (OLAP)

OLAP technologies allow data stored in a data mart to be subjected to analysis and ad hoc enquiry, using processes such as slice-and-dice, drill-down and roll-up. A data mart is typically a subset of data that is held in a larger data warehouse. The subset reflects the responsibilities of the business unit, department or team that owns the data mart. For example, a sales department would own a data mart containing only sales-related information. The data that are loaded into the data mart would depend on the sorts of analysis that users of the mart want to perform. OLAP is valuable to a range of CRM users who have different types of questions to ask of the data. Salespeople can analyze their territory to determine revenue and profitability by customer. Service people can analyze call response rates and times. Partner managers can analyze the performance of partners by comparing marketing fund approvals to partner-generated revenues.

Data that are to be analyzed using OLAP are stored in one or more star schema, as shown in Figure 12.5. A star schema separates data into facts and dimensions. Facts are quantitative data such as sales revenues and sales volumes. These facts have related dimensions. Dimensions are the ways in which facts can be disaggregated and analyzed. For instance, sales revenues might be broken down by the dimensions of geography and time period. Dimensions can be hierarchical. The geography dimension might contain the hierarchical levels of country, state and city; the time dimension might contain year, month and day levels.

OLAP helps users explain why facts are as they are, by reference to dimensions. For example, if sales in Germany are struggling, the user can drill down from national sales facts into sales by metropolitan area, to find out whether the problem lies in a particular region. By progressively drilling down into hierarchical levels it may become possible to spot the source of a problem. If the problem does not appear to be specific to a metropolitan region the analyst can explore other dimensions such as time and product class.

A star schema contains a central fact table surrounded by several dimension tables, giving it the appearance of a star, as in Figure 12.5. This data structure (central fact table surrounded by dimension tables) means it is possible to conduct many different types of analysis. Based on the tables shown in Figure 12.5, users could obtain answers to questions like these:

- What discounts are offered to customer X?
- How do the quantities shipped vary year by year?
- What are the total sales of product ABC?

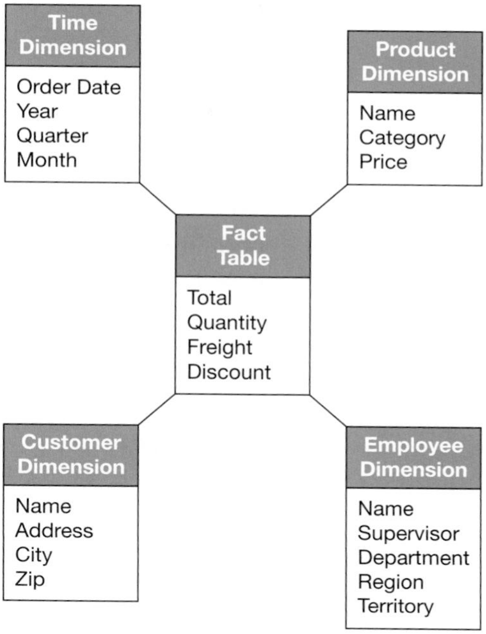

A data warehouse, unlike a data mart, will typically contain several star schemas, each organized around a central fact table based on customers, opportunities, service requests, activities and so on. The customer schema, for example, may contain information such as customer sales revenue figures, sales volumes, cost of sales, profit margins, discounts and promotional expense.

OLAP tools can also support decisions in real time. For example, propensity to buy measures can be delivered to a call centre agent whilst the customer is on the telephone. This allows a tailored offer to be made that is more likely to receive a positive response from the customer.

An important element in CRM analytics is the information delivery mechanism. Information can be made available on the desktop in a Web browser interface with graphical layout and drill-down. This approach requires the user to search for a result. Another method of delivery involves setting trigger points (e.g. when a customer logs more than a certain number of service calls in a month). The analytics application then pushes the related information to the user via email, SMS or another alert mechanism. This approach, also known as 'publish and subscribe', is a powerful management tool.

There are many players in the business analytics marketplace that offer users OLAP functionality.[18] Some major vendors are Tableau, Qlik, Microsoft, IBM, SAS, SAP and Oracle. Database vendors also provide OLAP functionality as part of an integrated offering.

Figure 12.5 Example of a star schema: fact table and dimensions[17]

Data mining

Data mining is the third way in which customer-related data can be interrogated. In the CRM context, data mining can be defined as follows:

Data mining is the application of descriptive and predictive analytics to large datasets to support the marketing, sales and service functions.

Although data mining can be performed on operational databases, it is more common that it is applied to the more stable datasets held in data marts or warehouses. Higher processing speeds, reduced storage costs and better analytics packages have made data mining more attractive and economical, and larger volumes of data have made data mining more useful, if not essential.

Data mining analytics work in a number of ways: by classification, estimation, prediction, affinity grouping, clustering, and description and visualization.[19]

Sometimes the purpose of analytics is simply to *describe* some phenomenon. A massive customer database with millions of records may need to be analyzed just so that managers get a better sense of who buys what in which channels. Descriptive analytics answer users' questions about 'What's going on here?' A good description reduces the complexity of a dataset and may motivate users to look for an explanation. Imagine a descriptive comparative analysis of the sales of different brands of hotdog. The analysis produces a ranking by sales, and the leading brand sells 300 per cent more than the second ranked brand. Managers would be motivated to investigate why. They might explore a number of possible explanations: better marketing campaigns, stronger distribution, better taste performance and more attractive price point. Further analysis would have to take place. The description has led to an explanation. Once a description has been produced, many analytics packages offer users an array of *visualization* tools such as charts, graphs, plots, maps, dashboards, hierarchies and networks of many kinds to help users understand the information. Outputs from analysis can also be exported into any of a large number of data visualization packages.

Analytics also delivers insight by *classifying* some newly observed entity into a pre-defined classification scheme. The simplest example is classifying a new customer as female or male. A more complex example is: you might have developed a hierarchy of existing customers based on their CLV, and created a word profile of each group. When you identify a potential new customer you can judge which group the prospect most resembles and assign the customer to that group. That will give you an idea of the prospect's potential value. From an analytics perspective, the existing hierarchy is a well-defined training set composed of pre-classified examples.

Whereas classification deals with discrete categories, *estimation* deals with continuous variables. A bank developing a marketing campaign for a new product might run its

CASE STUDY 12.4

DATA MINING AT MARKS & SPENCER

Data mining has proven to be a successful strategy for the UK retailer Marks & Spencer. The company generates large volumes of data from the ten million customers per week it serves in over 300 stores. The organization claims data mining lets it build one-to-one relationships with every customer, to the point that whenever individual customers come into a store the retailer knows exactly what products it should offer in order to build profitability.

Marks & Spencer believes two factors are important in data mining. First is the quality of the data. This is higher when the identity of customers is known, usually as a result of e-commerce tracking or loyalty programme membership. Second is to have a clear business goal in mind before starting data mining. For example, M&S uses data mining to identify 'high margin', 'average margin' or 'low margin' customer groups. The company then profiles 'high margin' customers. This is used to guide customer retention activities with appropriate targeted advertising and promotions. This technique can also be used to profile 'average margin' or 'low margin' customers who have the potential to be developed into 'high margin' customers.

customers through an estimation model and give each customer a score between 0 and 1 based on the probability that they will respond positively to an offer. Estimations such as these mean that the customers can be rank ordered for treatment to the campaign, with some customers below a given threshold not receiving the offer. Churn modelling is widely deployed by CRM practitioners; this also uses estimation models.

Prediction is particular application of either classification or estimation. All prediction problems can be recast as problems of classification or estimation, depending on whether the variable that is being predicted is categorical or continuous. CRM practitioners might want to predict whether a customer will refer a friend, increase their spending by 50 per cent next year or trade up to a fee-paid app. Prediction works by using training examples where the value of the variable that is to be predicted is already known (e.g. pay for an app) and there are a number of records where this action has already happened. A model is built based on historical data and the model applied to the customers whose actions are being predicted.

Analysts use *affinity grouping* procedures to find out which things go together. Affinity grouping is based on finding associations between data. CRM practitioners in retail widely conduct shopping basket analyses, which might, for example, reveal that customers who buy low fat desserts are also big buyers of herbal health and beauty aids, or that consumers of wine enjoy live theatre productions. Affinity groupings can be used to identify cross-selling opportunities, or plan store layouts so that associated items are located close to each other. One analyst at Wal-Mart, the American retailer, noted a correlation between diaper sales and beer sales, which was particularly strong on Fridays. On investigating further he found that fathers were buying the diapers and picking up a six-pack at the same time. The company responded to this information by locating these items closer to each other. Sales of both rose strongly.[20]

Whereas shopping basket analyses often rely on cross-sectional data (data collected at one point in time), another form of affinity grouping considers the association between data over time. Sequential patterns can be identified by analytics. Analysts look for 'if . . . then' rules in customer behaviour. For example, they might find a rule such as 'If a customer buys walking shoes in November, then there is a 40 per cent probability that they will buy rainwear within the next six months'.

Another form of analytics uses *clustering*. This involves taking a diverse dataset and finding the naturally occurring clusters within it. Cluster analysts do not try to fit new cases into a pre-defined model, as in the classification described above. The general objective of clustering is to minimize the differences between members of a cluster whilst simultaneously maximizing the differences between clusters. In other words, clustering techniques generally try to maximize both within-group homogeneity and between-group heterogeneity. Clustering techniques work by using a defined range of variables (fields) in the clustering procedure. CRM practitioners often attempt to cluster customer records into groups. For example, a customer segmentation project could take a wide range of transaction, demographic, lifestyle and behavioural data to cluster records (customers) into groups. Another clustering project might consider a narrower range of variables to find out how customers who complain differ from customers who do not complain. There are a number of clustering techniques, including cluster analysis, Classification and Regression Trees (CART) and Chi-square Automatic Interaction Detection (CHAID).[21] Once statistically homogenous clusters have been formed they need to be interpreted. Lifestyle market segments are outputs of cluster analysis on large sets of data. Cluster labels such as 'Young working-class families' or 'Wealthy suburbanites' are often used to capture the essence of the cluster.

These different approaches to data mining can be used in various sequences too. For example, you could use clustering to create customer segments, then within segments use transactional data to predict future purchasing and CLV.

According to Gartner Inc.'s analysis of vendors providing advanced analytics – which they define as 'the analysis of all kinds of data using sophisticated quantitative methods (for example, statistics, descriptive and predictive data mining, simulation and optimization) to produce insights that traditional approaches to business intelligence (BI) – such as query and reporting – are unlikely to discover' – the market leaders are SAS, IBM, Knime and RapidMiner.[22] There are many other vendors.

Directed and undirected data mining

There are two approaches to data mining.[23] Directed data mining (also called supervised, predictive or targeted data mining) has the goal of predicting some future event or value. The analyst uses input data to predict a specified output. For example: What is the probability that customers will respond positively to our next offer? Which customers are most likely to churn in the next year? What is the profile of customers who default on payment? Directed data mining stresses classification, prediction and estimation.

Undirected (or unsupervised) data mining is simply exploration of a dataset to see what can be learned. It is about discovering new patterns in the data. The analyst is not trying to predict or estimate some output. The following questions require undirected data mining: How can we segment our customer base? Are there any patterns of purchasing behaviour in our customer base? Undirected data mining uses clustering and affinity-grouping techniques.

Data mining procedures

We now introduce you to a number of common data mining techniques, as summarized in Table 12.3, organized by their use for directed or undirected data mining. This is not a complete list of all of the techniques used by data miners, and neither do we explore all the ramifications of these techniques here. We advise interested readers to refer to specialist authorities on data mining or business statistics.[24]

Table 12.3 Selected techniques used by data miners

Directed data mining techniques	Undirected data mining techniques
• Decision trees	• Hierarchical clustering
• Logistic regression	• K-means clustering
• Multiple regression	• Two-step clustering
• Discriminant analysis	• Factor analysis
• Neural networks	

First, we describe the directed data mining techniques. Remember that some of these techniques can only be used on particular types of data – nominal, ordinal, interval or ratio.

Decision trees are so called because the graphical model output of decision tree analysis has the appearance of an inverted root and branch structure. Decision trees work through a process called recursive partitioning. A dataset including the variable you are trying to predict, say purchase of life insurance, and a number of independent variables that you think might explain the purchase decision are assembled. The decision tree algorithm progressively partitions the dataset into groups according to a decision rule that aims to maximize homogeneity or purity of the response variable in each of the obtained groups. At each partitioning step an additional explanatory variable is used to partition the groups. This partitioning process is done recursively on each additional split until no further useful splits are found. When the recursive partitioning process is completed, a decision tree is formed. We provide an example in Chapter 5 of decision tree analysis being used to predict credit risk. The same process can be applied to predicting customer churn, response to marketing campaigns or referral of a friend. Decision trees can work with both categorical (nominal or ordinal) and continuous (interval or ratio) data.

Logistic regression measures the influence of one or more independent variables that are usually continuous (interval or ratio data) on a categorical dependent variable (nominal or ordinal data). The output of linear regression modelling reports regression coefficients that represent the effects of the predictor independent variables on the dependent variable. For example, you may develop a theory that the decision of a customer to upgrade to a new smart phone model will be predicted by the number of years the customer has been a user of the previous model, income, number of friends on Facebook, spending on data, and number of texts sent and received. A training model can be developed on a dataset that contains all these data. The coefficients computed by the algorithm reflect the relative influence of each independent variable on the target variable. Data for additional independent variables can be added to the model to improve its ability to predict the target behaviour. Sometimes removing variables from the equation also improves the predictive performance of the model. Rarely does a logistic regression predict that a customer will definitely buy (or churn, or visit a store, or default). Regression models indicate probabilities of the customer engaging in the target behaviour; outputs from regression can therefore be used to assign scores or propensities-to-act to the customer. A high propensity to buy would encourage a CRM practitioner to target that customer with an offer.

Multiple regression (like logistic regression) is a technique that uses two or more predictor variables to predict a dependent variable, but in the case of multiple regression the dependent variable is a continuous (interval or ratio) variable. For example, multiple regression can be used to predict sales revenues, customer profitability and repeat purchase rates. If you wanted to predict the number of subscribers to a cable TV channel, you might hypothesize that the following factors might be useful predictors: the kilowatt strength of the channel's alternative free-to-air signal, the number of homes in the channel's service area, the number of competing channels, the number of minutes of advertising on the channel relative to competitors, and channel subscription costs. Multiple regression modelling would indicate the relative influence of each of these variables. Model fit might be improved by progressively dropping the least influential variable from the equation until all the remaining variables are statistically significant predictors. You need to bear in mind the rubbish-in–rubbish-out rule. Multiple regression finds a statistical association between the independent and dependent variables. It does not tell you if your hypothesized model is correct.

Whereas regressions are essentially scoring models, *discriminant analysis* (DA) clusters observations into two or more classes. DA can be used to find out which variables contribute most to explaining the difference between groups. The technique can also be used to assign new cases to groups. For example, DA can use a person's scores on a range of predictor variables to predict the customer lifetime value group (high, medium or low) that the customer best fits.

Neural networks are another way of fitting a model to existing data for classification, estimation and prediction purposes. Despite the anthropomorphic metaphor of brain function, neural networks' foundations are machine learning and artificial intelligence.

Neural networks can produce excellent predictions from large, complex and imperfect datasets containing hundreds of potentially interactive predictor variables. However, neural networks can be difficult to understand as they are represented in complex mathematical equations, with many summations, nonlinear and exponential functions and parameters.[25] Neural networks need to be trained to recognize patterns on sample datasets. Once trained, they can be used to predict customer behaviour from new data. According to Michael Berry and Gordon Linoff, 'neural networks are a good choice for most classification and prediction tasks when the results of the model are more important than understanding how the model works'.[26]

We now turn to the undirected data mining techniques in Table 12.3. Clustering techniques identify natural groupings within a dataset. For example, customers can be grouped into segments based on the similarity between their patterns of buying behaviour. Shopping basket analysis also uses clustering to answer the question 'What items are bought together?' By adding a time dimension, clustering techniques can be used to identify patterns in the sequences of buying behaviour. In clustering techniques, there are no pre-defined classes or categories such as churners/non-churners. Clustering techniques group records according to the data input, so it is important for cluster modelling to give careful consideration to the fields of data that are to be clustered.

Hierarchical clustering is the 'mother of all clustering models'.[28] It works by assuming each record is a cluster of one and gradually groups records together until there is one super-cluster comprising all records. The results are presented in a table or dendrogram. Figure 12.6 is a dendrogram that groups export markets into clusters on the basis of historical sales, and the sales mix.

The managerial value of this sort of cluster analysis depends on what can be observed in the various clustering levels. In this case the analyst has decided that he can make sense out of three clusters (A, B and C in the illustration). Cluster A consists of Northern Ireland to Greece (from the top of the graph), B consists of Malaysia to Bangladesh and C Botswana to Uganda.

CHURN PREDICTION USING NEURAL NETWORKS[27]

Using a dataset from a mobile-phone service provider, analysis by neural network was performed to develop a churn prediction model. The dataset contained 20 fields of information about 2,427 customers, plus a field recording whether the customer had churned (left the company). The SPSS data mining software package (now owned by IBM) was used. The predictor variables were as follows:

1. *State*: categorical variable, for the 50 states and the district of Columbia.
2. *Account length*: integer-valued variable for how long account has been active.
3. *Area code*: categorical variable.
4. *Phone number*: essentially a surrogate key for customer identification.
5. *International Plan*: dichotomous categorical having yes or no value.
6. *Voice Mail Plan*: dichotomous categorical variable having yes or no value.
7. *Number of voice mail messages*: integer-valued variable.
8. *Total day minutes*: continuous variable for number of minutes customer has used the service during the day.
9. *Total day calls*: integer-valued variable.
10. *Total day charge*: continuous variable based on previous two variables.
11. *Total evening minutes*: continuous variable for minutes customer has used the service during the evening.
12. *Total evening calls*: integer-valued variable.
13. *Total evening charge*: continuous variable based on previous two variables.
14. *Total night minutes*: continuous variable for storing minutes the customer has used the service during the night.
15. *Total night calls*: integer-valued variable.
16. *Total night charge*: continuous variable based on previous two variables.
17. *Total international minutes*: continuous variable for minutes customer has used service to make international calls.
18. *Total international calls*: integer-valued variable.
19. *Total international charge*: continuous variable based on previous two variables.
20. *Number of calls to customer service*: integer-valued variable.

The neural network produced from these data predicted churn with 92.35 per cent accuracy (i.e. in 2,241 of 2,427 cases). The model allows the cellular service provider to predict possible churners and take proactive actions to retain valued customers.

K-means clustering is the most widely used form of clustering routine. It works by clustering the records into a predetermined number of clusters. The predetermined number is 'k'. The reference to 'means' refers to the use of averages in the computation. In this case it refers to the average location of the members of a particular cluster in n-dimensional space, where n is the number of fields that are considered in the clustering routine. The routine works by assigning records to clusters in an iterative process until the records are optimally clustered to create 'k' clusters. The optimal solution will both minimize the variance within a cluster

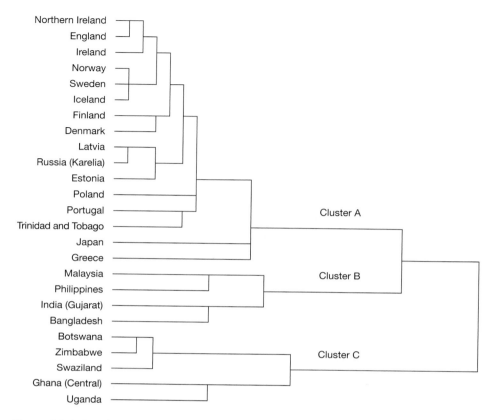

Figure 12.6 Dendrogram output from hierarchical clustering routine[29]

whilst simultaneously maximizing the distance between clusters. Unless there is good reason to specify a given number of clusters, a data miner may want to experiment with a number of different 'k' values and see what the analysis throws up. After the routine has produced the clusters, the user will want to profile and name each cluster, to make them more managerially useful. Figure 12.7 is an example of graphical output of k-means clustering, showing three clusters of records.

Two-step clustering combines predetermined and hierarchical clustering processes. At stage one, records are assigned to a predetermined number of clusters (alternatively you can allow the algorithm to determine the number of clusters). At step two, each of these clusters is treated as a single case and the records within each cluster subjected to hierarchical clustering. Two-step clustering can work well with large datasets. It is the only clustering procedure that works with a mixture of categorical and continuous data.

Factor analysis is a data reduction procedure. It does this by identifying underlying unobservable (latent) variables that are reflected in the observed variables (manifest variables). SERVQUAL, which you read about in Chapter 6, is a result of factor analysis. SERVQUAL is a technology for measuring and managing service quality. When SERVQUAL was

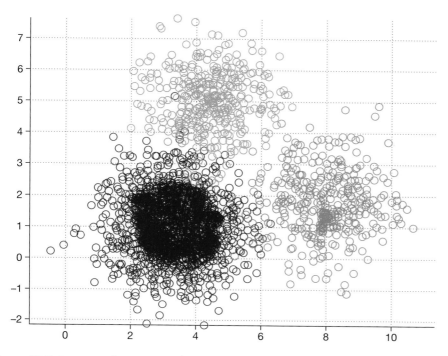

Figure 12.7 K-means clustering output[30]
Copyright © 2009, Michael Chen. All rights reserved.

developed there had been very little work done to investigate what customers understood by the expression 'service quality'. The researchers conducted many focus groups from which they extracted hundreds of statements about participants' views on service quality. A long questionnaire was then created that listed many of these statements. This was administered to a sample of people who completed Likert scales reporting their level of agreement or disagreement with the statements. The results were subjected to factor analysis, as a result of which ten components of service quality were identified. These ten latent variables (listed in Table 12.4) were hidden in the survey response data, and revealed only through factor analysis. Later, these were further reduced to five more inclusive factors.

The major analytics software vendors produce documentation that describes the various analytical tools that are available, and the uses to which they can be put.[31]

Table 12.4 SERVQUAL's latent variables revealed by factor analysis

Reliability	Communication
Responsiveness	Credibility
Competence	Security
Access	Understanding/knowing the customer
Courtesy	Tangibles

PRIVACY ISSUES

How organizations acquire, store, analyze and use customer data is an important issue for regulators; privacy and data protection are major concerns to legislators around the world. Customers are increasingly concerned about the amount of information commercial organizations have about them, and the uses to which that information is put. In fact, most consumers are not aware of just how much information is available to companies. When you use the Internet, small programmes called cookies are downloaded onto your hard drive from the sites you visit. With increasing legislation in this area (e.g. European Union's ePrivacy Directive, Article 5(3)),[32] companies need to secure permission to operate cookies and hold information on individual site visitors.

There have been two major responses to the privacy concerns of customers. The first is self-regulation by companies and associations. For example, a number of companies publish their privacy policies and make a commercial virtue out of their transparency. Professional bodies in fields such as direct marketing, advertising and market research have adopted codes of practice that members must abide by.

The second response has been legislation. In 1980, the Organization for Economic Cooperation and Development (OECD) developed a set of personal data protection principles.[33] Internationally, these principles provide the most commonly used privacy framework; they are reflected in existing and emerging privacy and data protection laws in the European Union, and serve as the basis for the creation of best practice privacy programmes and additional principles.

The OECD principles are as follows:

1   *Collection Limitation Principle.* Personal data should be obtained by lawful and fair means and, where appropriate, with the knowledge or consent of the data subject.

2   *Data Quality Principle.* Personal data should be relevant to the purposes for which they are to be used, and, to the extent necessary for those purposes, should be accurate, complete and kept up-to-date.

3   *Purpose Specification Principle.* The purposes for which personal data are collected should be specified not later than at the time of data collection and the subsequent use limited to the fulfilment of those purposes or other uses compatible with those purposes.

4   *Use Limitation Principle.* Personal data should not be disclosed, made available or otherwise used for purposes other than those specified except (a) with the consent of the data subject; or (b) by the authority of law.

5   *Security Safeguards Principle.* Personal data should be protected by reasonable security safeguards against such risks as loss or unauthorized access, destruction, use, modification or disclosure of data.

6   *Openness Principle.* There should be a general policy of openness about developments, practices and policies with respect to personal data. Means should be readily available of establishing the existence and nature of personal data, and the main purposes of their use, as well as the identity and usual residence of the data controller.

7   *Individual Participation Principle.* An individual should have the right: (a) to obtain from a data controller, or otherwise, confirmation of whether or not the data controller has data relating to him; (b) to have communicated to him, data relating to him (i) within a reasonable time; (ii) at a charge, if any, that is not excessive; (iii) in a reasonable manner; and (iv) in a form that is readily intelligible to him; (c) to be given reasons if a request made under subparagraphs (a) and (b) is denied, and to be able to challenge such denial; and (d) to challenge data relating to him and, if the challenge is successful, to have the data erased, rectified, completed or amended.

8   *Accountability Principle.* A data controller should be accountable for complying with measures that give effect to the principles stated above.

The United States Department of Commerce developed the *Safe Harbor* self-certifying legal framework to allow US organizations to comply with the EC Data Protection Directive. Because of the purpose, the framework's principles align closely with OECD's. There are seven *Safe Harbor* principles:

1   *Notice.* Organizations must notify individuals about the purposes for which they collect and use information about them. They must provide information about how individuals can contact the organization with any inquiries or complaints, the types of third parties to which it discloses the information and the choices and means the organization offers for limiting its use and disclosure.

2   *Choice.* Organizations must give individuals the opportunity to choose (opt out) whether their personal information will be disclosed to a third party or used for a purpose incompatible with the purpose for which it was originally collected or subsequently authorized by the individual.

3   *Onward Transfer (Transfers to Third Parties).* To disclose information to a third party, organizations must apply the notice and choice principles. Where an organization wishes to transfer information to a third party that is acting as an agent, it may do so if it makes sure that the third party subscribes to the *Safe Harbor* Privacy Principles or is subject to the Directive or another adequacy finding. As an alternative, the organization can enter into a written agreement with such third party requiring that the third party provide at least the same level of privacy protection as is required by the relevant principles.

4   *Access.* Individuals must have access to personal information about them that an organization holds and be able to correct, amend, or delete that information where it is inaccurate, except where the burden or expense of providing access would be disproportionate to the risks to the individual's privacy, or where the rights of persons other than the individual would be violated.

5   *Security.* Organizations must take reasonable precautions to protect personal information from loss, misuse and unauthorized access, disclosure, alteration and destruction.

6   *Data Integrity.* Personal information must be relevant for the purposes for which it is to be used. An organization should take reasonable steps to ensure that data are reliable for intended use, accurate, complete, and current.

7   *Enforcement.* In order to ensure compliance with the *Safe Harbor* principles, there must be (a) readily available and affordable independent recourse mechanisms so that each individual's complaints and disputes can be investigated and resolved and damages awarded where the applicable law or private sector initiatives so provide; (b) procedures for verifying that the commitments companies make to adhere to the *Safe Harbor* principles have been implemented; and (c) obligations to remedy problems arising out of a failure to comply with the principles. Sanctions must be sufficiently rigorous to ensure compliance by the organization. Organizations that fail to provide annual self-certification letters will no longer appear in the list of participants and *Safe Harbor* benefits will no longer be assured.

Safe Harbor is one of several cross-border data transfer options for organizations in the USA that conduct business in the EU. For an organization to employ *Safe Harbor* as a compliance mechanism, the organization must be subject to the Federal Trade Commission's or Department of Transportation's authority. *Safe Harbor* is a very popular option, particularly for handling customer data. Its use continues to grow, often serving as a starting point for many US organizations expanding their operations into the EU.

The World Wide Web Consortium (W3C) has established a Privacy Interest Group whose charter is to 'improve the support of privacy in Web standards by monitoring ongoing privacy issues that affect the Web, investigating potential areas for new privacy work, and providing guidelines and advice for addressing privacy in standards development'.[34] The group notes that the evolution of Web technologies has increased collection, processing and publication of personal data. Privacy concerns are raised more often as applications built on the Web platform have access to more sensitive data – including location, health and social network information – and users' activity on the Web is ubiquitously tracked. The W3C Privacy Activity coordinates standardization work to improve support for user privacy on the Web and develops general expertise in privacy-by-design for Web standards.

SUMMARY

This chapter has explored how organizations analyze and use customer-related data. We define analytical CRM as the process through which organizations transform customer-related data into actionable insight for either strategic or tactical purposes. Analysis of customer-related data supports strategic CRM by answering questions like 'Who are our most valuable customers?' and operational CRM by answering questions like 'What offer should we next make to the customer?' Analytical CRM supports strategic and tactical decision making by sales, marketing and service teams throughout the customer lifecycle. CRM analytics are commissioned and delivered to users in three ways: through standard reports, online analytical processing or data mining. Analytical methods for structured data – the type of data that typically resides in relational databases – are mature. Analytics for unstructured data are becoming more widely adopted. Textual analysis is the most widely deployed form of unstructured data analytics. Analytics for big data are still evolving. Big data are characterized by their volume, velocity and variety. These attributes make analysis challenging. Data mining technologies work in a number of ways: by describing and visualizing, classifying, estimating, predicting, affinity grouping and clustering. Managers and data miners need to understand the types of analysis that are appropriate for different levels of data – nominal, ordinal, interval and ratio. Privacy regulations place constraints on what can be done with customer-related data. Data analysts need to be aware of these constraints.

NOTES AND REFERENCES

1   http://www.ibm.com/smarterplanet/global/files/be–en_be–commerce–unica_casestudy_ing_021910.pdf (Accessed 2 June 2014).

2   Courtesy sap.com. Used with permission.

3   http://support.sas.com/software/products/txtminer/#s1=1 (Accessed 6 June 2014).

4   http://www.b-eye-network.com/view/12783 (Accessed 6 June 2014).

5   http://support.sas.com/resources/papers/proceedings14/1288–2014.pdf (Accessed 6 June 2014).

6   http://www.intel.com.au/content/dam/www/public/us/en/documents/solution-briefs/big-data-101-brief.pdf (Accessed 4 June 2014).

7   http://www.geektime.com/2013/10/24/the-3-vs-of-big-data-and-their-technologies/ (Accessed 6 June 2014).

8   See, for example, http://www.theinternetofthings.eu/.

9   http://www.forbes.com/sites/gregsatell/2014/01/03/why-most-marketers-will-fail-in-the-era-of-big-data/, and: http://www.digitaltonto.com/2013/what-is-big-data-and-what-do-we-do-with-it/ (Accessed January 2014).

10 Zikopoulos, P.C., Eaton, C., deRoos, D., Deutsch, T. and Lapis, G. (2012). *Understanding big data: analytics for enterprise class Hadoop and streaming data*. New York: McGraw-Hill.

11 http://www.sapbigdata.com/stories/ebays-early-signal-detection-system-runs-machine-learning-predictive-powered-by-sap-hana/ (Accessed 7 January 2014).

12 http://www.informationweek.com/big-data/big-data-analytics/big-data-success-3-companies-share-secrets/d/d-id/1111815?page_number=1 (Accessed 7 January 2014).

13 For more information: http://hadoop.apache.org/index.html. We note that IBM's publicity focuses on the value IBM adds to the open-source Hadoop, whereas SAP focuses upon its own solution (HANA) but identifies where and how it works with Hadoop; http://www.sapbigdata.com/analytics/.

14 Stephens, S.S. (1951). Mathematics, measurement and psychophysics. In S.S. Stephens (ed.). *Handbook of experimental psychology*. New York: Wiley.

15 Zikmund, W.G., McLeod, Jr., R. and Gilbert, F.W. (2003). *Customer relationship management: integrating marketing strategy and information technology*. Hoboken, NJ: John Wiley.

16 http://richardsbusinessblog.wordpress.com/category/bi/ (Accessed 8 June 2014).

17 http://www.dwreview.com/OLAP/Introduction_OLAP.html (Accessed 8 June 2014).

18 http://www.gartner.com/technology/reprints.do?id=1–1QLGACN&ct=140210&st=sb (Accessed 8 June 2014).

19 Berry, M.J.A. and Linoff, G.S. (2000). *Data mining: the art and science of customer relationship management*. New York: John Wiley

20 Dempsey, M. (1995). Customers compartmentalised. *Financial Times*, 1 March.

21 Saunders, J. (1994). Cluster analysis. In G.J. Hooley and M.K. Hussey (eds). *Quantitative methods in marketing*. London: Dryden Press, pp. 13–28.

22 http://www.gartner.com/technology/reprints.do?id=1–1QXWEQQ&ct=140219&st=sg (Accessed 8 June 2014).

23 Berry, M.J.A. and Linoff, G.S. (2000). *Data mining: the art and science of customer relationship management*. New York: John Wiley.

24 See, for example, Berry, M.J.A. and Linoff, G.S. (2000). *Data mining: the art and science of customer relationship management*. New York: John Wiley; Tsiptsis, K. and Chorianooulos, A. (2009). *Data mining techniques in CRM*. Chichester: John Wiley; Giudici, P. (2003). *Applied data mining*. Chichester: John Wiley.

25 Berry, M.J.A. and Linoff, G.S. (2000). *Data mining: the art and science of customer relationship management*. New York: John Wiley.

26 Berry, M.J.A. and Linoff, G.S. (2000). *Data mining: the art and science of customer relationship management*. New York: John Wiley, p. 128.

27 Sharma, A. and Panigrahi, P. (2011). A neural network based approach for predicting customer churn in cellular network services. *International Journal of Computer Applications*, 27(11), 26–31.

28 Tsiptsis, K. and Chorianooulos, A. (2009). *Data mining techniques in CRM*. Chichester: John Wiley.

29 http://thejuicepress.wordpress.com/about-marketing-research/cluster-analysis/dendrogram/ (Accessed 11 June 2014).

30 http://www.mathworks.com/matlabcentral/fileexchange/24616-kmeans-clustering (Accessed 6 June 2014).

31 See: http://www.sas.com/en_us/software/analytics.html; http://www-01.ibm.com/software/au/analytics/spss/; http://www.tableausoftware.com/, http://www.qlik.com/; http://www.sap.com/pc/analytics/strategy.html; http://www.microsoft.com/en-au/server-cloud/audience/business-analytics.aspx#fbid=CN0jGPCbOlx (Accessed 10 June 2014).

32 http://ec.europa.eu/ipg/basics/legal/cookies/index_en.htm.

33 http://oecdprivacy.org/ (Accessed 9 June 2014). See also Swift, R.S. (2001). *Accelerating customer relationships using CRM and relationship technologies*. Upper Saddle River, NJ: Prentice Hall.

34 http://www.w3.org/Privacy/ (Accessed 10 June 2014).

Part V

REALIZING THE BENEFITS OF CRM

So far, we have covered why firms are, or should be, interested in CRM as part of an overall strategic approach to managing the customer lifecycle, the tremendous opportunities afforded by new technology and business processes, and how CRM potentially benefits both customers and firms alike. However, extensive research from both business and technology perspectives concludes that neither the technology nor many CRM programmes generate meaningful business improvement. Numerous surveys of CRM's impact in the early 2000s, when the first wave of businesses had gone live with their CRM implementations, demonstrate that large numbers felt their investments had not been successful, even though many firms did not even measure the ROI of CRM investment! The Gartner Hype Cycle that we introduced in Chapter 9 applies broadly to CRM technologies. The Hype Cycle points to the tremendous initial excitement associated with innovative CRM technology, inflated expectations about what can be achieved, and the subsequent disillusionment and rethink that is evident in so much of technology-led change. Given that best-practice CRM technology is available on the open market from a vibrant, competitive and global set of technology vendors (e.g. IBM, Oracle, SAP, SAS, salesforce.com, to name but a few) it is unrealistic to expect that CRM technologies alone generate sustainable competitive advantage. Realizing business benefit from investment in CRM is the responsibility of management, not the IT vendor.

Chapter 13 covers the generation of a business case for CRM investment, the management of its benefits, planning the implementation and aligning the organization for its success. Chapter 14 focuses on the project management skills you will need to implement CRM programmes.

PLANNING TO SUCCEED

CHAPTER OBJECTIVES

After reading this chapter you will understand how to:

- Generate a business case for CRM aligned both to your strategic intention and the needs/behaviours of your customers.

- Identify and plan for the immediate operational benefits of CRM.

- Identify and plan for potential future benefits arising from improved operational effectiveness.

- Understand options for organizational structure to implement CRM strategy.

THE LOGIC OF THE BUSINESS CASE

Success or failure of CRM is often determined well before you start the programme; in preparing the business case, the outcome of the investment can be predetermined. Imagine going to the Board of your company and asking for $50 million over three years to develop/enhance a CRM programme. You have looked at a number of CRM programmes, spoken with peers, companies, suppliers and experts and have a good feel for the solutions, people and processes that you need to develop. These are relatively easy to estimate in terms of time and cost because CRM is a mature practice. You identify to your Board colleagues the win–win argument for CRM just as we have in Chapter 1. You explain how technology can generate a comprehensive view of each customer's history, enabling you to apply sophisticated analytics that enable you to manage customers according to their unique profile in real time, all with the expectation that you will be more profitable. The obvious questions are: How much incremental profit will you generate? What is the ROI? What is the risk?

The honest answer is that you don't yet know. Until you have engaged with customers interactively, learnt from them, experimented with real-time customization of offers, experienced the reduction of service costs and so on, you only know with certainty what CRM will cost. You have little idea about the size and timing of return. Typically, managers make heroic assumptions about customer retention rates, up-selling, cross-selling and cost-to-serve. Sometimes these are made on the basis of claimed but unproven best practice metrics provided by technology partners, and other times they are just assumptions based on cost, as if you were asking: 'What assumptions do I need to make for this investment to pay, and are they reasonable assumptions to make?' These estimated returns are put into a spreadsheet and discounted for the time value of money and a Net Present Value of the investment is determined.[1]

The traditional business case does not match the nature of CRM benefits

The practice of discounting cash flows does not suit investments in IT-enabled change, such as CRM.[2] Discounted cash flow (DCF) analysis or finding the Net Present Value (NPV) works by computing the difference between cash inflows and outflows discounted for the risk associated with that class of investment. Discounting allows one to compare inflows and outflows, typically occurring at different times through the project at a hypothetical time 'zero'. Where the NPV is positive, the real value of cash generated adjusted for risk is greater than the investment, and shareholder value is therefore created. This is the dominant model used by companies when allocating their investment funds, and is known as the Capital Asset Pricing Model (CAPM). If a company invests in numerous projects, each of which is expected to generate more real cash than its cost, then, over time, the value of the firm will rise.

The economic logic of the CAPM is sound. However, it is based on assumptions that are questionable in the context of large-scale CRM investments.

- Where CRM is a 'bet the business' imperative or a major, disruptive change in business strategy, the risk of failure is too great for 'expected value' decision making. If a company must become customer-centric quickly, then this is no longer one investment amongst many – it is a 'do or die' situation.

- The variance of outcomes is sufficiently predictable to make an expected value meaningful. When faced with discontinuous futures, scenario planning may be a better option than using 'expected value'. A CRM change programme that costs, for example, $100 million, might not generate one cent of incremental cash (loses $100 million) but, on the other hand, could transform the business fundamentally and generate $500 million (but nothing in between). DCF might show the investment has an expected value of $200 million but that is a meaningless figure for the Board; they either lose $100 million or gain $500 million.

- No complementary assets and capabilities are needed. CRM's impact on business performance is almost always in conjunction with, or mediated by, other capabilities such as excellent brand management,[3] customer-focused management,[4] employees,[5] new product development[6] and organizational responsiveness.[7] If these capabilities are not developed, the CRM programme might fail initially. However, over time it gathers so much customer insight that your new product development improves markedly. It is almost impossible to know that at the start, or estimate the benefits up-front. It is pure guesswork.

IT researchers have long recognized that investments in technology alone do not improve performance or economic output.[8] Whilst they too identify similar complementary assets and capabilities needed, they emphasize the role of the conscious management of the potential benefits from IT investments: the 'benefits realization' approach to managing CRM implementation.[9] The challenge of planning for CRM payback is that the returns tend to occur in two stages and the second stage does not automatically follow on from the first.[10] Typically, the first return on CRM investment is through improved operational performance. Duplicate databases are consolidated into a single view of the customer, front- and back-office integration is improved thus reducing costs, channels are integrated allowing the organization to serve customers anywhere at any time, self-service online reduces costs further, marketing campaigns are less costly to implement and may generate greater sales through improved customer selection. At this point, the company may declare success and manage the CRM for selective improvements over time. However, this improved operational performance likely has generated new CRM assets (databases, mining tools, customer relationships) and capabilities (data mining, database management, interacting with customers). These improved operational and analytic CRM assets and capabilities enable more ambitious strategic CRM initiatives: bigger changes to align the business to the needs of the most attractive customers in the market. Such benefits are said to be latent and staged or layered[11] and are realized over an extended time period.[12] Active benefits realization improves the return on IT investment.[13]

Given this staged or layered description of the benefits arising from CRM, then the discounted cash flow approach to valuing CRM investments is inadequate. Moreover, it takes the company's attention away from identifying and managing latent benefits over time to a focus on short-term cash flow generation from enhanced operational CRM (e.g. campaign management, reduced service costs). Typical business cases, based on capital expenditure logic, assume a linear and continuous relationship between activity and cash flow that can be discounted back to time zero and contrasted with the estimated investment. CRM benefits are discontinuous: some operational benefits are experienced early on and then there is a 'break' where management either realizes the latent benefits made possible by newly achieved customer insight and enhanced CRM capabilities – or not.

Such structure of benefit corresponds closer to another sort of investment analysis that is much more used in financial circles than in marketing circles: real options pricing models. You may be familiar with financial options; that is, the right to buy or sell an asset at some point in the future for a price you set today. For example, farmers agreeing a price for their harvest in advance guarantee sufficient income to carry on farming; the risk of turbulent markets is too much to accept for some farmers. Similarly, a food manufacturer may purchase options to buy raw materials at a fixed price for, say, six months hence, so as to have some certainty of costs. A *real* option is the right to buy or sell a physical asset, or even a business, at some point in the future.

A Board member may believe that customer-centricity could be the future of his business but is unwilling to completely change his business model at this time; he feels it is too risky, too unproven and, in any case, he has better opportunities in front of him. He could, however, build a limited CRM infrastructure, with databases, tools and analysts, to learn about customers and experiment with customization and marketing automation to see how it works. If customers do not respond, then he does not exercise the option to scale up to an expensive

CRM solution. He will only have lost the cost of the limited CRM infrastructure that is small versus the loss he would have made had he gone ahead with the bigger CRM investment and changes to the business model. However, if the limited CRM investment has demonstrated precisely how to make it work for his company, then he is very well placed to exercise the option to scale up. He has a blueprint for success, some capabilities, a management team in place and basic infrastructure. Implementing the more ambitious CRM programme is far less risky than doing it cold and will take far less time. This 'test market' of CRM, this investment in learning and building basic capabilities, can be considered a real option that is exercised only if CRM appears to have real promise. It limits the risk and exposure for the company but also provides it with the possibility to reap the rewards should CRM be 'right' in this environment.

If the idea of testing CRM before embarking on a full-blown change programme appeals, then how would you write a business case for it? How would you quantify the value of the learning that you have yet to acquire? The financial markets have long managed such investments. People may wish to participate in a stock's future growth potential without necessarily buying the stock outright, so they buy an option to buy that stock at a certain price in the future. Investment firms can price these options given the current share price, what you are willing to bet it will be in the future, how many months in the future and the risk in the market. For non-financial investments like CRM, the financial markets 'real options pricing' models provide a useful analogy and methodology.[14] The most popular of these models is called Black Scholes and you can find websites that will calculate the option value online – Apple even has a widget for this!

Real options have been demonstrated to work in the context of creating a business case for CRM.[15] The value of the real option can be added to the value of a traditional discounted cash flow that assumes a test followed by a full roll-out. By valuing the learning in the business, you are far more likely to design and manage CRM to learn from customers and to respond to what they are telling you. This contrasts to an approach you need to 'justify' the investment by assuming, even before engaging with customers, that they will wish to be cross-sold to, pay more, be more loyal and so on. We believe that the business case sets the vision and values for the CRM programme.

The Benefits Dependency Network

Testing CRM asks an obvious question: What will success look like? What are we looking for with respect to customer behaviour, selection, operating costs and so on? These questions mean that managers of CRM implementations must work out how to identify immediate and latent benefits of CRM and test for their presence. IT experts have developed a framework for doing that: the Benefit Dependency Network or BDN. It is a logical structure of connected activities and events that are associated with identified benefits. Figure 13.1 provides a simplified illustration of a BDN.

It is important that each benefit, for example 'increased conversion rate of leads-to-orders', has an owner in the business accountable for its achievement and empowered to work backwards through the dependency network to bring about the changes to activities and processes that are necessary for the benefit to be achieved. CRM solutions enable those activities but do not generate them automatically. Too often, CRM is seen as a technology

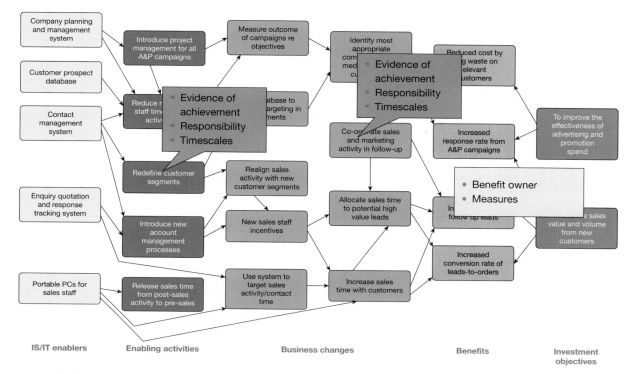

Figure 13.1 Benefit Dependency Network example[16]

implementation project whose success is determined by its functioning, rather than its delivery of business results. The BDN shifts management's thinking from technology to business benefits.

ORGANIZING FOR BENEFITS

First we have to acknowledge that there is a spectrum of CRM programmes and associated investments, ranging from buying a new campaign management tool to reorienting the organization's strategy and direction. We will focus on the larger scale implementations of CRM, those that bring about significant change to business processes, people's roles and perhaps even the organization's structure.

Alfred Chandler[17] is credited with the expression 'strategy before structure', suggesting that organizations should decide their strategic goals before designing the structure of the organization to bring about the achievement of those goals.

Companies adopting CRM as their core business strategy need to create an organizational structure that achieves three major outcomes through its marketing, selling and service functions:

1   The acquisition of carefully targeted customers or market segments.

2   The retention and development of strategically significant customers or market segments.

3   The continuous development and delivery of competitively superior value propositions and experiences to the selected customers.

This is the core of strategic CRM and it needs to be supported by the organization's structure. No structure is perfect and each entails trade-offs; however, firms embarking on a customer-centric strategy need to make these trade-offs in favour of encouraging teams from across their organization, and those in supplier and partner companies, to work together to deliver customized communications and offers to the most attractive customers.

Conventional customer management structures

We will start by considering a stand-alone company as it organizes to achieve these three CRM goals. This company is presented with a number of alternative structures:

1   Functional organization structure.
2   Geographic organization structure.
3   Product, brand or category organization structure.
4   Market or customer-based organization structure.
5   Matrix organization structure.

Functional structure

A functional structure has sales, marketing and service specialists reporting to a functional head such as a director or vice president of sales and marketing. The specialists might include marketing analyst, market researcher, campaign manager, account manager, service engineer and sales support specialist. Small to medium-sized businesses with narrow product ranges tend to prefer the functional organization. The three core disciplines that interface with customers – sales, marketing and service – may or may not coordinate their efforts, and share their customer knowledge by depositing it in a common customer database. From a CRM perspective it would be better if they did! Elsewhere in a functionally organized business will be other specialists whose decisions can impact on customer acquisition, retention and experience, for example, specialists in operations, human resources and accounts receivable. These experts also would benefit from having access to customer information. Very often, functional specialists feel a sense of loyalty to their discipline rather than their customers.

Geographic structure

A geographic structure organizes some or all of the three core customer management disciplines – marketing, selling and service – on territorial lines. Selling and service are more commonly geographically dispersed than marketing. International companies often organize geographically around the Americas, EMEA (Europe, Middle East and Africa) and Asia-Pacific regions. Smaller companies may organize around national, regional or local areas.

Where customers are geographically dispersed and value face-to-face contact with salespeople, there is a clear benefit in salespeople also being geographically dispersed. Where service needs to be delivered at remote locations, field service staff may also be distributed geographically. Because selling and service costs can be very high, companies try to find ways to perform these activities more cost-effectively. Some companies sell face-to-face to their most important customers and offer a telesales service to others. Others provide service through centralized contact centres that might either be outsourced or company-operated. Websites that enable customers to service their own requirements can also reduce cost.

One disadvantage of this approach, from a CRM perspective, is that there may be many different customer types in a single geographic area. A salesperson selling industrial chemicals might have to call on companies from several industries such as textiles, paint or consumer goods manufacturing. The applications of the sold product may be diverse; the buying criteria of the customers may be quite different. Some may regard the product as mission-critical; others may regard it insignificant. The problem is multiplied if a salesperson sells many products to many customer groups. The salesperson develops neither customer, nor product, expertise.

Product, brand or category structure

A product or brand organization structure is common in companies that produce a wide variety of products, especially when they have different marketing, sales or service requirements. This sort of structure is common in large consumer goods companies such as Procter and Gamble and Unilever, and in diversified business-to-business companies. Product or brand managers are generally responsible for developing marketing strategy for their products, and then coordinating the efforts of specialists in marketing research, advertising, selling, merchandising, sales promotion and service, to ensure that the strategic objectives are achieved. Normally, brand and product managers have to compete for company resources to support their brands. Resources are spread thinly across many brands and the company risks becoming focused on products rather than customers. Procter and Gamble found that brand managers became isolated, competing vigorously against each other, focusing on their own goals, rather than those of the corporation. Brands competed against each other, creating cannibalization.[18]

Many multi-brand companies have found that brand management makes it difficult to integrate the entire resources of the organization around the needs of customers. Brand management encourages competition between the company's product-brand offers rather than promote integrated customer offers. Product-brand companies lack coordination and have disregard for the value of the customer's time. The customer may also experience varying levels of service from the different brand or product managers. Some companies have tried to coordinate their product-marketing efforts by appointing product group managers to an oversight role or customer front end to the product brand structure to help customers navigate around the complex offers.

Most leading fast-moving consumer goods companies have moved to a category management structure. Kraft markets a number of different brands, including Louis Rich cold meat cuts and Oscar Mayer hot dogs. The company has category business directors who coordinate a team of functional experts focused on each major category (Figure 13.2). Brand managers sit on the category team. The category team works with a customer team that is dedicated to each major customer, to ensure that the category offer generates profit for both Kraft and the customer. The customer team works closely with customers to help them learn how to benefit more from intelligent product assortment, shelf position and promotion decisions. They also help retailers to better understand and exploit their own customer data.

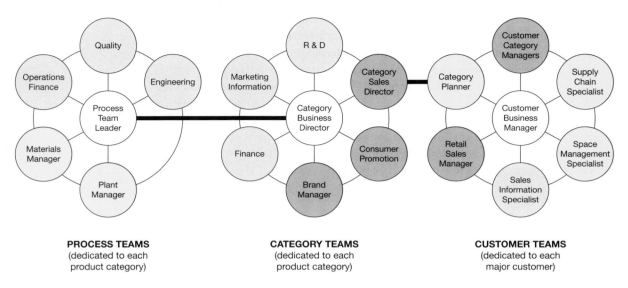

Figure 13.2 Category management at Kraft[19]

Also dedicated to each category is a process team that is responsible for ensuring that business processes are aligned with customer requirements. Typically, the process team addresses issues of quality management and logistics. This sort of structure attempts to integrate product, functional and customer considerations.

Market or customer structure

Market- or customer-based organization structures are common when companies serve different customers or customer groups that are felt to have different requirements or buying practices. Market- or customer-based managers come in many forms: market managers, segment managers, account managers and customer business managers, for example. The roles are responsible for becoming expert on market and customer requirements and for ensuring that the organization creates and delivers the right value proposition and experience to the customer. Recently, there has been a trend towards national, key or global account management that we look at in more detail later in the chapter.

Matrix structure

A matrix organization is often the preferred structural solution when a company has several different product lines serving several different customer groups. A matrix typically has market- or customer-based managers on one side, and product managers on the other side of the matrix as in Figure 13.3. In the high-tech industries, another common matrix structure is geography against industry. The sales team includes a sales person and a pre-sales consultant. Sales people are organized into geographic territories, but pre-sales consultants are organized by industry. This allows customers to have not only a geographically convenient point of face-to-face contact but also an industry specialist on whose expertise they can draw.

A variation that is commonly found in multi-channel organizations is the replacement of customer managers with channel managers. Multi-channel retailers can have several

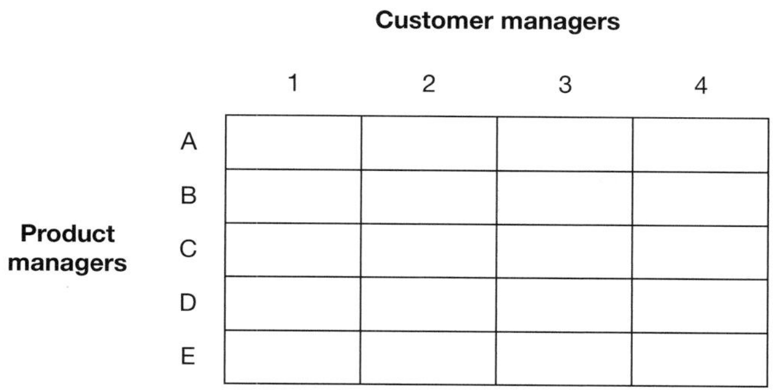

Customer managers

Figure 13.3 Matrix organization structure

routes to market: stores, catalogues, online retailing, perhaps even a TV shopping channel. Financial services institutions also have many channels: branch networks, call centres, agency outlets and corporate websites. Matrix organizations are thought to facilitate both horizontal and vertical communication, therefore improving coordination and reducing inefficiencies.

Market or customer managers in matrices are responsible for developing and maintaining profitable relationships with external customers. Generally, they view product managers in the matrix as suppliers. Sometimes the internal product manager will compete against external suppliers to become the market manager's preferred supplier. Then, market managers will form internal customer–supplier relationships, negotiate prices and agree service levels just as they would with outside suppliers. Pricing internal transfers can be a tricky decision. One of two approaches is taken: either the internal supplier sells at external market prices (as if they were marketing to an external customer, and aiming to make a profit), or they sell at an internally agreed transfer price that enables market managers to return a profit on their external transactions and relationships. This price then allows the market manager more flexibility in negotiating price with the external customer.

As an alternative to, or in some cases a prelude to, the development of a matrix organization, many companies have opted for the use of cross-functional teams. A cross-functional team is usually established when a project has implications that span normal functional, product or market lines. A cross-functional team is often used to consider the implications of the adoption of CRM. It will consist of experts from marketing, sales, service, technology, finance and general management.

NETWORK AND VIRTUAL ORGANIZATIONS

Business networks compete, not just stand-alone companies. Virgin Atlantic's network competes with the networks of American Airlines and British Airways. Indeed, some members of VA's network may also be part of BA's and AA's networks.

In this networked world, it is no longer a simple matter to know where an organization's boundary lies. This brings us to the role of IT in organizational design. The role of IT in a stable corporate environment is to allow senior management to control information and decision making.[20] As environments become more turbulent, and as companies attempt to forge network relationships, the role of IT has changed. Its role is now to provide information that enables the company and its network members to:

- Sense and respond rapidly to changes in the business environment.

- Collaborate to develop and deliver better customer value propositions.

- Enhance and share their learning about customers.

- Improve their individual and joint cost profiles.

Customers do not want to learn how the organizations they patronize are structured. They do not want to have queries rerouted from one silo or specialist to another in search of a solution. Customers who hear the words, 'That's not my department. I'll put you through to the right person', or find themselves looping through interactive voice response (IVR) menus in search of a solution are likely to be dissatisfied customers. Customers want their needs, demands and expectations to be met. Companies therefore need to create an organization structure that enables their products, services and information to be ubiquitously and immediately available in the channels that customers patronize. Traditional structures, particularly those that are function-, geography- or product-based, struggle to meet these standards.

Structures that are IT-enabled are more likely to meet customer requirements. For example, an online banking service is open every day and hour of the year. A typical branch-based service is open less than one-third of the time. If the branch network were to replicate the scale of the online service, it would require three times the staffing levels with a concomitant increase in management structure. Even then, this could not match the convenience of a home-accessed banking service, or its price. PWC reports that a branch-based transaction costs a bank 40 times the cost of an Internet transaction.[21] Some or all of these transaction cost savings can be passed on to customers as improved prices. For example, buying life insurance online is between 8 per cent and 15 per cent cheaper than buying through a bricks-and-mortar broker.[22]

At its most advanced, the IT-enabled organization is able to take any sales or service query from any customer in any channel and resolve it immediately. Among the preferred characteristics of such a design are:

- A customer interface that is consistent across channels and easy to use whatever the technology or device.

- A first point of contact that takes responsibility for resolving the query.

- A back-end architecture that enables the contact point to obtain relevant customer and product information immediately.

These IT-enabled structures eliminate the need for conventional silo-based geography-, function- and product-based arrangements.

PERSON-TO-PERSON CONTACTS

Interpersonal contacts between people from the seller and buyer dyad are important, whether they are conducted face-to-face or mediated by technology such as phone, chat and email. On the seller's side these contacts are important for identifying customer needs, requirements and preferences, for understanding and managing customer expectations, for solving problems and showing commitment. Over the life of a relationship, such personal contacts contribute to the reduction of uncertainty and the creation of close social bonds. Interpersonal communication also underpins the development of product and process adaptations that serve as investments in the relationship. These act as structural bonds.

Relationships between individuals on buyer and seller sides tend to be hierarchically matched.[23] Sales representatives meet with buyers, general managers meet with general managers. Researchers have also identified three main patterns of inter-organizational contact.[24]

1   *Controlled contact* pattern, where all contacts are physically channelled through a single point of contact, typically a salesperson on the seller's side or a buyer on the customer's side. This individual manages all the contacts on the other side of the dyad. There are two forms of this pattern: seller-controlled and buyer-controlled.

2   *Coordinated contact* pattern. Many different departments or individuals have direct personal contacts with departments or individuals on the other side, but there is one department or person, usually a buyer or sales representative, who is involved in and coordinates all these contacts. There are three forms of this pattern: seller-coordinated, buyer-coordinated and jointly coordinated.

3   *Stratified contact* pattern, where individuals and departments on both sides of the dyad manage their own contacts with their equivalents on the other side of the dyad.

These established patterns are breaking down under the influence of new technologies. Now it is possible to have many-to-many communications between contacts on the buyer's and seller's sides, enabled by Web technologies. The coordination of these contacts is one of the features of CRM application software. Modern customer communication requires the use of multi-channel consolidation infrastructures if all types of communication are to be consolidated into a single record of inter-organizational contact.

KEY ACCOUNT MANAGEMENT

Many B2B companies have adopted a market-based customer management structure variously called key account management, national account management, regional account management or global account management. We use the term key account management (KAM) to cover all four forms. KAM is a structure that facilitates the implementation of CRM at the level of the business unit.

A key account is an account that is strategically significant. This normally means that it presently or potentially contributes significantly to the achievement of company objectives, such as profitability. It may also be a high volume account, a benchmark customer, an inspiration or a door opener, as described in Chapter 5.

Companies choose one of two ways to implement KAM. Either a single dedicated person is responsible for managing the relationship, or a team is assigned, as in the Kraft example mentioned earlier. The team membership might be fully dedicated to a single key account, or may work on several accounts. Generally, this is under the leadership of a dedicated account director.

The motivation to adopt a KAM structure comes from recognition of a number of business conditions:

1   *Concentration of buying power* lies in fewer hands. Big companies are becoming bigger. They control a higher share of corporate purchasing. Smaller companies are cooperating to create purchasing power and leverage purchasing economies. Even major competitors are collaborating to secure better inputs. For example, Procter and Gamble and Unilever, rivals on the supermarket shelf, are cooperating to buy raw materials and input goods such as chemicals and packaging.

2   *Globalization.* As companies become global they want to deal with global suppliers, if only for mission-critical purchases. Global companies expect to procure centrally but require goods and services to be provided locally.

3   *Vendor reduction programmes.* Customers are reducing the number of companies they buy from, as they learn to enjoy benefits from improved relationships with fewer vendors.

4   *More demanding customers.* Customers are demanding that suppliers become leaner. This means they eliminate non-value adding activities. They want suppliers to supply exactly what they want. This may mean more reliable, more responsive customer services, and just-in-time delivery.

A supplier may decide that it wants to introduce a KAM system, but it is generally the customer who decides whether to permit this sort of relationship to develop. If customers feel that their needs are better met outside of a KAM-based relationship, they are unlikely to participate in a KAM programme.

According to one study, suppliers are finding considerable benefits in the adoption of KAM.[25]

- Doing large amounts of business with a few customers offers considerable opportunities to improve efficiency and effectiveness, thereby reducing transaction costs.

- Selling at a relationship level can spawn disproportionately high and beneficial volume, turnover and profit.

- Repeat business can be considerably cheaper to win than new business.

- Long-term relationships enable the use of facilitating technologies such as electronic data interchange (EDI) and shared databases.

- Familiarity and trust reduce the need for checking and make it easier to do business.

Although the research suggests major benefits for sellers, the companies that succeed at KAM are those that perform better at a whole range of management activities including selecting strategic customers, growing key accounts and locking out the competition.

> Companies that are most effective at developing strategic customer relationships spend more time and effort thinking about their customers' profiles, direction and future needs than the least effective. . . . [T]hey spend relatively less time and effort considering how their strategic customers will benefit themselves as suppliers.[26]

Concentration of buying power has led to buyers taking charge of relationships. Many companies have supplier accreditation and certification processes in place. To be short-listed as a potential supplier, vendors often have to invest in satisfying these criteria. Buyers increasingly have documented processes that compel vendors to deal with specific members of a decision-making unit at specific times in the buying process. Under these circumstances, sellers may not have the chance to exhibit their exceptional selling capabilities. What they must do, however, is demonstrate their relationship management capabilities.

KAM differs from regular business-to-business account management in a number of important ways. First, the focus is not on margins earned on each individual transaction; rather, the emphasis is on building a mutually valuable long-term relationship. The effect of this is that a more trusting, cooperative, non-adversarial relationship develops. Second, key account plans are more strategic. They look forward five or more years. Non-key accounts are subjected to mere tactical campaigning designed to lift sales in the short term. Third, the KAM (team) is in continuous contact, very often across several functions and at multiple levels of hierarchy. Special access is often provided to customer senior management. Contact with non-key accounts tends to be less frequent and less layered. Fourth, suppliers make investments in key accounts that serve as structural bonds. Indeed, even the allocation of a dedicated key account manager or team represents an investment in the customer. Additionally, suppliers are much more likely to adapt elements of their value proposition such as products, inventory levels, price, service levels and processes for key accounts. Some additional elements might be added to the value proposition for key accounts. This might include vendor-managed inventory, joint production planning, staff training and assistance with the customer's product development and marketing strategies.

KAM can be considered a form of investment management, where the manager makes decisions about which accounts merit most investment, and what forms that investment should take.

Researchers have made efforts to understand how KAM develops over time.[27] Figure 13.4 shows KAM developing through several stages as suppliers and customers become more closely aligned. As the relationship becomes more collaborative, and as the level of involvement between the two parties grows, the commitment to more advanced forms of KAM grows.

In the pre-KAM stage, a prospective key account – one that shows signs of being strategically significant – has been identified. In the early KAM stage, the new supplier has won a small share of customer spend and is on trial. The early KAM structure often takes the form of a bow-tie (Figure 13.5), in which the only contact is between single representatives

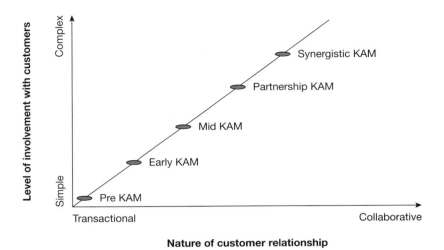

Figure 13.4 A model of KAM development

of each company, typically account manager and buyer. These contacts act as gatekeepers, liaising with their own colleagues as needed.

The bow tie is a very fragile arrangement. If either individual does not get on well with the other, the relationship might not evolve. If either moves on or retires, the relationship may dissolve. The ability of the supplier company to understand the customer depends on the skills of one person alone. If that person does not record what is known in a shared customer database, it might be lost for ever.

As it becomes clearer that the relationship is paying off for both parties, they develop stronger bonds. The supplier becomes a preferred, though not sole supplier. There are other, more senior, contacts between the organizations. As the relationship heads towards partnership KAM status, the relationship becomes more established. The customer views the supplier as a strategic resource. Information is shared to enable the parties to resolve problems jointly. Customers might invite suppliers to go 'open-book' so that cost structures are transparent. Pricing is stable and determined by the tenure and value of the relationship. Innovations are offered to key accounts first before being introduced to other customers. There is functional alignment, as specialists talk to their counterparts on the other side. There is much more contact between the companies at every level. The job of the key account manager is to coordinate all these contacts to ensure that the account objectives are achieved.

The most advanced form of KAM, identified as synergistic KAM, occurs when a symbiotic relationship has developed. As Figure 13.6 suggests, the boundaries between the two organizations are blurred as both sides share resources such as data and people to work on mutually valued projects. These might be cost-reduction projects, new product development projects, quality assurance projects or other ventures beyond the scope of their present relationship.

This developmental model does not mean to suggest that all KAM arrangements migrate along the pathway towards synergistic KAM. KAM will only advance as far as the parties want. If either party finds they are not benefiting from the arrangement, it can be reversed and

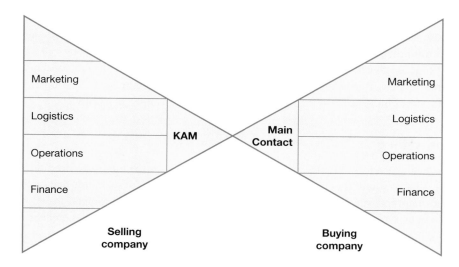

Figure 13.5 Bow-tie structure for early KAM[28]

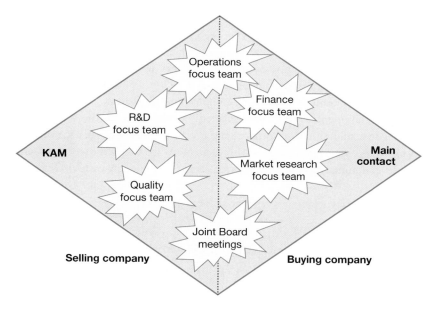

Figure 13.6 Virtual organization for synergistic KAM[29]

become more transactional. Key account status might be withdrawn if the customer ceases being strategically significant, purchases from a major competitor of the current supplier, becomes financially unstable, displays unethical behaviours or demands too many concessions, making the relationship unprofitable.

There are also situations that can lead to relationship dissolution. This might happen if the customer finds that the supplier has acted opportunistically, thereby breaking trust. Opportunistic behaviours might include ramping up price, betraying confidences to third parties, supplying the customer's major competitors or artificially restricting supply. Suppliers can also 'sack' customers, for example, when it is clear that there is no prospect of making a profit from the relationship even if it were to be re-engineered to reduce cost.

Progress along the KAM pathway may also be limited by either party's relationships with other companies. It may be impossible for a vending machine company to develop a strong relationship with PepsiCo, if it already has a strong relationship with Coca-Cola.

Team selling

Team selling is a form of selling that is often associated with the more advanced forms of KAM. A key account team is assembled that consists of a number of specialists that can sense and respond to customer concerns over a variety of issues. The team might, for example, include people from engineering, logistics, research and development, and sales. Collaborative team selling may even cross organizational boundaries. Representatives from two or more partnering organizations can come together to pitch for new business or service an established customer. Partner relationship management systems facilitate such arrangements by making customer, project and product information available to all partners.

These teams may be thought of as a multi-person selling centre, in much the same way that the customer has a multi-person buying centre, or decision-making unit. The selling centre might have a fixed composition throughout the relationship with the customer, though the make-up is more likely to vary. For example, at the beginning of the relationship a 'hunter' might initially win the account. Later a 'farmer' takes over and builds the team to maintain and manage the relationship for mutual benefit.

Major issues for team selling are the composition of the team, coordination of team efforts and measurement of team performance. Coordination can be achieved through conformance to a cultural norm (for example, a focus on customer satisfaction, or mutual benefit), formal rules and plans, deference to hierarchical direction, improved communication facilitated by committee meetings or IT. Intranets can be especially useful in this respect.

SUMMARY

CRM should not be planned and managed as an IT project; management focus should be on the benefits, not the technology. The way most companies assess investments through discounted cash flow analysis does not align well with how CRM benefits are realized. CRM benefits are both immediate (mostly operational) and latent; the latter can only develop once the initial CRM investments have paid off in the development of appropriate customer assets and relationship capabilities. The business case must somehow identify the potential for such latent benefits, emanating from the learning that occurs initially. Real options pricing provides a useful model for presenting the business case, given that latent benefits can only be realized if the company learns from the short-term experiences with CRM. Once the case is made, the organization must identify and plan the realization of CRM benefits and the Benefits Dependency Network is suggested as a tool for accomplishing that. The BDN will suggest organizational changes required that facilitate the realization of benefits. Often, organizations implementing CRM need to either move from product and functional structures to more customer-centric ones. In the business-to-business environment this may mean the development of Key Account Management.

NOTES AND REFERENCES

1   Copeland, T. and Weston, J. (1998). *Financial theory and corporate policy*. Reading, MA: Addison-Wesley.

2   Maklan, S., Knox, S. and Ryals, L. (2005). Using real options to help build the business case for CRM investment. *Long Range Planning*, 38(4), 393–410.

3   Morgan, N.A., Slotegraaf, R.J. and Vorhies, D.W. (2009). Linking marketing capabilities with profit growth. *International Journal of Research in Marketing*, 26(4), 284–93.

4   Vorhies, D.W., Orr, L.M. and Bush, V.D. (2010). Improving customer-focused marketing capabilities and firm financial performance via marketing exploration and exploitation. *Journal of the Academy of Marketing Science*, 39(5), 736–56.

5   Orr, L.M., Bush, V.D. and Vorhies, D.W. (2011). Leveraging firm-level marketing capabilities with marketing employee development. *Journal of Business Research*, 64(10), 1074–81.

6   Ernst, H., Hoyer, W.D., Krafft, M. and Krieger, K. (2010). Customer relationship management and company performance – the mediating role of new product performance. *Journal of the Academy of Marketing Science*, 39(2), 290–306.

7   Homburg, C., Grozdanovic, M. and Klarmann, M. (2007). Responsiveness to customers and competitors: the role of affective and cognitive organizational systems. *Journal of Marketing*, 71, 18–38; and Jayachandran, S., Hewett, K. and Kaufman, P. (2004). Customer response capability in a sense-and-respond era: the role of customer knowledge process. *Journal of the Academy of Marketing Science*, 32(3), 219–33.

8   Hitt, L. and Brynjoifsson, E. (1996). Productivity, business profitability, and consumer surplus: three different measures of information technology value. *MIS Quarterly*, June, 121–42.

9   Peppard, J., Ward, J. and Daniel, E. (2007). Managing the realization of business benefits from IT investments. *MIS Quarterly Executive*, 6(1), 1–17.

10 Peppard, J. and Ward, J. (2005). Unlocking sustained business value from IT investments. *California Management Review*, 48(1), 52–70.

11 Goh, K.H. and Kauffman, R. (2005). Towards a theory of value latency for IT investments. In *Proceedings of the 38th Annual Hawaii International Conference on System Sciences*. IEEE Computer Society, Washington, DC, pp. 1–9.

12 Devaraj, S. and Kohli, R. (2000). Information technology payoff in the health-care industry: a longitudinal study. *Journal of Management Information Systems*, 16(4), 41–67.

13 Braun, J., Mohan, K. and Ahlemann, F. (2010). How benefits from IS/IT investments are successfully realized: the role of business process know how and benefits management practice. In *ICIS 2010 Proceedings*. St Louis, pp. 1–13.

14 Damodaran, A. (1966). *Investment valuation*. New York: John Wiley.

15 Maklan, S., Knox, S. and Ryals, L. (2005). Using real options to help build the business case for CRM investment. *Long Range Planning*, 38(4), 393–410.

16 Professor J. Peppard, Cranfield School of Management. Used with permission.

17 Chandler, Jr, A.D. (1962). *Strategy and structure: concepts in the history of the industrial enterprise.* Casender, MA: MIT Press.

18 Martinsons, A.G.B and Martinsons, M.G. (1994). In search of structural excellence. *Leadership and Organization Development Journal,* 15(2), 24–8.

19 George, M., Freeling, A. and Court, D. (1994). Reinventing the marketing organization. *McKinsey Quarterly,* No. 4.

20 Whisler, T.L. (1970). *The impact of computers on organizations.* New York: Praeger.

21 www.pwc.com/en_US/us/financial-services/publications/viewpoints/assets/pwc-reinventing-banking-branch-network.pdf (Accessed 22 April 2014)

22 Brown, J.R. and Goolsbee, A. (2002). Does the Internet make markets more competitive? Evidence from the life insurance industry. *Journal of Political Economy,* 110(5), 481–507.

23 Cunningham, M.T. and Homse, E. (1986). Controlling the marketing–purchasing interface: resource development and organisational implications. *Industrial Marketing and Purchasing,* 1(2), 3–27.

24 Cunningham, M.T. and Homse, E. (1986). Controlling the marketing–purchasing interface: resource development and organisational implications. *Industrial Marketing and Purchasing,* 1(2), 3–27.

25 Policy Publications (1998). *Developing strategic customers and key accounts.* Bedford: Policy Publications (author, John Hurcombe).

26 Quotation attributed to John Hurcombe (author of *Developing strategic customers and key accounts.* Bedford: Policy Publications) in a press release.

27 Millman, A.F and Wilson, K.J. (1995). From key account selling to key account management. *Journal of Marketing Science,* 1(1), 8–21; Macdonald, M. and Rogers, B. (1996). *Key account management.* Oxford: Butterworth-Heinemann.

28 Millman, A.F and Wilson, K.J. (1995). From key account selling to key account management. *Journal of Marketing Science,* 1(1), 8–21; Macdonald, M. and Rogers, B. (1996). *Key account management.* Oxford: Butterworth-Heinemann.

29 Millman, A.F and Wilson, K.J. (1995). From key account selling to key account management. *Journal of Marketing Science,* 1(1), 8–21; Macdonald, M. and Rogers, B. (1996). *Key account management.* Oxford: Butterworth-Heinemann.

CHAPTER 14

IMPLEMENTING CRM

CHAPTER OBJECTIVES

By the end of this chapter you will be aware of:

- Five major phases in a CRM implementation.
- A number of tools and processes that can be applied in each phase of a CRM implementation.
- The importance of project management and change management throughout the implementation process.

INTRODUCTION

A focus on benefits and the appropriate organization structure with which to deliver them are necessary but not sufficient for CRM success. Also required is an effective project/ programme management plan for CRM implementation. In our experience, marketers are not often skilled programme managers; marketing expertise is based upon customer and competitor insight, co-creating innovative offers with partners and customers and communicating effectively with customers, not on managing organizational change. Change management is a very complex phenomenon that requires specialist expertise. It is not possible to cover this topic fully in one chapter; here, we highlight some aspects you will wish to consider when ready to implement CRM, so that you might seek out appropriate resources and advice to help you succeed.

We also note CRM professionals often distinguish between projects and programmes, with the latter being larger scale, more systemic changes. Given that readers of this book may be working across programmes and projects of varying complexity and change, we use the terms interchangeably.

In this chapter, we will look at the five major phases of a CRM implementation, and the processes and tools that can be used within those phases to ensure that CRM projects deliver what is expected of them.[1] Depending on the scope of the project some of these phases, processes and tools may not be required. The key phases are shown in Figure 14.1.

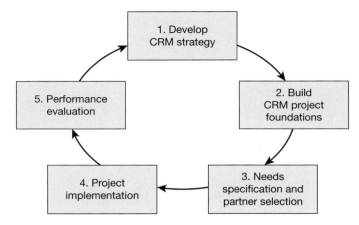

Figure 14.1 The five-step implementation process

1 *Develop the CRM strategy*

- situation analysis
- commence CRM education
- develop the CRM vision
- set priorities
- establish goals and objectives
- identify contingencies, resources and people changes
- agree the business case with the Board.

2 *Build CRM project foundations*

- establish governance structures
- identify change management needs
- identify project or programme management needs
- identify critical success factors
- develop risk management plan.

3 *Needs specification and partner selection*

- process engineering
- data review and gap analysis
- initial technology needs specification and research alternative solutions
- write request for proposals (RFP)
- call for proposals
- revised technology needs identification
- assessment and partner selection.

4 *Project implementation*

- refine project plan
- identify technology customization needs
- prototype design, test, modify and roll out.

5   *Performance evaluation*

- project outcomes
- business outcomes.

PHASE 1: DEVELOP THE CRM STRATEGY

CRM strategy can be defined as follows:

> **CRM strategy is a high level plan of action that aligns people, processes and technology to achieve customer-related goals.**

Situation analysis

Typically, a CRM programme starts in response to changes in the organization's customer strategy. It helps to have an organizing framework to guide your analysis. The comprehensive models of CRM that are described in Chapter 1 might be helpful. Another useful framework is the Customer Strategy Cube. This is a three-dimensional analysis of your company's served market segments, market offerings and channels (routes-to-market). The situation analysis answers the questions, 'Where are we now?' and 'Why are we where we are?' in terms of the three dimensions of the cube.

Figure 14.2 illustrates the customer strategy cube of a company that sells four different offerings to five different market segments through three different channels. Each block in this cube – there are 60 (5 × 4 × 3) of them – might be a potential business unit that would be subject to a situation analysis. In fact, most businesses do not operate in all potential blocks of their customer strategy cube. They operate selectively. For example, AMP sells financial

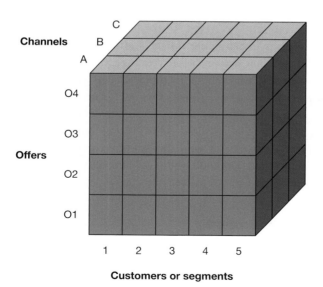

Figure 14.2 Customer strategy cube

products through a network of independent and tied financial planners. They do not sell direct-to-consumer. Not all offerings are sold to all market segments through all channels.

The situation analysis examines the three dimensions of the customer strategy cube independently and jointly. Questions such as the following are asked:

- *Customers or segments*: Which segments do we target? Which segments do we serve? What are our customer-related marketing and sales objectives? How much do we sell to customers? How satisfied are they? What is our market share? What is our share of customer spending? How effective are our customer acquisition strategies and tactics? How effective are our customer retention strategies and tactics? How effective are our customer development (cross-sell and up-sell) strategies and tactics? What are the customer touchpoints? What do our customers think about their experience of doing business with us? Which customer management processes have most impact on our costs or customer experience? Which technologies do we use to support our marketing, selling and service functions, and how well do they operate?

- *Market offerings*: Which products do we offer? What is our branding strategy? How well known are our offerings? Who do we compete against? What advantages or disadvantages do we offer vis-à-vis competitors? How do we augment and add value to our basic product offer? What benefits do customers experience from our offerings? How do our prices compare with competitors? What are our margins?

- *Channels*: Which channels do we use to distribute to our customers – direct and indirect? Which channels are most effective? What level of channel penetration do we have? Which channels are becoming more/less important? Where do our competitors distribute? What do channel partners think of their experience of doing business with us? What margins do channel members earn? Which channel management processes have most impact on our costs or channel member experience? How are our channels integrated to provide a seamless customer experience?

The goal of this audit is to get a clear insight into the strengths and weaknesses of the company's current customer strategy before creating a CRM vision. Data can be collected from executives, managers, customer-contact people, channel partners and, most importantly, customers. Business plans can be studied. One of the outcomes might be a customer interaction map, as in Figure 14.3, that identifies all customer touchpoints and the processes that are performed at those touchpoints. Normally, the interactions that have important impact on customer experience or your own costs become primary candidates for re-engineering and automation. The audit will serve as the start point for thinking about what you want to achieve from a CRM implementation.

Commence CRM education

CRM, as you have read in Chapter 1, is a term that means different things to different people. It is important that all stakeholders have a clear understanding of what CRM denotes. Your IT people might think that it is a technology project, marketers may think it is campaign management and salespeople may think it is a customer contact database. Sales management

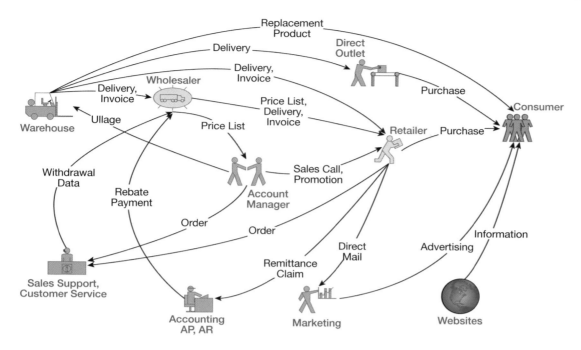

Figure 14.3 Customer interaction map

may think of CRM as enabling management of the sales pipeline, whilst service management may see CRM principally as a means of reducing cost. This is not problematic if the organization's CRM vision (see next section) is merely a collection of independent point solutions; however, if the firm is giving CRM more strategic consideration, the implications across the organization need to be understood by everyone and agreed.

Develop the CRM vision

Your CRM vision is a high-level statement of how CRM will change the way the business relates to its customers. The vision addresses the need for change and articulates a destination. Examples of CRM visions are:

- We will work with our members in a trust-based relationship to represent their interests, and to satisfy their needs for high value, security and peace of mind in motoring, travel and home.[2]
- We will build and maintain long-term relationships with valuable customers by creating personalized experiences across all touchpoints and by anticipating customer needs and providing customized offers.
- To be able to see all information in one place.[3]

The CRM vision gives shape and direction to CRM strategy. The CRM vision might be senior management's perspective based on what they learned from the education process, or it could be the product of a wider visioning process that engages more members of the company, and perhaps even customers and partners. The vision will eventually guide the development of measurable CRM outcomes.

Set priorities

CRM projects vary in their scope, and can touch on one or more customer-facing parts of your business – sales, marketing and service. Clear priorities for action, normally focused on cost reduction or enhanced customer experience, might fall out of the situation analysis, but more time and debate is often necessary. Priority might be given to projects that produce quick wins or are low cost. Longer-term priorities might prove more difficult to implement. For example, you may want to prioritize a new segment of customers based on their potential profitability. An impediment to that outcome would be your company's inability to trace costs of selling, marketing and service to customers. You may therefore need to prioritize the implementation of an activity-based costing system before performing the new segmentation.

Establish benefits expected – the goals and objectives

Goals and objectives emerge from the visioning and prioritizing processes. Although the terms 'goals' and 'objectives' tend to be used synonymously, we use the 'goal' to refer to a qualitative outcome and 'objective' to refer to a measurable outcome. For example, a CRM goal might be to acquire new customers. A related CRM objective would be to generate 200 additional qualified leads by Q4 of the next financial year.

As shown in Table 14.1, CRM goals generally cluster around three broad themes: enhancing customer satisfaction or loyalty, growing revenues or reducing costs. CRM strategies often pursue several goals simultaneously, for example increasing customer retention and reducing customer service costs.

Table 14.1 Strategic goals for CRM

Customer loyalty/satisfaction	Revenue growth	Cost reduction
Increase customer satisfaction	Increase sales revenues	Reduce cost of sales
Increase customer retention	Enhance cross-sell and up-sell opportunities	Reduce customer service costs
Increase customer loyalty	Increase customer profitability	Reduce marketing costs
Increase partner loyalty	Acquire new customers	Increase margins
	Increase marketing campaign response	
	Improve lead numbers and quality	

Identify contingencies, resources and people changes

The next step is to build a Benefits Dependency Network (BDN) around the goals. The BDN concept was explained in Chapter 13. The process of thinking about the business changes required in order to achieve the CRM goals is hugely important and ensures that the organization is aware of the scope of change required. Too often, CRM is seen as a marketing (or worse, an IT) project and a 'let them get on with it' attitude prevails. As the programme unfolds, customer managers will start demanding resources and changes to business processes. It is much better to have these matters aired and agreed before spending large amounts on CRM, only to find out that the organization is unable, or unwilling, to develop the complementary capabilities and resources needed to make CRM work.

This step will also ensure that you identify the people, process, organization changes and technology requirements for the goals and objectives to be achieved. You will return to these matters repeatedly as the project unfolds, but at this stage you need a general idea of the changes that are necessary, so that you can begin to identify costs, investments and timescales that form part of the business plan.

Agree the business case with the Board

Whilst we discussed the business case in Chapter 13, it is worth reprising it here. The business case is built around the costs and benefits (identifiable and latent) of CRM and answers the question: 'Why should we invest in this CRM project?'

The business case looks at both costs and revenues. CRM implementations can generate additional revenues in a number of ways. We break these out into benefits that are more likely to be immediately achievable and those that are latent; that is, they become apparent after the organization has developed complementary CRM assets and capabilities.

The costs of a CRM project extend well beyond the costs of CRM software. Additional costs might be incurred from systems integration, infrastructure costs, new desktop, laptop or handheld devices, software configuration, data modelling, beta-testing, helpdesk support,

Table 14.2 Immediate and latent benefits from CRM

Immediate benefits	Latent benefits
• More sales leads	• Unspecified new products and services arising from enhanced insight
• More revenues from cross-selling and up-selling	• Stronger customer partnerships
• Better margins (yield management)	Increased customer satisfaction delivering higher loyalty, willingness to pay and reduced costs-to-serve
• Lower cost-of-sales	• Realignment of assets to meet customer needs better
• Increased retention and recommendation	
• Lower cost of customer acquisition	

change management, project management, process re-engineering, software upgrades, training and consultancy services, let alone the opportunity costs of diverting your own staff members from their routine work. For a simple CRM project IT costs may represent one-quarter of total project costs; for a complex project IT costs may be as low as one-tenth of total project costs.

Some business cases are able to ignore technology costs. Many companies using enterprise software are already paying for CRM modules in their inclusive licence fees. A licensed SAP-user, for example, might be using enterprise software for back-office functions only. However, the licence fee permits the company to use the enterprise suite's CRM modules. No additional licence costs are incurred. Other companies that elect to deploy CRM through the SaaS approach, rather than installing software on their own hardware, treat CRM software as an operating expense. They simply treat software costs, based on a per-user monthly fee, as an operational expense that can be allocated to marketing, sales or service budgets.

Many of these costs and benefits are measurable, but there are also likely to be some important latent or strategic benefits that are much harder to value, for example development of a customer-centric way of doing business, better customer experience, improved responsiveness to changes in the market or competitive environments, more information sharing between business silos, more harmonious relationships with customers and the development of an information-based competitive advantage.

PHASE 2: BUILD CRM PROJECT FOUNDATIONS

Having created the CRM strategy, BDN and business case the next phase involves building the foundations for the CRM implementation.

Establish governance structures

CRM projects are designed and implemented by people. Governance structures (see Figure 14.4) need to be put in place to ensure that project roles and responsibilities are properly defined and allocated.

The Programme Director (PD) plays an important role in this structure. Ultimately, the PD has responsibility for ensuring that the project deliverables are achieved, and that project costs are controlled. The PD in larger projects is a full-time appointment. The PD has a boundary-spanning role – one foot is in the CRM Steering Committee, the other is in the Programme Team. Another key member of the Steering Committee is the executive sponsor. This is typically a Board-level senior executive who commits real time to the project and ensures that resources are made available. The Steering Committee makes policy decisions about the CRM implementation – for example, which technology to buy, which consultants to hire – and ensures that the implementation stays on track and within budget. Other senior executives may sit on the Steering Committee to ensure that the project remains business-focused and does not slide into being an IT-dominated project. The Programme Team is composed of representatives from the major stakeholders. They have the responsibility for implementing the project successfully. The stakeholder representatives may have their own advisory groups that ensure that stakeholder needs and concerns are known and brought to

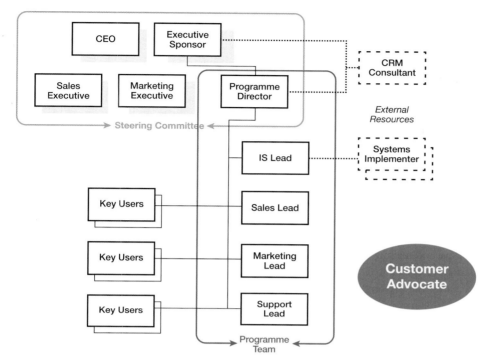

Figure 14.4 Governance structure[4]

the Programme Team. CRM implementations can impose considerable demands on a company's own internal IT resources which might be called on to perform several project-related roles. The lead developer role ensures that the CRM software is customized to meet the needs of users. The database developer role ensures that customer-related data held in disparate databases are made available to end-users in the form required for operational and analytical CRM applications. The front-end developer role ensures that the user interface is easy to understand and use.

It is not uncommon for CRM projects to import resources and talents to help deliver the project. This governance structure shows a CRM consultant working with the Steering Committee. It is unlikely that an in-house Steering Committee has sufficient experience of CRM project implementations. An experienced consultant can help the Steering Committee overcome problems as the project progresses. A systems implementer is also shown in this governance structure as an important external resource. For an installed CRM system, vendors generally supply technical help to ensure that the system is properly implemented. The implementer has a boundary-spanning role, being an employee of the vendor but working on site as the client's advocate.

A systems integrator may also be needed to align disparate systems into a coherent whole to support the project objectives. Systems integration can be defined as follows:

> **Systems integration is the practice of aligning and combining system components such as people, processes, technology and data for the achievement of defined outcomes.**

Very often, desired CRM outcomes are impeded by the poor interoperability of IT systems. For example, the IT system that supports Web operations may be incompatible with the IT system that supports the call centre. The result is that there may be two different databases containing important customer-related information. A systems integrator might be needed to programme the interface that links the two systems.

Finally, the governance chart shows that the voice-of-the-customer has to be heard in the project team. Customers of companies that implement CRM are important stakeholders, because their experience of doing business will change. Some CRM projects fail to deliver optimal outcomes because the project team fails to ask, 'What would the customer think?'

Identify change management needs

Even small CRM projects can prove challenging in terms of change management. A sales force automation project might involve centralizing data that are presently kept on individual reps' laptops, and making that information available to all in the team. Reps will have to learn to share. In a distributed sales force, these reps may have not even met each other. If they have to change their selling methodology, record keeping and reporting habits as well, there just might be some worry, if not outright resistance.

According to consultants Booz Allen & Hamilton, 'Leadership teams that fail to plan for the human side of change often find themselves wondering why their best-laid plans go awry.'[5] They describe change both in terms of top-down leadership and bottom-up buy-in, as does John Kotter whose eight-step approach to managing change is widely cited and deployed.[6] The eight steps are as follows:

1   Create a sense of urgency so that people begin to feel 'we must do something'.
2   Put together a guiding team to drive the change effort (this is the governance structure described above).
3   Get the vision right, and build supporting strategies.
4   Communicate for buy-in.
5   Empower action by removing organizational barriers to change.
6   Produce short-term wins to diffuse cynicism, pessimism and skepticism.
7   Don't let up, but keep driving change and promoting the vision.
8   Make change stick by reshaping organizational culture.

Kotter emphasizes that successful change management programmes adopt a see–feel–change approach. To bring about change it is necessary not only to get people to see the need for change, but also to feel so emotionally engaged that they want to change. He stresses the importance of emotional engagement with the programme's vision and strategies.

Organizational culture

The concept and composition of organizational culture is hotly contested. Organizational culture is a well-researched and complex phenomenon, and it is not possible to do it full justice in a section of a chapter in a book on CRM. However, with CRM project failure rates reported at high levels,[7] CRM leaders must be sensitive to the 'culture' in which they wish to implement CRM. We outline some aspects that we believe are important for project managers to understand.

In everyday language, organizational culture is what is being described when someone answers the question 'What is it like working here?' More formally, organizational culture can be defined as

A pattern of shared values and beliefs that help individuals understand organizational functioning and thus provide them with the norms for behavior in the organization.[8]

Essentially, organizational culture comprises widely shared and strongly held values. These values are reflected in patterns of individual and interpersonal behaviour, including the behaviour of the business leaders, and expressed in the norms, symbols, rituals and formal systems of the organization.

A number of studies indicate that organizational culture affects business performance.[9] Recent research has also shown that organizational culture is a predictor of CRM success.[10] Adhocracy, one of four organizational cultures identified in the Competing Values model (Figure 14.5), shows the strongest association with CRM success. Adhocracies are highly flexible, entrepreneurial, externally oriented organizations. Their core values are creativity and risk-taking.

Cameron and Quinn have developed a process for companies wishing to change their culture as indicated by the Competing Values model.[11] They suggest that cultural change may involve adjustment to the organization's structure, symbols, systems, staff, strategy, style of leaders and skills of managers, but emphasize that individual behavioural change is the key to culture change.

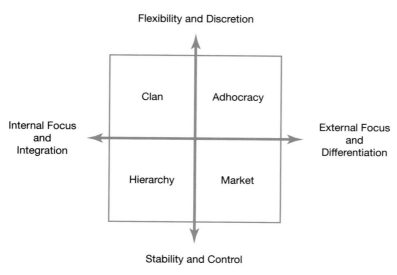

Figure 14.5 The Competing Values model of organizational culture[12]

Buy-in

As noted by John Kotter, buy-in operates at an emotional or intellectual (rational) level. Intellectual buy-in is where people know what has to be changed and understand the justification for the change. New technologies are adopted more quickly when users believe that the system will be easy to use. Emotional buy-in is where there is genuine heartfelt enthusiasm, even excitement, about the change. The matrix in Figure 14.6 shows the possibility of four employee segments, reflecting the presence or absence of emotional and rational buy-in. Champions are emotionally and rationally committed. Weak links are neither emotionally nor rationally committed. Bystanders understand the changes being introduced, but feel no emotional buy-in to the change. Loose cannons are fired up with enthusiasm but really do not understand what they have to do to contribute to the change. All these segments will be found in major change projects such as a CRM implementation.

The CRM project's vision and goals need to be accepted by each of these groups in different ways. The Programme Team's challenges are to encourage bystanders to become passionate about the project's goals, and to educate loose cannons on the reasoning behind CRM. Weak links can be truly problematic if they are in customer-facing roles or impact on customer experience. It has been said that it takes many years to win a customer's confidence and trust, but only one incident to break it. If efforts to win them over fail, weak links may need to be reassigned to jobs where there is no customer impact.

Identify project or programme management needs

CRM implementations can place considerable demands on project management skills and CRM project leaders need to understand their organization's capacity to manage complex change projects successfully.

The CRM project plan spells out the steps that will get you from where you are now (customer strategy situation analysis) to where you want to be (CRM vision, benefits, goals and objectives), on time and within budget. The CRM programme director generally performs the project management role, but sometimes it is outsourced to a consultant. A project plan

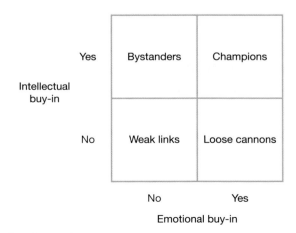

Figure 14.6 The buy-in matrix

Figure 14.7 CRM project Gantt chart[13]

sets out the tasks to be performed, the order in which they are to be performed, the time each will take, the resources required to perform the tasks (including people and money) and the deliverables from each task. Tools such as Gantt charts, Critical Path Analysis (CPA), Programme Evaluation and Review Technique (PERT) or network diagrams are useful tools for project managers. Some tasks will be performed in parallel, some in sequence. As the project rolls forward there will be periodic 'milestone' reviews to ensure that it is on time and on budget. A CRM project that has the goal of improving the productivity of marketing campaigns might be made up of a number of tasks or mini-projects, each with its own deliverable and time-line, including the following: market segmentation project, database development project, creation of a new campaign management process, management reports project, technology search and selection project, and a user training project.

Identify critical success factors

Critical success factors (CSFs) are the 'must haves' that underpin project success. Critical success factors can be defined as follows:

> **CSFs are attributes and variables that can significantly impact business outcomes.**

CRM consultants and vendors offer a range of opinions on CSFs, mentioning the following: a clear customer strategy that defines your company's offers, markets and channels; an organizational culture that promotes coordination and information-sharing across business units; an agreed definition of what counts as CRM success; executive sponsorship of the CRM programme's objectives; availability and use of pertinent, accurate, timely and usable customer-related information; a clear focus on people and process issues, not only technology; starting small with quick wins that are then promoted within the company as success stories; focus on automating processes that have major implications for costs or customer experience; and engagement of all stakeholders, including end-users and customers, in programme planning and roll-out.

There have been very few independent studies of CRM CSFs. Da Silva and Rahimi[14] conducted a single CRM case-study test of three CSF models that had originally been developed in the context of Enterprise Resource Planning (ERP) implementations. They found that CRM CSFs could be categorized as strategic and tactical. Strategic CSFs are encountered at the beginning of the project, while tactical CSFs become important later. Strategic CSFs include a clear CRM philosophy (we prefer the term 'vision'), top management commitment and project management expertise. Tactical CSFs include troubleshooting skills, good communications and software configuration.

Croteau and Li conducted an empirical assessment of CRM CSFs in 57 large Canadian organizations.[15] Focusing only on the technology element – therefore ignoring people and process issues – they conclude that the CSF most strongly associated with CRM success is an accurate and well-developed knowledge management system. This has to be supported by a suitable IT infrastructure which can capture, manage and deliver real-time customer, product and service information in order to improve customer response and decision making at all customer touchpoints. They also found that another important CSF is top management support.

Luis Mendoza and his colleagues conducted a qualitative study of CSFs that involved a panel of eight expert judges identifying 13 CSFs and 55 associated metrics covering people,

Table 14.3 Critical success factors for successful CRM strategies

Critical success factor		People	Process	Technology
1	**Senior management commitment**	X		
2	Creation of a multidisciplinary team	X	X	
3	Objectives definition	X		
4	Interdepartmental integration	X	X	
5	Communication of the CRM strategy to staff	X	X	
6	Staff commitment	X		
7	**Customer information management**			X
8	Customer service		X	X
9	Sales automation		X	X
10	**Marketing automation**		X	X
11	**Support for operational management**	X	X	X
12	Customer contact management	X		X
13	Information systems integration			X

Note: More important CSFs are **bold** typeface.

process and technology aspects of CRM strategy.[16] The CSFs and their alignment with people, process and technology appear in Table 14.3, the most important being highlighted in bold.

Develop risk management plan

Research suggests that a large number of CRM projects, perhaps as many as half or even two-thirds, fail.[17] Of course, there can be many potential causes of failure, ranging from outrageously ambitious objectives, through inadequate project management to resistance of end-users to the adoption of new technologies. At this step of the CRM implementation process, you will be trying to identify the major risks to achieving the desired outcomes. Once identified, you can begin to put risk-mitigation strategies and contingency plans in place. As you would expect, some risks reflect an absence of the CSFs identified above. Gartner Inc. names a number of common causes of CRM failure: management that has little customer understanding or involvement; rewards and incentives that are tied to old, non-customer objectives; organizational culture that is not customer-focused; limited or no input from customers; thinking that technology is the solution; lack of specifically designed, mutually reinforcing processes; poor-quality customer data; little coordination between departmental initiatives and projects; creation of the CRM team happens last, and the team is composed of IT people, but lacks business staff; no measures or monitoring of benefits, and lack of testing.[18]

Risk-mitigation strategies are your responses to these risks. Let's take the risk of management having little or no customer understanding. How might you respond to this? There are a number of things you could do – management could work in the front-line serving customers (executives at McDonald's do this), listen in to call centre interactions for at least one hour a week, or mystery shop your own and competitor organizations.

PHASE 3: NEEDS SPECIFICATION AND PARTNER SELECTION

Having built the CRM project foundations, the next phase involves specifying needs and selecting suitable partners.

Process engineering

The first task of phase 3 is to identify business processes that need attention – making them more effective or efficient, or flagging them as candidates for automation.

Business processes can be defined as follows:

> **A business process is a set of activities performed by people and/or technology in order to achieve a desired outcome. Business processes have a defined start and end point.**

Put more simply, business processes are how activities are performed by the company. Processes can be classified in several ways: vertical and horizontal; front office and back office; primary and secondary.

- *Vertical* processes are those that are located entirely within a business function. For example, the customer acquisition process might reside totally within the marketing department. *Horizontal* processes are cross-functional. New product development processes are typically horizontal and involve sales, marketing, finance and research and development groups.

- *Front-office* (or front-stage) processes are those that customers encounter. The complaints-handling process is an example. *Back-office* (or back-stage) processes are invisible to customers, for example the procurement process. Many processes straddle both front and back offices. The order-fulfilment process is an example: the order-taking part of the process is in the front office; the production scheduling part is back office.

A distinction is also made between primary and secondary processes. *Primary* processes have major cost implications for companies or, given their impact on customer experience, major revenue implications. The logistics process in courier organizations – from picking up a package through moving the package to delivering the package – constitutes about 90 per cent of the cost base of the business, and is therefore a primary process. Customers may have a different perspective on what is important. They typically do not care about back-office processes. They care about the processes they touch. In the insurance industry these are the claims process, the policy renewal process and the new policy purchase process. In the courier business they are the pick up, delivery and tracking processes.

Secondary processes have minor implications for costs or revenues, or little impact on customer experience.

Strategic CRM aims to build an organization that is designed to create and deliver customer value and experience consistently better than competitors to targeted customers. Designing processes that create value for customers is clearly vital to this outcome. 3M's customer promise is 'Practical and ingenious solutions that help customers succeed'. It does this in part through new product development processes that are designed to identify good ideas and bring them to the market quickly.[19] For 3M, the innovation process is a primary process that enables the company to differentiate itself from competitors.

Operational CRM involves the automation of the company's selling, marketing and service processes and generally requires the support of analytical CRM. Figure 14.8 shows the campaign management process for a particular customer offer made by First Direct, a UK-based online and telephone bank. It shows that the propensity of a customer to open a high interest savings account is determined by a scoring process that considers both demographic and transactional data. The propensity modelling process is an illustration of analytical CRM. If a target score is reached an offer is made either by the customer service agent during the phone call or at a later time by email. This automation of the selling process is an example of operational CRM.

Flowcharting, which is also known as blueprinting and process mapping, is a tool that can be used to make processes visible. The flowchart sets out the steps involved in performing the process. It may also identify the people (or roles) that contribute to the process, and the standards by which the process is measured, such as time, accuracy or cost. Processes always have customers, who may be either internal or external to a company. Customers receive process outputs. Workflow functionality is embedded into many CRM applications and is

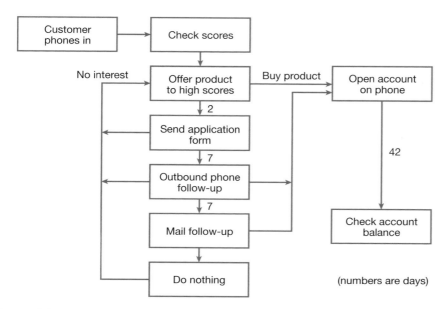

Figure 14.8 Campaign management process for high interest saving account

Table 14.4 Evaluating processes[20]

	Process rating
Best practice (superiority)	The process is substantially defect-free and contributes to CRM performance. Process is superior to comparable competitors' and other benchmarks
Parity	A good process which largely contributes to CRM performance
Stability	An average process which meets expectations with no major problems but which presents opportunities for improvement
Recoverability	The process has identified weaknesses which are being addressed
Criticality	An ineffective and/or inefficient process in need of immediate remedial attention

used for process mapping. Flowcharts can be used to identify fail points where a process frequently breaks down, redundancies and duplications. They can also be used for induction and training of new people, and for illustrating internal customer–supplier relationships.

Processes can be rated according to the degree to which they can be improved. It has been suggested, for example, that processes be rated according to the criteria in Table 14.4.

Data review and gap analysis

Having identified processes for attention, the next step is to review the data requirements for the CRM implementation, and to identify shortfalls.

Strategic CRM uses customer-related data to identify which customers to target for acquisition, retention and development, and what to offer them. Operational CRM uses customer-related data in the everyday running of the business, for example in handling billing queries in the contact centre, or mounting campaigns in the marketing department. Analytical CRM uses customer-related data to answer questions such as: 'Who are our most profitable customers?' and 'Which customers are most likely to churn?' The fundamental issue companies have to ask is: What customer-related data do we need to achieve the CRM programme's goals and objectives?

Members of the Programme Team should be well placed to answer the question 'What information is needed?' For example, the Programme Team's marketing lead would be expected to appreciate the information needs of marketers running event-based campaigns. Typically, these marketers want to know response rates to previous mailings broken down by customer group, the content of those offers, sales achieved by these mailings and the number of items returned unopened. They would also want to know the names and addresses of selected targets, their preferred method of communication (Mail? Email? Phone?), their preferred form of salutation (First name? Mr? Ms?) and what offers have been successful in the past.

At this stage of planning the CRM project, you are identifying the data that are needed for the defined CRM purposes, and creating an inventory of data that are currently available. The gap between what are available and what are needed may be quite significant. A useful distinction can be made between 'need-to-know' and 'like-to-know'; that is, between information *needed* for CRM purposes, and information that *might* be useful at some future point. Given the costs of developing and maintaining customer-related databases, companies need to be rigorous in screening data requirements. Another data review issue is the quality of the available data. It is one thing to have available data; it is another for that data to be of good quality. In general, higher quality data are required for operational CRM applications than for analytical CRM. Operational CRM systems interact with customers. If a customer service agent calls a customer with a gender-specific offer only to find that the expected Mr turns out to be a Ms the offer is almost bound to fail. On the other hand if there are gender errors in the customer record it makes little difference to the prediction of churn.

Initial technology needs specification and research alternative solutions

Earlier in this implementation process, you began to consider technology requirements. Now you can return to this question with a clearer focus on the process and data issues. There are a huge number of software applications that fall under the heading of CRM, many of which we discuss in Chapters 8–12. You now need to decide what applications will deliver your CRM vision and meet the business case requirements. You can learn about these applications by visiting vendor websites, joining online communities, such as www.customerthink.com, or attending physical or virtual (online) exhibitions.

The 'real options' approach to CRM investment that we discussed in Chapter 13 has implications for the decision to build, buy or rent the CRM applications that you choose. Your options are to build your CRM applications from scratch, to buy an on-premise site licence or pay a monthly per-user charge for an on-demand solution. If you opt to build from scratch you may find that some open-source modules provide much or all of what you need.

Open-source software is peer-reviewed software that gives CRM application developers the opportunity to view and evaluate source code. Open source advocates suggest that being able to modify source code leads to improved software with fewer bugs, and that free distribution leads to more developers working to improve the software. The second alternative is to license CRM applications. The final alternative is to pay a monthly per-user fee for an on-demand (hosted) solution.

Hosted or on-premise CRM

As the market for CRM software matures, companies have a choice of excellent products almost all of which are fit for purpose. An important decision is how to access CRM functionality. CRM software is distributed in two ways. It can be installed on your company's own servers or it can be accessed on another party's servers via the Internet. The former is known as on-premise, offline or installed CRM, an option that has been the preferred mode for many large-scale enterprises and early adopters of CRM. The alternative is known as hosted or online CRM, Web-service, the ASP (Application Service Provider) model, or the Software as a Service (SaaS) model.

The hosted option is becoming more popular as CRM solutions are adopted by mid-market and smaller enterprises. Some larger organizations are also opting for online CRM solutions, and many enterprises are using a hybrid mix of hosted and on-premise solutions, which is feasible when the underlying data model is the same.[21] Hosted CRM applications deliver very much the same functionality as their on-premise competitors, including advanced functionality for competitive intelligence, social media integration, pricing, content management, data warehousing, marketing analytics and workflow design.[22]

The choice of delivery model is often determined by consideration of total cost of ownership (TCO). TCO can be computed over different time periods, say one, three and five years. TCO may indicate that hosted is a better solution than on-premise for a small business's sales force automation project for ten sales reps. However, for a large-scale business transformation project with significant changes to business processes in sales, marketing and customer service, on-premise solutions may offer a better TCO. TCO of hosted solutions is largely a matter of the total number of seats (CRM users) using the CRM solution. Hosted solutions offer easy and immediate scalability, substitution of fixed cost with variable cost (lower risk), regular updates to the software's functionality freely provided by the cloud-based supplier, maintenance, user training and online support and, of course, virtually no support costs. TCO for on-premise solutions needs to consider additional costs such as systems integration (integrating the CRM technology with the business's back-office processes, for example), customization, user training, additional IT staff members, additional hardware (such as Web servers), support and periodic application upgrades.

There have been a number of published comparisons of the TCO of hosted versus installed,[23] and they vary in their conclusions. Some suggest the TCO of hosted CRM is superior; others say the TCO of installed CRM is superior, particularly over the longer term. The TCO of hosted versus installed clearly depends on the scope of the CRM project (ten users versus 500 users; point CRM solution versus enterprise-wide CRM deployment) and the timescale over which TCO is computed. Readers are therefore advised to consider their particular circumstances in computing TCO.

The decision to opt for hosted over on-premise, or vice versa, may be significantly dependent on answers to the following questions:

1   Are you willing to commit? Investing big money in a CRM programme and the necessary supporting software only makes sense if you know exactly what you want from it. If your business is unsure what it wants, or simply wants to learn from trial-and-error or experience, hosted solutions may be a better option.

2   Does your company have the in-house IT skill set to install, maintain and support an on-premise solution? The more complex the solution the more demanding it can be on IT resources.

3   Do you need systems integration? The more comprehensive the CRM project, the more likely it will need to integrate with other business technologies. For example, you might want your CRM system to 'talk to' or share data with back-end systems for finance, inventory management and order processing. Currently, on-premise solutions offer the best prospect of successful systems integration. Hosted CRM systems are not integrated with other user company technologies. However, hosted CRM providers are striving to increase their compatibility. Both hosted and on-premise CRM vendors offer pre-integrated functionality such as mapping systems (used by marketers) and global positioning systems (used by sales reps).

4   Is your business stable, growing or contracting? Some installed applications can be difficult and costly to scale up or down, as user numbers grow or contract, or as business cycles change. Hosted solutions do not present that problem.

5   What do you know about the technology partner? Big names like SAP, SAS, IBM and Oracle are likely to be around for the long haul. They provide both installed and hosted CRM solutions. Other hosted solutions brands such as salesforce.com and NetSuite are well established and have good reputations. You may feel you can trust your valuable customer-related data to these names, but not some of the less-established names. When you outsource customer data-storage to a hosted solutions provider, you are also outsourcing data security. You need to consider whether their security standards compare favourably to your own in-house data security.

In addition to the costs of CRM applications, businesses also need to consider hardware issues. What sort of device is best suited to sales, service and marketing users? Perhaps salespeople need a tablet or smart phone for easy portability, whereas the contact centre prefers desktops, and marketing people prefer laptop computers. Table 14.5 offers a comparison of tablet and laptop attributes.

Write request for proposals (RFP)

Before calling for proposals you need to write a detailed RFP. This document becomes the standard against which vendors' proposals are evaluated. It summarizes your thinking about the CRM programme and invites interested parties to respond in a structured way. Typical contents of the RFP include:

Table 14.5 Comparing laptops and tablets[24]

Attribute	Laptop	Tablet
Content	Full	Narrow
Size	XXXX	X
Portability	Moderate	High
Speed of input	Fast	Slow
On-screen legibility	XXXX	X
Stickiness	Moderate	High
Walk and use	No	Yes
Presentations	Excellent	Poor
Replacement cost	High	Moderate
Synchronization	Good	Excellent

1   Instructions to respondents.

2   Company background.

3   The CRM vision and strategy.

4   Strategic, operational and analytical CRM requirements.

5   Process issues:

    a   customer interaction mapping

    b   process re-engineering.

6   Technology issues:

    a   delivery model – SaaS, on-premise, blended

    b   functionality required – sales, marketing and service

    c   management reports required

    d   hardware requirements

    e   architectural issues

    f   systems integration issues

    g   customization issues

    h   upgrades and service requirements

    i   availability of free-trial periods.

7   People issues:

    a   project management services

    b   change management services

    c   management and staff training.

8   Costing issues – TCO targets.

9   Implementation issues – pilot, training, support, roll-out, time-line.

10 Contractual issues.

11 Criteria for assessing proposals.

12 Time-line for responding to proposals.

Call for proposals

The next step is to invite potential partners to respond to the RFP. You will see from the RFP contents that CRM projects sometimes require input from several process, people and technology partners. On the technology side, if your company is already paying for CRM modules as part of its enterprise IT system, you will certainly want to add this technology vendor to the list of those invited to respond. Between three and six potential technology vendors are typically invited.

Revised technology needs identification

Proposals from technology vendors will sometimes identify opportunities for improved CRM performance that you may not have considered. Perhaps there is some functionality or issue that you had not considered. For example, you might not have considered the need to provide implementation support to sales reps in the field. A vendor that indicates that they will be able to help reps learn the new technology in remote locations might be very attractive.

Assessment and partner selection

The next stage is to assess the proposals and select one or more partners. This task is generally performed by the Steering Committee. Assessment is made easier if you have a structured RFP and scoring system. There are two types of scoring system: unweighted and weighted. An unweighted system simply treats each assessment variable as equally important. A weighted system acknowledges that some variables are more important than others. These are accorded more significance in the scoring process. Some criteria, for example the availability of some essential functionality, may be so important that their absence prevents detailed consideration of the rest of the partner's proposal.

PHASE 4: PROJECT IMPLEMENTATION

So far, you have developed the CRM strategy, built the CRM project foundations, specified your needs and selected one or more partners. It is now implementation time!

Refine project plan

The first step of phase 4 requires you to cooperate with your selected partners in refining the project plan. Remember, this was originally defined without consideration of the needs and availability of your partners. You may find that your partner's consultants are already committed to other projects and that you will have to wait. Your partners will be able to help you set new milestones and refine the budget.

Identify technology customization needs

It is very common that off-the-shelf technology fails to meet all the requirements of users. Some vendors have industry-specific versions of their CRM software. Oracle, for example, offers a range of CRM suites for banking, retail, public sector and other verticals. Even so, some customization is often required. The lead developer, database developer and front-end developer, in partnership with vendors, can perform these roles.

Prototype design, test, modify and roll out

The output of this customization process will be a prototype that can be tested by users on a duplicated set, or a dummy set, of customer-related data. End-user tests will show whether further customization is required. Final adjustments to marketing, selling and service processes are made at this stage, and further training needs are identified and met. After a final review, a roll-out programme is implemented. In most companies this is a phased roll-out. A new contact management system might be rolled out to the key account team before other members of the sales team; a new campaign management module may be trialled on newer brands rather than established brands; a sales force automation system might be rolled out first to the 'champions', those identified earlier as buying in both emotionally and rationally. The idea is to iron out any problems before company-wide adoption.

PHASE 5: PERFORMANCE EVALUATION

The final phase of the CRM project involves an evaluation of its performance. How well has it performed? Two sets of variables can be measured: project outcomes and business outcomes/benefits realized. *Project outcomes* focus on whether the project has been delivered on time and to budget. Your evaluation of the *business outcomes* or benefits requires you to return to the project objectives, your definition of CRM success, and the business case and ask whether the desired results have been achieved.

If your single goal was to enhance customer retention rates, with a measurable lift from 70 per cent to 80 per cent, and this is accomplished then your CRM project has been successful. Congratulations! However, most projects have multiple objectives and it is common for some objectives to be achieved and others to be missed. Lead conversion by the sales team might rise, but lead generation by campaign managers might fall short of objective. A critical issue concerns the timing of any business performance evaluation. It can take users several months to become familiar with new processes, and competent in using new technology. Periodic measures of business outcomes can be taken over time, to ensure that the programme outcomes are achieved. Ongoing training, timed to coincide with software upgrades, can enhance business outcomes. In the short term it is generally impossible to assess whether the latent benefits specified in the business case have been achieved.

SUMMARY

In this chapter, you have learned about the five major phases of a CRM implementation, and the processes and tools that are used to ensure that CRM projects deliver what is expected of them. The key phases are: (1) Develop the CRM strategy; (2) Build the CRM project foundations; (3) Needs specification and partner selection; (4) Project implementation; and (5) Performance evaluation. CRM projects vary in scope, duration and cost, but it is always important to be clear about what business outcomes are desired, and to measure the performance of the CRM implementation accordingly.

NOTES AND REFERENCES

1   The content in this section is drawn from a number of sources. In addition to our own experiences, important contributions are made by John Turnbull, Managing Director of Customer Connect (www.customerconnect.com.au), and Gartner Inc. (www.gartner.com).

2   http://blogs.salesforce.com/ask_wendy/files/how_to_create_your_crm_vision_5.16.05.pdf (Accessed 26 June 2007).

3   https://vwcrmhandbook.pbworks.com/w/page/52098383/Basis%20of%20your%20strategy (Accessed 23 April 2014).

4   Courtesy of Customer Connect Australia www.customerconnect.com.au Used with permission.

5   http://www.boozallen.de/media/file/guiding_principles.pdf (Accessed 27 June 2007).

6   Kotter, J.P. and Cohen, D.S. (2002). *The heart of change: real-life stories of how people change their organizations.* Boston, MA: Harvard Business School Press.

7   Buttle, F. and Ang, L. (2004). ROI on CRM: a customer journey approach. www.crmsearch.com/crm-failures.php (Accessed 24 April 2014).

8   Deshpandé, R. and Webster, Jr, F.E. (1989). Organizational culture and marketing: defining the research agenda. *Journal of Marketing,* 53(January), 3–15.

9   Deshpandé, R., Farley, J.U. and Webster, Jr, F.E. (1993). Corporate culture, customer orientation, and innovativeness in Japanese firms: a quadrad analysis. *Journal of Marketing,* 57(January), 23–37.

10 Iriana, R., Buttle, F. and Ang, L. (2013). Does organizational culture influence CRM's financial outcomes? *Journal of Marketing Management,* 29(3/4), 467–93.

11 Cameron, K.S. and Quinn, R.E. (1999). *Diagnosing and changing organisational culture.* Reading, MA: Addison-Wesley.

12 Cameron, K.S., and Quinn, R.E. (1999). *Diagnosing and changing organisational culture.* Reading, MA: Addison-Wesley.

13 Enbu Consulting: http://www.enbuconsulting.com/products_projmgr.php?pgurl=projmgr (Accessed 23 April 2014).

14 Da Silva, R.V. and Rahimi, I.D. (2007). A critical success factor model for CRM implementation. *Inernational Journal of Electronic Customer Relationship Management,* 1(1), 3–15.

15 Croteau, Anne-Marie and Li, P. (2003). Critical success factors of CRM technological initiatives. *Canadian Journal of Administrative Sciences,* 20(1), 21–34.

16 Mendoza, L.E., Marius, A., Perez, M. and Griman, A.C. (2007). Critical success factors for a CRM strategy. *Information and Software Technology,* 49, 913–45.

17 Buttle, F. and Ang, L. (2004). ROI on CRM: a customer journey approach. http://www.crm2day.com/library/EpFlupuEZVRmkpZCHM.php; Davids, M. (1999). How to avoid the 10 biggest mistakes in CRM. *Journal of Business Strategy,* November/December, 22–6; http://www.crmsearch.com/crm-failures.php (Accessed 24 April 2014).

18 www.gartner.com

19 Treacy, M. and Wiersema, F. (1995) *The discipline of market leaders.* London: Harper Collins.

20 Adapted from Jones, P.A. and Williams, T. (1995). *Business improvement made simple.* Northampton: Aegis Publishing.

21 A data model is an abstract description of how data are organized in an information system or database.

22 For a review of hosted CRM, refer to Buttle, F. (2006). Hosted CRM: literature review and research questions. Macquarie Graduate School of Management, working paper 2006–1.

23 eMarketer (2005). *CRM spending and trends.* http://www.emarketer.com/Report.aspx?crm_aug05 (Accessed 21 August 2005); Meta Group (2004). Hosted CRM: the real cost. http://www.metagroup.com/us/displayArticle.do?oid=47816 (Accessed 11 November 2005); Kane, Robe (2004). The top 10 myths of hosted CRM. http://www.aplicor.com/4%20Company/10%20Myths%20of%20 Hosted%20CRM%20Whitepaper.pdf (Accessed 20 October 2005).

24 Courtesy of Customer Connect Australia www.customerconnect.com.au Used with permission.

Part VI

LOOKING TO THE FUTURE

CHAPTER 15

THE FUTURE

It has been approximately 30 years since the term relationship marketing (RM) appeared, at least in an academic context, promoting the idea that long-term relationships with customers make sound economic sense.[1] The RM pioneers presented a radical departure from the orthodoxy of transaction-focused product brand marketing that had dominated marketing since its origins. Just behind this new recognition of the importance of customer relationships, enterprise software emerged to make it feasible to build and manage relationships with customers at a scale and at a cost affordable for most organizations. At first, there was a debate as to what to call this new management practice, but ultimately customer relationship management won out and this technology-enabled customer management solution is now established as part of most companies' infrastructure.

Of course, pundits are always interested in 'what's new' and we have no shortage of candidates for our attention. Almost coincidental with CRM, we had the commercialization of the Internet as e-commerce, which is now becoming m-commerce (mobile commerce). The rise of Web 2.0 begat social media and, as of writing this book, Facebook has 1.2 billion subscribers,[2] a size that dwarfs any customer database built to date. YouTube estimates that 100 hours of video are uploaded to it every minute[3] and Twitter claims that 500 million Tweets are sent every day.[4] The amount of data being created is frankly hard to imagine but it seems that we are in a phase of exponential data growth. IBM suggests that we create 2.5 quintillion bytes of data daily, and that 90 per cent of the world's data has been created in the past two years.[5] The sheer volume of data being generated represents a huge challenge and opportunity for organizations.

But the rapid pace of technical innovation is, if anything, accelerating; and with it the explosion in the type and volume of data continues. Wearable technology and the 'Internet of Things' (IoT) will enable unprecedented levels of observation of customers (with attendant ethical issues) and of business processes.[6] Wearable technology includes Google Glass and 'smart' watches, both recently introduced to the market as of writing. The Internet of Things is a buzz-expression that describes putting relatively 'dumb' sensors in objects that can identify each object uniquely and then connecting them all to create an extremely intelligent system. Experts predict the IoT will spawn new solutions for supply chains, reducing food waste, enabling improved traffic management, healthcare monitoring and intelligent shopping.

There is a looming battle for control of this vast ocean of customer information. Jaron Lanier's *Who Owns the Future*[7] outlines a world where power moves up a data-rich hierarchy to what he calls the 'Siren Servers', the largest most comprehensive data repositories. Candidates for control of data, and hence the economy, include Google, Facebook, Amazon and perhaps big IT services firms such as IBM. The average citizen merely provides his or her intellectual property for free, fuelling the profits of the siren servers whilst impoverishing the middle class. Consider how the 'free' is displacing journalists, photographers, newspapers, musicians and, perhaps, with the advent of free online education, teachers. Countering that view are those advocating that individuals must take control of their own data through personal data stores (PDS) allowing them to limit what the siren servers access and/or charge them for their own data. Issues of privacy aside, information is power. PDS is a movement for returning that power to the people who generate those data.

CRM came about only when database technology permitted the 'single view of the customer' that could be understood effectively through data analytics and accessed by customer-facing service and salespeople in real time. CRM needs data, and currently most systems are built upon organizations' operational databases: customer records, sales data, service contact histories and so on. With the advent of social media and user-generated content, CRM vendors are trying to integrate out-of-company data into CRM, so-called 'social CRM'. It is challenging, these new forms of data are unstructured and plentiful; integrating them into the highly structured databases companies have is not a trivial task – this is one of the big data challenges.

Ownership of data is another issue facing CRM. If the valuable data are owned by Facebook, Google, etc., they will effectively disintermediate the customer from the firm. If consumers would rather interact with friends in Facebook to determine what it is that they wish to buy, order in the same application and share their experiences post-purchase, their relationship as the customer is at least shared with the technology firm if not 'owned' primarily by it. The dominant data owners will demand a share of the money that is flowing through the commerce occurring over their 'space'. Perhaps they will support insider offers that compete against outsiders and make the implementation of CRM much harder.

On the supply side, there are technologies that will transform the design, manufacture and distribution of goods. One of particular relevance to CRM is 'additive' or 3D printing, giving the ability to produce physical objects from a relatively small printer. Early designs were limited to simple objects produced by very large and expensive printers. But even as we write this chapter, the quality and complexity of what can be made is advancing rapidly, the size of the printers shrinking and their prices tumbling. Additive printing is now affordable and feasible for millions. With 3D printing, it is now possible to imagine truly customer-driven procurement processes starting with online collaboration to co-design a product and almost immediate manufacture and delivery. Zero inventory, zero logistics, no cost to manufacture borne by the supplier. This model potentially overturns the 200-year history of the ongoing industrial revolution and we cannot yet really imagine the new business models that this will create. The nature of the relationship between customer and supplier will certainly be affected by such a radical transformation of the supply chain.

With respect to CRM implementation, there is an unanswered question that we hear asked more and more: Is it better to have a data scientist lead CRM and teach her something about marketing, or better to have a sales marketer lead CRM and teach her enough about data science to extract value from the investment? From a research perspective, this is work to be done. Anecdotally, we hear the increasing demand from senior business leaders for new skills in marketing to make sense of the data being generated.

CRM as a set of business practices and a set of technologies will undergo considerable change over the next ten years. We think what remains constant is the relentless focus on helping customers extract value from companies' offers by listening, targeting, customizing and supporting them through the lifecycle of the relationship. This requires complementary assets and capabilities including data and analytical tools.

We have, in this book, tried to help you understand the rationale for investing in managing customer relationships, how to build the strategic, operational and analytical capabilities it requires, understand how to realize the benefits of CRM (both immediate and latent) and to organize and change for its successful implementation. The future will be every bit as challenging but we believe that most firms will still have a need to identify themselves to their best customers and engage in a learning relationship with them so that firms prosper and customers obtain the best solutions to their problems or needs.

NOTES AND REFERENCES

1 Berry, L. (2002). Relationship marketing of services – perspectives from 1983 and 2000. *Journal of Relationship Marketing*, 1, 59–77.

2 http://www.mondaynote.com/ (Accessed 15 April 2014).

3 http://www.youtube.com/yt/press/statistics.html (Accessed 27 April 2014).

4 https://about.twitter.com/company (Accessed 27 April 2014).

5 http://www-01.ibm.com/software/data/bigdata/what-is-big-data.html (Accessed 27 April 2014). We suggest that the statistic that 90 per cent of the data in the world has been created in the past two years is based upon equating data with bytes. This is not the same as the world's knowledge, valuable data, etc. Nonetheless, it is a measure of the rate of growth of data.

6 http://www.mckinsey.com/insights/high_tech_telecoms_internet/the_internet_of_things (Accessed 27 April 2014).

7 Lanier, J. (2013). *Who owns the future?* London: Allen Lane.

INDEX

3 Mobile 374
3 Mobile case study 198
3D printing 162, 388
3M 159, 198, 374
5-process model 21

ABC class service 112
account management 215–16
account value 128
ACORN 124–5
activity-based costing (ABC) 33, 133–5
activity links 48–9
activity management 216–17, 270–1
actor bonds 48
adhocracy 369
Adidas 162
ADT money-back service guarantee case study 171
advertising 67–70
affective advertising objectives 67–8
affective value 157
affiliation data 82
affinity groupings 327
affinity marketing 82
agent management 271–2
Air Canada case study 104
airlines 38, 94, 97; big data analytics 320; customer engagement 103; demarketing 112; gamification 104; Product-Service Systems 167; satisfaction–profit chain 46
Amazon 162–3, 183, 316
American Airlines 94, 136
American Customer Satisfaction Index (ACSI) 45, 45
American Express 93, 104–5
American Heart Association (AHA) case study 304

analytical CRM: customer acquisition 81–2; customer experience 201; customer lifecycle 313–16; customer-related data 15 see also customer-related databases; data configuration 311; data reviews 376; operational CRM and 374; overview 11–13, 310–12; strategy and tactics 312–13; structured and unstructured data 316–19
analytical insight 323
Anglo-Australian school 50–1
Apple 5, 165, 201, 320
Application Service Providers (ASPs) 17
apps 275
Arm and Hammer 60
Arnould, E. 199
Asian (guanxi) school 52
ASP (Application Service Provider) model 377–8
asset management 257
attitudinal loyalty 43
attractiveness 144–5
Audi Group 93
Australia and New Zealand Standard Industrial Classification (ANZSIC) 127
auto-diallers 243
auto manufacturers 18, 46, 60; warranties case study 318
automated call distribution (ACD) 278
automated routing 317
average handling time (AHT) 271
awareness 26
AXA Seguros e Inversiones (AXA) case study 12

B&Q 177
BA 112, 320
baking soda applications 60
balanced scorecard 44
Ballantyne, D. 50
banded packs 71
banking industry: affinity marketing 82; branch/internet costs 350; campaign management 374–5; case study 32; CRM and 18; customer acquisition 79; customer development 110; customer experience 199; customer portfolio management (CPM) 120; customer retention 87, 107; data warehousing 305; demarketing 111–12, 113; NBA 315; personalized communication 182; physical evidence value 178; satisfaction–profit chain 46; strategic switching 61; touchpoints 195; value 175
Barclays Bank case study 36
Basu, K. 43
Bayliss, T. 164–5
Beam Inc. 257
behavioural engagement 196
behavioural loyalty 42–3
benchmark customers 149
Benefit Dependency Network (BDN) 344–5, 365
benefit segmentation 125
benefits of CRM 364, 365–6
Benetton 305
Berger, P.D. 36
Berry, M. 330
BICC 59
big data 12
big data analytics 319–21

bivariate models 143–5
Black Scholes 344
blogs 180
Body Shop 105, *106*
bonding 99–102
Bonobos case study 81
bonus packs 71
Boots 96, 97
Booz Allen & Hamilton 368
Boston Consulting Group (BCG)
    matrix 147–8
boundary spanners 177
brand managers 347
branding 166
Branson, Richard 75
BT 59
bundling 112, 120, 166
business case for CRM: agreement
    365–6; logic of 341–5; performance
    evaluation 381; traditional 342–4
business markets 127
business markets segmentation
    126–30
business outcomes 381
business performance 44–7
business-to-business (B2B) *see also*
    customer portfolio management
    (CPM): activity-based costing 133;
    customer acquisition 64–7;
    customer attrition 59; customers
    121; prospecting 64–7; relationship
    resistance 37–8; theories 47–9
business-to-consumer (B2C) *see also*
    customer portfolio management
    (CPM): activity-based costing 133;
    company resistance 38; customer
    acquisition 67–77; customer
    attrition 59; customer resistance
    40–1; customers 121; data mining
    137; lead generation 67;
    relationships 39–40
Buttle, F. 20, 72
buy-in 370
buzgate *179*
buzz 72 *see also* word-of-mouth
    (WOM) influence

CACI 124
call centres 93, 201, 242–3, 267, 268;
    agent management 271–2
call for proposals 380
Cameron, K.S. 369

campaign management 80, *375*;
    customer development 110;
    definitions 235; marketing
    automation 7–8, 235–9
canvassing 67
Capital Asset Pricing Model (CAPM)
    342
capital equipment 11
car distribution 46
Carlzon, J. 195
case assignment applications 272
case management 272–3
cash-back 71, 99
categorical data 321, 323
category management organization
    structure 347–8
Caterpillar 107
census data 296–7
CEOExpress portal *65*
Chakraborty 317
Chandler, A. 345
change management needs 368–70
channel configuration 107
channel integration 110, 266–7
channel managers 348–9
channel silos 86
channels, value from 182–3
chat window *284*
CHEP 257
Chi-square Automatic Interaction
    Detection (CHAID) 138, 327
chocolate market 126
Christopher, M. 50
Church and Dwight 60
churn prediction case study 331
churn rates 29, 108–9
Classification and Regression Trees
    (CART) 138, 327
classification schemes 326
click-to-open rates (CTOR) 238, 294
closed-loop marketing (CLM) 234
cloud solutions providers 17
clustering techniques 137–8, 327–8,
    330
Coca-Cola 149; case study 279
cognitive advertising objectives
    67–8
cognitive engagement 196
cold calls 67, 75–6
collection schemes 99
commitment 26, 27, 28
Commitment–Trust Theory 52

Commonwealth Bank of Australia
    (CBA) 112, 305
communication objectives 67–8
communications programme 9
company websites 64–5
Competing Values model 369
competitions 71, 298
competitors 107, 123, 164
complaints 10, 109, 173–4
complaints management process
    175–6, 177
Compustat 46
computer telephony integration (CTI)
    278
conditional value 158
configurators 9, 160, 221–2; case study
    223
conformance to specification 167
consumer goods manufacturers 18
consumer markets 123–6;
    segmentation criteria 124
contact centres 266–7
contact management 9, 217
contact patterns 351
content management 244
continuous data 321–2, 323
contract management 273
conventional management structure
    346–9
Conversion Model (Hofmeyr) 62–3
conversion rates 70
cooperatives 86
corporate culture 107
cost-to-serve 34, 111, *143*, 143
Coupland, J. 199
coupons 71
craft customization 160
credit card companies 31–2, 33
credit rating services 79
credit risk 138–9
Critical Path Analysis (CPA) 371
critical success factors 371–3
Crosby, P. 167
cross-promotions 71
cross-selling 109–10
Croteau, A.-M. 372
Cunningham, M. 48
customer acquisition: Bonobos case
    study 81; business-to-business
    prospecting 64–7; business-to-
    consumer prospecting 67–77;
    campaign management 80; costs

133; CRM analytics support 81–2; event-based campaigns 80–1; key performance indicators 77–8; lead management 79–80; new customers 60–1; offers 78–9; overview 58–9; plans 59; portfolio purchasing 61–3; prospecting 63–72; right offers 78–9; strategies for 313; tracking referrals case study 75

customer attrition 59
customer-centric businesses 5, 6–7
customer clubs 97–8
customer communication, value from 179–82
customer communications management (CCM) 273–4
customer contact role 177
customer delight 90–3
customer development 314; strategies for 109–11
customer engagement 102–6, 195–6
customer experience (CX): concepts 195–7; CRM and 200; CRM software 202–5; CRM's influence 200–2; definitions 189–90; experience economy 189–90; explanation 189–94; IKEA case study 193; Kiwi Experience case study 192; layered model 194; management 197–200; planned 192–3; service marketing 190–1; Total Quality Management 193–4
customer-generated media (CGM) 180
customer insight 30–1
customer interaction map 363
customer journey 31
customer lifecycle 58–9, 313–16; analytics throughout 313–16 see also customer acquisition; customer retention
customer lifetime value (CLV): case study 32; computing 34–7, 314; customer acquisition 59, 81; definitions 32–3; estimation 135–6
customer loyalty 42–3
customer markets model 51
customer organization structure 348
customer-perceived value: branding 166; case study 171, 176; from channels 182; from customer communication 179–81; customization 159–63;

disintermediation 181; explanation 154–6; incremental benefits 165–6; interactivity 181; marketing mix 163–4; modelling 157–9; from people 177–8; personalization 181; personalization case study 182; from physical evidence 178–9; from processes 174–6; product innovation 164–5; product-service bundling 166; products and services 164; from service 167; service level agreements 172–3; service quality 167–71; service recovery programmes 173–4; sources of 159; value creation 153–4; value-in-exchange 156; value-in-experience 157; value-in-use 157

Customer Portfolio Analysis (CPA) 140
customer portfolio management (CPM): activity-based costing 133–5; architecture 204; bivariate models 143–5; Boston Consulting Group matrix 147–8; business markets 126–30; business-to-business 141–2; consumer markets 123–6; customer lifetime value 135–6; customer management strategies 150; customer portfolio models 142; data mining 137–41; education 362–3; future of 387–9; market segmentation 121–3; overview 120–1; sales forecasting 130–3; strategically significant customers 148–9; strategy 361; SWOT 147; trivariate models 146; vision 363–4
customer portfolio matrix 130, 143
Customer Referral Scheme (CRS) 74–5
Customer Referral Value (CRV) 34
customer-related databases: analytical insight 323–33; big data analytics 319–21; corporate customer-related data 290; customer lifecycle 313–16; data attributes 302–3; data integration 303–4; data marts 306–7; data warehousing 305–6; define functions 292–3; enhancing internal data 296–7; information fields 294–5; information requirements 293–5; information sources 295–8; knowledge

management 307–8; maintenance 301–2; market segmentation case study 297; overview 289–90; population 299–301; privacy issues 334–6; secondary and primary data 298–9; steps to develop 292; strategy and tactics 312–13; structured and unstructured data 290–2, 316–19; structured data 321–3; technology and operating system 298–9
customer relationship management (CRM) see also analytical CRM; operational CRM; strategic CRM: commercial contexts 18; constituencies 16–17; definitions 3–4, 15–16; misunderstandings 13–15; models 20–2; types 4
Customer Relationship Value (CRV) 35–6
customer retention: Air Canada case study 104; analytical CRM 314; bonding 99–102; candidates for 89; case study 102; context 106–7; customer delight 90–3; customer development strategies 109–11; customer engagement 102–6; customer-perceived value 94–9; economics 88–9; explanation 85–6; gamification 103–4; improving 28–9; JetBlue case study 103; key performance indicators 108; Korea Telecom case study 102; loyalty schemes case study 96; managing 87; overview 84–5; rates 30, 37, 86–7, 135–6; relational attachment 104–5; research 108–9; role of research 108–9; social bonds 100; strategies 90; structural bonds 100; termination 111–13; values-based attachment 105–6
customer satisfaction 41–2, 102, 109; levels 47; satisfaction–profit chain 45–7
customer segmentation 123–6, 256
customer self-service (CSS) 274–6
customer service: costs 133; explanation 262–3
Customer Service Excellence certification 264–6
Customer Strategy Cube 361–2
customer surveys 131
customer tenure 29, 30

customer value hierarchy 164
customization 110, 159–63
customized solutions 159

Da Silva, R.V. 372
data attributes 302–3
data creation 387
data integration 303–4
data marts 306–7, 324
data mining: case study 326; customer
    development 110; customer
    portfolio management (CPM)
    137–41; definitions 325; descriptive
    analysis 326; directed data mining
    328, 329–30; overview 11–12;
    procedures 328–33; segmentation
    17; statistical routines 258–9;
    undirected data mining 328, 330–3;
    warehoused data 316–17
data ownership 388
data protection 334–6
data reviews 375–6
data transformation 305, *306*
data types 321–3
data validation 300
data warehousing 305–6, 325
database marketing 14
Dawkins, P.M. 88–9
de-duping data 300–1
decision trees 138–9, *140*, 329
decomposition forecasting 132
defection rates 86
Dell Computers 91
Dell, Michael 18
Deloitte's 74
demarketing 111
descriptive analysis 326
Dial Eco-Smart case study 236
dialogue 50
Dick, A.S. 43
digital analytics 248–51
Digital Analytics Association (DAA)
    250
digital marketing 244
direct mail campaign management
    237–8
Direct Marketing Association 238
direct-to-customer (DTC) channels
    64
direct-to-customer (DTC)
    communication 181
directed data mining 329–30

discount rates 135–6; LTV and 35, 35
discounted cash flow (DCF) analysis
    342
discounts 71
discriminant analysis (DA) 330
disintermediation 181
Disney 16, 305
dissolution 26
Do Not Call registers 243
document management 217–18, 257
Dolby Laboratories 257
door openers 149
door-to-door sales 76
Dow chemical 174
down-selling 110
Driver and Vehicle Licensing Agency
    (DVLA) case study 19
Dun & Bradstreet 304
Dunnhumby 17
Dwyer, R. 26, 31, 51
Dyer, J. 49, 51
Dyno Nobel 131

easyJet 175
economic development 189–90
Economic Value to the Customer
    (EVC) 156
Eircom case study 29
Eismann 74
electronic data interchange (EDI) 30,
    101
email 181–2
email campaign management 238–9,
    240, *259*, *295*
Email Experience Council 238
email marketing 66, 76
email response management systems
    (ERMS) 276–7
emotional engagement 196
emotional value 158
engineer-to-order 161
enterprise portals 178
Enterprise Resource Planning (ERP)
    183, 213, 312, 372
epistemic value 158
equity bonds 101
equity theory 173
escalation 277–8
estimation 326–7
ethical concerns, customer retention
    107
ethnography 198–9

event-based campaigns 8, 75, 80–1,
    110; marketing automation
    239–40
event management 218; case study
    219
expansion 26
expectations 91, 92
expectations–disconfirmation model
    42
Experian 296
experience mapping 197–8
exploration 26
exponential smoothing 132
EXQ 194

Facebook 17, 180, 246
factor analysis 332–3
family lifecycle (FLC) 124–5
fashion industry 8, 75
field service 267
Filtrex case study 245
financial bonds 101
Fiocca, R. 144, 145
first call resolution (FCR) 272
First Direct 110, 175, 374, *375*
first-time fix rate (FTFR) 282
fitness for purpose 167
flexibility of applications 203
flowcharting 374
Ford, F. 48
Forrester Research 196, 238, 275
free gifts 99
free premiums 71
free publicity 75
free trials 71
Freight Traders case study 227
frequency 69–70
frequent flier programmes (FFP) 94,
    97
front-office processes 374
Frontier Bank 113
functional organization structure
    346
functional quality 168
functional silos 86
functional value 157–8

Gadde, L.-E. 48
gamification 103–4
Gantt charts 371
gap analysis 375–6
Gartner competency model 21–2

Gartner Inc. 3–4, 236, 246, 251, 252, 274, 292, 328, 373
GE 11, 167
general ledger costing 133–4
General Motors 32
geo-demographic classification schemes 124–5
geographic bonds 100, 101
geographic organization structure 346–7
Gilmore, J. 189–90, 191
Giordano 159
global account management 351–6
goals 364
Google 70, 245; Google Analytics 75, 250, *251*
Googlebot 245
governance structures 366–8
governments 19
graphical user interface (GUI) 228
Groeger, L. 72
Grönroos, C. 49, 168, 193
GSK 159
guanxi 52, 66
Gümmesson, E. 49
Gupta, S. 135

Häagen-Dazs 123
Hadoop 321
Håkansson, H. 48
Hammersley, M, 198
hardware 214
Harley Davidson 105
Harley Owners Group (HOG) 98
healthcare 107, 178
Heartlanders 297
Heide, J. 51
Helgesen, O. 46
help desks 267
heterogeneity, intangibility, perishability and inseparability (HIPI) 190–1
Hewlett Packard 241
hierarchical clustering 330, *332*
hierarchical databases 291
high future lifetime value customers 148
high performance systems 203–4
high volume customers 149
Hofmeyr, J. 62–3
Holbrook, M. 158
Honda case study 6

hospitals 178
hosted CRM 377–8
hotel industry 125
HPES case study 241
Hunt, S. 27, 51, 52
Hype Cycle 246–7, 292

iBeacon 320
IBM 11, 12, 128, 174, 298, 388
ICEE Company case study 270
identification of business 123
IDIC model 20
IHS 93
IKEA 97, 193
implementation: CRM strategy 361–6; five-step process 359–61; needs specifications 373–80; performance evaluation 381; project foundations 366–73; project implementation 380–1
inbound communications management (ICM) 278, *283*
incentive management 218
incremental benefits, customer-perceived value 165–6
Industrial Marketing and Purchasing (IMP) school 47–9
Information Technology Infrastructure Library (ITIL) 267
Information Technology Service Management (ITSM) 267
ING case study 315
innocent 73
inspirations 149
insurance companies 31, 33, 78, 85–6
integrated customer communication 110
integrated marketing management 251–2
Intel 159
interactions 49–50
interactive episodes 25
interactive technologies 181–2
Interactive Voice Response (IVR) 10, 201, 243, 272, 275, 278
interactivity 181
intermediaries 182–3
International Customer Service Standard *265*, 266
International Standard Industrial Classification (ISIC) 126–7; codes 127

Internet of Things 319, 320, 387–8
interval data 322
invoicing applications 278
IT, misunderstandings 14–15

Jap, S. 51
JetBlue case study 10, 103
job management applications 278–9, *280*
John Lewis Partnership 89
Joint Industry Committee for National Readership Surveys (JICNARS) 124
Juran, J.M. 167
JUST EAT case study 248
Just-In-Time (JIT) 48, 101
justice 173–4

k-means clustering 331–2, *333*
Kahneman, D. 155
KANA 280
Kano, Noriaki 92–3
Kanthal 142
Kaspersky Lab 276
Keaveney, S. 108
Keller and Heckman case study 219
Kellogg's 99
key account management (KAM) 177, 351–6
key performance indicators (KPI) 44, 252
keyword marketing 244–5
Kids & Cul-de-Sacs 297
kiosks 275
Kiwi Experience case study 192
Klaus and Maklan 194
knowledge-base self-service 279–80
knowledge-based bonds 101
knowledge management 307–8
Korea Telecom case study 102
Kotler, P. 5
Kotter, J. 368, 370
Kraft 347–8
Kumar, V. 34
Kwik Fit 93

Lanier, J. 388
lead allocation 79
lead management 9, 218–20; customer acquisition 79–80; prospect scoring 313–14
lead nurturing 79
lead qualification 79

lead tracking 79
leadership 368
leading indicators 132
Lee, J. 34
legal bonds 101
Lehmann, D. 135
Levitt, T. 123, 164
Lexus 75
LG 159
Li, P. 372
Likert scale 323, 333
LinkedIn 66
Linoff, G. 330
Lodish, L. 70
logfile analysis 248–9
logistic regression 329
lotteries 71
low prices 159
loyalty management 253–4
loyalty schemes 15, 94–7, 137, 298
Lucozade 165
Lusch, R. 50

management consultants 17
margin multiple 135–6
market identification 123
market organization structure 348, 351–6
market segmentation 121–3; business markets 126–30; case study 129, 297; consumer markets 123–6; customer-related databases 297–8; marketing automation 235, 255; value assessment 129–30
marketing analytics 258–9
marketing automation (MA) 7–8; asset management 257; benefits 232–4; campaign management 235–7; case study 232; content management 244; customer segmentation 256; definitions 231–2; Dial Eco-Smart case study 236; digital marketing 244; direct mail campaign management 237–8; document management 257; email campaign management 238–9; event-based campaigns 239–40; Filtrex case study 245; functionality 234; integrated marketing management 251–2; JUST EAT case study 248; keyword marketing 244–5; lead generation 243; loyalty management 253–4; market segmentation 255; marketing analytics 258–9; marketing optimization 241–2; marketing performance management 252–3; marketing resource management 253; online marketing 244; partner marketing 255; product lifecycle management 256–7; search engine optimization 245–6; social media marketing 246–50; software applications 234; Staples case study 232; telemarketing 242–3; trigger marketing 240–1; workflow development 259
marketing costs 30
marketing, definitions 49
marketing mix 163
'Marketing Myopia' (Levitt) 123
marketing optimization 110, 241–2
marketing performance management 252–3
marketing processes 14
marketing resource management 253
Marketing Science Institute (MSI) 73
Marks and Spencer case study 326
mass customization 160–3
Master Data Management 303
match-to-order 161
matrix organization structure 348–9
MBAs 164
McCarthy, E. 163
McDonald, M. 25
McDonald's 60, 159; customer experience 189; physical evidence value 178; segmentation criteria 125
MCI 61–2
McKinsey 31, 111, 159
mean time to resolve (MTTR) 282
Member-Get-Member (MGM) schemes 33, 74–5
Mendoza, L. 372
merchandising 73–4
merge-purge *300*, 301
Meta Group 202
Meyer-Waarden, R.C. 97
Microsoft Canada 255
Microsoft Dynamics 17, 225
middleware 303

mobile coupons 71
moments of truth 195
Morgan, R. 27, 51, 52
moving averages forecasting 132
Müller, M. 162
multi-channel marketing 236–7
multi-product bonds 101
multiple regression 329–30
MySpace 246
mystery shopping 197

Nasr, N.I. 36
national account management 351–6
National Australia Bank 195
NatWest Bank case study 120, 199
Naudé, P. 48
Nectar 94–5, 253–4
needs specifications 373–80
Nestlé's mother and baby club 98
Net Present Value (NPV) 342
Netflix 162–3
NetSuite 17, *255*
network databases 291
network organizations 349–51
networking 65–6
neural networks 139–40, 330; case study 331
new customer discounts 34
new customers: acquisition 59; new-to-category 60, 61; new-to-company 60–1; portfolio purchasing 61–3
next best action (NBA) 315–16
next best offer (NBO) 8, 250, 316
Nielsen 296, 297
Nippon Conlux 149
nominal data 321, 322
Nordic model of service quality 168
Nordic School 49–50
Nordstrom 159
Normann, R. 195
North American Industry Classification System 127
North American school 51–2
not-for-profit sector 18–19
Nypro 111

objectives 364
office equipment 86, 107
on-premise CRM 377–8

one-to-one marketing 181
online analytical processing (OLAP) 258, 282, 312, 316–17, 324–5; databases 293
online clothing companies 32
online marketing 244
online sources of leads 64–5
online transaction processing (OLTP) databases 293
operating systems 298–9
operational CRM *see also* marketing automation (MA); sales force automation (SFA); service automation: customer experience 201; data reviews 375–6; overview 7, 7–11, 12, 311–12, 374
operations management 14
opportunity management 9, 220
optimization 110
Oracle: chat window *284*; contact management *217*; inbound communications management *283*; loyalty management *254*; multi-channel marketing *237*; pipeline management *222*; service analytics 282; SFA *213*; workflow development 225
order management 220–1
ordinal data 322, 323
Organization for Economic Cooperation and Development (OECD) 334–5
organizational culture 368–9 *see also* Competing Values model
organizational structure 345–9
outbound communications management 280
ownership expectations 107

page-tagging 249
Parasuraman, A. 168–9, 193
Parasuraman, Zeithaml and Berry (PZB) model of service quality 193
Pareto principle 135, *141*
participant observation 199–200
partner marketing 255
partner relationship management (PRM) 11
partner selection 373–80
party plans 75
patronage rewards 99
pay-per-click (PPC) marketing 245

Payne, A. 50
Payne and Frow model of CRM 21
Peck, H. 50
peer-to-peer self-service (P2PSS) 275
people management (HR) 14
Peppers & Rogers 17
Peppers, D. 20, 181
perceived risk 39, 155–6
performance evaluation 381
person-to-person contacts 351
personal data stores (PDS) 388
personal referrals 64
personalized communication 181, 182; marketing automation 235
Petre, M. 189
physical evidence, value from 178–9
Piller, F. 162
Pine, J. 189–90, 191
pipeline management 221, *222*
pitchers 77
portals 65, 178, 183, 275
portfolio purchasing 61–3
portfolios, overview 119–21
positive interpersonal relationships 100
postcode segmentation 124
PR (public relations) 66
predictive analytics 81–2, 138, 327
predictive dialling 280–1
price increases 112
primary data collection 298
primary processes, business 374
priorities for action 364
priorities for improvement (PFIs) 91–2
privacy 334–6
Privacy Interest Group 336
PRIZM 297
process bonds 101
process engineering 373–5
process evaluation 375
process innovation 175
processes, value from 174–6
Procter and Gamble 347
product-based value 164–6
product configuration 9, 160, 221–2; case study 223
product encyclopedias 221
product innovation 159, 164–5
product integration 77

product lifecycle management 256–7
product organization structure 347–8
product-oriented businesses 5
product placement 77
product-service bundling 166
Product-Service Systems (PSSs) 167
product silos 85–6
product visualisation 222–3
production-oriented businesses 5
profit margins 33
profit per customer 37
programme directors (CRM) 366–8, 370–1
Programme Evaluation and Review Technique (PERT) 371
Programme Team 366–7, 376
programmes/projects 359
project bonds 101
project foundations 366–73
project implementation 380–1
project management needs 370–1
project outcomes 381
projects 359
promotional activities 66
propensity modelling process 374
propensity to buy 35, 81
propensity-to-switch 128
proposal generation 223
proposals assessment 380
proposals, call for 380
prospect lists 67
prospecting 63–4; business-to-business 64–7; business to consumer 67–77
prototypes 381
psychic costs 155
publicity 66
purchasing practices 107
PWC 350

qualitative sales forecasting 131
quality model 92–3
quality of service 167–71
query-based reports *324*
Query By Example (QBE) 302
queuing and routing applications 281
Quinn, R.E. 369
quotation management 223–4

Radicati Group 276
Rahimi, I.D. 372
RATER variables 168–9, 173, 193–4

ratio data 322
RBS case study 199
reach 69–70
real options 343, 344, 376
rebates 71, 99
Recency–Frequency–Monetary value 43, 80, 109, 125, 295
Recommend-A-Friend (RAF) schemes 74–5
referral schemes 74–5, 77, 88
regional account management 351–6
registrations 298
regression forecasting 132–3
Reichheld, F.F. 31–2, 33, 88–9, 102, 193
reintermediation 183
relational attachment 104–5
relational databases 11–12, 291
relationship marketing (RM) 49, 387
relationships: business performance 44–7; changes within 26; commitment 27; company resistance 37–8; customer loyalty 42–3; customer resistance 40–1; customer satisfaction 41–2; customer viewpoints 39–41; with customers 28–32; definitions 24–5; difficulty of managing 144; key account management 351–6; quality 28; relative strength 145; strategies for 150; termination 111–13; theories 47–52; trust 26–7
reputational quality 168
request for proposals (RFP) 378–80
resources, definitions 49
response rates 70
restaurants 91–2
retention 28–9, 30
RightNow 17, 201
risk 39, 155
risk management plans 373
Rochdale Pioneers 94
Roche case study 9
Rogers, M. 17, 181
Rolls-Royce 11, 167
root cause analysis 318

Saatchi and Saatchi 159
sacrifices 154

Safe Harbor 335–6
Safeway 95
sales force automation (SFA): 8–9; adoption 226–7; benefits 226–7; case study 227; definitions 212–13; eco-system 213–15; Keller and Heckman case study 219; motivations 227; overview 8–9, 211–22; Product Configurator case study 223; reports 224, 225; sales performance 227–8; software functionality 215–26; vendors 213
sales forecasting 9, 130–3, 314; applications 224; moving averages 132
sales management reporting 224
sales-oriented businesses 6
sales promotions 70–2, 98–9
sales team estimates 131
salesforce.com 224
samples 70–1
Samsung 74
SAP 303, 317
SAS 137, 195, 317
Sasser, Jr., W.E. 31–2, 33, 193
satisfaction–profit chain 41, 45–7
scalability of systems 204
Scandinavian Airlines 170
scenario testing 242
scheduling applications 281
Schwab, C. 71
scripting 281
search engine optimization 244–6
search engines 64, 183
SECOM case study 176
secondary processes 374
self-checkout 275
self-liquidating promotions 99
self-service 274–6, 279–80
selling process stages 8–9
SEMMA (Sample, Explore, Modify, Model, Assess) 137
Sen, A. 306
sentiment analysis 317, 318
service analytics 281–2
service automation 10; activity management 270–1; agent management 271–2; benefits 268–70; case study 270; Coca-Cola case study 279; contract management 273; customer communications management

273–4; customer self-service 274–6; customer service 262–3; customer service excellence 264–6; definitions 266; email response management systems 276–7; escalation 277–8; explanation 266–8; functionality 271; inbound communications management 278; Interactive Voice Response 10, 201, 243, 272, 275, 278; invoicing applications 278; job management applications 278–9; knowledge-base self-service 279–80; outbound communications management 280; predictive dialling 280–1; queuing and routing applications 281; scheduling applications 281; scripting 281; service analytics 281–2; service history 269; service level management 282–3; service quality modelling 263–4; software applications 270; spare parts management 283; voice biometrics 283; web collaboration 284; workflow development 284
service centre automation case study 279
Service-Dominant Logic (SDL) 50
service guarantees 171
service level agreements 172–3
service level management (SLM) 282–3
service marketing 190–2
service quality 167–8, 263–4; theories 168–71, 193
service recovery programmes 173–4
service, role of 49
service, value from 167–74
SERVPERF 170–1
SERVQUAL model 168–71, 193–4, 332–3
Shapiro, B. 144
share-of-wallet (SOW) 44, 44, 61, 128
Shell 95
Sheth, J. 51, 158
Shouldice Hospital 107
Siebel Systems Inc. 3
Siebel, Tom 3
silos 85–6
Singapore Airlines 159
single view of the customer (SVOC) 211

situation analysis 361–2
Six-Markets Model 51
Smith, A. 156
SMS messages 76
Snehota, I. 48
social bonds 100, 101
social CRM 13
social engagement 196
social grading 124
social media 10, 13, 17, 72–3, 183;
  analytics 250; customer-company
  communication 180; prospecting
  65–6
social media marketing 246–8
social risk 155
social value 158
software applications 202–5
Software as a Service (SaaS) 17, 377–8
Southwest Airline 180–1
Spa'kle 101
Spam 276
spare parts management 283
SPSS 137
SQM Group 272
Standard and Poor's 46
standard reports 258, 323, *324*
Staples case study 232
star schemas 324, *325*
STARTS 302–3, 307–8
statistical procedures, in CRM 316–18
Steering Committee 366–7
Stevens, S. 322
strategic CRM 5–7, 15, 311, 374,
  375–6 *see also* customer experience
  (CX); customer portfolio
  management (CPM)
strategic goals 345, 364
strategic importance 144
strategic switching 61–3, 64
strategically significant customers
  148–9
strategy analytics 312–13
Strengths, Weaknesses, Opportunities
  and Threats (SWOT) 147
strip-mining 201–2
structural bonds 100
structured databases 290–2; analytics
  for 316, 321–3
Structured Query Language (SQL)
  302
Subaru Owners Club 98
subscriptions 298

SugarCRM *294*, 295
supermarkets 81, 96, 108
supply chain management (SCM) 213
Swatch the Club 98
Swedish Customer Satisfaction
  Barometer (SCSB) 45
synchronization 268
synergistic KAM 354–5
SYNGENTA AG case study 129
systems integration 367

tactics for CRM 312–13
targeting 235
team selling 356
technical quality 168
technological bonds 101
technological innovations 387–8
technology customization 381
technology requirements 376–8
technology revisions 380
technology solution vendors 18
telecommunications 86;
  satisfaction–profit chain 46;
  strategic switching 61–2
telemarketing 67, 75–6, 242–3
tenure 29, 30
termination 111–13
terms of trade 133
territory management 224–5
Tesco 137, 140; Clubcard 137
text analytics 317
Text Miner 317
third sector 18–19
timber industry case study 149
time-series forecasting 131–2
total cost of ownership (TCO) 155–6,
  377
total customer experience (TCE)
  189
total quality management (TQM)
  48, 193–4
touchpoints 195
Toyota 159
Transaction Cost Economics 154
Treacey, M. 159
trend analysis 318
trigger marketing 240–1
Triplet of Relationship Marketing
  49–50
Trouble-ticket *273*
trust 26–7, 28
Turnbull, P. 146

Tversky, A. 155
Twitter 10–11, 17, 180–1, 250, 387
two-step clustering 332

undirected data mining 330–3
United Nations Statistics Division
  126–7
universities 19
UNIX 298
unstructured data 12, 268, 292–3,
  316–19; big data analytics 319–21
unstructured databases 290–2;
  analytics for 316–19
up-selling 109–10
US Bancorp 35
US Xpress Enterprises case study 306
usability of applications 203
usage attributes 124, 125
user attributes 124
utility companies 29

validation of data 300
value 50; from channels 182–3; from
  customer communication 179–82;
  customer-perceived value 157–9;
  definitions 154, 156; marketing mix
  163; from people 177–8; from
  physical evidence 178–9; from
  processes 174–6; from products
  164–6; from service 167–74; sources
  of 159
value chain 20–1
value creation 153–4
value-in-exchange 156
value-in-experience 157
value-in-use 157
value ladder 31
value propositions 120, 121–3, 159,
  201
value retention 87
values-based attachment 105–6
values-based bonds 101
Vargo, S. 50
Vendor Managed Inventory (VMI)
  101, 154–5
verification of data 300
vertical processes 374
Villanueva, J. 78
Virgin 75, 106
Virgin Atlantic 349
virtual organizations 349–51
virtual resellers 183

Vodafone 86
voice biometrics 283
volume consumed 125–6
vouchers 98

Wal-Mart 159; production-oriented
    businesses 5
warranties case study 318
Watson, R.T. 305
wearable technology 387
web analytics 248–9
web collaboration 284
web portals 178

web self-service 275
weighted average cost of capital
    (WACC) 35, 135–6
Westpac case study 182
What Digital Camera 69
Who Owns the Future (Lanier) 388
Wiersema, F. 159
Williamson, O. 154
Woodburn, D. 25
word-of-mouth (WOM) influence 34,
    72, 78, 88
workflow development 225–6, 259,
    284

workflow functionality 235, 374–5
working capital costs 133
World Wide Web Consortium (W3C)
    336

Xerox 174, 175

Young Digerati 297
YouTube 387

Zeithaml, V. 157, 193
Zolkiewski, J. 146
zone of delusion 25